MW01012540

THE HANDBOOK FOR

THE NEW Art and Science OF TEACHING

ROBERT J. MARZANO

A joint publication

555 North Morton Street
Bloomington, IN 47404
800.733.6786 (toll free) / 812.336.7700
FAX: 812.336.7790

email: info@SolutionTree.com
SolutionTree.com

Visit **go.SolutionTree.com/instruction** to download the free reproducibles in this book.

Printed in the United States of America

Library of Congress Cataloging-in-Publication Data

Names: Marzano, Robert J., author. | Marzano, Robert J. New art and science of teaching.
Title: The handbook for the new art and science of teaching / Robert J. Marzano.
Description: Bloomington, IN : Solution Tree Press, [2019] | Companion volume to The new art and science of teaching. | Includes bibliographical references and index.
Identifiers: LCCN 2018014071 | ISBN 9781947604315 (perfect bound)
Subjects: LCSH: Effective teaching--United States. | Classroom management--United States. | Teaching--Aids and devices. | Learning, Psychology of.
Classification: LCC LB1025.3 .M3424 2019 | DDC 371.102--dc23 LC record available at https://lccn.loc.gov/2018014071

Solution Tree
Jeffrey C. Jones, CEO
Edmund M. Ackerman, President

Solution Tree Press
President and Publisher: Douglas M. Rife
Editorial Director: Sarah Payne-Mills
Art Director: Rian Anderson
Managing Production Editor: Kendra Slayton
Senior Production Editor: Suzanne Kraszewski
Senior Editor: Amy Rubenstein
Proofreader: Miranda Addonizio
Text and Cover Designer: Laura Cox
Editorial Assistant: Sarah Ludwig

Visit **go.SolutionTree.com/instruction** to download the free reproducibles in this book.

Table of Contents

Reproducibles are in italics.

About the Author

Robert J. Marzano, PhD, is the cofounder and chief academic officer of Marzano Research in Denver, Colorado. During his fifty years in the field of education, he has worked with educators as a speaker and trainer and has authored more than forty books and two hundred articles on topics such as instruction, assessment, writing and implementing standards, cognition, effective leadership, and school intervention. His books include *The New Art and Science of Teaching*, *Leaders of Learning*, *Making Classroom Assessments Reliable and Valid*, *A Handbook for Personalized Competency-Based Education*, and *Teacher Evaluation That Makes a Difference*. His practical translations of the most current research and theory into classroom strategies are known internationally and are widely practiced by both teachers and administrators.

Dr. Marzano received a bachelor's degree from Iona College in New York, a master's degree from Seattle University, and a doctorate from the University of Washington.

To learn more about Robert J. Marzano's work, visit marzanoresearch.com.

Introduction

The New Art and Science of Teaching has a long history, dating back to the 1980s, when my colleagues and I synthesized the research and theory that would become the foundation for this book. In the ensuing years, my colleagues and I developed texts that explored research-supported instructional strategies—namely, *Dimensions of Thinking* (Marzano et al., 1988) and *A Different Kind of Classroom* (Marzano, 1992). However, some believed that the strategies themselves would guarantee enhanced student learning. As this is simply not the case, I set about to create an instructional model that would tie the strategies together in an interactive manner that would allow them to work in concert. And *The Art and Science of Teaching* (Marzano, 2007) was born.

As I have stated before, effective teaching is not merely following a set of preprogrammed instructional strategies. Rather, the strategies are techniques that the teacher uses to create lessons that optimize student learning. In this way, teachers are artists in using skill and savvy to develop unique creations that are not scripted but true to their individuality. And like any artist, teachers must continuously better their skill using the most up-to-date techniques based on research and theory. *The New Art and Science of Teaching* (Marzano, 2017) represents the current knowledge of effective teaching and draws from the past and is rooted in the present while turning an eye toward the future.

The New Art and Science of Teaching

The model of effective instruction has been updated in several ways. I have added two categories ([1] Strategies That Appear in All Types of Lessons and [2] Assessment) and arranged the categories into three overarching segments: (1) feedback, (2) content, and (3) context. *Feedback* refers to the information loop between the teacher and the students that provides students with an awareness of what they should be learning and how they are doing. *Content* refers to lesson progression, which allows students to move from an initial understanding of context to application of content while continuously reviewing and upgrading their knowledge. *Context* refers to the following student psychological needs: engagement, order, a sense of belonging, and high expectations.

Additionally, I have rearranged some of the elements that appear in each design area to eliminate redundancy and added some new elements. As an example of rearrangement to eliminate redundancy, the element of *organizing students to interact* (now in the category Strategies That Appear in All Types of Lessons) is a combination of three separate content-related elements from the original framework: (1) *organizing students to interact with new knowledge*, (2) *organizing students to practice and deepen knowledge*, and (3) *organizing students for cognitively complex tasks*. New elements include *generating and defending claims*, *motivating and inspiring students*, and both elements within the Assessment category. The model now encompasses 43 elements and 332 strategies.

Perhaps the greatest change to the model is that it takes a student-outcomes perspective as opposed to the teacher-outcomes perspective of *The Art and Science of Teaching*. This focus on student outcomes makes intuitive sense since the instructional strategies are meant to generate certain mental states and processes in students' minds to thus enhance their learning. Table I.1 depicts these specific mental states and processes.

Table I.1: Teacher Actions and Student Mental States and Processes

	Teacher Actions	Student Mental States and Processes
Feedback	Providing and Communicating Clear Learning Goals	1. Students understand the progression of knowledge they are expected to master and where they are along that progression.
	Using Assessments	2. Students understand how test scores and grades relate to their status on the progression of knowledge they are expected to master.
Content	Conducting Direct Instruction Lessons	3. When content is new, students understand which parts are important and how the parts fit together.
	Conducting Practicing and Deepening Lessons	4. After teachers present new content, students deepen their understanding and develop fluency in skills and processes.
	Conducting Knowledge Application Lessons	5. After teachers present new content, students generate and defend claims through knowledge application tasks.
	Using Strategies That Appear in All Types of Lessons	6. Students continually integrate new knowledge with old knowledge and revise their understanding accordingly.
Context	Using Engagement Strategies	7. Students are paying attention, energized, intrigued, and inspired.
	Implementing Rules and Procedures	8. Students understand and follow rules and procedures.
	Building Relationships	9. Students feel welcome, accepted, and valued.
	Communicating High Expectations	10. Typically reluctant students feel valued and do not hesitate to interact with the teacher or their peers.

Source: Marzano, 2017.

The teacher actions and student mental states and processes translate nicely into a set of questions that help teachers plan units and lessons within those units. In *The New Art and Science of Teaching*, these are referred to as design questions. Table I.2 depicts these.

Table I.2: Design Questions

	Design Areas	Design Questions
Feedback	1. Providing and Communicating Clear Learning Goals	How will I communicate clear learning goals that help students understand the progression of knowledge they are expected to master and where they are along that progression?
	2. Using Assessments	How will I design and administer assessments that help students understand how their test scores and grades are related to their status on the progression of knowledge they are expected to master?

Content	3. Conducting Direct Instruction Lessons	When content is new, how will I design and deliver direct instruction lessons that help students understand which parts are important and how the parts fit together?
	4. Conducting Practicing and Deepening Lessons	After presenting content, how will I design and deliver lessons that help students deepen their understanding and develop fluency in skills and processes?
	5. Conducting Knowledge Application Lessons	After presenting content, how will I design and deliver lessons that help students generate and defend claims through knowledge application?
	6. Using Strategies That Appear in All Types of Lessons	Throughout all types of lessons, what strategies will I use to help students continually integrate new knowledge with old knowledge and revise their understanding accordingly?
Context	7. Using Engagement Strategies	What engagement strategies will I use to help students pay attention, be energized, be intrigued, and be inspired?
	8. Implementing Rules and Procedures	What strategies will I use to help students understand and follow rules and procedures?
	9. Building Relationships	What strategies will I use to help students feel welcome, accepted, and valued?
	10. Communicating High Expectations	What strategies will I use to help typically reluctant students feel valued and comfortable interacting with me and their peers?

Source: Marzano, 2017.

These ten design questions and the general framework with the three categories provide a road map for lesson and unit planning that not only points to specific strategies but also ensures a focus on student outcomes.

Table I.3 (page 4) depicts the forty-three elements embedded in the ten design areas found within the three general categories, thus illustrating the comprehensive network of *The New Art and Science of Teaching* model.

Additionally, each element involves multiple strategies. In all, *The New Art and Science of Teaching* model includes over 332 specific instructional strategies embedded in the 43 elements. This brings us to the need for this handbook.

The Handbook

This handbook is set up to guide you through the model. The three categories make up the parts to this book. Each chapter covers a design area with elements assigned to their appropriate chapters. Within each element are strategies that will help you master the element. However, keep in mind that the strategies are not meant to be a checklist nor hard-and-fast rules to follow. The strategies can be effective means of implementing the goals of the element, but each teacher must discover what works best for him or her—make the art your own. The appendix (page 329) offers two reproducibles that support your implementation of each of the forty-three elements. "Tracking Progress Over Time" (page 330) helps teachers set goals related to their proficiency with each element and track their progress toward these goals over the course of a unit, semester, or year. The "Strategy Reflection Log" (page 331) provides teachers a space to write down their thoughts and reflect on the implementation process for specific strategies related to each element.

Decades of research have provided practical and actionable steps for implementation, and these are shared with you in the form of reproducibles, tips, and examples throughout the strategies. Many of these resources come from *The Marzano Compendium of Instructional Strategies* (Marzano Research, 2016), a rich, frequently updated online resource for K–12 teachers, instructional coaches, teacher mentors, and administrators to

Table I.3: Elements Within the Ten Design Areas

Feedback	Content	Context
Providing and Communicating Clear Learning Goals 1. Providing scales and rubrics 2. Tracking student progress 3. Celebrating success **Using Assessments** 4. Using informal assessments of the whole class 5. Using formal assessments of individual students	**Conducting Direct Instruction Lessons** 6. Chunking content 7. Processing content 8. Recording and representing content **Conducting Practicing and Deepening Lessons** 9. Using structured practice sessions 10. Examining similarities and differences 11. Examining errors in reasoning **Conducting Knowledge Application Lessons** 12. Engaging students in cognitively complex tasks 13. Providing resources and guidance 14. Generating and defending claims **Using Strategies That Appear in All Types of Lessons** 15. Previewing strategies 16. Highlighting critical information 17. Reviewing content 18. Revising knowledge 19. Reflecting on learning 20. Assigning purposeful homework 21. Elaborating on information 22. Organizing students to interact	**Using Engagement Strategies** 23. Noticing and reacting when students are not engaged 24. Increasing response rates 25. Using physical movement 26. Maintaining a lively pace 27. Demonstrating intensity and enthusiasm 28. Presenting unusual information 29. Using friendly controversy 30. Using academic games 31. Providing opportunities for students to talk about themselves 32. Motivating and inspiring students **Implementing Rules and Procedures** 33. Establishing rules and procedures 34. Organizing the physical layout of the classroom 35. Demonstrating withitness 36. Acknowledging adherence to rules and procedures 37. Acknowledging lack of adherence to rules and procedures **Building Relationships** 38. Using verbal and nonverbal behaviors that indicate affection for students 39. Understanding students' backgrounds and interests 40. Displaying objectivity and control **Communicating High Expectations** 41. Demonstrating value and respect for reluctant learners 42. Asking in-depth questions of reluctant learners 43. Probing incorrect answers with reluctant learners

Source: Marzano, 2017.

fully implement *The New Art and Science of Teaching* framework. This handbook is meant to set you up for success with this model, and as such, it provides you with a strong starting point from which to let your artistic instincts flourish.

Here you are given the science. Now, you provide the art.

PART I

Feedback

CHAPTER 1

Providing and Communicating Clear Learning Goals

Effective feedback begins with clearly defined and clearly communicated learning goals. The goal of this design area is for students to understand the progression of knowledge they are expected to master and where they are along that progression. Teachers are able to meet that goal by answering the question, How will I communicate clear learning goals that help students understand the progression of knowledge they are expected to master and where they are along that progression? The three elements and associated strategies in this chapter help the teacher do just that.

Element 1: Providing Scales and Rubrics

An effective educator provides a clearly stated learning goal accompanied by a scale or rubric that describes levels of performance relative to the learning goal. Research has shown that setting goals or objectives increases student achievement (Lipsey & Wilson, 1993; Walberg, 1999; Wise & Okey, 1983).

To be successful, students must understand what they are expected to achieve and how to get there. The best vehicle for delivering that knowledge is a proficiency scale. Element 1 underscores the necessity of providing both proficiency scales and rubrics; however, we will focus on proficiency scales here. A scale is more general and describes a progression of knowledge or skills. Rubrics are typically created for a specific project or task and describe details that are applied to the assignment rather than the skill. Figure 1.1 provides an example of a proficiency scale.

LANGUAGE Context Clues *Grade 6*	
4.0	In addition to Score 3.0, the student demonstrates in-depth inferences and applications that go beyond what was taught.
3.5	In addition to score 3.0 performance, the student has partial success at score 4.0 content.
3.0	The student will use context (for example, the overall meaning of a sentence or paragraph or a word's position or function in a sentence) as a clue to the meaning of a grade-appropriate word or phrase (L.6.4a).

Figure 1.1: Sample proficiency scale for English language arts standard.

continued →

LANGUAGE Context Clues *Grade 6*	
2.5	The student has no major errors or omissions regarding score 2.0 content and partial success at score 3.0 content.
2.0	The student will recognize or recall specific vocabulary, such as: • *Clue, context, function, meaning, paragraph, phrase, position, sentence, word* The student will perform basic processes, such as: • Demonstrate the use of context clues using structured sentences in isolation
1.5	The student has partial success at score 2.0 content, but major errors or omissions regarding score 3.0 content.
1.0	With help, the student has partial success at score 2.0 content and score 3.0 content.
0.5	With help, the student has partial success at score 2.0 content but not score 3.0 content.
0.0	Even with help, the student demonstrates no understanding or skill.

There are six strategies within this element.

1. Clearly articulating learning goals
2. Creating scales or rubrics for learning goals
3. Implementing routines for using targets and scales
4. Using teacher-created targets and scales
5. Creating student-friendly scales
6. Identifying individual student learning goals

The following sections will explore each strategy to provide you with guidelines to effectively implement this element. Read through each before creating a plan for your classroom. Teachers may use the strategies individually or in combination. Remember, these are not merely activities to be checked off; they are methods of creating a practice that combines your art with the science of providing scales and rubrics. Reflect on your use of each strategy by filling out the "Strategy Reflection Log" on page 331.

Clearly Articulating Learning Goals

Before we set learning goals, we must understand exactly what they are. Learning goals state what students will know or be able to do at the end of the learning period. They are not the activities or assignments; rather, these are tasks that are meant to support students in achieving the learning goals.

Teachers acquire the goals from their standards documents and write them in such a way that creates clarity for both teacher and student. Consider the following formats for learning goals.

Declarative knowledge: Students will understand ____.

Procedural knowledge: Students will be able to ____.

These two formats allow teachers to unpack sometimes complicated standards into simple sentences that clarify the action or knowledge a student is expected to be able to demonstrate at the end of the learning period. For example, "Students will understand how the antebellum period affected the Civil War," or "Students will be able to design and execute an experiment that demonstrates Newton's second law of motion."

Teachers communicate these learning goals for each assignment. In turn, each assignment must directly relate to the learning goal. In this way, both teachers and students understand the purpose of an assignment.

Creating Scales or Rubrics for Learning Goals

Teachers embed the learning goal in a proficiency scale. The learning goal itself is the target for score 3.0. Teachers then articulate a simpler learning goal for score 2.0, and a more complex goal for score 4.0 (see figure 1.2).

4.0	**More complex learning goal** In addition to score 3.0, the student demonstrates in-depth inferences and applications that go beyond what was taught.
3.5	In addition to score 3.0 performance, the student has partial success at score 4.0 content.
3.0	**Target learning goal**
2.5	The student has no major errors or omissions regarding score 2.0 content and partial success at score 3.0 content.
2.0	**Simpler learning goal**
1.5	The student has partial success at score 2.0 content, but major errors or omissions regarding score 3.0 content.
1.0	**With help, the student has partial success at score 2.0 content and score 3.0 content.**
0.5	With help, the student has partial success at 2.0 content but not score 3.0 content.
0.0	**Even with help, the student demonstrates no understanding or skill.**

Figure 1.2: Proficiency scale template.

Using the template in figure 1.2, follow these four steps to create your own proficiency scale.

1. Identify a target learning goal. This goal will become the score 3.0 content in the scale. For example, "Students will describe complex causal relationships in grade-appropriate passages."
2. Identify knowledge that is simpler than the target learning goal and a prerequisite to achieving the target learning goal. This content will become the score 2.0 level of the scale. For example, based on the example in step 1, a simpler goal could be, "Students will identify literary clues that signal a cause-effect relationship in a specific grade-appropriate text." Score 2.0 often includes more than one content statement, as the simpler content might include vocabulary terms as well as several basic facts or processes.
3. Identify knowledge that is more complex than the learning goal. This content will become the score 4.0 level of the scale. Content at this level goes beyond what teachers will directly teach in class and often includes complex comparisons, generalizations, or application of knowledge to real-world problems. Continuing the example, a more complex learning goal could be, "Students will explain the relationship between complex causal relationships in one story and those in other stories." Some teachers, schools, and districts prefer to simply state, "Students will make inferences and applications beyond what was taught," rather than explicitly stating a specific level 4.0 learning goal. Either approach is acceptable.
4. Include generic descriptions of other levels. Scores 1.0 and 0.0 are general statements, rather than content specific, and do not change. The same goes for half-point scores, if teachers use them.

Implementing Routines for Using Targets and Scales

Routines provide several benefits to the classroom. In relation to element 1, routines encourage students' attentiveness to learning targets and proficiency scales; they help students relate their learning back to the targets and scales; and they help teachers focus their lessons on the goals set in targets and scales. How might you develop a routine to include targets and scales? Following are a few examples.

Begin and end every lesson by relating the activity or task back to the learning target and relating the learning target back to the scale. This should involve a brief review of the scale and should not take more than several minutes of class time. Extend this activity by giving students the opportunity at the end of class to explain how they see the lesson relating to the target and the scale.

Post a copy of the scale and learning target in the same place every day so it is accessible to students. Students should instinctually know where to look for a scale and target during every class. For example, teachers can write the learning target for the day on the whiteboard and create cork boards for the various scales students might want to reference during class. Additionally, teachers can make individual copies of scales for students to use during class or at home.

Create a routine that helps relate the lesson to the learning goal. For example, before a lesson, write and strategically place sticky notes around the classroom to remind yourself to relate the content back to the target and scale. Ask students individually or in groups to brainstorm how the lesson relates to the learning goal during a pause in instruction or near the end of class. Teachers can also ask students to give a quick signal to request an explanation whenever they aren't certain how the lesson relates to the target and scale.

The main benefit of establishing such routines is to reinforce the idea of a learning progression. Teachers can reinforce learning progressions in a number of ways: by asking students to summarize their progress toward a learning target at the end of a week, class period, or unit; by having students relate what they have just learned to their previous understanding or knowledge of the subject; or by asking students to identify where they are on a scale before leaving the classroom. Teachers should consistently engage students in activities that help them understand that they are getting closer to the goal with every lesson.

Using Teacher-Created Targets and Scales

Once you've spent the time and energy creating the scales, you must use them as a foundation for instruction; otherwise, that precious time has been wasted. For example, for a lesson with brand-new content, you might plan your lesson to first focus on score 2.0, which would be considered the daily learning target. Once you've established that the students are able to successfully meet this goal, move up to the set learning goal of score 3.0 content.

Of course, to effectively implement targets and scales, you must be sure that students understand the learning progressions. Introduce or review the concepts of learning targets and proficiency scales in a general way before relating them directly to the content they'll need to master. You may also consider using past student work to exemplify each level of the scale. Throughout instruction, relate assignments and activities back to the learning target or scale to help students absorb these concepts and become fluent in their use.

Consider extending your use of targets and scales by putting them in the students' hands. Ask students to set goals based on a target or scale. Or, ask students to describe how their actions contribute to their mastery of the target. Another option is to have students determine for themselves where they are on the scale and what they need to do to get to the next level.

Creating Student-Friendly Scales

In this strategy, the teacher asks students to translate the scale into student-friendly language. After explaining the target, simpler (2.0), and more complex (4.0) learning goals, the teacher divides the students into groups of three or four to write out their own versions of each of these levels. The teacher then compiles the students' suggestions, presents the rewritten scale to students for feedback and comments, and revises as necessary.

The benefits of this strategy are twofold. First, the students' responses help the teacher to better identify the students' understanding of both the target and the scale. Second, students are better able to internalize the learning progression having done this work rather than just viewing the scale on a whiteboard or poster.

Figure 1.3, based on Robert J. Marzano's (2006) work in *Classroom Assessment and Grading That Work*, shows student-friendly wording of each score on a proficiency scale.

4.0	I know (can do) it well enough to make connections that weren't taught, and I'm right about those connections.
3.5	I know (can do) it well enough to make connections that weren't taught, but I'm not always right about those connections.
3.0	I know (can do) everything that was taught (the easy parts and the harder parts) without making mistakes.
2.5	I know (can do) all the easy parts and some (but not all) of the harder parts.
2.0	I know (can do) all the easy parts, but I don't know (can't do) the harder parts.
1.5	I know (can do) some of the easier parts, but I make some mistakes.
1.0	With help, I know (can do) some of the harder parts and some of the easier parts.
0.5	With help, I know (can do) some of the easier parts but not the harder parts.
0.0	I don't know (can't do) any of it.

Source: Marzano, 2006.

Figure 1.3: Example of a student-friendly proficiency scale.

Identifying Individual Student Learning Goals

The teacher asks students to identify and record a personal learning goal that interests them and that relates to the teacher-identified learning goals. Students state their personal learning goals using the following formats.

When this unit is completed, I will better understand ____________________.

When this unit is completed, I will be able to ____________________.

Instead of creating a proficiency scale for their personal goals, students can use the following generic scale to examine their progress.

4 = I did even better than the goal I set.
3 = I accomplished my goal.
2 = I didn't accomplish everything I wanted to, but I learned quite a bit.
1 = I tried, but I didn't really learn much.
0 = I didn't really try to accomplish my goal.

Figure 1.4 (page 12) can provide your students with guidance in setting and tracking their personal learning goals.

Student Progress Chart

Name: ______________________________

Learning Goal: ______________________________

Initial Score: ______________________________

Goal Score: ____________________ by ____________________

Specific things I am going to do to improve: ______________________________

____

____

____

Score on Learning Goal	a	b	c	d	e	f	g	h	i	j
4										
3										
2										
1										
0										

Date

a. ____________________ f. ____________________

b. ____________________ g. ____________________

c. ____________________ h. ____________________

d. ____________________ i. ____________________

e. ____________________ j. ____________________

Figure 1.4: Student progress chart.

Visit **go.SolutionTree.com/instruction** *for a free reproducible version of this figure.*

Monitoring Element 1

Specific student responses and behaviors allow the teacher to determine whether this element is being implemented effectively and producing the desired effects.

- Students can describe how they have progressed on a scale.
- Students can explain the learning goal for the lesson.
- Students can describe how their current activities relate to the learning goal.
- Students can explain the progression of levels of performance on the scale.

Use this list to monitor student responses to element 1.

To monitor your own use of this element, use the scale in figure 1.5 in combination with the reproducible "Tracking Teacher Actions: Providing Scales and Rubrics" (page 23). As with other proficiency scales, level 3 or higher is the goal.

4 Innovating	I adapt behaviors and create new strategies for unique student needs and situations.
3 Applying	I provide scales and rubrics, and I monitor the extent to which my actions affect students' performance.
2 Developing	I provide scales and rubrics, but I do not monitor the effect on students.
1 Beginning	I use the strategies and behaviors associated with this element incorrectly or with parts missing.
0 Not Using	I am unaware of strategies and behaviors associated with this element.

Figure 1.5: Self-rating scale for element 1—Providing scales and rubrics.

The following examples describe what each level of the scale might look like in the classroom.

- **Not Using (0):** A teacher does not typically articulate learning goals in her class. When she does, she does not embed those goals in a scale.
- **Beginning (1):** A teacher posts a learning goal embedded in a scale but does not review the goal or scale with his class or explain how daily assignments relate to the learning goal.
- **Developing (2):** A teacher has established a routine for using learning goals and scales. At the beginning and end of each lesson, she describes how the content in the lesson relates to a specific part of the scale. However, the teacher does not make sure students understand how to use the scale and isn't sure if the routine is having an impact on students' understanding of their progress.
- **Applying (3):** A teacher presents learning goals and scales and asks his students to translate scales into student-friendly language. He leads students in defining unfamiliar terms then puts them into small groups to generate specific, action-oriented descriptions of each level of the scale. He monitors each group to make sure each student understands the scale and the concept of a learning progression. Once the students have an understanding of the learning goals and scale, the teacher checks to ensure that students can describe how the scale relates to classroom activities.
- **Innovating (4):** A teacher has had a great deal of success introducing and using proficiency scales with her class. However, some students who are English learners are having difficulty understanding the different levels of knowledge depicted in the scale. To help ensure that these students can use the scale, the teacher asks a friend of hers to translate the scale into the students' native language, which in this case is Spanish. She also pairs monolingual Spanish speakers with students who speak both Spanish and English when discussing the various levels of the scale.

Element 2: Tracking Student Progress

An effective educator facilitates tracking student progress on one or more learning goals using a formative approach to assessment. Research has shown that feedback—making students aware of their progress toward learning goals—is associated with an increase in student achievement (Bangert-Drowns, Kulik, Kulik, & Morgan, 1991; Bloom, 1976; Haas, 2005; Haller, Child, & Walberg, 1988; Kumar, 1991; Lysakowski & Walberg, 1981, 1982; Tennenbaum & Goldring, 1989; Walberg, 1999). Feedback is particularly effective when accompanied by clear goals and when given frequently (Bangert-Drowns, Kulik, & Kulik, 1991; Marzano, 2007). Element 2 focuses on assessing students often and giving them feedback on how they are progressing toward their goals. There are seven strategies within this element.

1. Using formative scores
2. Designing assessments that generate formative scores
3. Using individual score-level assessments
4. Using different types of assessments
5. Generating summative scores
6. Charting student progress
7. Charting class progress

The following sections will explore each strategy to provide you with guidelines to effectively implement this element. Read through each before creating a plan for your classroom. Teachers may use the strategies individually or in combination. Remember, these are not merely activities to be checked off; they are methods of creating a practice that combines your art with the science of tracking student progress. Reflect on your use of each strategy by filling out the "Strategy Reflection Log" on page 331.

Using Formative Scores

Using formative scores throughout a unit of instruction helps teachers and students monitor progress and adjust as necessary. This strategy works in conjunction with proficiency scales, as the class is familiar with the levels of learning progression featured on the scales. Teachers give assessments periodically throughout a unit or term, which allows students to progress up the scale.

To create assessments that generate formative scores, the teacher designs assessment tasks that correspond to 2.0, 3.0, and 4.0 content (as specified on the scale for each learning goal). For 2.0 content, forced-choice or selected-response tasks (multiple-choice, matching, true or false, or fill-in-the-blank items) are common. For 3.0 and 4.0 content, short- or extended constructed-response tasks (short written or oral responses, essays, oral reports, demonstrations, or performances) are common.

The teacher then grades these assessments using scores from the proficiency scale. When students review their scores, they know where they are on the learning progression and what they need to do to get to the next level.

Designing Assessments That Generate Formative Scores

An assessment for formative scores should contain items or tasks that correspond directly to levels 2.0, 3.0, and 4.0. Level 2.0 items and tasks address basic details and processes that are relatively easy for students. These items are often forced-choice recognition and recall questions or fill-in-the-blank items. Level 3.0 items and tasks address ideas and processes that are more complex but were still taught directly in class. Level 3.0 informational items and tasks are often open ended and ask students to write a few sentences. Level 4.0 items and tasks require students to make inferences or applications that go beyond what was taught in class. These items ask students to generate original ideas and often take the form of comparing, classifying, creating analogies, or analyzing errors.

An assessment may cover more than one proficiency scale. If this is the case, the teacher must provide formative scores for each scale represented on the assessment; otherwise, the score is not able to be used formatively.

Planning an assessment system to generate formative scores involves the teacher identifying which topics to assess, when to assess them, and whether a specific assessment will address more than one topic. Although a teacher does not have to identify every assessment to use for each topic for a grading period, it is useful to rough out a general plan. For example, the following chart in figure 1.6 from *Classroom Assessment and Grading That Work* by Robert J. Marzano (2006) depicts a general plan for assessing six topics (each with its own proficiency scale) over a nine-week period. Xs denote when the teacher will assess a topic. As the class will assess more than one topic most weeks, the teacher might choose to give multiple separate assessments or one that covers numerous topics.

Week	Topic					
	1	2	3	4	5	6
1	X	X				
2		X	X			
3	X		X			
4				X		X
5					X	
6				X	X	X
7	X	X	X			
8				X	X	X
9	X	X	X	X	X	X

Source: Marzano, 2006.

Figure 1.6: General plan for assessing six measurement topics over nine weeks.

Using Individual Score-Level Assessments

Assessments for formative scores do not always have to cover the whole range of the associated proficiency scale; some can evaluate only one level of a scale (for example, only 2.0 content). Such assessments allow students to progress at their own pace through the levels of the scale.

Since this strategy requires the teacher to use assessments that evaluate only one level of a scale, the teacher should design several assessments during an instructional unit. For example, the teacher could design three assessments to be given over the course of a unit. The first assessment comes near the beginning of the unit and covers only score 2.0 content. For this assessment, the highest score students could receive would be a 2.0 because the assessment only addresses this level of the scale. The second assessment comes later in the unit, after the teacher has covered the target content, and is focused on level 3.0 knowledge. At the end of the unit, the teacher provides an assessment that covers score 4.0 content. Of course, students must first demonstrate competence with a level before being given an assessment at the next level. With this approach, the whole class progresses together. The teacher continues teaching and assessing a level of content until the whole class (or close to it) has mastered that level.

Using Different Types of Assessments

Teachers use different types of assessments to collect formative scores. Each has its time and place in the classroom.

Obtrusive assessments interrupt the normal flow of activity in the classroom. The most common is the traditional pencil-and-paper tests involving true-or-false, multiple-choice, fill-in-the-blank, and constructed-response items. However, this category also includes demonstrations, performances, and probing discussions between the teacher and a student.

Unobtrusive assessments do not interrupt the flow of instruction, and students might not even be aware the teacher is assessing them. Such assessments typically involve the teacher observing students, in person or via recording. They are most easily applied to content that is procedural or involves a skill, strategy, or process.

Student-generated tasks are a powerful alternative to the other two categories of assessments—and are the most underutilized in classrooms. Students generate their own tasks to demonstrate competence for specific levels of the scale. This approach is often used when a student receives a score on a teacher-designed assessment and wants to move up to the next score value on a proficiency scale. He then develops an idea for a task to show he has mastered the content of the next level and presents it for teacher approval. Student-generated assessments help develop student agency because they give some decision-making power to those being assessed.

Generating Summative Scores

A summative score indicates a student's status at the end of a specific interval of time such as a grading period. There are four different approaches to assigning summative scores.

- **Approach 1:** Each assessment over a specific interval of time allows students to score at the 2.0, 3.0, or 4.0 level. The students graph their scores throughout the unit, and the teacher uses that group of scores to assign a summative score at the end of the unit.
- **Approach 2:** The first assessment within a specific interval of time allows students to score at the 2.0, 3.0, or 4.0 level. After the first assessment, students move at their own pace, taking individual score-level assessments to move up to the next level.
- **Approach 3:** The teacher administers individual score-level assessments to the entire class, only moving up to the next level once the majority of students in the class has mastered the content at the current level.
- **Approach 4:** The teacher assigns scores at the end of each unit, but students are allowed to improve those scores at any time during the year by demonstrating their competence at higher score levels, usually using student-generated assessments.

For this strategy, teachers can use one or more of these different approaches to generating summative scores for a specific proficiency scale.

Charting Student Progress

Students set goals relative to a specific scale at the beginning of a learning period and track their scores on that scale, using a chart the teacher provides, such as that in figure 1.7.

The teacher can then assign a summative score to the student for the scale at the end of the learning period.

Charting Class Progress

In this strategy, the teacher uses a whole-class tracking chart to get a snapshot of the percentage of students who scored at proficient or above for a particular assessment. See figure 1.8 for an example.

Individual teachers or teams of teachers can use these aggregated data to identify future instructional emphases. If the data indicate that an insufficient percentage of students in a particular grade level are at or

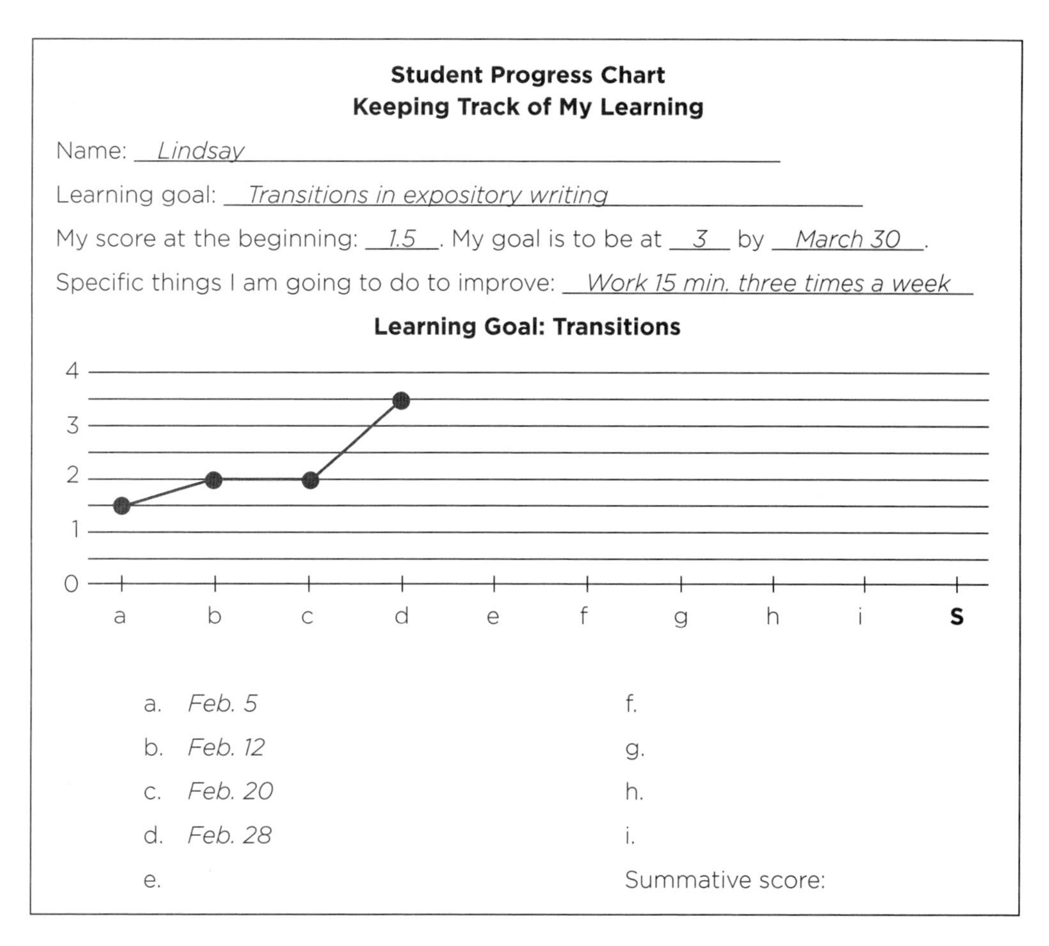

Source: Marzano, 2010.

Figure 1.7: Student progress chart.

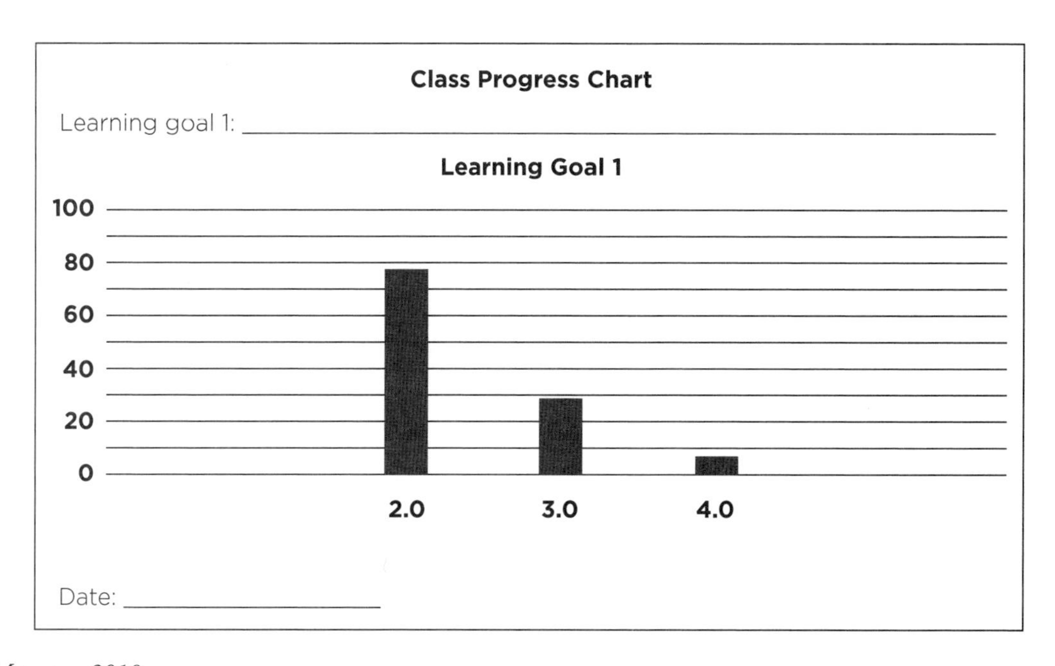

Source: Marzano, 2010.

Figure 1.8: Class progress chart.

above the designated performance standard, then teachers at that grade level might mount a joint effort to enhance student progress for the learning goal.

Monitoring Element 2

Specific student responses and behaviors allow the teacher to determine whether this element is being implemented effectively and producing the desired effects.

- Students can describe how they have progressed on a particular proficiency scale.
- Students periodically update their status on a proficiency scale.
- Students can describe what they need to do to get to the next level of performance.

Use this list to monitor student responses to element 2.

To monitor your own use of this element, use the scale in figure 1.9 in combination with the reproducible "Tracking Teacher Actions: Tracking Student Progress" (page 24). As with other proficiency scales, level 3 or higher is the goal.

4 Innovating	I adapt behaviors and create new strategies for unique student needs and situations.
3 Applying	I track student progress, and I monitor the extent to which my actions affect student learning.
2 Developing	I track student progress, but I do not monitor the effect on student learning.
1 Beginning	I use the strategies and behaviors associated with this element incorrectly or with parts missing.
0 Not Using	I am unaware of strategies and behaviors associated with this element.

Figure 1.9: Self-rating scale for element 2—Tracking student progress.

The following examples describe what each level of the scale might look like in the classroom.

- **Not Using (0):** A teacher does not track student progress or encourage students to track their own progress. Each unit's final grade is based on a single assessment or the average of a number of assessments.
- **Beginning (1):** A teacher hands out a chart to her students and tells them that they can track their progress toward a goal using the scores from different assignments. However, the students are uncertain about what they need to do to improve their status. Students resist completing the activity regularly because they don't see a good reason to write down their scores when the teacher already does so in her gradebook.
- **Developing (2):** A teacher uses a formative approach to assessment to measure how well his students understand the content. He designs a proficiency scale for the unit or set of lessons, and creates assessments for 2.0, 3.0, and 4.0 content. The teacher shares the proficiency scale with the class and explains how assessments will correlate to the levels of the scale. However, he makes little or no attempt to determine the extent to which students are aware of their status and growth on the scale.
- **Applying (3):** A teacher uses various types of assessments to track student progress on the scale throughout the unit. She systematically meets with students to discuss their growth and what they can do to move to the next level of the scale.
- **Innovating (4):** A teacher uses different types of assessments to measure student progress on the scale. While most students seem to understand how to use the scale and how they

are progressing, a few seem confused or uninterested in tracking their progress. The teacher periodically meets with these students to help them understand how they are doing and what they can do to increase their relative position on the scale.

Element 3: Celebrating Success

An effective educator provides students with recognition of their current status and their knowledge gain relative to the learning goal. Research has shown that reinforcing students' effort increases student achievement (Hattie, Biggs, & Purdie, 1996; Kumar, 1991; Marzano, 2018; Schunk & Cox, 1986; Stipek & Weisz, 1981). Helping students see a direct relationship between how hard they work and how much they learn is an important part of reinforcing effort (Deci, Koestner, & Ryan, 2001; Deci, Ryan, & Koestner, 2001; Marzano, 2007). Element 3 focuses on celebrating to emphasize effort and growth. There are three strategies within this element.

1. Status celebration
2. Knowledge gain celebration
3. Verbal feedback

The following sections will explore each strategy to provide you with guidelines to effectively implement this element. Read through each before creating a plan for your classroom. Teachers may use the strategies individually or in combination. Remember, these are not merely activities to be checked off; they are methods of creating a practice that combines your art with the science of celebrating success. Reflect on your use of each strategy by filling out the "Strategy Reflection Log" on page 331.

Status Celebration

The teacher celebrates each student's final status (or summative score) at the end of each unit (or at any point in time). Perhaps the teacher recognizes all the students who achieved a final score of 3.0, all the students who achieved a final score of 3.5, and all the students who achieved a final score of 4.0. Following are examples of status celebrations.

- **Certificates:** Hand out certificates to students who achieved their end-of-term goal during a special recognition ceremony at the end of a quarter or semester.
- **Snack parties:** Host a snack party during lunch, during recess, or after school for students or classes who achieved a particular goal for the term.
- **Success banners or posters:** Have students sign and draw pictures on a banner that commemorates individual or class achievements at the end of the term.
- **Student honor roll:** Post the names of students who achieved final scores of 3.0, 3.5, and 4.0 for a particular learning target or unit on a class website or in the classroom.
- **Field trip:** Allow students to participate in an educational, end-of-term field trip. Perhaps consider allowing students to brainstorm possible destinations. If possible, choose destinations that relate to the topics covered over the course of the unit or term.
- **Friday Fun Club:** One Friday a month, allow students who achieved a particular final score on a unit to spend the last hour of the day or class period playing academic games.
- **Film Club:** Invite students who achieved a particular score on a unit to attend the screening of a film that relates to the content covered in class. The club could convene at the end of a school day or over the course of one class period.

Knowledge Gain Celebration

The teacher celebrates knowledge gain, which is the difference between a student's initial and final scores for a learning goal. This is one of the most powerful aspects of formative assessment—it allows students to see their progress over time. Recognizing and celebrating knowledge gain in addition to or in place of final status gives virtually every student something to celebrate because every student will increase his or her knowledge relative to specific learning goals. The teacher recognizes a student who started at a 1.5 and ended at 3.0 in the same way as a student who began with a score of 2.5 and ended with a score of 4.0; the teacher recognizes both students for a knowledge gain of 1.5. Following are examples of knowledge gain celebrations.

- **Demonstrations:** Ask the student to demonstrate to the class how he or she answered or solved a difficult question on a test or assignment. Have the student explain the reasoning behind the answer. If the student is uncomfortable presenting in front of the class, ask if you can present the student's thinking and acknowledge his or her success in class.
- **Charts:** Have students create a graph that demonstrates their progress over the course of a semester. Ask students to set learning goals for themselves and chart their progress toward their goal. When students meet or exceed a goal, add their names to a poster in the classroom that lists all of the students who achieved their learning goals.
- **Student work board:** Use a corkboard to display examples of good student work. Announce which papers, assignments, or tests will go up on the corkboard weekly or bi-weekly and ask the whole class to give those students a round of applause.
- **Student of the month award:** Give a student of the month award to a student who has shown great improvement, shared knowledge with others, or worked exceptionally hard to master new content. Create a certificate for the student, and post his or her name and picture, if available, in the classroom or on a class website. Below the student's name or picture, describe in a sentence or two why that student was chosen as the student of the month.
- **Class progress goals:** Set a class goal that every student will raise his or her score a certain amount by the end of a unit or semester. Encourage students who have already met their goals to work with students who may be struggling. Chart the progress of the class on a poster in the room or online on a class website. If the goal is met, organize a party for the class at the end of a class period, during lunch, or after school with drinks and snacks.

Verbal Feedback

The teacher emphasizes each student's effort and growth by specifically explaining what he or she did well on a task. The teacher should avoid attributing accomplishments to innate intelligence, talent, or other fixed characteristics. Appropriate phrases to use when giving verbal feedback include the following.

- "You tried very hard on this—good job."
- "You put a lot of effort into this—nice work."
- "You were very focused while working on this—way to go."
- "You were well prepared for this; keep up the good work."
- "You really thought through this, and it paid off."
- "You came very well informed about this—excellent work."
- "You were ready for this—very good."

Consider the following five tips for providing growth-minded feedback (Marzano Research, 2016).

1. Emphasize the student's effort or preparation for the task.
2. Describe how the student's approach helped the student succeed.

3. Try acknowledging a different student every day.
4. Speak enthusiastically about the student's achievements or improvements.
5. Acknowledge students' hard work in front of peers, parents, and other teachers when possible.

Teachers can provide verbal feedback during the following scenarios (Marzano Research, 2016).

- At the end of a successful class period, they stand by the door, compliment the class on their hard work and effort, and give them high fives as they leave the classroom.
- They can write an email to a parent after a student turns in an exemplary assignment or shows improvement, letting the parent know how well the student is doing.
- They can leave a personalized note at the bottom of an assignment or on the student's desk that compliments the student's efforts or work in class.
- They can read a passage from a student's test answer, essay, or other written assignment in front of the class and explain what that student did well.

Monitoring Element 3

Specific student responses and behaviors allow the teacher to determine whether this element is being implemented effectively and producing the desired effects.

- Students demonstrate pride regarding their accomplishments.
- Students appear to strive for higher scores on a proficiency scale.
- Students say they enjoy celebrations.

Use this list to monitor student responses to element 3.

To monitor your own use of this element, use the scale in figure 1.10 in combination with the reproducible "Tracking Teacher Actions: Celebrating Success" (page 25). As with other proficiency scales, level 3 or higher is the goal.

4 Innovating	I adapt behaviors and create new strategies for unique student needs and situations.
3 Applying	I celebrate success, and I monitor the extent to which my actions affect students.
2 Developing	I celebrate success, but I do not monitor the effect on students.
1 Beginning	I use the strategies and behaviors associated with this element incorrectly or with parts missing.
0 Not Using	I am unaware of strategies and behaviors associated with this element.

Figure 1.10: Self-rating scale for element 3—Celebrating success.

The following examples describe what each level of the scale might look like in the classroom.

- **Not Using (0):** A teacher does not provide verbal feedback to students to indicate that she has noticed their efforts or achievements. Additionally, she does not celebrate students' successes in front of their peers or parents.
- **Beginning (1):** A teacher celebrates the academic achievements of students who consistently score high on class assignments, but he does not acknowledge other students' knowledge gains or provide verbal feedback to encourage their continued growth.

- **Developing (2):** A teacher purposefully provides written and verbal feedback to all students and publicly acknowledges their successes or growth over the term. However, she does not collect data to monitor whether her feedback encourages continued progress or motivates her students.
- **Applying (3):** A teacher uses feedback and classwide celebrations to encourage students' improvement and to celebrate their success at the end of the term. He notes which of his behaviors incite changes in students' motivation and efforts and if students appear proud of their accomplishments at the end of the term.
- **Innovating (4):** A teacher uses knowledge gain celebrations to celebrate student achievements. When one student struggles to improve or seems unmotivated in class, the teacher works with the student individually to set knowledge gain goals that they can track and celebrate together. The teacher also creates opportunities for students to share their knowledge with the class.

Action Steps

Use the "Tracking Teacher Actions" reproducibles that follow (pages 23–25) to monitor your implementation of each element in this chapter.

Additionally, visit the appendix (page 329) for the reproducible "Tracking Progress Over Time" (page 330), which helps teachers set goals related to their proficiency with each element and track their progress toward these goals over the course of a unit, semester, or year. Also, the "Strategy Reflection Log" (page 331) in the appendix provides a space to write down your thoughts and reflect on the implementation process for specific strategies related to each element. Finally, visit **go.SolutionTree.com/instruction** for both student surveys and teacher surveys, the results of which provide feedback about your proficiency with each element.

Tracking Teacher Actions: Providing Scales and Rubrics

The teacher can use this form to plan his or her usage of strategies related to the element of providing scales and rubrics.

Check Strategies You Intend to Use	Strategies	Description of Instructional Plan
	Clearly Articulating Learning Goals	
	Creating Scales or Rubrics for Learning Goals	
	Implementing Routines for Using Targets and Scales	
	Using Teacher-Created Targets and Scales	
	Creating Student-Friendly Scales	
	Identifying Individual Student Learning Goals	

Source: Adapted from Marzano Research. (2016). Marzano compendium of instructional strategies. *Centennial, CO: Author.*

Tracking Teacher Actions: Tracking Student Progress

The teacher can use this form to plan his or her usage of strategies related to the element of tracking student progress.

Check Strategies You Intend to Use	Strategies	Description of Instructional Plan
	Using Formative Scores	
	Designing Assessments That Generate Formative Scores	
	Using Individual Score-Level Assessments	
	Using Different Types of Assessments	
	Generating Summative Scores	
	Charting Student Progress	
	Charting Class Progress	
	Other:	
	Other:	

Source: Adapted from Marzano Research. (2016). Marzano compendium of instructional strategies. *Centennial, CO: Author.*

Tracking Teacher Actions: Celebrating Success

The teacher can use this form to plan his or her usage of strategies related to the element of celebrating success.

Check Strategies You Intend to Use	Strategies	Description of Instructional Plan
	Status Celebration	
	Knowledge Gain Celebration	
	Verbal Feedback	
	Other:	
	Other:	
	Other:	

Source: Adapted from Marzano Research. (2016). Marzano compendium of instructional strategies. *Centennial, CO: Author.*

CHAPTER 2

Using Assessments

Assessment is a feedback mechanism for both students and teachers. Assessments should provide students with information about how to advance their understanding of content and teachers with information about how to help students do so.

The goal of this design area is for students to understand how test scores and grades relate to their status on the progression of knowledge they are expected to master. Teachers are able to meet that goal by answering the question, How will I design and administer assessments that help students understand how their test scores and grades are related to their status on the progression of knowledge they are expected to master? The two elements and associated strategies in this chapter help the teacher do just that.

Element 4: Using Informal Assessments of the Whole Class

An effective educator uses informal assessments to get a general sense of how the class is doing regarding a specific topic. Research shows that classroom assessments should be frequent and formative in nature, encourage students to improve, and give students a clear picture of their progress on learning goals (Bangert-Drowns, Kulik, Kulik, & Morgan, 1991; Bangert-Drowns, Kulik, & Kulik, 1991; Black & Wiliam, 1998; Crooks, 1988; Fuchs & Fuchs, 1986; Kluger & DeNisi, 1996; Natriello, 1987). Teachers should use assessment data to provide students with evidence that effort on their part results in higher scores (Marzano, 2006). There are four strategies within this element.

1. Confidence rating techniques
2. Voting techniques
3. Response boards
4. Unrecorded assessments

The following sections will explore each strategy to provide you with guidelines to effectively implement this element. Read through each before creating a plan for your classroom. Teachers may use the strategies individually or in combination. Remember, these are not merely activities to be checked off; they are methods of creating a practice that combines your art with the science of using informal assessments of the whole class. Reflect on your use of each strategy by filling out the "Strategy Reflection Log" on page 331.

Confidence Rating Techniques

In this strategy, the students rate how confident they are in their understanding of a topic in the moment with direct input. The teacher uses this immediate feedback to determine what areas of the content are causing students difficulty. Following are a few ways students can rate their confidence quickly and easily.

- **Hand signals:** Hand signals provide an effective means for determining students' confidence because they require little preparation. The teacher gives the class quick instruction on predetermined hand signals before a lesson begins. Students might give a thumbs-up to indicate confidence with the material, a thumbs-down to indicate lack of confidence, or a thumbs-sideways to indicate uncertainty.
- **Polling technology:** Polling technology (clickers or smartphone apps) can be a fun and versatile means for students to rate their confidence with the material. Websites such as Poll Everywhere (www.polleverywhere.com) allow the teacher to set up confidence rating questions and then ask students to answer them using the text function of their cell phones or by visiting a specific link and voting online.
- **Color-coded cards:** Color-coded cards can be as simple as slips of colored construction paper. To use this strategy, a teacher can provide students with a system of different colored cards and have students keep them in a single stack on their desks. For example, a green card could indicate that students are confident with the material, a yellow card could indicate uncertainty, and a red card could indicate that they want the teacher to stop and re-explain a difficult point. During the lesson, students place the colored card that corresponds to their level of confidence with the material on top of the stack.

Voting Techniques

The teacher provides specific questions or prompts and asks students to vote on answers. Typically, such questions have a true-or-false or multiple-choice format. Teachers can use this to spur class discussion or simply gauge classwide competence with the content. Students can vote using confidence rating techniques or other methods such as the following.

- **Use tokens:** Using tokens to indicate answers can be an especially fun way for K–5 students to vote in the classroom. To use tokens, set up several cans or jars and provide students with a token (a coin or other small object) to place in the containers. Label each container with a different possible answer to a question. Ask students to deposit their tokens one by one, or ask the whole class to deposit their tokens at the same time. When all the tokens have been deposited, the teacher can then ask students to indicate which container they think has acquired the most votes.
- **Vote with your feet:** The teacher asks several students to provide possible answers to a difficult question. Those students then stand at different locations around the room, while the rest of the class gets out of their seats and stands near the student they think gave the right answer. Allowing two to three minutes for students to make their decision will encourage them to talk among themselves as they make their way around the room. This can induce impromptu class discussions and afford students the opportunity to get up and move around for a short time while staying focused on the content.

Response Boards

The teacher asks students to respond to a question—usually multiple choice, true or false, or short answer—using an erasable whiteboard or response card. He or she can then quickly scan the responses to get a good idea of the class's competence with the content. As this is meant to be a quick check for understanding, train yourself to look for the following.

- **Missing information:** The absence of types of information can reveal as much as their presence. The answers to many questions can be phrased in a variety of ways, and when students are unsure about particular concepts they tend to avoid using those concepts in their answers. Pay special attention to whether students are avoiding using certain ideas in their answers, as this can be a hidden indicator that they are having difficulty with those concepts.
- **Key words:** Proper use of relevant vocabulary is a necessary step to greater understanding of a topic. Looking for the presence of key words in students' answers can be a quick way of assessing whether they have a basic grasp of the content. Pay attention to how students use key words, as the misuse of certain words or phrases can indicate that students are struggling with the material.
- **Procedural clues:** For answers involving several steps or components, look for words that indicate order or progression. Words and phrases like *before*, *then*, *next*, or *in addition* can indicate that students are grasping the procedural nature of certain skills or are beginning to understand the relationships between different concepts. Of course, check to make sure that the procedures and associations are being described correctly.
- **Justifications:** One way to assess students' level of competency is to check for justifications in their answers. The use of words and phrases like *because* or *resulting in* show that students are beginning to understand the why and how of an answer and not just the what. Correct justifications for answers indicate that students are forming a more comprehensive understanding of the material.
- **Extrapolation:** A major indicator that students are mastering a content area is that they are able to apply the principles of the content to hypothetical situations. In other words, they not only know the correct answer to the specific question posed but can employ that knowledge to answer other similar questions. Look for if-then statements to assess whether students are understanding the concepts underlying the material.

Unrecorded Assessments

In this strategy, teachers administer assessments that students then score themselves. Teachers do not record individual scores in a gradebook, but they use the scores as a whole to see how well the class is doing. Unrecorded assessments are useful in providing students direct, immediate feedback about their progress. Use the template in figure 2.1 (page 30) to help guide students in reflecting on their assessment.

Monitoring Element 4

Specific student responses and behaviors allow the teacher to determine whether this element is being implemented effectively and producing the desired effects.

- Students readily engage in whole-class assessment activities.
- Students can describe the status and growth of the class as a whole.
- Students seem interested in the entire class's progress.
- Students appear pleased as the whole class's performance improves.

Use this list to monitor student responses to element 4.

To monitor your own use of this element, use the scale in figure 2.2 (page 30) in combination with the reproducible "Tracking Teacher Actions: Using Informal Assessments of the Whole Class" (page 37). As with other proficiency scales, level 3 or higher is the goal.

The following examples describe what each level of the scale might look like in the classroom.

- **Not Using (0):** A teacher only uses assessment to record grades for individual students.

Student Assessment Scoring Sheet

Name: ______________________________ Date: ____________

Topic: ______________________________

Section 1 score: ________ / ________

Section 2 score: ________ / ________

Section 3 score: ________ / ________

Overall score: ________ / ________

In which areas do you think you did well?

In which areas do you think you need improvement?

Are there any areas or questions that you completely did not understand?

Source: Marzano Research, 2016.

Figure 2.1: Student assessment scoring sheet.

Visit ***go.SolutionTree.com/instruction*** *for a free reproducible version of this figure.*

4 Innovating	I adapt behaviors and create new strategies for unique student needs and situations.
3 Applying	I use informal assessments of the whole class to determine students' proficiency with specific content, and I monitor the extent to which students respond to assessment-guided feedback and instruction.
2 Developing	I use informal assessments of the whole class to determine students' proficiency with specific content, but I do not monitor the effect on students.
1 Beginning	I use the strategies and behaviors associated with this element incorrectly or with parts missing.
0 Not Using	I am unaware of strategies and behaviors associated with this element.

Figure 2.2: Self-rating scale for element 4—Using informal assessments of the whole class.

- **Beginning (1):** A teacher administers informal assessments of the whole class, but those assessments are not focused on specific content important for students to learn.
- **Developing (2):** A teacher uses informal assessments of the whole class to provide students with feedback about how they are doing but does not attempt to determine if this feedback is useful to the students.
- **Applying (3):** A teacher uses informal assessments of the whole class to provide students with feedback about how they are doing and monitors their responses in order to adjust his classroom instruction.
- **Innovating (4):** A teacher uses various informal assessments of the whole class to provide students with feedback about how they are doing. When she notices that some students are

reluctant to indicate their confidence with the material in the whole-class setting, she has brief conversations with those students at their desks to gauge their confidence.

Element 5: Using Formal Assessments of Individual Students

An effective educator uses a variety of formal assessments to determine individual students' proficiency with specific content at specific points in time, which are then translated into scores and recorded in a gradebook. Research has shown that gathering and using student assessment data to provide feedback and develop knowledge and skill improves student achievement (Black & Wiliam, 1998). Ideally, teachers and students use assessment data in a loop as they focus on a specific learning target, collect data about and evaluate learning in relation to the target, and then take steps to move closer to the target (Brookhart & Nitko, 2007). Feedback to students, an important element of assessment, is also associated with student achievement gains (Hattie & Timperley, 2007).

There are seven strategies within this element.

1. Common assessments designed using proficiency scales
2. Assessments involving selected-response or short constructed-response items
3. Student demonstrations
4. Student interviews
5. Observations of students
6. Student-generated assessments
7. Response patterns

The following sections will explore each strategy to provide you with guidelines to effectively implement this element. Read through each before creating a plan for your classroom. Teachers may use the strategies individually or in combination. Remember, these are not merely activities to be checked off; they are methods of creating a practice that combines your art with the science of using formal assessments of individual students. Reflect on your use of each strategy by filling out the "Strategy Reflection Log" on page 331.

Common Assessments Designed Using Proficiency Scales

Teachers who teach the same content at the same level work together in teams to create common formative and summative assessments that provide students with feedback. Consider the following four steps.

1. Create a proficiency scale for the topic that will be the focus of the common assessment.
2. Design an assessment that includes items and tasks for score 2.0, 3.0, and 4.0 content.
3. Score the assessment individually or in cooperation with the other teachers and discuss the results for all students who have taken the common assessment.
4. Identify those students with common needs based on the assessment results, and group students for instruction according to their needs.

Assessments Involving Selected-Response or Short Constructed-Response Items

The teacher administers assessments that employ selected-response and short constructed-response items. Constructed-response items require students to generate a correct answer as opposed to merely recognizing one. Short-answer assessments and oral responses are examples of constructed-response assessments. Following are six types of selected-response items (Marzano, 2006).

1. **Traditional multiple choice:** Provides a stem and alternatives, some of which are distractors and one of which is the correct choice

2. **Matching:** Provides multiple stems and multiple options
3. **Alternative choice:** Provides a stem and two choices that are quite similar
4. **True or false:** Provides statements that must be judged as true or false
5. **Fill in the blank:** Provides a stem for which only one correct answer is reasonable
6. **Multiple response:** Allows for two or more correct responses

Student Demonstrations

The students generate presentations that demonstrate their understanding of a topic. Different content areas lend themselves more readily to certain types of demonstrations. For example, subject areas that focus on physical skills (such as physical education, art, and music) frequently use student demonstrations. For those content areas where demonstrations are primarily mental in nature the teacher might ask a student to think aloud while he or she is using the skill, strategy, or process.

Ask students the following questions during or after a demonstration (Marzano Research, 2016).

- "What specific skills were you demonstrating?"
- "What parts do you think you did well?"
- "On which parts did you struggle?"
- "What would you do differently if you were to do it again?"

Student Interviews

During student interviews, the teacher holds a conversation with individual students about a specific topic and then assigns a score to each student that depicts his or her knowledge of the topic. Following are tips for interviewing students.

- **Have a clear progression to the interview:** Instead of asking the student to tell you everything he or she knows about a particular topic, start with the score 2.0 content in the proficiency scale for that topic and then move up through score 3.0 and 4.0 content.
- **Prompt for further information:** If a student can't think of anything else to say, gently prod him or her for further information using the proficiency scale as a prompt.
- **Revisit previous statements:** Ask a student to recall topics from earlier in the conversation. Help him or her make connections with the current topic by asking, "How is what you said earlier affected by what we're talking about now?" Or, you might simply ask the student to explain a previous topic over again. Revisiting a topic can help the student recall information he or she missed the first time around.
- **Ask the student to defend conclusions:** When a student draws an inference, makes a prediction, or otherwise states a conclusion, ask him or her to defend or justify the statement. Explore gaps in reasoning by asking, "How did you form that conclusion from this particular information?" Encourage him or her to think about alternative possibilities by asking, "How might these same events have resulted in a different outcome?" or "What sort of information might disprove your conclusion?"

Observations of Students

The teacher observes students interacting with the content and assigns a score that represents their level of knowledge or skill regarding the specific topic observed. Students may display their proficiency through demonstration or verbally in response to the teacher's questions. For example, a teacher may observe a student incorrectly executing the order of operations when working a mathematics problem. The teacher might point out the mistake and then observe the student rework the problem with the correct method.

A template, like the one in figure 2.3, can help to record your observations.

Teachers can use this chart during class to quickly record their unobtrusive observations of students, which can be transferred to the gradebook later.

Student Name	What I Observed	Score on the Proficiency Scale

Source: Marzano Research, 2016.

Figure 2.3: Student observation chart.

Visit **go.SolutionTree.com/instruction** *for a free reproducible version of this figure.*

Student-Generated Assessments

The teacher invites students to devise ways they will demonstrate competence on a particular topic at a particular level of the proficiency scale. Student-generated assessments provide a wide variety of ways in which students can demonstrate competence. Use the template in figure 2.4 to help guide students in planning for their assessment.

Student-Generated Assessment Planning Guide

Name: ______________________________

Learning goal or topic: ______________________________

I want to demonstrate that I am at the __________ level of the proficiency scale for this topic.

To achieve this level, I have to understand or be able to do (describe the score level content in your own words):

I will demonstrate my understanding or skill by (describe your student-generated assessment):

Examples:

- Writing an essay
- Demonstrating a process
- Explaining a concept to my teacher
- Making a model
- Creating a multimedia project

My student-generated assessment proves my understanding or skill because:

Source: Marzano Research, 2016.

Figure 2.4: Student-generated assessment planning guide.

Response Patterns

The teacher identifies response patterns at score 2.0, 3.0, and 4.0 levels as opposed to adding up points to create an overall score on an assessment. This generative score indicates the content on which students are doing well and the content on which they must improve to move to the next level. There are three approaches a teacher might use to examine response patterns.

1. **Percentage scores:** In this method, the teacher computes percentage scores for each score level. For example, say a student acquires 88 percent of the possible points for the score 2.0 level, 50 percent of the points for the score 3.0 level, and 15 percent of the points for the score 4.0 level. Examining the overall pattern, the teacher then determines how well the student performed overall in reference to the scale. This is done by making decisions about the student's proficiency moving from score 2.0 through score 4.0. The score 2.0 percentage is 88 percent, so the teacher concludes that the student obtained at least a score of 2.0 on the assessment. Next, the student's percentage score for the 3.0 content was 50 percent. The teacher concludes that this is not enough to warrant an overall score of 3.0, but it is enough to warrant a score of 2.5. The teacher stops at this point. If a student has not provided enough evidence to warrant a score at one level, then he or she is not scored at the next level up.
2. **Response codes:** With this approach, each student's response on each item is coded as *correct*, *partially correct*, or *incorrect*, as opposed to assigning points to each item. For more specificity, a teacher can use *high partial* and *low partial* in place of *partially correct*. After scoring individual items, the teacher determines the pattern of responses and assigns a score accordingly. For example, if a student's answers are correct on all items of the score 2.0 section of the test, partially correct on two items of the score 3.0 section of the test, correct on the third item of the score 3.0 section, and incorrect on the two items of the score 4.0 section of the test, that student would receive a score of 2.5.
3. **Flowcharts:** A flowchart is a type of diagram that represents a process. Steps are placed in boxes, and the boxes are connected with arrows, leading one through a progression of boxes based on a series of answers to yes or no questions. Using a flowchart, teachers can easily, consistently, and uniformly score the assessments of the whole class. Teachers can use the flowchart in figure 2.5 to score an assessment using a proficiency scale.

Monitoring Element 5

Specific student responses and behaviors allow the teacher to determine whether this element is being implemented effectively and producing the desired effects.

- Students can explain what the score they received on an assessment means relative to a specific progression of knowledge.
- Students can explain what their grades mean in terms of their status in specific topics.
- Students propose ways they can demonstrate their level of proficiency on a scale.

Use this list to monitor student responses to element 5.

To monitor your own use of this element, use the scale in figure 2.6 in combination with the reproducible "Tracking Teacher Actions: Using Formal Assessments of Individual Students" (page 38). As with other proficiency scales, level 3 or higher is the goal.

The following examples describe what each level of the scale might look like in the classroom.

- **Not Using (0):** A teacher does not use assessments that address the content that is being taught.
- **Beginning (1):** A teacher conducts formal assessments of individual students and records their scores in the gradebook, but he does not frequently use those assessments to provide students with helpful feedback about their progress toward learning goals.

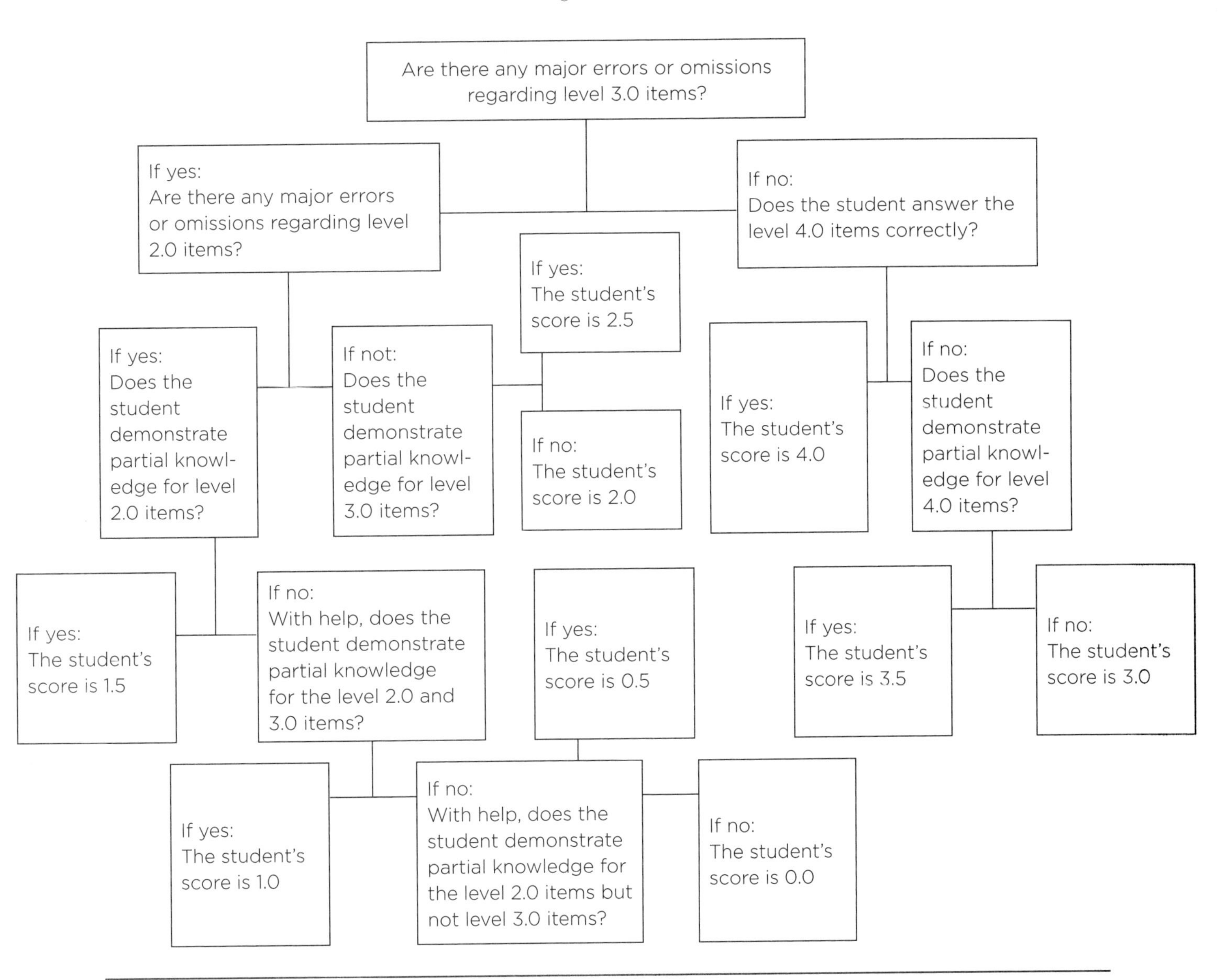

Figure 2.5: Flowchart for proficiency scale.

4 **Innovating**	I adapt behaviors and create new strategies for unique student needs and situations.
3 **Applying**	I use formal assessments of individual students to determine students' proficiency with specific content, and I monitor the extent to which students respond to assessment-guided feedback and instruction.
2 **Developing**	I use formal assessments of individual students to determine students' proficiency with specific content, but I do not monitor the effect on students.
1 **Beginning**	I use the strategies and behaviors associated with this element incorrectly or with parts missing.
0 **Not Using**	I am unaware of strategies and behaviors associated with this element.

Figure 2.6: Self-rating scale for element 5—Using formal assessments of individual students.

- **Developing (2):** A teacher conducts frequent formal assessments of individual students and records their scores in the gradebook. She provides students with clear feedback about their progress, though she does not monitor whether students respond to that feedback with improved understanding of the content.
- **Applying (3):** A teacher conducts frequent formal assessments of individual students and records their scores in the gradebook. He provides them with clear feedback about their progress, and his monitoring of their assessment scores allows him to refine his classroom instruction for further improvement.
- **Innovating (4):** A teacher uses various strategies to conduct frequent formal assessments of individual students in order to provide them with clear feedback that will help them improve their understanding of the content. When her classroom observations reveal that one of her students seems to be struggling with the assessments, she seeks alternative forms of assessment that provide the student with different ways to demonstrate his understanding.

Action Steps

Use the "Tracking Teacher Actions" reproducibles that follow (pages 37–38) to monitor your implementation of each element in this chapter.

Additionally, visit the appendix (page 329) for the reproducible "Tracking Progress Over Time" (page 330), which helps teachers set goals related to their proficiency with each element and track their progress toward these goals over the course of a unit, semester, or year. Also, the "Strategy Reflection Log" (page 331) in the appendix provides a space to write down your thoughts and reflect on the implementation process for specific strategies related to each element. Finally, visit **go.SolutionTree.com/instruction** for both student surveys and teacher surveys, the results of which provide feedback about your proficiency with each element.

Tracking Teacher Actions: Using Informal Assessments of the Whole Class

The teacher can use this form to plan his or her usage of strategies related to the element of using informal assessments of the whole class.

Check Strategies You Intend to Use	Strategies	Description of Instructional Plan
	Confidence Rating Techniques	
	Voting Techniques	
	Response Boards	
	Unrecorded Assessments	
	Other:	
	Other:	

Source: Adapted from Marzano Research. (2016). Marzano compendium of instructional strategies. *Centennial, CO: Author.*

Tracking Teacher Actions: Using Formal Assessments of Individual Students

The teacher can use this form to plan his or her usage of strategies related to the element of using formal assessments of individual students.

Check Strategies You Intend to Use	Strategies	Description of Instructional Plan
	Common Assessments	
	Selected-Response and Short Constructed-Response Items	
	Student Demonstrations	
	Student Interviews	
	Observations of Students	
	Student-Generated Assessments	
	Response Patterns	
	Other:	

Source: Adapted from Marzano Research. (2016). Marzano compendium of instructional strategies. *Centennial, CO: Author.*

PART II

Content

CHAPTER 3

Conducting Direct Instruction Lessons

In a direct instruction lesson, a teacher is presenting new content. Teachers generally teach simpler content, including factual information, vocabulary, and details from the proficiency scales directly. This method of instruction is most effective at communicating new and simpler content because it allows teachers to guide students through unfamiliar concepts and lays the foundation for more complex explorations of the topic.

The goal of this design area is for students to understand, when content is new, which parts are important and how the parts fit together. Teachers are able to meet that goal by answering the question, When content is new, how will I design and deliver direct instruction lessons that help students understand which parts are important and how the parts fit together? The three elements and associated strategies in this chapter help the teacher do just that.

Element 6: Chunking Content

Based on student needs, an effective teacher breaks the content into small chunks (that is, digestible bites) of information that students can easily process. Research has shown that information in small pieces allows students to hold it in working memory long enough to process it (Good & Brophy, 2003; Linden et al., 2003; Mayer, 2003; Rosenshine, 2002). The teacher should present chunks of information in a logical sequence, and he or she should determine the size of each chunk by how much students already know about the content (Marzano, 2007).

There are three strategies within this element.

1. Using preassessment data to plan for chunks
2. Presenting content in small, sequentially related sets
3. Allowing for processing time between chunks

The following sections will explore each strategy to provide you with guidelines to effectively implement this element. Read through each before creating a plan for your classroom. Teachers may use the strategies individually or in combination. Remember, these are not merely activities to be checked off; they are methods of creating a practice that combines your art with the science of chunking content. Reflect on your use of each strategy by filling out the "Strategy Reflection Log" on page 331.

Using Preassessment Data to Plan for Chunks

Based on students' initial understanding of new content, the teacher presents new content in larger or smaller chunks. How much the students know about the topic determines how big, or small, the chunks will be. Preassessments can be either informal (such as those presented in element 4) or more structured, hard-copy assessments that include problems that represent the levels of the proficiency scale.

If students scored well in a specific area on a preassessment, the teacher presents that information as part of a larger chunk. When presenting information about which students displayed misconceptions or little prior knowledge on the preassessment, the teacher can use smaller chunks.

Presenting Content in Small, Sequentially Related Sets

Next, the teacher delivers the chunks. If presenting new declarative knowledge, the chunks include concepts and details that logically go together. If presenting new procedural knowledge, the chunks include steps in a process that go together. While executing the chunking process, the teacher monitors student understanding. If the students seem confused, before moving to the next chunk, the teacher stays with the content until understanding is achieved.

Allowing for Processing Time Between Chunks

The teacher provides a structured time for students to work together to process chunks of content. For example, a teacher has students work in groups of three. Students decide who will be member A, member B, and member C. The teacher presents the first chunk of information, and member A summarizes it. Members B and C add to what A has already said, and each group identifies elements of the chunk they are still confused about. The teacher takes questions from the whole class to clarify these confusions and then asks each group to predict what the next chunk will be about. The teacher presents the next chunk, and groups repeat the process, except that member B summarizes and members A and C add information. After the teacher presents the third chunk, groups repeat the process again, with member C summarizing, and members A and B adding information.

Monitoring Element 6

Specific student responses and behaviors allow the teacher to determine whether this element is being implemented effectively and producing the desired effects.

- Students actively engage in processing content between chunks.
- Students can explain why the teacher stops at specific points during a presentation of new content.
- Students appear to understand the content in each chunk.

Use this list to monitor student responses to element 6.

To monitor your own use of this element, use the scale in figure 3.1 in combination with the reproducible "Tracking Teacher Actions: Chunking Content" (page 62). As with other proficiency scales, level 3 or higher is the goal.

The following examples describe what each level of the scale might look like in the classroom.

- **Not Using (0):** A teacher introduces a new unit by giving a class-long lecture. She only pauses when a student raises his hand to ask a question and does not give the students time to process new or difficult knowledge.
- **Beginning (1):** A teacher does not plan in advance where he will pause when reading a short story with his students. He decides to pause every few sentences, which disrupts the narrative and causes his students to lose track of the story's plot.
- **Developing (2):** A teacher purposefully presents the introduction to a new unit in small chunks by breaking the important concepts of the unit into categories. However, she does not use

4 Innovating	I adapt behaviors and create new strategies for unique student needs and situations.
3 Applying	I chunk content, and I monitor the extent to which my actions affect students.
2 Developing	I chunk content, but I do not monitor the effect on students.
1 Beginning	I use the strategies and behaviors associated with this element incorrectly or with parts missing.
0 Not Using	I am unaware of strategies and behaviors associated with this element.

Figure 3.1: Self-rating scale for element 6—Chunking content.

any techniques to verify that the students are processing and understanding each chunk of information.

- **Applying (3):** A teacher employs the chunk processing strategy to teach students new information. He observes and engages with the different groups in the room to make sure that every group member is participating and grasping the content. The teacher moves on to the next chunk when he is satisfied that the class understands what was just taught.
- **Innovating (4):** A teacher observes her class after describing each step of a complex procedure and asking them to try it out. She looks for students who appear to be struggling with the steps so that she can modify her instructional approach. She pairs one struggling student with a student who appears to be successfully implementing the step and then asks the partner who is doing the step correctly to demonstrate and explain it to the other student.

Element 7: Processing Content

During breaks in the presentation of content, an effective teacher engages students in actively processing new information. Research has shown that some processing macrostrategies (such as reciprocal teaching) increase student achievement (Rosenshine & Meister, 1994). Processing macrostrategies combine several individual research-based strategies (such as summarizing, questioning, or predicting) to help students actively process information (Marzano, 2007).

There are eight strategies within this element.

1. Perspective analysis
2. Thinking hats
3. Collaborative processing
4. Jigsaw cooperative learning
5. Reciprocal teaching
6. Concept attainment
7. Think-pair-share
8. Scripted cooperative dyads

The following sections will explore each strategy to provide you with guidelines to effectively implement this element. Read through each before creating a plan for your classroom. Teachers may use the strategies individually or in combination. Remember, these are not merely activities to be checked off; they are methods of creating a practice that combines your art with the science of processing content. Reflect on your use of each strategy by filling out the "Strategy Reflection Log" on page 331.

Perspective Analysis

This strategy was originally developed by Robert J. Marzano (1992) in *A Different Kind of Classroom: Teaching With Dimensions of Learning*. The teacher asks students to consider multiple perspectives on new knowledge using perspective analysis. Topics might include controversial political topics, school- and community-related issues, or historical perspectives, to name a few. This strategy involves five steps, each with a corresponding question.

1. **Identify your own position on a controversial topic:** What do I believe about this?
2. **Determine the reasoning behind your position:** Why do I believe that?
3. **Identify an opposing position:** What is another way of looking at this?
4. **Describe the reasoning behind the opposing position:** Why might someone else hold a different opinion?
5. **When you are finished, summarize what you have learned:** What have I learned?

Students then consider a different position on the topic and the reasoning behind it.

Thinking Hats

Edward de Bono (1999) originally developed this strategy in *Six Thinking Hats*. The teacher asks students to process new information by imagining themselves wearing any one of six different-colored thinking hats. Students should use multiple hats when examining one chunk of new content as a way of developing a more thorough understanding of the information. Depending on the hat they wear, students look at new knowledge in a slightly different way, as follows.

1. **White hat (neutral and objective perspectives):** When wearing the white hat, students examine facts and figures related to the new information without drawing conclusions or interpreting them.
2. **Red hat (emotional perspectives):** When wearing the red hat, students express how they feel about the new information but should still refrain from judging either the topic or their feelings.
3. **Black hat (cautious or careful perspectives):** When wearing the black hat, students look for weaknesses or risks that stem from the new information. (Some teachers have expressed concern about using the color black for this hat. If students might be offended, the teacher should use a different color hat for these perspectives.)
4. **Yellow hat (optimistic perspectives):** When wearing the yellow hat, students look for positive and valuable aspects of the new information.
5. **Green hat (creative perspectives):** When wearing the green hat, students generate new ideas or create novel solutions to problems using the new information.
6. **Blue hat (organizational perspectives):** When wearing the blue hat, students reflect on their thinking processes and decide what perspectives they would like to take (in other words, what hats they would like to put on) as they interact with new information.

Figure 3.2 outlines the six thinking hat perspectives.

Collaborative Processing

The teacher asks students to meet in small groups to summarize the information just presented, ask clarifying questions, and make predictions about upcoming information. After allowing the students to interact in small groups, the teacher can lead the whole class in a discussion of their summaries, questions, and predictions.

Since collaborative processing requires students to interact with peers, accurately summarize content, predict content, and clarify challenging information, students' ability to comfortably use all elements of the collaborative processing strategy may need to develop over time. Use figure 3.3 to track students' use of the collaborative processing strategy. If students seem stuck at the beginning or developing stages, evaluate which behaviors need to be strengthened through modeling, coaching, or instruction.

Jigsaw Cooperative Learning

The teacher organizes students in teams of equal size (for example, five members) and the content into as many categories as there are team members (for example, five categories). Once students are in their groups,

White Hat	Red Hat	Black Hat
Examine: Factual information Figures, tables, charts, and graphs Evidence for information given Important details **Ask:** What information is provided? What information is missing? What does this tell me?	**Examine:** Emotional reactions to information Initial responses to information Hunches about information **Ask:** What are my initial reactions to this information? How do I feel about this? What are my hunches about this?	**Examine:** Possible risks associated with information Weaknesses in the information Downsides or negative implications **Ask:** Are there are any errors or weaknesses in this information? What are the negative implications? What problems do I see?
Yellow Hat	**Green Hat**	**Blue Hat**
Examine: Positive aspects of new information The strengths or value of information Benefits and advantages **Ask:** What are the positive aspects of this information? How is this beneficial? Why is one aspect preferable over the other?	**Generate:** New ideas Possible solutions for problems associated with information Recommendations or alternative suggestions **Ask:** What is my recommended solution? Are there alternative solutions? What are my new ideas?	**Reflect on:** Thoughts about the information Perspectives on the content Which hat would help strengthen understanding **Ask:** What kind of thinking would help me understand this? What is the next step? How can I summarize what I understand?

Source: Marzano Research, 2016.

Figure 3.2: Thinking hats.

Beginning	Developing	Desired Student Responses
☐ The student listens to peers but does not frequently add to discussions or take notes. ☐ The student seems confused about which information is pertinent to include in a summary. ☐ The student relies on other members in the group to provide predictions, summaries, and questions. ☐ The student resists answering questions and will only answer if the teacher directly asks.	☐ The student appears to be engaged in the conversation and takes notes on what peers say and new content. ☐ The student is able to generate a summary that includes pertinent information. ☐ The student takes on different roles in the discussions but may make mistakes in implementation. ☐ The student volunteers answers to questions but may not answer in a way that reveals a strong perspective on the new content.	☐ The student is engaged in the conversation and builds on other students' thoughts. ☐ The student is comfortable leading the group in organizing and recording new content. ☐ The student generates summaries and recognizes what information may be missing in a summary. ☐ The student actively predicts, summarizes, clarifies, and creates questions. ☐ The student willingly shares opinions, answers, and ideas when responding to another student's questions or comments.

Figure 3.3: Recognizing students' use of the collaborative processing strategy.

the teacher assigns each student a topic about which he or she will become an "expert." Once students each have their expert topic, groups disband and students with the same expert topic meet together in expert groups to investigate the topic, share their findings, ask questions of each other and the teacher, and discuss their ideas. After each student has become an expert on his or her topic, the original groups re-form and students each present their expert knowledge to the other members of the group. Other group members can ask questions of the expert or the teacher as they learn the new information.

Consider the following tips when implementing jigsaw cooperative learning activities.

- Plan in advance which topics each group will be responsible for and which students will be grouped together.
- Before students begin researching their topics, ask them to consider what they already know about their topic. As they gather information, they should make connections between what they are learning and what they already know.
- Provide students with sources where they can get more information on their topic. These resources could be a chapter in a class textbook, a website, or a short article.
- Ask students to take notes or use a graphic organizer to record the important details they learn about their topic. Students should consider which information is important to share with their groups as they are researching.
- Provide multiple opportunities for students to discuss what they have learned with their classmates. Students can discuss new information with their expert groups, their primary groups, and the class as a whole at the end of the jigsaw cooperative learning activity.
- When students begin sharing information with their groups, ask them to consider if what they are saying is contributing to the group's knowledge. Are they framing what they have learned in a way that other students can understand? Remind students that their classmates may not have the same background knowledge on the topic, so it is important that they provide sufficient details.
- As each group discusses new information, encourage students to make linkages between the different areas they explored. Students can describe how each topic relates to the other topics and how their new knowledge about each aspect contributes to their understanding of the unit as a whole.

Reciprocal Teaching

Small groups of students, with one student designated as the discussion leader, use this strategy to interact with new information. Before the teacher presents a chunk of new information, members of the group generate predictions about the content. After the teacher presents the chunk of content, the discussion leader asks the group questions about the information presented, and the members of the group discuss each question. After the questions have been discussed, someone from the group (not the discussion leader) summarizes the content presented so far, and the members of the group make predictions about the upcoming chunk of content, beginning the cycle again. The role of discussion leader should rotate from student to student so each student has the opportunity to generate questions about the content and practice facilitating the group's discussion.

Figure 3.4 can help guide their discussions.

Concept Attainment

The teacher asks students to identify, compare, and contrast examples and nonexamples of a concept. Examples of a concept should clearly display the attributes of the concept, and nonexamples should clearly not have attributes of the concept. Concept attainment is ideal to use when examining a complex topic that may be difficult to explain or define. It also works well when examining categories of objects or concepts. For example, teachers can use this strategy to examine different animal classes, a group of shapes, a part of

Discussing in Groups

During reciprocal teaching and other group discussions, it can be helpful to predict, question, clarify, and summarize information. This chart can help your group complete each of these processes successfully.

Predict	Question	Clarify	Summarize
Key words: *Guess, hypothesize, estimate, assume, infer, speculate, project* Describe what you have already learned about the topic. Take note of the purpose of the text or lesson. What is it trying to teach or show you, and how can that help you guess what information will come next? Use headings, pictures, and titles to help you predict what the text or teacher will discuss. Explain your reasons for your predictions. Adjust your prediction if new information seems to have proven it wrong.	**Key words:** *Ask, examine, explore, inquire, evaluate, challenge, investigate* Ask questions using who, what, where, why, when, and how. Challenge yourself and your classmates to find the main ideas in the content or text. Examine what the main idea, subject, or theme is an example of. Ask questions about something that is unclear or confusing. Evaluate why you might be learning this. How does it relate to the class, the subject area, and your life?	**Key words:** *Explain, define, reread, monitor, refine, simplify, sharpen* Use a dictionary or glossary to define a term that is new or challenging. Reread the text to gather more information. Break down a complex idea into parts and examine each part individually. Listen to your classmates and teacher's ideas to refine your own understanding. Ask questions about their thinking if it seems unclear. Draw a picture or diagram to help you understand a complex process or idea.	**Key words:** *Sum up, decide, conclude, judge, determine, review, surmise, organize* Look for the who, what, where, when, why, and how. Omit unnecessary information, and determine which information is most important to understanding the main ideas. Describe what you think the author or teacher wants you to know. Link what you have learned to what you already know. Explain your conclusions about the topic.

Source: Marzano Research, 2016.

Figure 3.4: Discussing in groups.

Visit ***go.SolutionTree.com/instruction*** *for a free reproducible version of this figure.*

speech, an artistic movement, or a genre of music. Additionally, this strategy can help students visualize correct and incorrect behaviors or uses of a procedure in the classroom. Once students seem comfortable with the patterns presented, ask them to generate their own examples and nonexamples to add to a class list.

Consider the following tips for using this strategy in your classroom.

- Organize examples and nonexamples into a simple chart to help students visualize patterns. If students are creating their own examples and nonexamples, ask them to record their choices in a graphic organizer.
- When asking students to define a mystery concept, begin first with examples and nonexamples that are simple and seem to parallel one another. These should give the students an idea of what is being contrasted. Instead of providing all of the examples at once, give two or three at a time and provide students with time to reflect on possible patterns.
- As you provide more examples, the students' understanding of what is being defined should sharpen. Elements might become more abstract as students' knowledge deepens.

- Avoid choosing examples and nonexamples with trivial differences that might confuse students.
- Instead of having students guess what the mystery concept is out loud, ask them to create their own examples and nonexamples that fit the pattern. Students can write their examples on the class chart to aid students who have not yet guessed the concept.

Think-Pair-Share

Frank Lyman (1981) originally developed this strategy. The teacher asks students to think critically about a question, pair up with another classmate to come to a consensus on their answer to the question, and then share their responses with other groups or the whole class. Limiting the amount of time for the thinking and pairing steps of the strategy can motivate students to make quick decisions and explain their thinking succinctly (for example, a teacher might give students thirty seconds to think of an answer and then three minutes to discuss with their partner). Since the procedure for this strategy is relatively simple, a teacher can implement it in a lesson either at planned points or informally as the need arises. The teacher can monitor the use of this strategy by observing students as they discuss topics, asking students to provide written summaries of their responses, or having pairs of students present their thinking to the whole class.

Figure 3.5 can help guide students' use of this strategy.

Name: ______________________________

Class: ______________________________

- Think about what you already know about the subject.
- Examine why you think this way.
- Try to make connections to other ideas or experiences.
- Write out or draw your thoughts.

- Share your ideas with your partner.
- Listen to your partner's ideas.
- Find similarities and differences between what you both believe.
- Decide what you will want to share with the class.

- Describe your answers or ideas to the class.
- Create a diagram or presentation that shows your classmates what you think.
- Write down what you learned and how the activity helped you understand the new information.

Source: Marzano Research, 2016.

Figure 3.5: Think-pair-share guidelines.

Visit **go.SolutionTree.com/instruction** *for a free reproducible version of this figure.*

Scripted Cooperative Dyads

Donald Dansereau (1988) originally developed this strategy. The teacher presents a new chunk of information or asks students to read a short excerpt of a text. As they read or listen, students take notes about the main idea and key details of the content. Then, the teacher breaks students up into groups of two and assigns each student to act either as the recaller or the listener. In their groups, the recaller summarizes the content, without looking at his or her notes, while the listener adds missing information and corrects any errors in the recaller's summary. Students should switch between the roles of recaller and listener after each chunk of information.

While this strategy may seem simple to implement, students' attention can easily become centered on getting the procedure right rather than on the processing of new content. To prepare students for using this strategy, teachers can review the following skills in class.

- **Taking notes and annotating:** Comprehensive notes are essential to the implementation of scripted cooperative dyads. Model different strategies for note-taking that will help students efficiently record the key ideas from texts and presentations. One simple technique teachers can share with students at all grade levels is two-column notes. In this strategy, students draw a line to separate the right and left sides of their notepaper. In the right column, students write the main ideas or concepts discussed in the content, and in the left column students write important details that refine their understanding of those main ideas. In addition to asking students to take notes, teachers can also encourage the annotation of texts through the use of symbols, sticky notes, or different colored highlighters.
- **Summarizing:** Students' summaries should build on and relate to the information they recorded in their notes. Ask students to try to describe the who, what, where, when, why, and how of information. Students looking for errors in their partners' summaries should also focus on these details. Teachers can have students practice their verbal summarization skills by giving them only a limited amount of time to summarize new content. If students are new to providing verbal summaries, teachers can also allow them to freewrite their ideas and the points they would like to make before asking them to present their summaries. Students should not refer to notes during their freewrite but try to come up with points from memory.
- **Acting as the listener:** When students take on the listener role, they will need to critically engage with what their partner is saying and look through their notes for refining or additional information. While students might think the listener role is easier because they will have their notes in front of them, in fact, the listener role requires students to enact multiple processes at once and is equally as challenging as the recaller role. The listener must actively cross-check facts, procedures, and key ideas the recaller brings up and politely correct their partners when appropriate. Additionally, listeners should listen for information that they might have missed or didn't quite understand when they were taking notes. In this way, scripted cooperative dyads are an exchange of information and ideas that should challenge students to examine what they know and understand about the topic.

Monitoring Element 7

Specific student responses and behaviors allow the teacher to determine whether this element is being implemented effectively and producing the desired effects.

- Students appear to be actively interacting with the content.
- Students volunteer predictions.
- Students can explain what they have just learned.
- Students voluntarily ask clarification questions.

Use this list to monitor student responses to element 7.

To monitor your own use of this element, use the scale in figure 3.6 (page 50) in combination with the reproducible "Tracking Teacher Actions: Processing Content" (page 63). As with other proficiency scales, level 3 or higher is the goal.

4 Innovating	I adapt behaviors and create new strategies for unique student needs and situations.
3 Applying	I engage students in processing content, and I monitor the extent to which my actions affect students.
2 Developing	I engage students in processing content, but I do not monitor the effect on students.
1 Beginning	I use the strategies and behaviors associated with this element incorrectly or with parts missing.
0 Not Using	I am unaware of strategies and behaviors associated with this element.

Figure 3.6: Self-rating scale for element 7—Processing content.

The following examples describe what each level of the scale might look like in the classroom.

- **Not Using (0):** A teacher does not provide opportunities for students to make predictions, summarize, or ask clarification questions about new content. After introducing new content, instead of providing time for the students to process what they have just experienced, the teacher uses direct instruction to introduce another piece of new information.
- **Beginning (1):** A teacher asks her students to use the thinking hats strategy to examine a new concept discussed in class. She encourages the students to use the thinking hats to deepen their responses and understanding but does not walk them through the process of using one hat at a time. Students fill out a worksheet using the hat descriptors but are not given the opportunity to discuss their conclusions or summarize how using the hats helped them better understand the new concept.
- **Developing (2):** A teacher uses the strategy of reciprocal teaching to help his students engage with new ideas in a unit on energy and motion. Within each reciprocal teaching group, he designates one student the discussion leader and asks that the other students answer the discussion leader's questions, clarify difficult information, and summarize the new content. After the first round of reciprocal teaching, he asks for the groups' summaries and predictions and moves on to the next chunk of new information. He does not monitor how well students executed the strategy or if it helped them increase their understanding.
- **Applying (3):** A teacher uses collaborative processing to introduce his students to a unit on triangles. He separates the students into groups and explains the overall process and their individual roles. The teacher models how the process works with several volunteers. After presenting each chunk of new content, he observes and assists the students as they implement the collaborative processing strategy. At the end of class, the teacher takes an informal survey to find out if the students found the strategy helpful and if they would use that strategy again.
- **Innovating (4):** A teacher uses the jigsaw cooperative learning strategy with her class during a unit on the French Revolution. She separates the class into groups of three and assigns each person in the group an effect of the revolution to investigate. As the students meet in their expert groups, she checks in, answers the groups' questions, and asks each student to record his or her research. When students reconvene with their original groups, they compile their research into a chart that they can share with the class and teacher. Because the class was extremely successful with this strategy, she extends the activity and their learning by adding a class discussion about which effects of the French Revolution have most shaped modern-day beliefs and society.

Element 8: Recording and Representing Content

An effective teacher engages students in activities that help them record their understanding of new content in linguistic ways or represent the content in nonlinguistic ways. Research has shown that representing information linguistically (summaries and notes) is associated with student achievement gains (Bangert-Drowns, Hurley, & Wilkinson, 2004; Crismore, 1985; Ganske, 1981; Hattie et al., 1996; Henk & Stahl, 1985; Marzano, Gnadt, & Jesse, 1990; Pflaum, Walberg, Karegianes, & Rasher, 1980; Raphael & Kirschner, 1985). Research has also shown that representing information nonlinguistically (models, pictures, mental images) increases student achievement (Guzzetti, Snyder, Glass, & Gamus, 1993; Haas, 2005; Hattie et al., 1996; Lovelace, 2005; Mayer, 1989; Nesbit & Adesope, 2006; Powell, 1980; Stahl & Fairbanks, 1986). When information is both linguistic and nonlinguistic, students process information more thoroughly and deeply.

There are eleven strategies within this element.

1. Informal outlines
2. Summaries
3. Pictorial notes and pictographs
4. Combination notes, pictures, and summaries
5. Graphic organizers
6. Free-flowing webs
7. Academic notebooks
8. Dramatic enactments
9. Mnemonic devices
10. Rhyming pegwords
11. Link strategies

The following sections will explore each strategy to provide you with guidelines to effectively implement this element. Read through each before creating a plan for your classroom. Teachers may use the strategies individually or in combination. Remember, these are not merely activities to be checked off; they are methods of creating a practice that combines your art with the science of recording and representing content. Reflect on your use of each strategy by filling out the "Strategy Reflection Log" on page 331.

Informal Outlines

In an informal outline, students use indentation to indicate the relative importance of ideas. They write big ideas at the left side of the paper, and indent and list details under the big idea to which they pertain. Students can also use numbering, bullets, or Roman numerals to organize information and display its relative importance. Figure 3.7 can help guide students in writing informal outlines.

Informal Outline

Name: ______________________ Topic or title: ______________________

1. Main idea: ______________________
   - Detail: ______________________
   - Detail: ______________________
2. Main idea: ______________________
   - Detail: ______________________
   - Detail: ______________________
3. Main idea: ______________________
   - Detail: ______________________
   - Detail: ______________________

Source: Marzano Research, 2016.

Figure 3.7: Informal outline template.

Visit **go.SolutionTree.com/instruction** *for a free reproducible version of this figure.*

Summaries

The teacher asks students to summarize content. Summarizing requires that students record the critical content from a text or lesson. Summarization techniques often require multiple complex cognitive processes and should be directly taught and modeled for students. Figure 3.8 is a scale that describes different phases of summarization mastery that teachers can use to measure students' ability to summarize content.

Score 4.0	Students summarize critical information in their own words and generate their own conclusions about the information.
Score 3.0	Students summarize critical information in their own words and demonstrate a clear understanding of the information.
Score 2.0	When responding to prompts from the teacher, students are able to identify critical information in a text or lesson.
Score 1.0	When responding to prompts from the teacher, students struggle to identify critical content or information.

Figure 3.8: Proficiency scale for summarization.

Consider using the following summarization activities in your classroom.

- Use summary frames to structure students' early attempts at summarization. A summary frame is a series of questions that focus on important elements of the content. Students answer the questions and then use their responses to generate a summary. For example, in a summary frame for a short story, the teacher might create a series of questions that ask students to list the setting, characters, main conflict, and resolution of the story.
- Show students how supplementary information, such as headings, images, and graphs, in visual presentations of content and texts can help them decipher what the main idea and key details are.
- Practice basic summarizing techniques by asking students to describe the plot of a familiar movie or story in one or two sentences. Remind students that it is not necessary to retell the whole plot; they should simply try to tell listeners the most important information in their own words. For extra support, ask students to list the who, what, where, when, and why of the plot before giving their summary.
- Ask students to use a simple graphic organizer to find the main idea and key details from a short presentation or text. Using an organizer can help students understand what kind of information is important to highlight in a summary. For extra support, provide students with the main idea before the start of the lesson and have them fill in the key details.
- When students begin summarizing content, ask them to think about what they would tell someone who had missed class to help them understand the important ideas from a lesson. Have them practice what they would say with a partner. To encourage students to condense their summaries to only the most critical details, have partners time each other to see if they can summarize ideas in thirty seconds or less.

Pictorial Notes and Pictographs

The teacher asks students to use pictorial notes and pictographs to illustrate new content. Pictorial notes may serve as an accompaniment to written notes or, in some cases, as the primary note-taking form. Figure 3.9 is an example of pictorial notes.

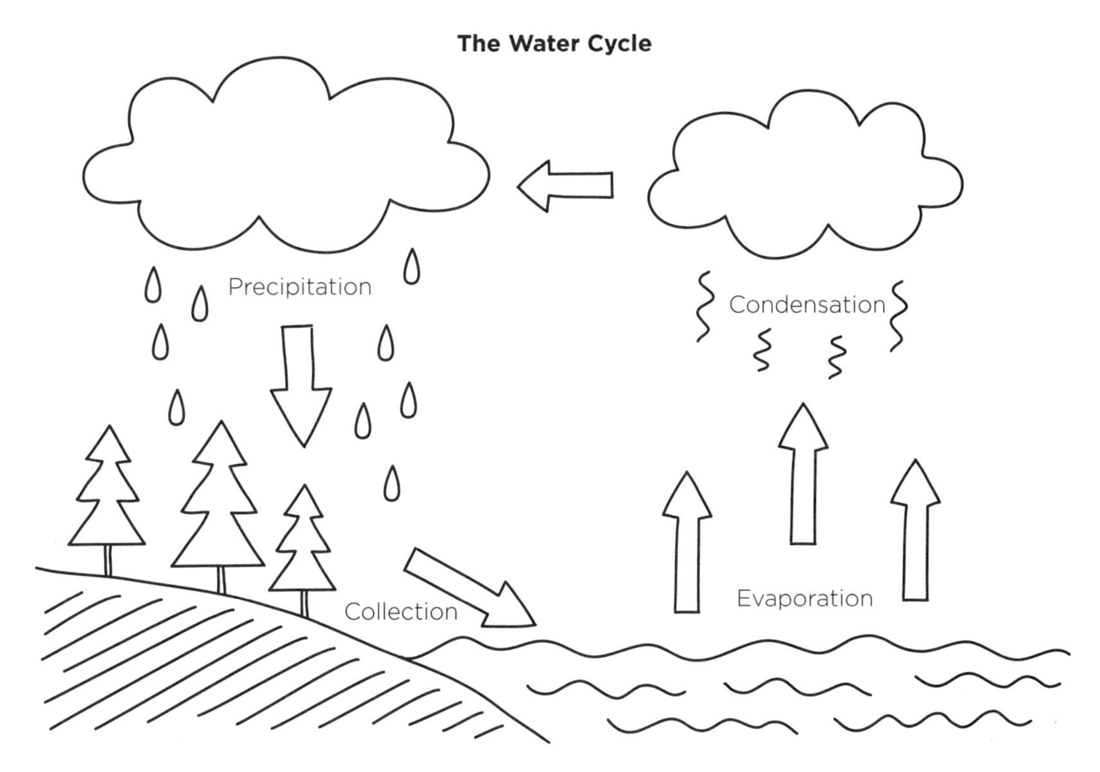

Source: Marzano Research, 2016.

Figure 3.9: Example of pictorial notes.

Pictographs, like pictorial notes, may be accompanied by text for clarification. Pictographs often represent data in mathematical charts. In place of numbers, images indicate how much of a certain item each category has. Additionally, pictographs can be simple drawings that express words or phrases. Pictographs can use any kind of image for any amount, as long as there is a clear key that defines the symbols for the students and teacher.

Figure 3.10 is an example of a pictograph that compares the number of apples harvested from three orchards. Students could draw this kind of chart before completing a word problem that uses these data.

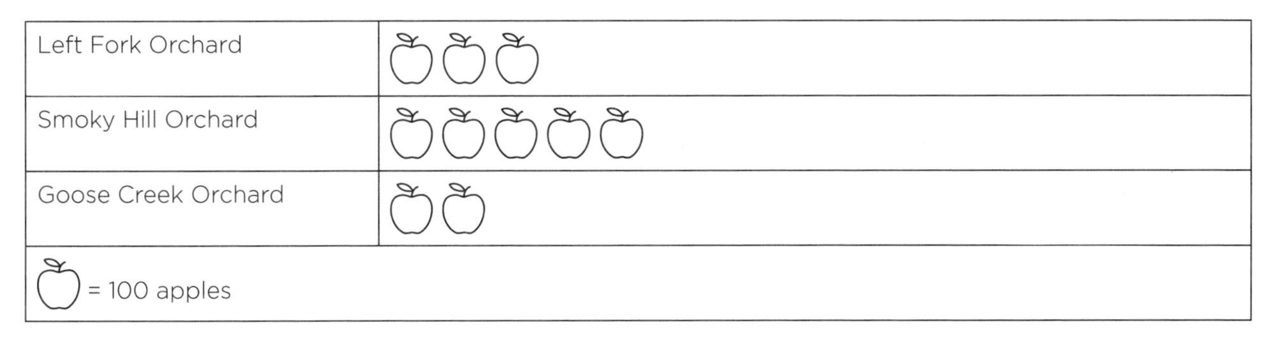

Left Fork Orchard	
Smoky Hill Orchard	
Goose Creek Orchard	
= 100 apples	

Source: Marzano Research, 2016.

Figure 3.10: Sample pictograph.

Combination Notes, Pictures, and Summaries

This strategy combines notes, pictures, and summaries. Students record written notes about the content in the left-hand column of a chart, pictographs or pictorial representations of the content in the right-hand column, and a summary of the content in the lower section of the chart. Figure 3.11 can guide students' use of this strategy.

Combination Notes Organizer

Name: ____________________

Subject: ____________________

Notes	**Picture**
Summary:	

Source: Marzano Research, 2016.

Figure 3.11: Combination notes organizer.

Visit **go.SolutionTree.com/instruction** *for a free reproducible version of this figure.*

Graphic Organizers

Students record their knowledge using graphic organizers that correspond to specific patterns commonly found in information. Common text structures include sequence, description, comparison, causation, and problem/solution. Find graphic organizers for these structures in figures 3.12, 3.13, 3.14, 3.15, and 3.16 (pages 55–56). Teachers can combine nonlinguistic representations with other note-taking strategies (like combination notes, pictures, and summaries).

Sequence Graphic Organizer

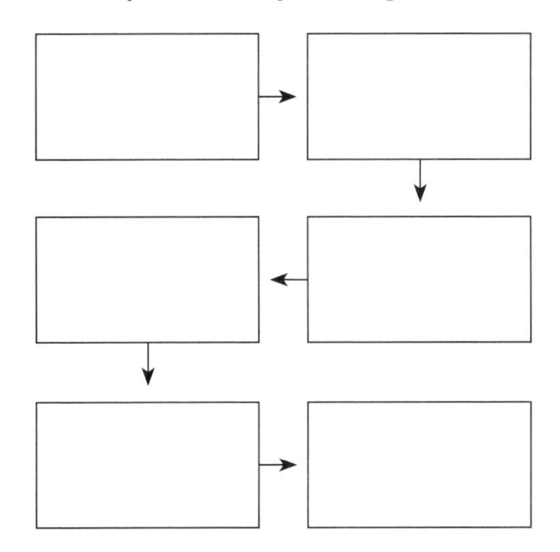

Source: Marzano Research, 2016.

Figure 3.12: Sequence graphic organizer.

Visit **go.SolutionTree.com/instruction** *for a free reproducible version of this figure.*

Description Graphic Organizer

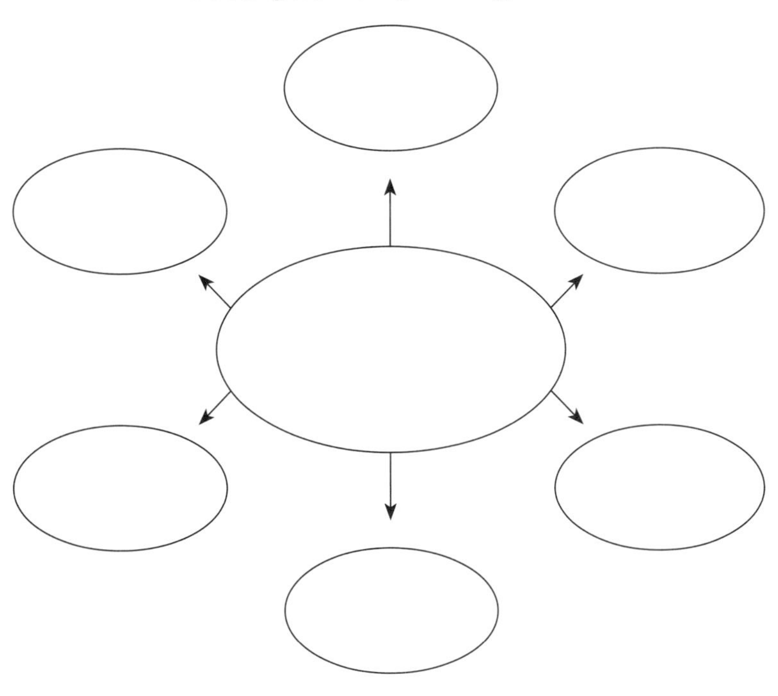

Source: Marzano Research, 2016.

Figure 3.13: Description graphic organizer.

Visit **go.SolutionTree.com/instruction** *for a free reproducible version of this figure.*

Comparison Graphic Organizer

Source: Marzano Research, 2016.

Figure 3.14: Comparison graphic organizer.

Visit **go.SolutionTree.com/instruction** *for a free reproducible version of this figure.*

Causation Graphic Organizer

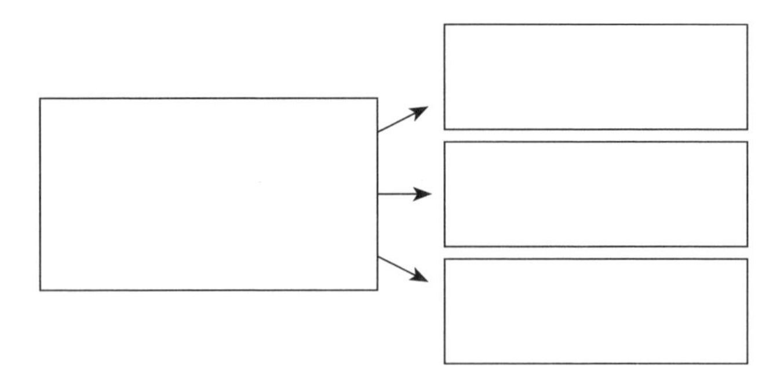

Source: Marzano Research, 2016.

Figure 3.15: Causation graphic organizer.

Visit **go.SolutionTree.com/instruction** *for a free reproducible version of this figure.*

Problem/Solution Graphic Organizer

Problem:

1.	2.	3.

Solution:

Source: Marzano Research, 2016.

Figure 3.16: Problem/solution graphic organizer.

Visit **go.SolutionTree.com/instruction** *for a free reproducible version of this figure.*

Free-Flowing Webs

In this strategy, students place big ideas in central circles and then use lines to connect big ideas to smaller circles that contain important details about each big idea. Unlike a simple description graphic organizer, a free-flowing web should connect multiple subtopics by showing how they relate to a central topic. A free-flowing web works well for organizing students' knowledge about an advanced concept or process. Teachers can ask students to complete a free-flowing web individually, but it can also serve as a group or whole-class review activity. Figure 3.17 shows a free-flowing web for the topic of pollution.

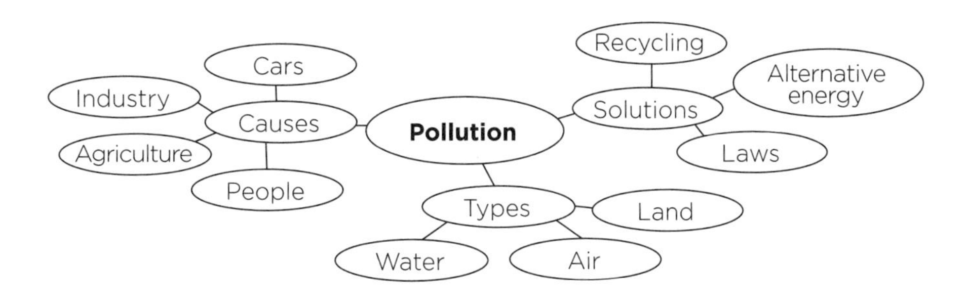

Figure 3.17: Sample free-flowing web.

Visit **go.SolutionTree.com/instruction** *for a free reproducible version of this figure.*

Following are possible uses for a free-flowing web.

- To compare the causes, effects, and possible solutions for a major global, political, or cultural issue
- To delineate different opinions in an argument or perspectives on a topic
- To diagram the steps, uses, purposes, and origins of a procedure
- To map the setting, players, and effects of an important historical event
- To describe the major story elements (such as plot, characters, setting) of a book or short text
- To compare the different subcategories within a category

Academic Notebooks

Students compile their notes to provide a permanent record of their thinking and make corrections to their thinking as they review previous entries. Students should date their entries and record reactions, questions, answers, and assessments of their progress. They can also make entries reflecting their conclusions and insights.

Figure 3.18 can help guide students' use of this strategy.

Academic Notebook Entry

Name: ______________________ Date: ______________

Subject: ______________________ Topic: ______________________

Details about what I learned:

1. ______________________
2. ______________________
3. ______________________

Summary of what I learned:

Questions I have about what I learned:

Figure 3.18: Template for a page entry in an academic notebook.

Visit **go.SolutionTree.com/instruction** *for a free reproducible version of this figure.*

Dramatic Enactments

For this strategy, students role-play characters or act out scenes, processes, or events. They can also use their bodies to create symbols for concepts such as radius, diameter, and circumference. While dramatic enactments can be highly engaging for students, they can be superficial if handled incorrectly. For example, if students are simply given roles with lines to read from a script, no deeper understanding of the content is taking place. Teachers must budget time in class for students to explain the explicit connections between their enactments and the content they represent. Consider the following tips for effective dramatic enactments.

- Students must have a strong understanding of the content before performing a dramatic enactment. While students can engage in research and more extensive investigation of a topic before performing a dramatic enactment, if this is a new strategy in the classroom, it may be beneficial to directly teach key information. Creating dramatic enactments can also help clarify and distinguish content for students, but only if they have the requisite background knowledge.
- Dramatic enactments should engage students' creativity and critical thinking skills. Dramatic enactments often ask students to reimagine content as something else or create a metaphor between content and movement. This concept might be challenging for students at first, so provide several examples for students to watch or help them map out a plan for their enactment before practicing it. If possible, save recordings of previous years' enactments or find a similar activity online that students can reference while working on their project.
- Students should be able to describe the choices they made in their dramatic enactments. Teachers can ask students to write a short summary of why they chose to structure their enactment the way they did or have students explain their reasoning verbally for the class.
- Dramatic enactments should encourage students to explore different perspectives, cultures, time periods, and characters. Dramatic enactments can be particularly useful to help students put themselves in someone else's shoes. Teachers can have students create short dramatic enactments that explore unique perspectives and then ask students how the dramatic enactment helped them better understand that perspective.
- Dramatic enactments should not focus on students' acting or performance abilities. Not all students will feel comfortable with the idea of performing in front of their peers. Teachers should encourage students to present clearly and confidently but remind them that the enactment is primarily about engaging with the content and learning from their own as well as their classmates' performances.

Mnemonic Devices

A teacher can use mnemonic devices to help students remember, record, and represent critical content. Mnemonic devices often link content to symbols, imagery, or patterns of sound to strengthen the memory of the user. A teacher can lead students in the use of mnemonic devices to encourage their continued engagement with content. Following are examples of mnemonic devices.

- **Acronym mnemonics:** Probably the most common acronym mnemonic is ROY G BIV, which represents the spectrum of colors found in the rainbow (red, orange, yellow, green, blue, indigo, violet). Students can create their own acronym mnemonic by using the first letters from a series of words to create a new word. Acronym mnemonics can be helpful when trying to remember items that belong to a category or steps in a process or procedure.

- **Music mnemonic:** Music has long been a useful mnemonic device; many students learn the alphabet or the quadratic equation using a melody. Advertisers also frequently take advantage of this mnemonic by setting their slogans to catchy melodies. For best use of this strategy, set a list of steps or facts to a song or melody that most students will be familiar with. Students can create their own music mnemonics by using the melody of a nursery rhyme, pop song, or common folk song to help them remember facts, dates, processes, and other lists of information. Extend this activity by having students create a short music video to accompany their music mnemonic.
- **Image mnemonic:** Unlike pictorial notes, an image mnemonic may not represent a fact or concept directly but may instead capitalize on the sound or other qualities of the concept to create a memorable, often silly, image. Students draw an image to help them remember content. For example, in order to remember that pi is the ratio of the circle's circumference to its diameter, a student might draw a whole pie balancing on top of half a pie. In this kind of mnemonic, while it is important to create a memorable image, it is equally important that the student is able to link the image to the fact or concept to remember, so it is essential that the connection between the image and content is not too tenuous.
- **Spelling mnemonic:** Students can create their own spelling mnemonics to help them remember the spelling of words that they often forget. This activity works well for distinguishing between two words that are very similar in spelling or sound. Teachers and students can use images, pithy phrases, or other devices to design a spelling mnemonic. One example of a spelling mnemonic, "you always want two desserts, but you only want one desert," helps students remember that *dessert* has two of the letter *s* and *desert* only has one.

Rhyming Pegwords

Students use this strategy to remember a list of facts or information. The method uses a set of concrete images that rhyme with the numbers one through ten, such as the following.

One is a bun.

Two is a shoe.

Three is a tree.

Four is a door.

Five is a hive.

Six is a stack of sticks.

Seven is heaven.

Eight is a gate.

Nine is a line.

Ten is a hen.

To remember a fact or piece of information, a student associates it with one of the concrete images. For example, a student might want to remember the following list of information about ancient Egyptian civilization.

1. Egyptian civilization developed along the Nile River in Africa.
2. The Egyptians used a system of writing called hieroglyphics.
3. The Egyptians built the pyramids as burial places for their pharaohs.

To remember these facts, the student might connect the first item to the image for the number one, a bun. He or she might picture a hot dog bun with the Nile River flowing through the center of it. The second item would be connected to the image for the number two, a shoe—perhaps a shoe with hieroglyphs written on the side of it. The third item in the list would be connected to the image of a tree, for the number three. The student might imagine a tree whose leaves and branches had been trimmed to create a pyramid shape. These images help the student ensure that he or she has remembered all the items in the list. This strategy is especially helpful with long lists of facts or lists that must be recalled in a certain order.

Link Strategies

Students use this strategy to remember facts or information by first creating symbols or substitutes for important ideas and then linking those symbols or substitutes together in a narrative. A symbol is an image that reminds one of important information, like a rainbow to represent the concept of an arc. A substitute is a word that is easy to picture and sounds like the information one is trying to remember, like the word ark to remember the concept of the arc of a circle.

For example, consider the scientific process. There are generally six steps in the process: (1) ask a question, (2) do background research, (3) construct a hypothesis, (4) test the hypothesis by doing an experiment, (5) analyze the data and draw a conclusion, and (6) report the results. The link strategy might produce the following narrative and symbols.

Prince Science went on a *quest* with his handy *magnifying glass* to look for the magic *hippo*. He went through many *perils* but trusted his horse, *Dart, to draw him to the hippo's conclave*. Afterward, the hippo and the prince developed quite the *rapport*.

- **Quest:** *Quest* sounds like question and stands in for the first step of the scientific process.
- **Magnifying glass:** *Magnifying glass* stands in as a symbol for research.
- **Hippo:** *Hippo* is a substitute for the word *hypothesis*.
- **Perils:** *Perils* is a substitute for the word *experiment*, because it sounds similar.
- **Dart and the hippo's conclave:** The phrasing of this sentence is meant to sound like and be a substitution for *data* and *draw a conclusion*.
- **Rapport:** *Rapport* is a substitute for *report*.

Monitoring Element 8

Specific student responses and behaviors allow the teacher to determine whether this element is being implemented effectively and producing the desired effects.

- Students produce summaries that include critical information.
- Students produce nonlinguistic representations that include critical information.
- Students can explain their linguistic and nonlinguistic representations.
- Students remember the critical content from previous lessons.

Use this list to monitor student responses to element 8.

To monitor your own use of this element, use the scale in figure 3.19 in combination with the reproducible "Tracking Teacher Actions: Recording and Representing Content" (page 64). As with other proficiency scales, level 3 or higher is the goal.

4 Innovating	I adapt behaviors and create new strategies for unique student needs and situations.
3 Applying	I have students record and represent content, and I monitor the extent to which my actions affect students' performance.
2 Developing	I have students record and represent content, but I do not monitor the effect on students.
1 Beginning	I use the strategies and behaviors associated with this element incorrectly or with parts missing.
0 Not Using	I am unaware of strategies and behaviors associated with this element.

Figure 3.19: Self-rating scale for element 8—Recording and representing content.

The following examples describe what each level of the scale might look like in the classroom.

- **Not Using (0):** A teacher expects that her students will take notes if they need to, but she does not provide them with any kind of strategies to do so.
- **Beginning (1):** A teacher asks his students to use combination notes to record critical information from a lesson. However, students are unfamiliar with the summarizing part of the organizer, and because the teacher does not model or explain techniques for summarizing, many leave that section of their notes blank.
- **Developing (2):** A teacher teaches her class a mnemonic for remembering different units of measurement. She uses the mnemonic effectively throughout the unit, but she doesn't try to determine if it enhanced their recall of the content.
- **Applying (3):** A teacher has his class use academic notebooks to record information, ideas, and reflections. He encourages students to write notes and record their ideas as diagrams or drawings. At the end of every unit, the teacher asks students to go back through their notes to amend any misunderstandings and respond to hypotheses made earlier in the unit. He then collects the academic notebooks and reviews them to see how the students' entries compare to their assessment answers and scores.
- **Innovating (4):** A teacher asks her class to use graphic organizers to record and represent critical content. First, she provides students with several templates they can use to record their notes and explains each purpose. She then puts students into small groups to complete their graphic organizers. As they complete their graphic organizers, she walks around the room, checking in with specific students who she knows have been having difficulty with the content. At the end of the lesson, she asks each group to explain why students chose their graphic organizer and what it helped them understand about the content.

Action Steps

Use the "Tracking Teacher Actions" reproducibles that follow (pages 62–64) to monitor your implementation of each element in this chapter.

Additionally, visit the appendix (page 329) for the reproducible "Tracking Progress Over Time" (page 330), which helps teachers set goals related to their proficiency with each element and track their progress toward these goals over the course of a unit, semester, or year. Also, the "Strategy Reflection Log" (page 331) in the appendix provides a space to write down your thoughts and reflect on the implementation process for specific strategies related to each element. Finally, visit **go.SolutionTree.com/instruction** for both student surveys and teacher surveys, the results of which provide feedback about your proficiency with each element.

Tracking Teacher Actions: Chunking Content

The teacher can use this form to plan his or her usage of strategies related to the element of chunking content.

Check Strategies You Intend to Use	Strategies	Description of Instructional Plan
	Using Preassessment Data to Vary the Size of Each Chunck	
	Presenting Content in Small Chunks	
	Chunk Processing	
	Other:	
	Other:	

Source: Adapted from Marzano Research. (2016). Marzano compendium of instructional strategies. *Centennial, CO: Author.*

Tracking Teacher Actions: Processing Content

The teacher can use this form to plan his or her usage of strategies related to the element of processing content.

Check Strategies You Intend to Use	Strategies	Description of Instructional Plan
	Perspective Analysis	
	Thinking Hats	
	Collaborative Processing	
	Jigsaw Cooperative Learning	
	Reciprocal Teaching	
	Concept Attainment	
	Think-Pair-Share	
	Scripted Cooperative Dyads	
	Other:	
	Other:	

Source: Adapted from Marzano Research. (2016). Marzano compendium of instructional strategies. *Centennial, CO: Author.*

Tracking Teacher Actions: Recording and Representing Content

The teacher can use this form to plan his or her usage of strategies related to the element of recording and representing content.

Check Strategies You Intend to Use	Strategies	Description of Instructional Plan
	Informal Outlines	
	Summaries	
	Pictorial Notes and Pictographs	
	Combination Notes, Pictures, and Summaries	
	Graphic Organizers	
	Free-Flowing Webs	
	Academic Notebooks	
	Dramatic Enactments	
	Mnemonic Devices	
	Rhyming Pegwords	
	Link Strategies	
	Other:	
	Other:	

Source: Adapted from Marzano Research. (2016). Marzano compendium of instructional strategies. *Centennial, CO: Author.*

CHAPTER 4

Conducting Practicing and Deepening Lessons

Once teachers introduce content through direct instruction, they must further develop student knowledge. Practicing and deepening lessons encourage students to investigate a topic more rigorously. During these lessons, students begin developing the ability to employ skills, strategies, and processes fluently and accurately. Teachers can utilize these lessons to assist students in connecting their understanding of the topic with previously learned content and to facilitate the practice of essential skills.

The goal of this design area is for students to deepen their understanding and develop fluency in skills and processes after teachers present new content. Teachers are able to meet that goal by answering the question, After presenting content, how will I design and deliver lessons that help students deepen their understanding and develop fluency in skills and processes? The three elements and associated strategies in this chapter help the teacher do just that.

Element 9: Using Structured Practice Sessions

When the content involves a skill, strategy, or process, an effective teacher engages students in practice activities that help them develop fluency. Research has shown that practicing skills, strategies, or processes increases student achievement (Bloom, 1976; Feltz & Landers, 1983; Kumar, 1991; Ross, 1988). Effective practice is more than repetition; it involves students gradually learning and then shaping the steps of a process. Teachers should thoughtfully design and guide this process (Anderson, 1982, 1995; Fitts & Posner, 1967).

There are eight strategies within this element.

1. Modeling
2. Guided practice
3. Close monitoring
4. Frequent structured practice
5. Varied practice
6. Fluency practice
7. Worked examples
8. Practice sessions prior to testing

The following sections will explore each strategy to provide you with guidelines to effectively implement this element. Read through each before creating a plan for your classroom. Teachers may use the strategies individually or in combination. Remember, these are not merely activities to be checked off; they are methods of creating a practice that combines your art with the science of using structured practice sessions. Reflect on your use of each strategy by filling out the "Strategy Reflection Log" on page 331.

Modeling

When teachers present any skill, strategy, or process to students, they should first model it for them. This involves the teacher walking through the steps involved in the skill, strategy, or process. The modeling process can include a number of steps and can incorporate different media to make content engaging and easy to comprehend. Teachers can use the following techniques to model a skill, strategy, or process for students.

- Demonstrating a skill, strategy, or process step by step
- Verbally explaining each step of a skill, strategy, or process
- Showing a video that demonstrates a procedure or process
- Showing a completed example with significant parts labeled for students
- Demonstrating several different ways a student can effectively perform a skill, strategy, or process
- Providing multiple completed examples
- Pointing out common errors in completed examples
- Performing an error while demonstrating a skill, strategy, or process and then explaining why it was incorrect

In addition to these modeling techniques, teachers can use think-alouds to explain why and how to use a skill, strategy, or process. Each time they enact a step in a procedure, they should explain why they are performing this step, how they are going to perform this step, and how students can recognize when they need to use the procedure. Think-alouds should also help students relate the procedure to what they already know. Students can use think-alouds to explain their own decisions if they demonstrate a procedure for the class or the teacher.

Guided Practice

Guided practice involves well-structured opportunities for students to engage in new skills, strategies, or processes. During these opportunities, activities move from very simple to more complex versions of the skill, strategy, or process. Figure 4.1 can help guide your use of this strategy.

Skill, strategy, or process to be taught: ______________________

Write down the type of guided practice activities to be used in this unit in the far left column, moving from simple to complex versions of the skill. Indicate with an "X" which days will incorporate guided practice of this activity. Fill in dates in the topmost row.

	Day 1	Day 2	Day 3	Day 4	Day 5	Day 6	Day 7	Day 8
Practice activity 1:								
Practice activity 2:								

How will I draw connections between the simple and complex versions of this procedure?

How will I further assist students who are struggling with the procedure even after guided practice?

Source: Marzano Research, 2016.

Figure 4.1: Guided practice planning guide.

Visit **go.SolutionTree.com/instruction** *for a free reproducible version of this figure.*

Close Monitoring

When students are learning a new skill, the teacher provides a highly structured environment and monitors student actions very closely to correct early errors or misunderstandings. As students become more adept with a skill, strategy, or process, the teacher encourages them to monitor their own progress and evaluate their own performances.

Use the following techniques to implement close monitoring in the classroom in a way that scaffolds the attainment of a skill, strategy, or process for students.

- Break procedures or processes into steps or chunks so that students can easily practice each piece.
- Model each step of the procedure or process.
- Ask students to work independently only when you have completed modeling the step so that you are available to observe their actions.
- Observe students as they practice each step. Only move on to the next step in a procedure or process after every student has completed the first step correctly.
- Gradually move students from simple examples to more difficult examples. One way to do this is to have students simply imitate or replicate your actions at first and then gradually have them execute the skill, strategy, or process on their own.
- When students are first learning processes or skills, ask them to repeat information in chorus. As students grow familiar with the information, call on individual students for answers or explanations to a question.
- Stop the whole class when you notice a pattern of errors in the students' performance of a skill, strategy, or process. Explain the errors to the class and have them practice that specific element of the procedure several times.
- Once students are able to complete the skill, strategy, or process independently, place students in small groups and have them complete several problems within the group. Ask each group member to contribute to the completion of the task and speak up if the group has made an error.

Frequent Structured Practice

When students are learning a new skill or process, the teacher first provides a clear demonstration of it. After this demonstration, students should have frequent opportunities to practice discrete elements of the skill or process and the process as a whole in situations where they have a high probability of success. Students should experience success multiple times before moving away from this type of practice. Figure 4.2 (page 68) can help guide your use of this strategy.

Varied Practice

Once students have engaged in frequent structured practice, they begin practicing a skill or process in more challenging situations. Students should still experience success, but they might need to work a bit harder than was necessary during frequent structured practice. During this type of practice, the teacher should encourage students to monitor their progress with the skill or process and to identify their strengths and weaknesses.

Students are ready to begin practicing a skill, strategy, or process in more challenging and varied situations when they can:

- Summarize how to perform the skill, strategy, or process
- Explain when to use the skill, strategy, or process
- Write out a step-by-step procedure for performing the skill, strategy, or process
- Describe the general use of the skill, strategy, or process
- Execute the skill, strategy, or process independently

Frequent Structured Practice Planning Chart

I will initially introduce the procedure or skill on ______________________________.

I will have students practice this procedure or skill ______ times over the course of ______ weeks.

By ______________________________, I expect all students to be able to use this skill or procedure.

Date	Practice Activity	Observations or Results

Do student artifacts show that they are easily using this skill correctly by the last practice session?

How will I deepen students' understanding and use of this skill or process?

Source: Marzano Research, 2016.

Figure 4.2: Frequent structured practice planning chart.

Visit **go.SolutionTree.com/instruction** *for a free reproducible version of this figure.*

Once a teacher is certain that students are ready to vary their use of the skill, strategy, or process, he or she can design more difficult practice problems.

Fluency Practice

Once students are comfortable with a skill or process and have experienced success with it in a wide range of situations, they engage in independent practice in which they focus on performing the skill or process skillfully, accurately, quickly, and automatically. The teacher can assign this type of practice with a skill or process as homework. Students can track their progress over time by keeping self-monitoring charts, such as the one in figure 4.3.

Worked Examples

While students are practicing skills and processes, the teacher provides them with problems or examples that have already been worked out so they receive a clear image of the correct procedure. To implement this strategy, create a written script to accompany each worked example to help students understand what is being demonstrated. After students have reviewed the script, have them answer several questions that ask them to explain what the worked example shows and to demonstrate their understanding of the example. These questions help students reflect on and review the steps outlined in the worked example.

For example, in the following worked example (figure 4.4) of adding fractions with different denominators, the teacher has provided a script outlining each step in the process.

Following the worked example, the teacher might ask these questions.

- "Is it possible to add two fractions with different denominators? Explain your answer."
- "What is one way we can find a common denominator?"
- "What do we have to do to the numerator when we find the common denominator?"

Student Fluency Progress Chart

Name: ______________________________

Skill or process: ______________________________

Progress Measurement	Practice Session				
	1	2	3	4	5
Number of items in my practice set					
Number of items performed correctly					
Number of minutes to complete the items					

How comfortable do I feel performing this skill, strategy, or process compared to when I first learned it?

What did I do to increase my fluency? Are there any techniques or tricks I learned that were particularly helpful?

Rate your fluency using the following scale.

Beginning	Intermediate	Fluent
I am comfortable attempting a skill, strategy, or process independently. I may need to write out the steps for performing the skill, strategy, or process, or refer to notes as I am practicing.	I am comfortable performing the skill, strategy, or process. I may struggle from time to time with difficult examples, but perform easier examples with ease.	I can use the skill, strategy, or process with no guidance and perform all aspects correctly. I can adapt the skill, strategy, or process to solve a range of problems efficiently.

Source: Marzano Research, 2016.

Figure 4.3: Student fluency progress chart.

Visit **go.SolutionTree.com/instruction** *for a free reproducible version of this figure.*

One Method for Adding Fractions With Different Denominators	
$\frac{3}{4} + \frac{1}{2} = ?$	In order to add two fractions, their denominators must match. When the denominators of two fractions in an addition problem are different, we must first find the fractions' common denominator.
$\frac{3}{4} + \frac{1}{2} = ?$ $4 \times 2 = 8$ New denominator = 8	One way to find a common denominator is to multiply the two denominators. The product of the two numbers will be the new denominator.
$\frac{3}{4} \times \frac{2}{2} = \frac{6}{8}$ $\frac{1}{2} \times \frac{4}{4} = \frac{4}{8}$ So, $\frac{6}{8} + \frac{4}{8} = ?$	However, since we multiplied the denominators, we must also multiply the numerators. In order to keep the fractions proportional, we must do what we did to the denominators to the numerators.
$\frac{6}{8} + \frac{4}{8} = ?$ $6 + 4 = 10$ So, $\frac{6}{8} + \frac{4}{8} = \frac{10}{8}$	Now that the denominators are the same, we can add the fraction like we normally would. This means that we add the numerators only and leave the denominators the same.

Figure 4.4: One method for adding fractions with different denominators.

Practice Sessions Prior to Testing

The teacher sets up a practice schedule to ensure that students have a chance to review and practice skills and processes before they are tested or retested on them. Relate the practice to a learning goal or scale using the following tips.

- Tell students which content will be tested on the assessment.
- If students have been charting their progress throughout the unit, have them estimate their current position on the proficiency scale and decide what score they would like to earn on the assessment. Ask students to propose ways they can practice skills and achieve their individual learning goals. Students can also provide explanations for why their activities are good ways to practice a skill, strategy, or process.
- Identify independent or group practice activities students can complete to strengthen their mastery of the learning goal. Have students complete the activities in class or ask them to perform them at home and monitor their ability to complete the tasks. Ask students to rate how fluently they were able to complete a task by providing them with a scale to measure their success.
- Create group practice sessions that review an important skill or process specifically addressed by the learning target or scale. Sessions may be required, or they can be offered as an optional practice activity.
- Create a calendar of practice dates and sessions that will prepare the class for the assessment. Post this calendar in the classroom or on a class website to help students plan for the practice sessions.

Monitoring Element 9

Specific student responses and behaviors allow the teacher to determine whether this element is being implemented effectively and producing the desired effects.

- Students actively engage in practice activities.
- Students ask questions about the procedure.
- Students increase their competence with the procedure.
- Students increase their confidence in their ability to execute the procedure.
- Students increase their fluency in executing the procedure.

Use this list to monitor student responses to element 9.

To monitor your own use of this element, use the scale in figure 4.5 in combination with the reproducible "Tracking Teacher Actions: Using Structured Practice Sessions" (page 89). As with other proficiency scales, level 3 or higher is the goal.

4 Innovating	I adapt behaviors and create new strategies for unique student needs and situations.
3 Applying	I use structured practice sessions, and I monitor the extent to which my actions affect students.
2 Developing	I use structured practice sessions, but I do not monitor the effect on students.
1 Beginning	I use the strategies and behaviors associated with this element incorrectly or with parts missing.
0 Not Using	I am unaware of strategies and behaviors associated with this element.

Figure 4.5: Self-rating scale for element 9—Using structured practice sessions.

The following examples describe what each level of the scale might look like in the classroom.

- **Not Using (0):** A teacher often assigns homework that asks his students to perform new skills, strategies, or processes after he introduces them. The teacher does not model procedures before students perform them and does not set aside additional time in class to practice processes and skills.
- **Beginning (1):** A teacher engages her students in fluency practice of summarizing short texts. Before asking the students to summarize, the teacher demonstrates the skill but does not engage the students in trying the skill. During the fluency practice, the teacher creates strict time limits for the students to generate and write down their summaries, and some of the students are not able to complete the fluency activities in the allotted time.
- **Developing (2):** The teacher models the long division procedure for his students. He describes each step of the procedure as he performs it on the whiteboard and explains when students will need to use this procedure. Afterward, he asks students to solve the same problem using the methods he has described. The teacher then presents additional examples and asks students to solve them with increasing levels of independence. Over the next few days, he provides similar practice sessions. However, he does not have a way of monitoring whether this strategy has helped students understand the procedure better or develop their fluency with the procedure.
- **Applying (3):** A teacher schedules practice sessions before assessments to help students succeed. She creates a scale and asks students to rate their level of comfort and certainty for various processes from recent lessons. She then conducts special practice sessions to go over the procedures that students are unsure about. After the practice sessions, she asks students to rate their comfort levels again. The teacher is careful to stagger the practice sessions so that there is enough time for students to become fluent in the processes before test day.
- **Innovating (4):** A teacher uses varied practice to challenge his students. He creates a series of word problems and asks students to work in groups of two to complete the set of problems. The teacher monitors how quickly each group seems to be moving forward and reminds groups who appear to be struggling of an important step or procedure they could use to solve the problem. There are two sets of students who finish their word problems quickly, so he asks them to write out a step-by-step guide of what they did and why to share with the class later.

Element 10: Examining Similarities and Differences

When content is informational, an effective teacher helps students deepen their knowledge by examining similarities and differences. Research has shown that identifying similarities and differences is associated with a gain in student achievement (Alexander, White, Haensly, & Crimmins-Jeanes, 1987; Baker & Lawson, 1995; Gick & Holyoak, 1980, 1983; Halpern, Hansen, & Reifer, 1990; Lee, n.d.; McDaniel & Donnelly, 1996; Raphael & Kirschner, 1985; Ross, 1988; Stone, 1983). Comparing, classifying, finding patterns, and identifying relationships are basic activities that require students to examine similarities and differences (Marzano, 2007).

There are fourteen strategies within this element.

1. Sentence-stem comparisons
2. Summaries
3. Constructed-response comparisons
4. Venn diagrams
5. T-charts
6. Double-bubble diagrams
7. Comparison matrices
8. Classification charts
9. Dichotomous keys
10. Sorting, matching, and categorizing
11. Similes
12. Metaphors
13. Sentence-stem analogies
14. Visual analogies

The following sections will explore each strategy to provide you with guidelines to effectively implement this element. Read through each before creating a plan for your classroom. Teachers may use the strategies individually or in combination. Remember, these are not merely activities to be checked off; they are methods of creating a practice that combines your art with the science of examining similarities and differences. Reflect on your use of each strategy by filling out the "Strategy Reflection Log" on page 331.

Sentence-Stem Comparisons

Students complete sentence stems that ask them to compare and contrast various people, places, events, concepts, or processes. These comparisons can be general or specific, as shown in the following examples.

- **General:** House cats are similar to lions because __________. House cats are different from lions because __________.
- **Specific:** Sherlock Holmes and Miss Marple are both characters who enjoy solving mysteries, but they are different because __________.

Consider using the following stem formats in your use of this strategy.

- __________ and __________ are similar because they both __________.
- __________ and __________ are different because __________ is __________, but __________ is __________.
- __________ and __________ are both __________, but different because __________.
- __________ is similar to __________ because __________. They are different from each other because __________.
- __________ is similar to __________ but different from __________ because __________.

Summaries

A summarizer is a simple graphic organizer that students can use to examine the similarities and differences between two items. It generally has three columns: the left column explicates features that are only found in the first item; the far-right column lists features that are only found in the second item; the middle column should list characteristics that are similar between the two items and include a sentence that summarizes the items' similarities. Teachers can use this graphic organizer to help students clearly articulate similarities and differences and practice summarizing. Figure 4.6 provides an example.

Topic 1: Corn	Summary Box	Topic 2: Cotton
	Thousands of years ago, cotton and corn were grown as domesticated crops in distant regions of the world, but today both are staple U.S. crops because of their diverse uses. Corn, which grows on tall stalks, is largely seen throughout the Midwest, while cotton, which grows on bushy shrubs, is a prominent crop of the American Southwest.	
Differences	**Similarities**	**Differences**
Grows on vertical stalks	Used to produce a wide array of food, chemical, and household products	Grows on leafy shrubs

Primarily grown throughout the Corn Belt in the Midwest	Grown in the United States	Grown in the South and Southwest
Originated as a crop in Central America	Existed as domestic crops for thousands of years	Domesticated by multiple cultures; exact origin is unknown

Figure 4.6: Example of a completed summarizer.

Constructed-Response Comparisons

A constructed-response comparison is a student-generated written response that describes the similarities and differences between two items or ideas. This strategy begins with a simple request by the teacher: "How is __________ similar to and different from __________?" Students must decide which similarities and differences to include in their responses and how to best frame their analysis. More advanced constructed responses can ask students to draw conclusions and indicate why it is important to understand the similarities and differences between the two items.

Figure 4.7 can help guide students' use of this strategy.

Comparison Words and Phrases

Look for these words and phrases to identify when a text or speaker is referring to similarities and differences. Use these words and phrases yourself when talking or writing about similarities and differences.

Words and Phrases That Indicate Similarities	Words and Phrases That Indicate Differences
• Similarly • Both • In a similar manner • Just like • In the same way • Likewise • Just as • Also • Furthermore • As well as • Alike • Have in common • Share the same	• In comparison • In contrast • On the contrary • On the other hand • Conversely • Whereas • While • Unlike • However • Yet • Instead of • Although • Rather • The antithesis of

Source: Marzano Research, 2016.

Figure 4.7: Comparison words and phrases.

Visit **go.SolutionTree.com/instruction** *for a free reproducible version of this figure.*

Venn Diagrams

Students use these visual tools to compare and contrast two or three people, places, events, concepts, or processes. Students can use Venn diagrams for specific, general, abstract, or concrete comparisons. Students write similarities where circles intersect, and they write characteristics unique to the comparison items where the circles do not intersect.

T-Charts

Students can use T-charts to compare two objects, ideas, events, or people. Students fill in a T-shaped graphic organizer by writing two topics across the top and details that describe each on either side of a dividing line. Then, once students have gathered several characteristics for each item, they look for similarities and differences between the two items. In several short sentences, students should explain the similarities and differences they see in their T-chart. Additionally, after completing their explanation, students can draw conclusions about the essential similarities and differences between the two things. The conclusion should not list all of the similarities and differences but simply sum up what the student recognizes as the fundamental similarities and differences between the two items. It can be helpful if students write parallel characteristics on each side of the T-chart. For example, when comparing Australia and the United States, students might write the continent each country is found on as the first characteristic. By writing the characteristics in parallel, students will easily be able to identify the similarities and differences between the two items after filling in the T-chart.

Double-Bubble Diagrams

Students use this type of diagram to compare the attributes of two people, places, events, concepts, or processes. They write the two things being compared in large circles on the left and right sides of a page. They list common attributes in smaller circles in the center of the page that connect to both large circles. They write unique attributes in smaller circles at the left and right edges of the page that connect only to the larger circle to which they apply.

See figure 4.8 for a template you can use in your classroom.

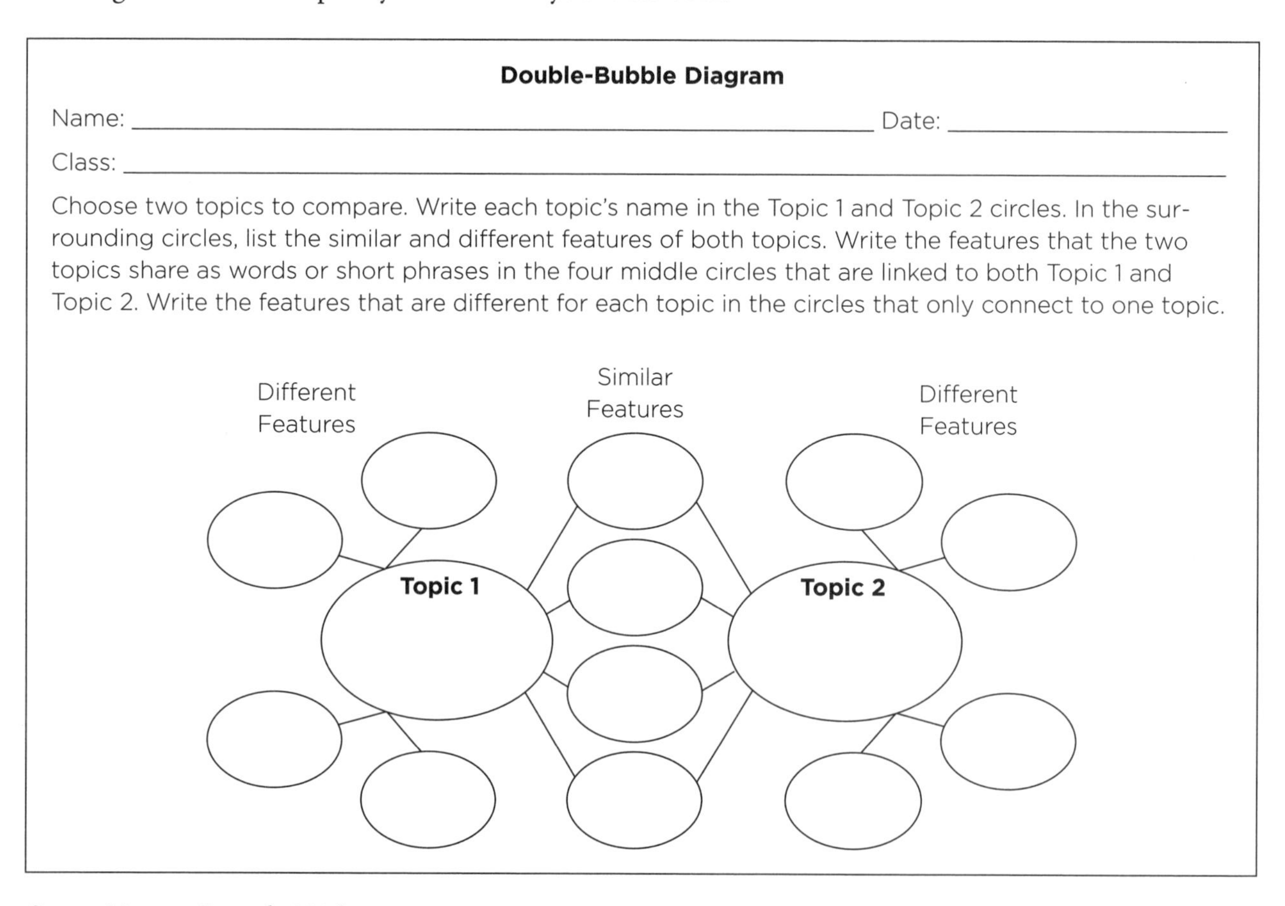

Double-Bubble Diagram

Name: ______________________ Date: ______________

Class: ______________________

Choose two topics to compare. Write each topic's name in the Topic 1 and Topic 2 circles. In the surrounding circles, list the similar and different features of both topics. Write the features that the two topics share as words or short phrases in the four middle circles that are linked to both Topic 1 and Topic 2. Write the features that are different for each topic in the circles that only connect to one topic.

Source: Marzano Research, 2016.

Figure 4.8: Double-bubble diagram template.

Visit **go.SolutionTree.com/instruction** *for a free reproducible version of this figure.*

Comparison Matrices

A comparison matrix is an analysis tool that allows students to compare several items by arranging the items' characteristics side by side. Both elementary and secondary students identify elements they wish to compare and write them at the top of each column in a grid. Next, using a matrix like the one in figure 4.9, students identify attributes they wish to compare and write them in the rows. Then, in each cell, students record information related to each attribute for each element. Finally, students summarize what they learned by comparing the elements.

Comparison Matrix

Name: ______________________________ Date: ______________

Class: ____

	Element:	Element:	Element:
Attribute:			
Attribute:			
Summary:			

Source: Marzano Research, 2016.

Figure 4.9: Comparison matrix template.

Visit **go.SolutionTree.com/instruction** *for a free reproducible version of this figure.*

Classification Charts

Students can use classification charts (like the one in figure 4.10) to group like items together based on their characteristics. The teacher creates a chart with several categories listed across the top and asks students to fill in examples that fit in each category. Students can pair up or form groups to share their charts with their peers, discuss and explain why they classified items as they did, and modify their charts after hearing others' perspectives. Students should then describe in a short paragraph the characteristics that unite each column of elements.

Classification Chart

Name: ______________________________ Date: ______________

Class: ____

Category:	Category:	Category:

In a few sentences, explain why you classified your examples into each of the three categories.

Source: Marzano Research, 2016.

Figure 4.10: Classification chart template.

Visit **go.SolutionTree.com/instruction** *for a free reproducible version of this figure.*

Dichotomous Keys

A dichotomous key is a graphic organizer that refines students' understanding of two or more concepts or objects by delineating different characteristics of each. Generally, the dichotomous key moves from broad characteristics that apply to multiple objects to more detailed characteristics as a way to clearly define the item being examined. Students can create dichotomous keys as either simple tables (figure 4.11) or flow charts (figure 4.12). This strategy is particularly useful when comparing multiple items that fit within the same category and might appear very similar on the surface. Students commonly use this strategy to distinguish between similar organisms in science, but teachers can adapt it for any subject that requires students to distinguish among items in the same category. Students can practice using this strategy with familiar items before moving on to more complex concepts and topics.

Step	Description	If Yes
1a	Has two sets of parallel sides	Is classified as a parallelogram, go to step 2a
1b	Does not have two sets of parallel sides	Is not classified as a parallelogram, do not continue
2a	Has four congruent sides	Go to step 3a.
2b	Does not have four congruent sides	Is classified as a rectangle
3a	Has four right angles	Is classified as a square
3b	Does not have four right angles	Is classified as a rhombus

Figure 4.11: Example of a dichotomous key simple table.

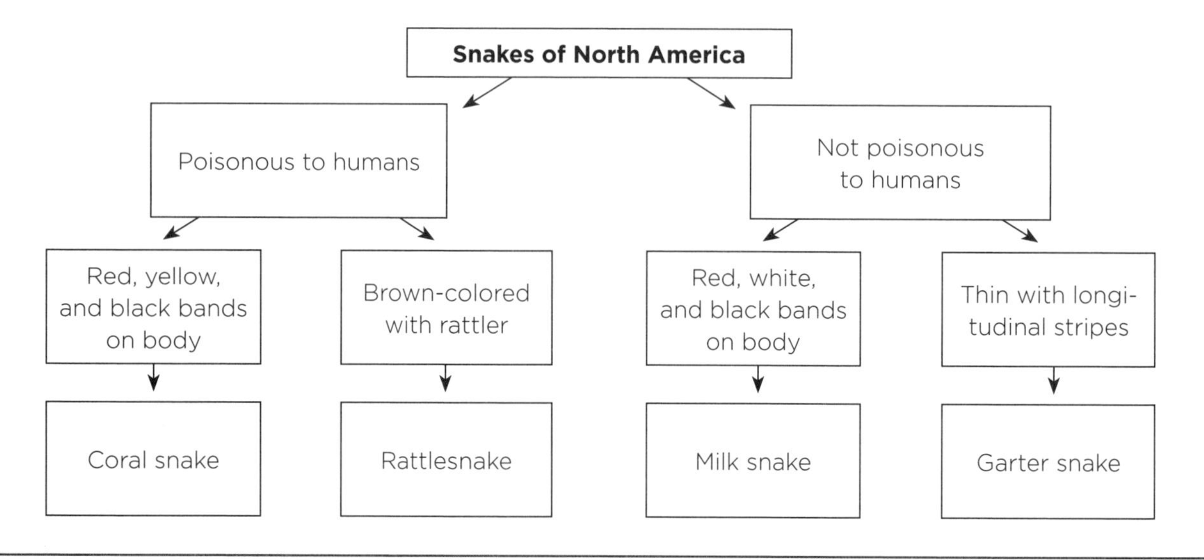

Figure 4.12: Example of a dichotomous key flow chart.

Sorting, Matching, and Categorizing

Teachers can ask students to participate in activities that require them to sort, match, and categorize content. When sorting, students should place items into specific, predetermined categories. When matching, students should match two things that are equivalent to one another. For example, they might match a picture or symbol with a word, a definition with a term, two mathematical equations with the same solution, or a synonym with a word. When categorizing, students should group elements into two or more categories and explain the reasoning behind their categorization. Teachers can ask students to complete these kinds of activities individually, in groups, or as a class. Teachers can also structure sorting, matching, and categorizing activities through the use of graphic organizers, worksheets, or other visual representations.

Following are examples of sorting, matching, and categorizing activities.

- **Defining vocabulary or terms:** This strategy works well when instructing students on important vocabulary or terms for a unit. When students are beginning to learn the definition of the term, teachers can have them match the word to its written definition, to an illustration of the term, or to a synonym. As students' understanding deepens, they should be able to sort the terms into categories. For example, in an English language arts class the teacher might ask students to sort words under the appropriate part of speech, and in a science class a teacher could have students sort terms under the type of animal or process they describe.
- **Understanding symbols:** A number of subject areas use symbols to represent ideas or processes. Students can use this strategy to familiarize themselves with the use, purpose, and definition of important symbols. For example, in a music class, students could match different musical symbols to their use, or they could categorize different instruments by which clef (the musical symbol used to indicate the pitch of written music notes) the music for the instrument uses.
- **Classifying objects that could belong to the same category:** Sorting and categorizing objects into more specific categories helps students understand which features define a particular set of objects. For example, for a unit on the solar system, a teacher could ask students to sort planets as gas giants, dwarf planets, or ice giants and have them explain which features of each planet cause them to belong to that category. Through this kind of activity, students learn that even objects within the same category, such as planets, can have a diverse range of features.

Similes

In this strategy, students state comparisons using *like* or *as*. Students can generate similes to help them understand how new knowledge relates to previous knowledge. They might include an explanation of why one object is like the other and can revise their similes after discussing them with their peers. Teachers can introduce similes by comparing new knowledge to something students are already familiar with. For example, when teaching a lesson on adding fractions, a teacher might state, "Adding fractions with different denominators is like trying to add apples and oranges," in order to show students that the denominators must be the same when adding fractions. Visit **go.SolutionTree.com/instruction** for the reproducible "Similes" to introduce students to this strategy.

Metaphors

With this strategy, students state comparisons using metaphors. In a metaphor, comparisons are stated as direct relationships—one thing is another—for example, *life is a journey*. Metaphors are sometimes abstract and can be extended to include more than one comparison. Students should explain why their metaphors are appropriate. When deepening students' knowledge of a subject, the teacher can instruct students to create metaphors that relate the new content to something they understand well. For example, when discussing the Silk Road and the Mongol Empire, students could state, "The Silk Road was a bridge between Eastern and Western cultures." Visit **go.SolutionTree.com/instruction** for the reproducible "Metaphors" to introduce students to this strategy.

Sentence-Stem Analogies

Students can use sentence stems to create comparisons that describe specific relationships between two items or concepts. Analogies always take this form: "Item 1 is to item 2 as item 3 is to item 4." The teacher might also present students with the first two terms of an analogy and ask them to fill in the second two terms, for example: "A coach is to an athlete as __________ is to __________." Visit **go.SolutionTree.com/instruction** for the reproducible "Sentence-Stem Analogies" to introduce students to this strategy.

Visual Analogies

The teacher asks students to use visual organizers to help them make analogies. The students create an analogy and specify the type of relationship the analogy is expressing. Many students are visual learners and working with content in a visual can help reinforce the meaning. Visit **go.SolutionTree.com/instruction** for the reproducible "Visual Analogies" to introduce students to this strategy.

Monitoring Element 10

Specific student responses and behaviors allow the teacher to determine whether this element is being implemented effectively and producing the desired effects.

- Students understand the similarities and differences between the elements being compared.
- Students ask questions about the similarities and differences between the elements being compared.
- Students can explain how the activities deepened their knowledge.

Use this list to monitor student responses to element 10.

To monitor your own use of this element, use the scale in figure 4.13 in combination with the reproducible "Tracking Teacher Actions: Examining Similarities and Differences" (page 90). As with other proficiency scales, level 3 or higher is the goal.

4 Innovating	I adapt behaviors and create new strategies for unique student needs and situations.
3 Applying	I engage students in examining similarities and differences, and I monitor the extent to which students deepen their knowledge.
2 Developing	I engage students in examining similarities and differences, but I do not monitor the effect on students.
1 Beginning	I use the strategies and behaviors associated with this element incorrectly or with parts missing.
0 Not Using	I am unaware of strategies and behaviors associated with this element.

Figure 4.13: Self-rating scale for element 10—Examining similarities and differences.

The following examples describe what each level of the scale might look like in the classroom.

- **Not Using (0):** A teacher does not ask her students to classify or describe similarities and differences to deepen their understanding of concepts taught in class. The teacher does ask students to describe concepts in order to refine their understanding of topics but does not provide opportunities for students to compare these descriptions to descriptions of other concepts.
- **Beginning (1):** A teacher asks his students to use a Venn diagram to compare two events they have been discussing in class. However, the teacher fails to describe how to use a Venn diagram

and assumes that his students will be able to complete the activity on their own and understand what it means.

- **Developing (2):** A teacher instructs her students to use a comparison matrix to compare three characters from a novel they have been reading. After the students have completed their matrices, they discuss what they have found. However, the teacher does not take note if their discussions indicate that their knowledge has developed.
- **Applying (3):** A teacher puts his students into groups of three to complete a classification chart. Once all of the students have completed their charts, he asks them to present their chart to the class and explain their reasoning. As the students present, he encourages the rest of the class to ask clarifying questions and listens to make sure the students' understanding is more complete as a result of the activity.
- **Innovating (4):** A teacher asks the class to create a visual analogy illustrating a relationship between organisms. When some students appear to be struggling with the activity, she puts them into a small group and asks them to describe the relationships first and then choose a relationship together that they can illustrate. After they choose a relationship, the teacher asks the students if they can think of something they have observed in their lives that behaves similarly. Once the students have completed the assignment, the teacher asks all of the students to hang their visual analogies on the wall and then the class goes through and identifies which relationship is being depicted in each analogy.

Element 11: Examining Errors in Reasoning

This element helps deepen students' understanding of content by having them examine their own reasoning or the overall logic of information presented to them. Research has shown that errors are sometimes present in students' understanding of content (Brown & Burton, 1978). The best way to correct those errors is for students to re-examine the content for accuracy (Clement, Lockhead, & Mink, 1979; Tennyson & Cocchiarella, 1986). Philosophers have identified the following four types of errors in thinking: (1) faulty logic, (2) attack, (3) weak reference, and (4) misinformation (Johnson-Laird, 1983; Johnson-Laird & Byrne, 1991; Toulmin, Rieke, & Janik, 1981).

There are twelve strategies within this element.

1. Identifying errors of faulty logic
2. Identifying errors of attack
3. Identifying errors of weak reference
4. Identifying errors of misinformation
5. Practicing identifying errors in logic
6. Finding errors in the media
7. Examining support for claims
8. Judging reasoning and evidence in an author's work
9. Identifying statistical limitations
10. Using student-friendly prompts
11. Anticipating student errors
12. Avoiding unproductive habits of mind

The following sections will explore each strategy to provide you with guidelines to effectively implement this element. Read through each before creating a plan for your classroom. Teachers may use the strategies individually or in combination. Remember, these are not merely activities to be checked off; they are methods of creating a practice that combines your art with the science of examining errors in reasoning. Reflect on your use of each strategy by filling out the "Strategy Reflection Log" on page 331.

Identifying Errors of Faulty Logic

In this strategy, students find and analyze errors of faulty logic. Errors of faulty logic refer to situations in which a conclusion is not supported by sound reasons. Specific types of errors in this category include the following.

- **Contradiction:** Presenting conflicting information—for example, saying that downloading music illegally should be punished more harshly while also arguing that internet providers and the government shouldn't be allowed to collect information about internet users
- **Accident:** Failing to recognize that an argument is based on an exception to a rule—for example, if a person argued that Scotland has a warm and sunny climate based on the weather during her one-week vacation there
- **False cause:** Confusing a temporal (time) order of events with causality or oversimplifying the reasons behind some event or occurrence—for example, superstitious beliefs such as wearing a certain shirt so that your favorite team will win
- **Begging the question:** Making a claim and then arguing for the claim by using statements that are simply the equivalent of the original claim—for example, saying that Namibia is the most beautiful country because it has the prettiest landscape
- **Evading the issue:** Changing the topic to avoid addressing the issue—for example, if a student defends himself against accusations of cheating on a test by saying that he always does his homework and never breaks curfew
- **Arguing from ignorance:** Arguing that a claim is justified simply because its opposite has not been proven true—for example, claiming that a certain subatomic particle must not exist because we haven't discovered it yet
- **Composition:** Asserting something about a whole that is true of only its parts—for example, creating a stereotype about a whole group of people based on the actions or traits of a few people from that group
- **Division:** Making a claim about individual parts based on the fact that it is generally true of the whole—for example, saying that because you dislike sandwiches, you must dislike tomatoes

Identifying Errors of Attack

Students find and analyze errors of attack. Errors of attack happen when a person focuses on the context of an argument, rather than the argument itself, in trying to refute the other side. That is, instead of using evidence and sound reasons to argue a point, a person ignores counterevidence and attacks the person who is arguing for the other side. Types of errors in this category include the following.

- **Poisoning the well:** Being so completely committed to a position that you explain away absolutely everything that is offered in opposition to your position—for example, refusing to accept that studies on the potential negative effects of drinking coffee are scientifically valid
- **Arguing against the person:** Rejecting a claim using derogatory statements (real or alleged) about the person who is making the claim—for example, stating that an opponent was fired from her job during an unrelated debate
- **Appealing to force:** Using threats to establish the validity of a claim—for example, threatening to expose unflattering information about an opponent to make the opponent surrender the argument

Identifying Errors of Weak Reference

Students find and analyze errors of weak reference. An error of weak reference occurs when a person uses information from untrustworthy or irrelevant sources to support an argument. Specific types of these errors include the following.

- **Sources that reflect biases:** Consistently accepting information that supports what we already believe to be true or consistently rejecting information that goes against what we believe to be true—for example, only reading articles from newspapers and websites that align with one's own political leanings
- **Sources that lack credibility:** Using a source that is not reputable for a given topic—for example, citing something that a movie star said in a debate about the causes of a disease
- **Appealing to authority:** Invoking authority as the last word on an issue—for example, treating a police officer's opinion as absolute truth in a discussion of gun laws
- **Appealing to the people:** Attempting to justify a claim based on its popularity—for example, justifications that begin "everyone knows" or "everyone agrees"
- **Appealing to emotion:** Using a "sob story" as proof for a claim—for example, justifying making a mistake by talking about the sad and stressful things that have happened lately

Identifying Errors of Misinformation

Students find and analyze errors of misinformation. Errors of misinformation occur when a person uses incorrect information in support of an argument. Following are types of misinformation errors.

- **Confusing the facts:** Using information that seems to be factual but that has been changed in such a way that it is no longer accurate—for example, citing demographic information that is ten or twenty years old
- **Misapplying a concept or generalization:** Misunderstanding or wrongly applying a concept or generalization to support a claim—for example, applying the generalization that Democrats are fiscally liberal to an individual Democrat's personal spending habits

Practicing Identifying Errors in Logic

Teachers can use practice exercises to help students identify errors in logic. These exercises can serve as a stepping stone for students as they progress from the basic step of understanding various errors in reasoning to the goal of recognizing them in everyday life. Typically, these exercises will describe a scenario in a few sentences and ask students to identify the reasoning error present in the scenario. Students might select the answer in a multiple-choice or matching format, or teachers can ask them to recall the answer from memory.

Provide students with the exercises in figure 4.14 (page 82) to practice identifying errors in reasoning.

Finding Errors in the Media

The teacher provides students with footage of political debates, televised interviews, commercials, advertisements, newspaper articles, blogs, and other sources and asks them to find and analyze errors in reasoning that underlie the messages therein. Following are resources for such media.

- **Intelligence Squared Debates (intelligencesquaredus.org):** Oxford-style debates over controversial current issues in which two panels of experts attempt to change the audience members' minds with evidence and reasoned arguments for and against a topic
- **Stanford University's Political Communication Lab (pcl.stanford.edu):** Archived political campaign advertisement videos and research on political rhetoric and media

Exercises for Practicing Identifying Errors in Reasoning

1. Connor's family has a dog that is almost twenty years old. When his friend's dog dies, Connor asks his mom how it could have happened. "His dog was only twelve," Connor says. "He should have lived a lot longer."
2. Jamie and Lewis are discussing the AIDS epidemic. "Maybe someday they'll find a cure," Jamie says. "There is no cure for AIDS," Lewis says. "They haven't found one yet, have they? And they've tried for a long time. That means there is no cure."
3. James is working on an essay for class, and Jamal asks him why he is writing it out by hand instead of using the computer. James says that the last time he used the computer he got a bad grade, so now he writes everything by hand first and types it on the computer later.
4. Annabelle and Zelda are assigned to debate whether or not Woodrow Wilson was a good president of the United States. Zelda goes first and presents her argument for why Wilson was a good president. When it is Annabelle's turn to speak, she begins by saying, "Since you all know Zelda, you'll understand that she is wrong, because she is always so rude."
5. Taylor asks Gale why she is wearing a jacket with a hole in the elbow. Gale tells him it is the new style. "Look around," she says. "Everyone is doing it."
6. Sasha has written a paper about the presidency of Ronald Reagan. Her teacher notices that most of the people Sasha quotes in the paper said that he was an excellent president. Almost all of them were people who worked very closely with him, and the quotes were recorded when they were still working for him.
7. Lawrence says he wants to get a master's degree in business administration after going to college, and Charlotte says she thinks that's great. "What kind of business do you want to go into?" she asks. Lawrence replies, "I don't want to go into business, I just want to make more money. People with MBAs make more money."

Answers: 1—Accident; 2—Arguing from ignorance; 3—False cause; 4—Arguing against the person; 5—Appealing to the people; 6—Using sources that reflect bias; 7—Misapplying a concept or generalization

Source: Marzano Research, 2016.

Figure 4.14: Exercises for practicing identifying errors in reasoning.

Visit **go.SolutionTree.com/instruction** *for a free reproducible version of this figure.*

- **Real Clear Politics (realclearpolitics.com):** Aggregated commentary, news, and statistics representing a full range of political viewpoints
- **Vintage Ad Browser (vintageadbrowser.com):** Large image collection of advertisements, including propaganda posters, sorted by subject or topic

Examining Support for Claims

Students examine the support provided for a claim by analyzing the grounds, backing, and qualifiers that support it. Grounds are the reasons given to support a claim and backing is the evidence, facts, or data that support the grounds, while qualifiers address exceptions or objections to the claim. Defining the structure of the argument and identifying how the support presented for a claim relates to that claim can help students determine whether the claim is valid.

Figure 4.15 can help guide students' use of this strategy.

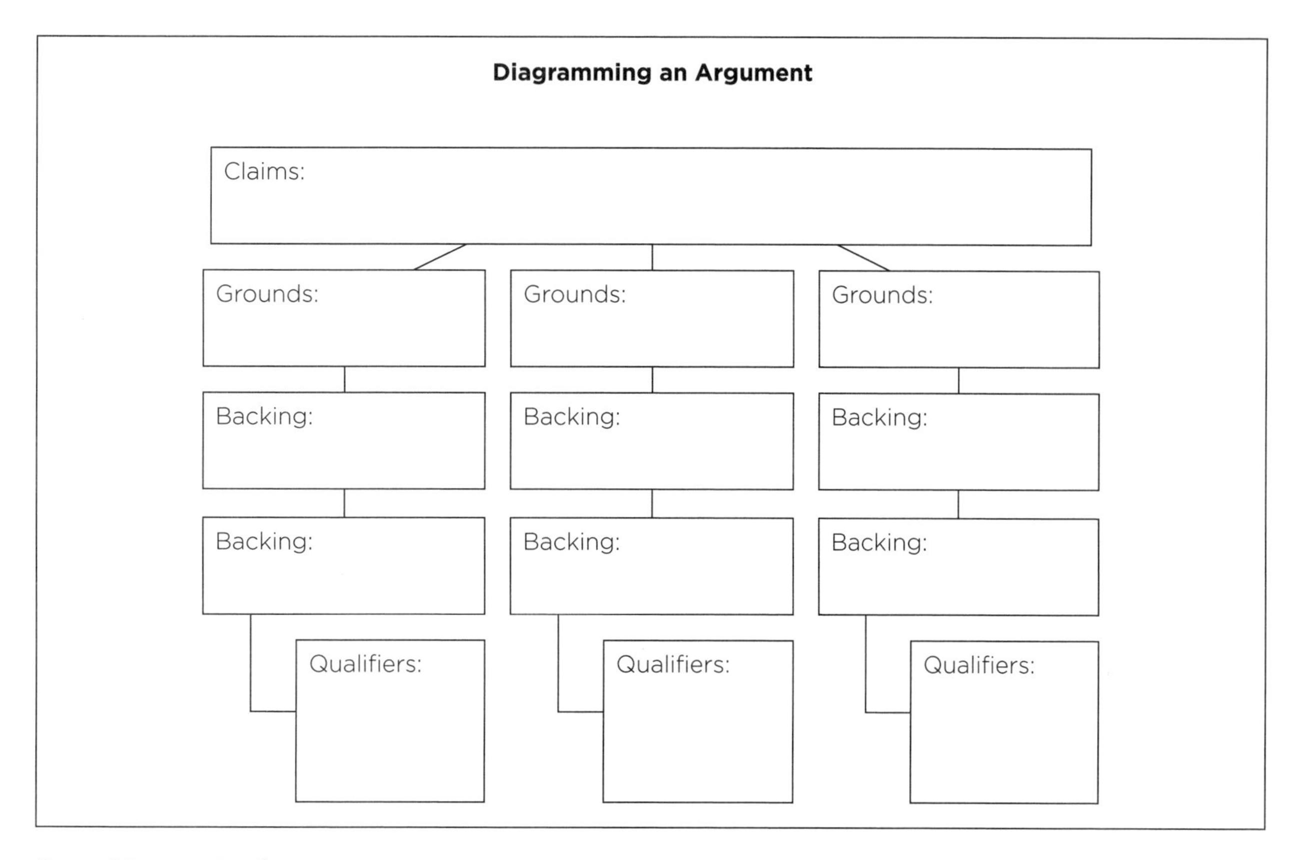

Source: Marzano, 2016.

Figure 4.15: Diagramming an argument.

Visit **go.SolutionTree.com/instruction** *for a free reproducible version of this figure.*

Judging Reasoning and Evidence in an Author's Work

Students apply their knowledge of reasoning and argumentation to delineate and evaluate the arguments presented in a text. To delineate an argument, students read a text and identify the claim, grounds, backing, and qualifiers. To evaluate an argument, students must decide whether the reasoning is valid or logical (containing no errors) and whether the supporting evidence is sufficient and relevant. If the evidence is sufficient, there is enough of it; if the evidence is relevant, it is related to the claim.

Provide students with the following questions to guide their use of this strategy (Marzano Research, 2016).

- What is the author's claim?
- What grounds does the author use to support that claim?
- What backing backs up the grounds?
- What qualifiers does the author give?
- Does the argument contain logical errors?
- Is the evidence sufficient?
- Is the evidence relevant?

Identifying Statistical Limitations

Students find and analyze errors that commonly occur when using statistical data to support a claim. Following are the major types of statistical limitations students should be aware of.

- **Regression toward the mean:** An extreme score on a measure is most commonly followed by a more moderate score that is closer to the mean—for example, an area that receives far more rain in a year than is normal will probably receive a more average amount of rain in the following year.
- **Errors of conjunction:** It is less likely that two or more independent events will occur simultaneously than that they will occur in isolation—for example, the probability of being struck by lightning *and* falling off a cliff while hiking is less than the probability of being struck by lightning *or* the probability of falling off a cliff.
- **Keeping aware of base rates:** Using the general or typical patterns of occurrences in a category of events as the basis on which to predict what will happen in a specific situation—for example, if a golfer shoots over par on the first ten holes of a course, then shoots one under par on the eleventh hole, it is probably unwise to predict that he or she will shoot under par on the rest of the holes.
- **Understanding the limits of extrapolation:** Realizing that using trends to make predictions (that is, extrapolating) is a useful practice as long as the prediction does not extend beyond the data for which trends have been observed—for example, if a teacher has been tracking one class's level of understanding using formative assessment, he or she can't necessarily extrapolate that information onto another class.
- **Adjusting estimates of risk to account for the cumulative nature of probabilistic events:** Realizing that even though the probability of a risky event might be highly unlikely, the probability of the event occurring increases with time and the number of events—for example, the more often a person breaks the speed limit while driving, the more likely it is that he or she will get caught.

Using Student-Friendly Prompts

To help students remember to examine arguments for errors in reasoning, teachers can use prompts and questions phrased in nontechnical language. Especially with K–2 students or students who are just learning these skills, it may be more effective to remind students, for example, to look for *getting off topic* rather than *evading the issue.*

Provide students with the following ten student-friendly prompts for finding errors in reasoning (Marzano Research, 2016).

1. Does this argument make assumptions that are inaccurate?
2. Is there enough information in this argument to support this conclusion?
3. Is the information that supports the argument accurate?
4. Is this person letting his or her own opinions about the topic determine what conclusions he or she draws or what information he or she uses to support those conclusions?
5. Does this argument get off topic or make points that are unrelated to the main point?
6. Does this argument assume that something that happened once or twice is true all the time?
7. Does this argument assume that the second of two events was caused by the first, just because it happened after?
8. Is this person ignoring the possibility that he or she could be wrong or ignoring all the evidence that the other side presents?
9. Does this person say unkind things about people who disagree with his or her point of view?
10. Does this argument use emotions instead of reasons?

Anticipating Student Errors

When presenting content, teachers can prevent confusion or missteps by pre-emptively addressing common errors. When planning a lesson or assignment, the teacher identifies errors that students are likely to make. Then, during the presentation of content, the teacher alerts students to the potential problems. For example, when a teacher introduces the process for finding the area of a right triangle, he recalls from previous years that students sometimes have difficulty identifying the base and height if the triangle has been rotated. He shows an example on the board in which the hypotenuse could be mistaken for the height and leads a discussion of why is this an error.

When planning for this strategy, consider the following questions (Marzano Research, 2016).

- What content are you covering?
- In your experience, what are common errors that students make with this content?

Then, for each error, create an example that demonstrates the error and allows you to correct it.

Avoiding Unproductive Habits of Mind

Habits of mind are ways we regularly approach situations. Unproductive habits of mind are those that hinder us from completing complex tasks. Conversely, productive habits of mind are those that help us complete complex tasks. Productive habits of mind include the following.

- **Staying focused when answers and solutions are not immediately apparent:** This disposition is typically executed when students are trying to solve a complex problem. It starts by recognizing the frustration felt because they can't find an answer or solution and are about to give up on the task. Upon this realization, they then re-engage in the task even though they are experiencing ambiguity.
- **Pushing the limits of one's knowledge and skills:** Students typically execute this disposition during long-term projects. It begins with students recognizing that they have set goals that are limited by their natural tendency to operate within their zone of comfort. Upon this realization, they then adjust their goals such that their accomplishment will require the students to acquire new knowledge and skills.
- **Generating and pursuing one's own standards of excellence:** This disposition is typically executed when students are trying to create a product. It starts by consciously thinking of how the product will look when it is complete and the standards by which the students will judge how well they did. While considering standard conventions for the product, students might adjust them so that they coincide with their personal level of development.
- **Seeking incremental steps:** This disposition is typically executed when students are learning something new that involves a number of interacting parts. Rather than trying to grasp the entire system as a whole, they continually strive to understand small subsets of the entire system. With the acquisition of each subset, they examine how it affects their understanding of the system as a whole and make adaptations in their thinking as necessary.
- **Seeking accuracy:** This disposition is typically executed when students are gathering information about a topic. It begins with their analysis of the source of the information they are receiving. If they are not completely sure of the accuracy of a source they then consult other sources they are more sure contain accurate information about the topic.
- **Seeking clarity:** This disposition is typically executed when students are trying to understand something new. It begins with students asking themselves if they have any confusion regarding

the information they have processed thus far. If they do, then they stop taking in new information and seek clarification from whatever resources are available.

- **Resisting impulsivity:** This disposition is typically executed when students wish to respond to some stimulus or form a conclusion based on new information they have processed. It begins with students realizing that they have an urge to respond or form a conclusion without collecting more information. They briefly pause and think about their response or conclusion with an eye toward making revisions.
- **Seeking cohesion and coherence:** This disposition is typically executed when students are creating something that has a number of interacting parts. Seeking cohesion means that they are continually monitoring the extent to which relationships between component parts are solid and stable and making adjustments if they are not. Seeking coherence means that students are continually monitoring whether the interaction of the parts is producing the desired effect and making adjustments if it is not.

Unproductive habits of mind are ways of approaching situations that are the opposite of the productive habits of mind. For example, while a productive habit of mind would be staying focused when we are trying to solve a complex problem, an unproductive habit of mind would be quitting as soon as we get frustrated. While a productive habit of mind would be pushing ourselves out of our comfort zone when working on a long-term project, an unproductive habit of mind would be backing down any time we notice that we are uncomfortable executing our current level of knowledge and skill.

Table 4.1 can help you determine whether you are using productive or unproductive habits of mind.

Table 4.1: Self-Analysis of Habits of Mind

Habit of Mind	Situation	Self-Analysis Question
Staying focused when answers and solutions are not immediately apparent	You are trying to solve a problem that is very difficult.	Am I giving up because I can't find the answer right away?
Pushing the limits of your knowledge and skills	You are working on a complex project or goal that takes a long time.	Am I stopping because I have to acquire new knowledge or skills to accomplish this?
Generating and pursuing your own standards of excellence	You are working on a complex project or goal that takes a long time.	Have I identified what the final product should look like in order for me to feel that I have done my best?
Seeking incremental steps	You are working on a complex project or goal that takes a long time.	Am I breaking the big project into small pieces that can be more easily accomplished?
Seeking accuracy	You are seeing, hearing, or learning something new.	Am I doing something or asking questions to determine if the new information is accurate?
Seeking clarity	You are seeing, hearing, or learning something new.	Am I aware of when I'm getting confused and stopping to ask questions or do something to clarify things?
Resisting impulsivity	You have to make a decision or react to something.	Am I aware that I'm acting without thinking about my actions and then stopping for a moment to examine my conclusions?
Seeking cohesion and coherence	You are creating something that has a lot of related parts.	Am I making sure that all the pieces fit together and work toward a common goal?

Source: Marzano, 2016.

Visit **go.SolutionTree.com/instruction** *for a free reproducible version of this figure.*

Monitoring Element 11

Specific student responses and behaviors allow the teacher to determine whether this element is being implemented effectively and producing the desired effects.

- Students actively identify and analyze their own errors.
- Students actively identify and analyze others' errors.
- Students can describe and exemplify the different types of errors one might make.
- Students can explain how the activities have increased their understanding of the content.

Use this list to monitor student responses to element 11.

To monitor your own use of this element, use the scale in figure 4.16 in combination with the reproducible "Tracking Teacher Actions: Examining Errors in Reasoning" (page 91). As with other proficiency scales, level 3 or higher is the goal.

4 Innovating	I adapt behaviors and create new strategies for unique student needs and situations.
3 Applying	When content is informational, I engage students in activities that require them to examine their own reasoning or the logic of information as presented to them, and I monitor the extent to which students are deepening their knowledge.
2 Developing	When content is informational, I engage students in activities that require them to examine their own reasoning or the logic of information as presented to them, but I do not monitor the effect on students.
1 Beginning	I use the strategies and behaviors associated with this element incorrectly or with parts missing.
0 Not Using	I am unaware of strategies and behaviors associated with this element.

Figure 4.16: Self-rating scale for element 11—Examining errors in reasoning.

The following examples describe what each level of the scale might look like in the classroom.

- **Not Using (0):** A teacher generally assumes that students probably have errors or misconceptions about content but does not provide them with opportunities to examine their reasoning.
- **Beginning (1):** A teacher points out errors in reasoning to her students when they become apparent in the course of a discussion or assessment. However, she gives them little or no opportunity to examine their own thinking.
- **Developing (2):** A teacher asks students to examine their own thinking—as well as information presented to them—for errors as a preventive measure. However, he does not keep track of student outcomes, so he isn't sure how well it is working.
- **Applying (3):** A teacher helps her students examine errors in reasoning by teaching them to find errors in the media and examine the support for claims that they read about. She records instances of erroneous thinking and is able to see that they are decreasing over time.
- **Innovating (4):** A teacher notices that while most of her students have markedly improved in their ability to detect errors in reasoning, several students are still struggling. In particular, they are having trouble determining whether support for a claim is sufficient. The teacher shows these students how to diagram an argument as a way to visually assess the support for a claim.

Action Steps

Use the "Tracking Teacher Actions" reproducibles that follow (pages 89–91) to monitor your implementation of each element in this chapter.

Additionally, visit the appendix (page 329) for the reproducible "Tracking Progress Over Time" (page 330), which helps teachers set goals related to their proficiency with each element and track their progress toward these goals over the course of a unit, semester, or year. Also, the "Strategy Reflection Log" (page 331) in the appendix provides a space to write down your thoughts and reflect on the implementation process for specific strategies related to each element. Finally, visit **go.SolutionTree.com/instruction** for both student surveys and teacher surveys, the results of which provide feedback about your proficiency with each element.

Tracking Teacher Actions: Using Structured Practice Sessions

The teacher can use this form to plan his or her usage of strategies related to the element of using structured practice sessions.

Check Strategies You Intend to Use	Strategies	Description of Instructional Plan
	Modeling	
	Guiding Practice	
	Close Monitoring	
	Frequent Structured Practice	
	Varied Practice	
	Fluency Practice	
	Worked Examples	
	Practice Sessions Prior to Testing	
	Other:	
	Other:	

Source: Adapted from Marzano Research. (2016). Marzano compendium of instructional strategies. *Centennial, CO: Author.*

Tracking Teacher Actions: Examining Similarities and Differences

The teacher can use this form to plan his or her usage of strategies related to the element of examining similarities and differences.

Check Strategies You Intend to Use	Strategies	Description of Instructional Plan
	Sentence-Stem Comparisons	
	Summaries	
	Constructed-Response Comparisons	
	Venn Diagrams	
	T-Charts	
	Double-Bubble Diagrams	
	Comparison Matrices	
	Classification Charts	
	Dichotomous Keys	
	Sorting, Matching, and Categorizing	
	Similes	
	Metaphors	
	Sentence-Stem Analogies	
	Visual Analogies	
	Other:	
	Other:	

Source: Adapted from Marzano Research. (2016). Marzano compendium of instructional strategies. *Centennial, CO: Author.*

Tracking Teacher Actions: Examining Errors in Reasoning

The teacher can use this form to plan his or her usage of strategies related to the element of examining errors in reasoning.

Check Strategies You Intend to Use	Strategies	Description of Instructional Plan
	Identifying Errors of Faulty Logic	
	Identifying Errors of Attack	
	Identifying Errors of Weak Reference	
	Identifying Errors of Misinformation	
	Practicing Identifying Errors in Logic	
	Finding Errors in the Media	
	Examining Support for Claims	
	Judging Reasoning and Evidence in an Author's Work	
	Identifying Statistical Limitations	
	Using Student-Friendly Prompts	
	Anticipating Student Errors	
	Avoiding Unproductive Habits of Mind	
	Other:	
	Other:	

Source: Adapted from Marzano Research. (2016). Marzano compendium of instructional strategies. *Centennial, CO: Author.*

CHAPTER 5

Conducting Knowledge Application Lessons

A third type of content lesson a teacher might employ involves knowledge application. Knowledge application lessons encourage students to move beyond the content and begin generating their own claims and conclusions. In these lessons, teachers facilitate students' exploration of their knowledge by providing guidance and resources. Ultimately, knowledge application lessons not only help students master the content but also help them examine the intrinsic ideas within content and how these concepts might apply to the overarching unit.

The goal of this design area is for students to generate and defend claims through knowledge application tasks after teachers present new content. Teachers are able to meet that goal by answering the question, After presenting content, how will I design and deliver lessons that help students generate and defend claims through knowledge application? The three elements and associated strategies in this chapter help the teacher do just that.

Element 12: Engaging Students in Cognitively Complex Tasks

An effective teacher engages students in complex tasks that require them to generate and defend conclusions. Research has shown that generating and testing hypotheses is associated with student achievement gains (El-Nemr, 1980; Hattie et al., 1996; Ross, 1988; Sweitzer & Anderson, 1983; Walberg, 1999). Projects that involve investigating or solving a problem increase students' understanding of principles and application of knowledge (Gijbels, Dochy, Van den Bossche, & Segers, 2005). Cognitively complex tasks require students to question their current knowledge and adjust it to accommodate their findings (Guzzetti et al., 1993).

There are seven strategies within this element.

1. Experimental-inquiry tasks
2. Problem-solving tasks
3. Tasks to examine the efficiencies of multiple methods of problem solving
4. Decision-making tasks
5. Investigation tasks
6. Invention tasks
7. Student-designed tasks

The following sections will explore each strategy to provide you with guidelines to effectively implement this element. Read through each before creating a plan for your classroom. Teachers may use the strategies individually or in combination. Remember, these are not merely activities to be checked off; they are methods of creating a practice that combines your art with the science of engaging students in cognitively complex tasks. Reflect on your use of each strategy by filling out the "Strategy Reflection Log" on page 331.

Experimental-Inquiry Tasks

The teacher uses experimental-inquiry tasks to teach students how to make predictions, test them, examine the results, evaluate the results, and reflect on the process to come to a defensible conclusion. Observations, experiments, surveys, and interviews are all appropriate data-collection techniques for this type of task. The teacher can ask students to answer the following questions as they engage in experimental-inquiry tasks.

- What is my prediction?
- How will I test my prediction?
- What do I expect to see if my prediction is correct?
- What actually happened?
- Did my prediction come true?
- How has my thinking changed?
- What conclusions can I defend?

Figure 5.1 can help guide students' use of this strategy.

Experimental-Inquiry Notes Template

The question I am investigating is ______________________________.

My hypothesis is that if ______________ then ______________ will occur because of______________________________.

To test my hypothesis I will do the following things:

1.

2.

3.

As I conduct my experiment I notice:

The results of my experiment show:

My observations and results lead me to these conclusions:

Experimental-Inquiry Model

Observation

Relevant Theory or Rule

Prediction

Experiment

Results

Source: Marzano Research, 2016.

Figure 5.1: Experimental-inquiry notes template.

Visit **go.SolutionTree.com/instruction** *for a free reproducible version of this figure.*

Problem-Solving Tasks

The teacher uses problem-solving tasks to teach students how to set a goal, identify obstacles or constraints to reaching that goal, find solutions, predict which solution is most likely to work, test their prediction, examine the results, evaluate the results, and reflect on the process. Students answer the following questions as they engage in problem-solving tasks.

- What is the goal?
- What obstacle or constraint makes it difficult to accomplish the goal?
- What are some ways I might overcome the obstacle or the constraint?
- Which solution do I predict will work best, and why?
- What actually happened?
- Do the results fit with my original prediction?
- If not, how should my thinking change regarding the problem?
- What are my conclusions?

Figure 5.2 can help guide students' use of this strategy.

Problem-Solving Map

Name: ____

Problem or goal:		
Possible Solution 1 Advantages and Disadvantages	Possible Solution 2 Advantages and Disadvantages	Possible Solution 3 Advantages and Disadvantages
Which solution do I predict will work best?		
Solution 1 Results	Solution 2 Results	Solution 3 Results
Do my results match my prediction? Why or why not?		
My conclusions:		

Source: Marzano Research, 2016.

Figure 5.2: Problem-solving map.

Visit **go.SolutionTree.com/instruction** *for a free reproducible version of this figure.*

Tasks to Examine the Efficiencies of Multiple Methods of Problem Solving

In this strategy, the teacher asks students to use logic to evaluate multiple methods of problem solving. Students will determine which method is most effective or efficient by comparing aspects of each. This strategy is common in mathematics, science, and the social sciences.

Provide students with a task using the methods of problem solving and directions or resources to help them use each method of problem solving. Ask students to record their observations and results using graphic organizers or written summaries, then have them explain why they think one method is better than another. Have students analyze their conclusions by asking themselves a series of questions that require them to reflect on why or how they got their results.

- "Is all of the information I started with correct?"
- "Did I complete each method from start to finish?"
- "Am I sure I performed all of the processes correctly?"
- "Is there a clear cause-and-effect relationship, or am I assuming that one exists?"
- "Do I have more experience with one method that makes it more likely that I would prefer it?"
- "Would I come to the same conclusion if I evaluated each method again?"
- "How would I explain my reasoning to a classmate? What evidence from my notes can I provide to defend my conclusion?"

Decision-Making Tasks

The teacher uses decision-making tasks to teach students how to identify possible alternatives, outline the criteria on which each alternative will be judged, apply the criteria to each alternative, and select the most appropriate alternative. To complete these tasks, students can use a decision-making matrix, such as the one in figure 5.3.

Decision-Making Matrix Worksheet

Criteria	Alternatives			
0—Does not meet the criterion at all **1—Meets criterion slightly** **2—Meets criterion** **3—Strongly meets criterion**				
Totals				

How do your totals compare with what you expected?

How do your results reveal something new about the items you were examining?

Source: Marzano Research, 2016.

Figure 5.3: Decision-making matrix worksheet.

Visit **go.SolutionTree.com/instruction** *for a free reproducible version of this figure.*

Students answer the following questions as they engage in decision-making tasks.

- What alternatives am I considering?
- What criteria am I using to select among alternatives?
- What do I predict will be the best alternative?
- Which alternatives came out on top?
- Do the results fit with my original prediction?
- If not, how should my thinking change?
- What are my conclusions?

Investigation Tasks

The teacher uses investigation tasks to teach students how to identify a concept, past event, or future hypothetical event; identify what is already known about the subject of investigation; identify confusions or contradictions; and develop a plausible resolution to the confusions or contradictions. Students answer the following questions as they engage in investigation tasks.

- Am I focusing on something that has to be defined better, something that happened in the past, or something that might possibly happen?
- What do I think I will find out?
- What is known about my subject?
- What confusions or contradictions exist about my subject?
- What do I think is the resolution to these confusions and contradictions?
- Did my findings fit with my original prediction?
- If not, how should my thinking change?
- What are my conclusions?

Students can also use a graphic organizer, such as that in figure 5.4, to record information.

<table>
<tr><td colspan="2">Concept or scenario:</td></tr>
<tr><td>Known or agreed on:</td><td>Confusions or contradictions:</td></tr>
<tr><td colspan="2">Resolution:</td></tr>
</table>

Figure 5.4: Graphic organizer for investigation tasks.

Invention Tasks

In this strategy, the teacher asks students to design a product that achieves a specific goal, solves a problem, or makes a task easier. Students consider what design will best suit the purposes and requirements of the task and then develop a prototype. Students then test the prototype in order to determine how effectively it meets their expectations and if it can be improved. This process may require multiple rounds of brainstorming, planning, creating, and troubleshooting. Ultimately, students should design a product, tool, or other invention that meets the standards of the task. Following is the full seven-step process for invention tasks.

1. **Set a goal for the task:** Teachers should set a specific goal for the task and describe how that goal relates to the current learning target or learning progression. Make the goal specific and attainable for students, so that they have a way to measure their progress toward the goal. For example, a teacher might ask students to create a mousetrap-powered car that can travel at least five meters as part of a physics unit.

2. **Establish rules and specific criteria for the task:** Teachers should explain what specifically students should or should not do when designing their inventions. For example, teachers might want to outline which materials students are allowed to use, which general processes or calculations they should consider when completing their project, and what students will need to do to succeed on the project. To make criteria explicit, teachers can create a scale or rubric to show how students' inventions will be evaluated.
3. **Help students brainstorm first steps:** Teachers should lead students in a discussion of what their first steps will be. Students might begin by sketching or describing an initial design for the project or several possible designs for a project. Encourage students to use graphic organizers and lists to compare different components, materials, and designs they might use for their prototypes.
4. **Ask students to create a list of their next steps:** Once students think they have identified a suitable design and the materials they will need, ask them to describe what specific steps they will take to make sure they complete the task successfully and on time. Students can set deadlines for each step. Remind students to consider any measurements or calculations they need to do before they construct their prototype, and encourage them to give themselves extra time to test out the invention before the project's due date.
5. **Facilitate development of the invention:** Teachers can provide time in class for students to work on their inventions and ask questions about their progress. Additionally, teachers can set up extra resources to guide students in their development of their prototypes. For example, teachers can create an online forum where students ask and answer each other's questions about steps in the invention process, address commonly asked questions in class, or meet one on one with students who are struggling with the assignment.
6. **Have students demonstrate the use of their invention:** At the end of the project, have students show what their invention does and explain how it meets the criteria of the assignment. Allow the class to ask questions about the invention after each student's presentation.
7. **Ask students to reflect on their work and what could be improved:** Have students explain what they learned through the invention process and what, if anything, they would do differently if they were to do the project again. Additionally, teachers can ask students to explain what changes could make their prototypes more effective and what they learned by listening to other students talk about their process and inventions.

Figure 5.5 can help guide students' use of this strategy.

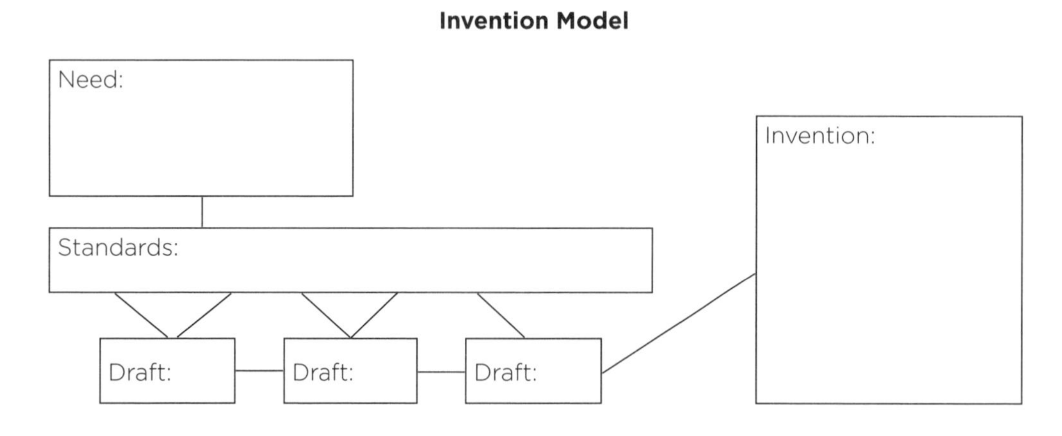

Figure 5.5: Invention model template.

Visit **go.SolutionTree.com/instruction** *for a free reproducible version of this figure.*

Student-Designed Tasks

The teacher asks students to design a task that deepens their understanding of a topic that interests them and relates to the class's learning target or unit. Students should be comfortable performing cognitively complex tasks independently before a teacher implements this strategy. Students will need to set a goal for their task, explain how it relates to content, and determine the best method for meeting their goal. The teacher can guide students in their tasks by setting up parameters or expectations for the completed product.

Ask students the following questions to help guide their use of this strategy.

- "What question or problem will your cognitively complex task address?"
- "What kind of cognitively complex task will you use to find a solution or learn more information?"
- "What do you predict you will learn about this topic?"
- "What steps will you take to complete this task? Please outline the process you will use and your schedule for completing those steps."
- "Will you need any materials or support to complete your project?"
- "How will you make sure your task meets the expectations for this project?"

Monitoring Element 12

Specific student responses and behaviors allow the teacher to determine whether this element is being implemented effectively and producing the desired effects.

- Students are clearly engaged in their cognitively complex tasks.
- Students can explain the conclusions they have generated.
- Students can defend their conclusions.
- Students have produced artifacts from the cognitively complex task.

Use this list to monitor student responses to element 12.

To monitor your own use of this element, use the scale in figure 5.6 in combination with the reproducible "Tracking Teacher Actions: Engaging Students in Cognitively Complex Tasks" (page 113). As with other proficiency scales, level 3 or higher is the goal.

4 Innovating	I adapt behaviors and create new strategies for unique student needs and situations.
3 Applying	I engage students in cognitively complex tasks, and I monitor the extent to which my actions affect students.
2 Developing	I engage students in cognitively complex tasks, but I do not monitor the effect on students.
1 Beginning	I use the strategies and behaviors associated with this element incorrectly or with parts missing.
0 Not Using	I am unaware of strategies and behaviors associated with this element.

Figure 5.6: Self-rating scale for element 12—Engaging students in cognitively complex tasks.

The following examples describe what each level of the scale might look like in the classroom.

- **Not Using (0):** A teacher does not engage her students in cognitively complex tasks. She does engage students in practicing skills and procedures but does not create activities that encourage students to apply their knowledge.

- **Beginning (1):** A teacher asks his students to conduct an experimental-inquiry task. However, he decides to make the task simpler by providing his students with a hypothesis to examine and sharing the correct results of the experiment with his students before they begin the task. Because he shares the expected results of the experiment, his students are able to easily discover when they make a mistake during the procedure, but they do not genuinely predict, revise their thinking, or come to new conclusions while performing the task.
- **Developing (2):** A teacher presents her students with a problem and asks them to brainstorm possible solutions to the problem. The teacher encourages the students to logically predict which solution might be the best and to test out each possible solution to see what happens. The students try out their solutions, but the class period ends before the class can discuss their conclusions and problem-solving methods. The teacher does not come back to the discussion during the next class, so she is not sure how well students applied their knowledge or how their learning progressed as a result.
- **Applying (3):** A teacher asks his class to design a rocket that uses Alka-Seltzer as fuel. He begins by helping students plan and generate ideas for the construction and materials needed for the rocket. He then allows the students to work in small groups to put together their rockets. On the last day of the unit, each group shows the class how its rocket works. After the presentations, the class discusses what it learned from making the rockets, observing the rockets, and listening to classmates talk about their rockets' construction.
- **Innovating (4):** A teacher asks her students to investigate a specific time period as part of a unit on world history. The teacher instructs each student to design an investigation question to help them learn more about the cultural, social, and technological aspects of the time period and place they are examining and then predict what they will find out during their research. The teacher creates a step-by-step procedure for students who are struggling with the investigation project as well as a number of prompts to help them generate ideas about their topic. Students then create a presentation that incorporates a visual component (such as a poster, PowerPoint presentation, or a diorama) to illustrate the complexity of that time period and culture. After the presentations, the teacher holds a group discussion in order to learn how students' perceptions of certain time periods were changed.

Element 13: Providing Resources and Guidance

An effective teacher acts as resource provider and guide as students engage in cognitively complex tasks. Research has shown that activities involving cognitive dissonance (a discrepancy between current knowledge and observations) increase student achievement (Guzzetti et al., 1993; Marzano, 2018). Models of statistical inference, effective argumentation, and logical errors can guide students as they use data, provide evidence, and verify their claims (Marzano, 2007).

There are nine strategies within this element.

1. Using proficiency or scoring scales
2. Providing resources
3. Providing informational handouts
4. Teaching research skills
5. Conducting interviews
6. Circulating around the room
7. Collecting informal assessment information
8. Offering feedback
9. Creating cognitive dissonance

The following sections will explore each strategy to provide you with guidelines to effectively implement this element. Read through each before creating a plan for your classroom. Teachers may use the strategies individually or in combination. Remember, these are not merely activities to be checked off; they are methods of creating a practice that combines your art with the science of providing resources and guidance. Reflect on your use of each strategy by filling out the "Strategy Reflection Log" on page 331.

Using Proficiency or Scoring Scales

The teacher asks students to use a proficiency or scoring scale to monitor their progress toward a learning goal over the course of a cognitively complex task. The scale should contain the target learning goal, a simpler learning goal, and a more complex learning goal. See figure 5.7 for an example of a proficiency scale for student progress on a task.

Score 4.0	I can list the steps of my task, say which step I'm on, and explain what I could do differently to improve my performance.
Score 3.0	I can list the steps of my task, say which step I'm on, and explain what I'm doing well.
Score 2.0	I can list the steps of my task and say which step I'm on, but I'm not sure how well I'm doing.
Score 1.0	I don't know the steps of my task or what I'm supposed to do next.

Figure 5.7: Sample scale for student progress on a task.

Providing Resources

When asking students to complete a cognitively complex task, the teacher provides resources that students will need to succeed at that task. In many cases, these resources will be informational—books, websites, videos, diagrams, and so on. In other cases, these resources might be more material—models or building materials. The teacher must also collect these resources in a place where students can access and use them as needed. This collection is often fairly broad, allowing students to select the information or materials they think they need from among numerous relevant options. Consider the following tips for providing resources.

- Collect books, articles, and other print resources on the topic at hand and use a designated bookshelf to store them all together. This shelf might be located in the classroom or in the school library if you plan to give students time to work there.
- If various students are working with different topics, use sticky notes or another temporary system to color-code resources by topic. If students are working at various reading levels or levels of a proficiency scale, a similar system can be used to denote the level of each resource.
- Collect online resources and share links with students. This might involve a playlist of videos on YouTube, a set of links on a social bookmarking site such as diigo.com, or simply a list of relevant websites.
- Provide nonlinguistic representations of important information. This might include pictures, videos, diagrams, or models. In addition, you could provide interactive representations of relevant content, such as a chemistry modelling set that allows students to build molecules.

Providing Informational Handouts

Provide students with informational handouts that they can keep and refer back to if they have questions about a long-term project or cognitively complex task. For example, a list of frequently asked questions and their answers can help students independently resolve confusion. This allows the teacher to more efficiently provide resources and guidance to the whole class. A syllabus for a project or unit is another example of an informational handout—it provides students with a road map for what they will be doing and learning throughout the project or unit.

The following questions (and their answers) might be helpful to include on an informational handout for a specific project or task (Marzano Research, 2016).

- What is the topic of this project?
- What learning goal is associated with this project?
- What are the timelines or due dates associated with the task or project?
- When will students be working on the project? How much class time will be provided? How much work will they do on their own?
- At the end of this project or task, will students have created a product (essay, presentation, model, or other tangible result)? If so, what is the final product?
- What are the steps for completing this project?
- What does successful completion of this project look like?
- Is there a proficiency scale for this task or project?
- How will students be expected to track their progress or demonstrate completion of various steps?
- Where will students get the information and materials needed to complete the task or project?
- If students have further questions or need more information, what other resources are available?

Teaching Research Skills

Teachers can and should consider instructing students in how to independently find resources and information that will help them complete cognitively complex tasks. Information and skills that can help students begin to develop their research abilities include the following.

- **Awareness of what types of resources are available:** Students are probably aware of books and the internet but may not know about other types of resources such as scholarly journals or newspaper archives.
- **Knowing where to access different types of resources:** Students need to know about databases and collections that can provide access to resources, such as school and local libraries and online databases of academic articles.
- **Effective search terms:** Because even many physical resource collections are electronically searchable, students need to be familiar with effective search practices and how to alter their search terms to return more or less specific results.
- **Assessing the reliability of a source:** Students must develop the habit of evaluating the validity of sources, especially on the internet, by looking at who provided the information and how credible they are.
- **Verifying information:** Students should learn to seek out numerous sources on a topic. The more sources verify the information, the more accurate it is likely to be.
- **Looking for a range of perspectives:** Many topics that students research will have a variety of opinions and perspectives associated with them. Students should avoid collecting biased or one-sided information by intentionally looking for a range of perspectives.
- **Primary and secondary sources:** Students should understand the terms *primary source* and *secondary source* and be able to recognize situations in which one may be more useful than the other.
- **Recording information:** Students should use effective note-taking skills to record key information from various sources, which will help solidify the information in their memories and enable them to use the information later.
- **Citing sources:** Students must know how to credit the sources of information through paraphrasing, direct quotations, in-text citations, and reference lists.

Consider the following student guidelines for successful research (Marzano Research, 2016).

- **Use multiple sources:** Look for information in different places, such as libraries (school, local, and so on), online research databases, specialized search engines like Google Scholar, and websites run by experts on your topic.
- **Try a range of possible keywords and search terms:** Broaden or narrow your results by adjusting search terms to be more or less specific. Search for keywords that are associated with your main topic, such as synonyms, causes and effects of the topic, categories that your topic fits into, or specific examples of general topics.
- **Check the relevance of information:** When you find information, double-check that it is related to your main topic or research question. If you cannot explain the connection in two sentences or less, the information might be irrelevant.
- **Check the reliability of sources:** Make sure you know who is providing the information and consider whether that person or organization is credible and unbiased. Look for books published by reputable authors and publishers, peer-reviewed scholarly articles, and websites of expert organizations. Avoid sources that are issued with little or no certification process, such as blogs, wikis, and self-published books. If you are not sure about the reliability of a source, try to verify the information using another source.
- **Manage the amount of material you need to read:** If you find a lot of information on a topic, break it into manageable chunks to make it easier to read and process.
- **Think about the information you are gathering:** Be sure to think critically about the information that you find. Consider whether there are contradictions within the information, whether it answers your research question completely, and whether it accurately represents the complexity of the topic (including facts, opinions, varying perspectives, controversies, and so on).

Conducting Interviews

The teacher conducts interviews with students to keep track of their progress as they work on cognitively complex tasks and projects. The teacher might use a checklist or scoring scale to guide each interview and to help the students plan their next steps.

In organizing student interviews, dedicate one class period to student interviews and ask the rest of the class to work quietly on their projects if they are not in an interview. Create a sign-up sheet with blocks of time for each student or student group and have students sign up for slots in advance. If there is not enough time in the class period to meet with all students, set aside blocks of time after school or during lunch. Alternatively, teachers can conduct interviews over several class periods, with a portion of each class devoted to interviews. Participation in the interviews can either be voluntary or an expectation for all students.

Before students attend their interview sessions, ask them to prepare any questions or concerns they have about the project. Instruct them to bring along any research, planning documents, and notes that they would like to discuss. If many students appear to be struggling on the same step or process in their task, it may be worthwhile to conduct a classwide direct instruction lesson or provide additional resources.

Consider the following interview questions.

- How comfortable do you feel completing this task?
- What kind of questions do you have so far about your project?
- Do you have a plan for your project?
- What have you done so far? What will you do next?
- How are you keeping track of your progress?

- What parts of this task do you think will be difficult to complete or implement?
- Are you struggling with the completion or implementation of any tasks?
- Which element of this task do you need the most help with?
- What materials do you need in order to complete this project?
- How will you check to see if your ideas are correct?
- How will you represent your results?
- How long do you believe it will take you to complete this task?
- Do you think you have enough time to complete this task?
- What kind of resources or materials could I provide to help you with your project?
- Do you feel like you were well prepared to do this task?
- How do you think this task relates to what you've been learning in class?

Circulating Around the Room

The teacher walks around the room while students work, allowing them to easily request assistance. While students might typically indicate that they need help by raising their hand, if multiple students need help at once, it can be difficult to make sure that every student's needs are addressed. The following are several ways a teacher can make sure every student is able to utilize available resources and teacher support to the fullest extent.

- Create an interactive list that students can write or type their names on while waiting for the teacher's assistance. The list can be on the whiteboard, or it can be a digital list that students access from iPads or their smartphones. The teacher should assist students in the order that their names appear on the list and remove or mark off their names after helping them.
- Create a visible signal that quickly and quietly indicates when a student needs help. For example, provide students with brightly colored index cards and have the students fold them in half into tent shapes so that the cards stand upright on their desk. When a student places a card on the desk, it means that he or she needs assistance.
- Encourage students to review their notes, check their textbooks, or look for information online while they wait for help. Students could also be allowed to ask their neighbor for assistance while they wait.
- If students have stopped working for a long period of time, check in to make sure they aren't struggling. Ask them what they have done so far and what they plan to work on next. If they can't specifically state what they have done or plan to do, provide them with a checklist to complete or remind them of their scale for the project, and then come back later to check on their progress.

Collecting Informal Assessment Information

The teacher examines student assessments to anticipate student needs and make helpful resources immediately available. Students who are not comfortable asking for resources (or who are not able to determine what type of resources or help they need) can benefit from easily available or offered resources. Consider the following types of assessments to determine where guidance is needed.

- **Class polls:** The teacher can take a quick informal poll to gauge students' understanding of a task or process. For example, a teacher can have students use smartphones to respond to a poll, or a teacher can take a simple thumbs-up, thumbs-down poll to measure understanding on a variety of topics. Aggregate results to see what most of the class is struggling with and which resources would be the most helpful.

- **Class discussions:** Have students discuss their tasks or projects in small groups or as a class. Circulate around the room, and listen to students' responses and the concerns they share. The information teachers gather from these discussions can inform future support and can help determine whether more instruction is needed, if students need clarification, or if additional resources could help them complete their work.
- **Multistage assignments:** Have students turn in parts of cognitively complex assignments before completing the whole assignment. Use these artifacts to help measure how well students are understanding the components, procedures, and purposes of their tasks. Rather than grading these early progress assignments, use them to provide new guidance and resources and then allow students to revise their thinking before they finish the project.
- **Student self-assessment:** Ask students to describe how comfortable they feel with the task so far and if they feel like they have access to enough resources to complete their work. The self-assessment can be a few questions on a handout, a response paragraph students have to write before leaving the classroom, or a poll.
- **Preassessment:** Before assigning a cognitively complex task, give students a preassessment that measures how familiar they are with certain processes, concepts, and resources that are available to them. If students are unsure of what to do when they struggle with a problem, design a procedure that will provide multiple avenues of support. Preassessments can also be used to anticipate the needs of students and which content they will need the most support to understand.

Offering Feedback

In this strategy, the teacher offers feedback to students about their overall performance on cognitively complex tasks and makes specific suggestions regarding how students can complete their tasks. Consider the following tips for providing effective feedback.

- Provide specific feedback that acknowledges both the strengths and weaknesses in a student's work. If the student was successful, point out aspects of the task that were well done or comment on the student's obvious effort and preparation. If the student was unsuccessful, point out aspects of the task that were done well and aspects that were done poorly or comment positively on effort and preparation or question the student about the lack of effort and preparation.
- Give feedback that indicates next steps or a course of action the students can take to improve. If possible, give the students an example of an action they haven't done that you believe could help them.
- If students don't appear to be engaging with the feedback, try wording it another way or being more specific. Students may not comprehend the language you're using or may not understand exactly what you expect.
- Set clear expectations through the use of learning goals and established rules and procedures. Whenever possible, give students the opportunity to see and understand their progress, their mistakes, and their achievements. Track student progress using a classwide chart or charts specific to each student and acknowledge when students reach a certain level or achieve a goal relative to their cognitively complex tasks.
- Give feedback frequently and consistently. Feedback is an exceptional tool for monitoring and encouraging student growth and should be given regularly.

Creating Cognitive Dissonance

When creating cognitive dissonance, the teacher seeks out information that does not align with students' hypotheses and presents that information to students to help them identify and correct errors in their thinking. For example, if a student's hypothesis is that the best solution to a problem involves building a model, the teacher might present the student with information showing that the components required to build the model are more expensive than the student's budget constraints will allow, prompting the student to rethink and revise his or her solution. When students revise a hypothesis, teachers can have them consider their original hypothesis, the new information that conflicts with that hypothesis, and how it affects what the student originally thought and ask them to write a new one.

Monitoring Element 13

Specific student responses and behaviors allow the teacher to determine whether this element is being implemented effectively and producing the desired effects.

- Students seek out the teacher for advice regarding their projects.
- Students can explain how the teacher's actions help them with their projects.
- Students are actively working on their complex tasks, making adaptations as they do so.

Use this list to monitor student responses to element 13.

To monitor your own use of this element, use the scale in figure 5.8 in combination with the reproducible "Tracking Teacher Actions: Providing Resources and Guidance" (page 114). As with other proficiency scales, level 3 or higher is the goal.

4 Innovating	I adapt behaviors and create new strategies for unique student needs and situations.
3 Applying	I provide resources and guidance, and I monitor the extent to which my actions affect students' performance.
2 Developing	I provide resources and guidance, but I do not monitor the effect on students.
1 Beginning	I use the strategies and behaviors associated with this element incorrectly or with parts missing.
0 Not Using	I am unaware of strategies and behaviors associated with this element.

Figure 5.8: Self-rating scale for element 13—Providing resources and guidance.

The following examples describe what each level of the scale might look like in the classroom.

- **Not Using (0):** A teacher does not actively try to provide resources and guidance. He expects that students will volunteer questions if they have any. He typically stays at his desk while students work and uses assessments only to provide scores, not feedback or guidance.
- **Beginning (1):** A teacher begins providing feedback to her students as a way to provide guidance when they are engaged in complex tasks. However, she does not provide feedback consistently and doesn't give specific, actionable feedback. Her feedback is often so general that students aren't sure exactly what they need to do differently or what they need to improve.
- **Developing (2):** A teacher makes himself available to students who need help and moves around the room as they work, looking for students who appear to be struggling. He takes the time to

work one-on-one with students and suggest resources the students can use. However, he doesn't check back in to make sure students are learning what they need to from that resource.

- **Applying (3):** A teacher walks around the room asking students questions to measure how well they are understanding cognitively complex tasks. She uses this information to determine with which parts of the task students need more support to complete. Based on the responses she receives, she provides extra digital resources, study sessions, and one-on-one meetings to help her students. She then reviews classroom artifacts, such as drafts, outlines, and worksheets, to make sure the resources she provided are having the desired effect.
- **Innovating (4):** A teacher sets up individual interviews with his students to learn about their progress on an experimental-inquiry task. After speaking with several students, he realizes that many are struggling with similar aspects of the project and decides to design an online resource the students can reference as they work. He also spends part of one class showing students how they can plan out their task and possible ways they can share their results with the class. He creates a checklist for students to use as they work, and he routinely checks in with students to see how much progress they have made and which parts of the checklist they have completed.

Element 14: Generating and Defending Claims

The ultimate purpose of engaging students in cognitively complex tasks is to provide opportunities for them to generate new conclusions and provide evidence for their conclusions. Research has shown that students who discuss controversial issues in safe, open, and respectful environments are more likely to participate in democratic processes later in life and feel more confident in their ability to influence decisions made in groups (Hahn, 1998). Well-defended claims include support such as grounds, backing, and qualifiers (Marzano & Heflebower, 2012; Toulmin, 2003). Learning to articulate one's ideas clearly and respectfully is a critical part of responsible communication (Michaels, O'Connor, & Hall, 2010).

There are seven strategies within this element.

1. Introducing the concept of claims and support
2. Presenting the formal structure of claims and support
3. Generating claims
4. Providing grounds
5. Providing backing
6. Generating qualifiers
7. Formally presenting claims

The following sections will explore each strategy to provide you with guidelines to effectively implement this element. Read through each before creating a plan for your classroom. Teachers may use the strategies individually or in combination. Remember, these are not merely activities to be checked off; they are methods of creating a practice that combines your art with the science of generating and defending claims. Reflect on your use of each strategy by filling out the "Strategy Reflection Log" on page 331.

Introducing the Concept of Claims and Support

Even though people make claims and provide support quite naturally, it is important to introduce the concept of claims and support to students so that they might engage with it more consciously and rigorously. At first, it is enough to introduce the idea that a claim is simply something one believes to be true. Students should be able to provide reasons for their beliefs and be able to provide evidence for those reasons. Reasons and evidence for claims are referred to as support.

One of the easiest ways to help students generate claims and support is to provide them with sentence prompts like the following.

Claim: I believe that ___________.
Reasons: I believe this because ___________.
Evidence: My evidence for this is ___________.

Students can complete these sentence stems and share them with the whole class or in small groups.

At the primary level, students might use versions of the prompts such as the following.

Claim: My new idea is ___________.
Reasons: I think this because ___________.
Evidence: What I actually saw was ___________.

These stems are for things students can actually observe, such as what happens to a plant growing in the classroom, the behavior of ants in an ant colony, or the habits of birds nesting in a tree outside the classroom.

Presenting the Formal Structure of Claims and Support

When students are familiar with the general concept of claims and support, the teacher can provide them with the more formal distinctions. Specifically, at a formal level, support for a claim should include grounds, backing, and qualifiers.

- **Grounds:** Initial reasons for a claim. Students should provide grounds that answer the question, Why do you think your claim is true?
- **Backing:** Additional information about grounds that helps establish their validity. Backing is more specific, in-depth evidence, such as research-based data, expert opinions, and facts.
- **Qualifiers:** Exceptions to claims. The number of qualifiers needed for a claim can help determine the certainty of a claim.

Diagramming an argument can help guide students' use of claims and support. See figure 4.15 (page 83).

Generating Claims

A claim is a new idea or opinion. Claims can take many forms. They can express an opinion that a certain action is necessary. They can express an opinion that something is good or bad, important or unimportant. They can express an opinion that something is better or worse than something else. It is useful to present students with claims like the following and have them identify the underlying message in each claim.

- Students should attend school year-round.
- Football is an unhealthy sport.
- Colorado is the best place to live in the United States.

It is also important to help students differentiate claims and facts. Claims are usually statements with which others may agree or disagree; facts are statements that can be verified.

Providing Grounds

Grounds are the initial reasons for a claim. Grounds answer the question, Why do you think your claim is true? To help students provide grounds for their claims, have them add the word *because* to the end of their claims and then ask them to finish their sentences. The portion of the sentence following *because* is grounds for the claim. For example:

- Students should attend school year-round because they often forget what they learned in school over the summer.

- Football is an unhealthy sport because players often suffer serious injuries.
- Colorado is the best place to live in the United States because it has so many ski resorts in a relatively small area.

Providing Backing

Backing provides specific information about grounds that help establish their validity. In some cases, backing is simply a more in-depth discussion of the grounds. There are three types of information that generally make good backing: (1) expert opinion, (2) research results, and (3) factual information.

Table 5.1 explores the three types of backing.

Table 5.1: The Three Types of Backing

Type of Backing	Definition	Examples
Expert opinion	A statement made by an individual who is recognized as an expert in his or her field.	Someone with a doctorate in climatology and years of field-research experience offers an opinion on the severity of global warming. An experienced and successful director of Broadway plays offers an opinion on the quality of an acting performance. An official at the U.S. Federal Reserve offers an opinion on the state of the economy.
Research results	Data collected through methodical investigation or through scientific experiments that are designed to test a hypothesis. Conclusions based on research results are not as unanimous and definitive as facts, but they come closer as more studies yield the same findings.	A U.S. Census Bureau report on wage equality found that working women's full-time earnings are approximately 75 percent of working men's earnings. The results of a meta-analysis show that use of academic games in the classroom is associated with a gain of 20 percentile points in student achievement. The National Center for Injury Prevention and Control conducted a study and found that one out of five high school students are bullied at school.
Factual information	Information that has evidential support and is generally acknowledged to be proven or true.	The state flower of Montana is the bitterroot. The American Civil War began in 1861 and ended in 1865. Ladybugs help plants by eating pests such as aphids.

Source: Marzano Research, 2016.

Generating Qualifiers

Qualifiers are exceptions to claims that indicate the degree of certainty for the claim. Often, as students research a topic, they will find information that supports a particular claim and other information that does not. Rather than ignoring information that does not support a particular claim, students can use nonsupporting information to specify situations in which their claim might not apply or address potential objections to their claim as part of their argument. To help students generate qualifiers, teachers can ask them to collect a wide range of evidence for a claim. Then, students can sort that evidence into two categories: (1) evidence that supports the claim and (2) evidence that does not support the claim. They should sort evidence supporting the claim into grounds (which are more general) and backing (which is more specific). Students can use evidence that does not support the claim to generate qualifiers.

A chart like figure 5.9 can help students classify the information they find.

Classifying Information

Name: ______________________________ Date: ______________

Class: ______________________________

As you conduct research about your claim, sort the information into supporting and nonsupporting categories. Then, use the supporting information to write grounds and backing and use the nonsupporting information to write qualifiers.

Supporting Information	Nonsupporting Information
Grounds and Backing	**Qualifiers**

Source: Marzano Research, 2016.

Figure 5.9: Template for classifying information.

Visit **go.SolutionTree.com/instruction** *for a free reproducible version of this figure.*

Formally Presenting Claims

Once students have an understanding of the nature of claims and support (that is, grounds, backing, and qualifiers) teachers should provide them with opportunities to generate claims and present their support. Of course, this can and should be done in an ad hoc manner during class discussion, but there should also be times when students are provided with opportunities to more formally generate and defend claims. These claims can come from their work on cognitively complex tasks: experimental inquiry, problem solving, decision making, investigation, and invention.

Figure 5.10 can help students self-assess their presentations.

Student Self-Assessment for Formally Presenting Claims

Name: ______________________________ Date: ______________

Class: ______________________________

After a formal presentation of a claim and support, use this form to self-assess your efforts.

	What I Did Well	What I Can Improve On
My claim		
My grounds		
My backing		
My qualifiers		

Source: Marzano Research, 2016.

Figure 5.10: Student self-assessment for formally presenting claims.

Visit **go.SolutionTree.com/instruction** *for a free reproducible version of this figure.*

Monitoring Element 14

Specific student responses and behaviors allow the teacher to determine whether this element is being implemented effectively and producing the desired effects.

- Students can generate claims based on their cognitively complex tasks.
- Students can provide grounds.
- Students can provide backing for grounds.
- Students can provide qualifiers.
- Students can describe why generating and supporting claims helps them learn more deeply and rigorously.

Use this list to monitor student responses to element 14.

To monitor your own use of this element, use the scale in figure 5.11 in combination with the reproducible "Tracking Teacher Actions: Generating and Defending Claims" (page 115). As with other proficiency scales, level 3 or higher is the goal.

4 Innovating	I adapt behaviors and create new strategies for unique student needs and situations.
3 Applying	I engage students in activities that require them to generate and defend their own claims, and I monitor the extent to which students are applying their knowledge.
2 Developing	I engage students in activities that require them to generate and defend their own claims, but I do not monitor the effect on students.
1 Beginning	I use the strategies and behaviors associated with this element incorrectly or with parts missing.
0 Not Using	I am unaware of strategies and behaviors associated with this element.

Figure 5.11: Self-rating scale for element 14—Generating and defending claims.

The following examples describe what each level of the scale might look like in the classroom.

- **Not Using (0):** A teacher presents information to students through direct instruction. She explains the supporting evidence for various ideas, but she does not give students the chance to engage in this process themselves.
- **Beginning (1):** A teacher asks students to generate and defend claims but neglects to teach them how to identify sound claims and good support, so the process is not very productive.
- **Developing (2):** A teacher instructs her students in how to generate and defend claims and often incorporates the process into her lessons. She does not, however, monitor whether or not this has caused students to demonstrate increased understanding of the content.
- **Applying (3):** A teacher has implemented this element into his social studies class by having students generate and defend claims about current events. By looking at student scores on various measurement topics over time, he is able to see that since he started including this activity, more students have developed the skills to apply their knowledge and are therefore reaching the 4.0 level of the proficiency scale more often.
- **Innovating (4):** A teacher regularly uses generating and defending claims to help students apply new knowledge, and she monitors students' success with the process. She notices that some students are having difficulty nuancing their arguments or acknowledging exceptions to their claims. To remedy this, she modifies the process so that students start by collecting all the information they can find related to their claim and then sort it into supporting evidence and qualifiers.

Action Steps

Use the "Tracking Teacher Actions" reproducibles that follow (pages 113–115) to monitor your implementation of each element in this chapter.

Additionally, visit the appendix (page 329) for the reproducible "Tracking Progress Over Time" (page 330), which helps teachers set goals related to their proficiency with each element and track their progress toward these goals over the course of a unit, semester, or year. Also, the "Strategy Reflection Log" (page 331) in the appendix provides a space to write down your thoughts and reflect on the implementation process for specific strategies related to each element. Finally, visit **go.SolutionTree.com/instruction** for both student surveys and teacher surveys, the results of which provide feedback about your proficiency with each element.

Tracking Teacher Actions: Engaging Students in Cognitively Complex Tasks

The teacher can use this form to plan his or her usage of strategies related to the element of engaging students in cognitively complex tasks.

Check Strategies You Intend to Use	Strategies	Description of Instructional Plan
	Experimental-Inquiry Tasks	
	Problem-Solving Tasks	
	Tasks to Examine the Efficiencies of Multiple Methods of Problem Solving	
	Decision-Making Tasks	
	Investigation Tasks	
	Invention Tasks	
	Student-Designed Tasks	
	Other:	
	Other:	

Source: Adapted from Marzano Research. (2016). Marzano compendium of instructional strategies. *Centennial, CO: Author.*

Tracking Teacher Actions: Providing Resources and Guidance

The teacher can use this form to plan his or her usage of strategies related to the element of providing resources and guidance.

Check Strategies You Intend to Use	Strategies	Description of Instructional Plan
	Using Proficiency or Scoring Scales	
	Providing Resources	
	Providing Informational Handouts	
	Teaching Research Skills	
	Conducting Interviews	
	Circulating Around the Room	
	Collecting Informal Assessment Information	
	Offering Feedback	
	Creating Cognitive Dissonance	
	Other:	
	Other:	

Source: Adapted from Marzano Research. (2016). Marzano compendium of instructional strategies. *Centennial, CO: Author.*

Tracking Teacher Actions: Generating and Defending Claims

The teacher can use this form to plan his or her usage of strategies related to the element of generating and defending claims.

Check Strategies You Intend to Use	Strategies	Description of Instructional Plan
	Introducing the Concept of Claims and Support	
	Presenting the Formal Structure of Claims and Support	
	Generating Claims	
	Providing Grounds	
	Providing Backing	
	Generating Qualifiers	
	Formally Presenting Claims	
	Other:	
	Other:	

Source: Adapted from Marzano Research. (2016). Marzano compendium of instructional strategies. *Centennial, CO: Author.*

CHAPTER 6

Using Strategies That Appear in All Types of Lessons

There are a number of strategies that commonly appear in all three types of lessons: (1) direct instruction, (2) practicing and deepening lessons, and (3) knowledge application lessons. Teachers can use these strategies to systematically guide students through the learning of content and to provide students with multiple opportunities to more deeply engage with and understand curriculum. When teachers use these strategies in tandem with one another, they can provide cohesion to lessons and longer units.

The goal of this design area is for students to continually integrate new knowledge with old knowledge and revise their understanding accordingly. Teachers are able to meet this goal by answering the question, Throughout all types of lessons, what strategies will I use to help students continually integrate new knowledge with old knowledge and revise their understanding accordingly? The eight elements and associated strategies in this chapter help the teacher do just that.

Element 15: Previewing Strategies

An effective teacher engages students in activities that help them link what they already know to the new content about to be addressed and facilitates these linkages. Research has shown that previewing techniques such as advanced organizers and cues (direct links between previous and new content) improve student achievement (Bloom, 1976; Crismore, 1985; Guzzetti et al., 1993; Hattie, 1992; Lott, 1983; Luiten, Ames, & Ackerson, 1980; Ross, 1988; Stone, 1983; Walberg, 1999; Wise & Okey, 1983). Previewing is especially important for students with low background knowledge (Mayer, 1979; West & Fensham, 1976).

There are thirteen strategies within this element.

1. Informational hooks
2. Bell ringers
3. What do you think you know?
4. Overt linkages
5. Preview questions
6. Brief teacher summaries
7. Skimming
8. Teacher-prepared notes
9. K-W-L strategy
10. Advance organizers
11. Anticipation guides
12. Word splashes
13. Preassessments

The following sections will explore each strategy to provide you with guidelines to effectively implement this element. Read through each before creating a plan for your classroom. Teachers may use the strategies individually or in combination. Remember, these are not merely activities to be checked off; they are methods of creating a practice that combines your art with the science of previewing strategies. Reflect on your use of each strategy by filling out the "Strategy Reflection Log" on page 331.

Informational Hooks

Informational hooks are activities teachers design to stimulate interest in a lesson's content. These activities might include anecdotes, video clips, audio clips, newspaper headlines, and other short attention-grabbing media to spark students' attention. The teacher might also present unusual information or personal stories related to the lesson topic. Hooks typically occur at the beginning of class. Consider the following questions when planning informational hooks (Marzano Research, 2016).

- What content am I presenting?
- What is the most interesting aspect of that content?
- What anecdotes or personal stories can I tell about the content?
- What video clips related to the content can I show?
- What audio clips related to the content can I play?
- What unusual information about this content can I present?
- What other attention-grabbing media (even unrelated to the content) can I use to pique students' interest?

Bell Ringers

As their name implies, bell ringers are activities at the very beginning of a class period that students are to engage in as soon as, or even before, the bell rings. Teachers can use bell ringers to have students practice or review content as a way to activate background knowledge before a new lesson. Following are examples of bell-ringer activities.

- **Quick quiz:** The teacher prepares a quick quiz (three to five questions) covering previously learned material that relates to, or serves as a foundation for, the day's new material. Quiz questions might be printed on handouts, given orally, or written on the board.
- **Group quiz:** Similar to a quick quiz, a group quiz involves students taking a short assessment of previously learned material that relates to upcoming material. In this case, however, students should work together in small groups to answer the questions. Questions should be more complex, requiring the group to discuss and decide on an answer. Teachers should preassign groups so students can begin work quickly.
- **Discussion question:** The teacher writes a single discussion question on the board. Students gather in preassigned groups, discuss the question, and formulate a group response. At the beginning of class, the teacher asks each group for its response, with the option of carrying the responses into a larger class discussion. Discussion questions can cover previously learned material, but questions might also introduce upcoming material or issues.
- **Summarization:** The teacher asks students to write summaries describing previously learned material. This might be material not covered in a long while (essentially serving as a review), a summarization of an entire unit or topic (helping students to synthesize a coherent picture of the material), or material covered the previous day (to keep that material fresh in students' minds). Summarization topics should relate to the day's upcoming new material and be written on the board so that students can begin as soon as they arrive. Teachers may collect and review summaries or add them to students' academic notebooks.

- **Student questions:** The teacher asks students to write down any questions they may have about previously learned material or the day's upcoming new material (in which case the teacher needs to identify the day's material verbally or on the board). The teacher may collect the questions and quickly review them to inform the direction of the day's instruction, or he or she may call on students to present their questions during a short class discussion period. This may also be combined with the summarization activity.

What Do You Think You Know?

The simplest way to preview new content is to ask students what they think they know about a topic. In this strategy, the teacher asks students to individually write down what they already know about an upcoming topic. After each student has created an individual list, the teacher asks students to pair up and discuss their previous knowledge and ideas. Each pair of students creates a list of its most original or most important knowledge and ideas, using examples where appropriate. Finally, pairs share their lists, and the teacher creates a whole-class list of what students already know about upcoming content. Visit **go.SolutionTree.com/instruction** for the reproducible "What Do You Think You Know?" to help guide students' use of this strategy.

Overt Linkages

The teacher helps students make overt links between content they have previously studied in class and new content being presented by overtly explaining the connections. For example, the teacher might say, "When you read the section in the chapter about percolation, keep in mind that it is similar to what happened in our last experiment, where the soil acted as a filter as the water seeped through it."

Preview Questions

The teacher asks questions about upcoming content to pique students' curiosity and activate their prior knowledge. Although students may not know the answers to the questions because they have not yet learned the new content, the questions help signal what information they should be listening for as the teacher presents new content.

Figure 6.1 can help guide students' use of this strategy.

Preview Question Handout

Name: ______________________ Date: __________

Topic: ______________________

Before the lesson begins, fill in the left-hand column with your best answer to the preview question. Then, during the lesson, take notes in the right-hand column when you learn new information about the preview question. Finally, at the end of the lesson, use your notes to summarize what you now know about the topic in the space provided.

Preview question:	
My answer to the preview question:	What I am learning:
What I know now:	

Source: Marzano Research, 2016.

Figure 6.1: Preview question handout.

Visit **go.SolutionTree.com/instruction** *for a free reproducible version of this figure.*

Brief Teacher Summaries

In this strategy, the teacher provides students with an oral or written summary of content that he or she is about to present. He or she also links upcoming content to past content. This helps students see key ideas and patterns and follow those ideas as the teacher presents more detailed information. To create a summary, teachers should consider the following about an upcoming lesson or unit: main ideas or patterns, key details, key terms or phrases, and things students need to remember or keep in mind.

Skimming

An effective teacher helps students skim written information on an upcoming topic by teaching them to look at major section headings and subheadings and asking them to analyze those headings to pick out main ideas and important concepts in the passage. The teacher might also ask students to try to summarize a passage after skimming it, record how well they think they already understand the new content, and predict what they will learn during an upcoming presentation of the new content. To help students successfully skim a text, teachers can have them record five headings; subheadings; topic sentences; and bolded, italicized, or repeated terms and phrases. Then, students can summarize the information, looking for central themes or ideas, and write down any questions they have about the topic.

Teacher-Prepared Notes

Using this strategy, the teacher provides an outline (including the main idea, key points, and new vocabulary) of the content to students before beginning to present new information. After presenting new information and reviewing the outline, the teacher should allow students to ask questions. This can help clear up initial confusion or misconceptions that students have about new content.

K-W-L Strategy

Donna M. Ogle (1986) originally developed the K-W-L strategy. The teacher uses this strategy before presenting new content. The letters of K-W-L stand for *know*, *want to know*, and *learned*. First, students identify what they know about the topic, and the teacher records this information under K on a chart. Then, students list what they want to know about a topic, and the teacher records this information under W on a chart. Finally, after a lesson, students identify and list things they have learned, which are recorded under L. At this point, the teacher and students examine what was written in the K column in an attempt to identify initial misconceptions about the content. Visit **go.SolutionTree.com/instruction** for the reproducible "K-W-L Worksheet."

Advance Organizers

The teacher creates a visual representation or graphic organizer showing the structure and organization of new content and illustrating how new content connects to information previously learned in class. Students can use this organizer to ask questions before the presentation of new content, to identify what they already know about new content, and to connect new content to their personal interests. Following are types of organizers.

- **Topics and details chart:** In a table, students fill in main ideas or topics at the top of each column. In the cells of each column, they fill in key details related to that topic. As they record details in subsequent columns, they can draw lines between various cells to denote connections or similarities.
- **Description chart:** Students write the topic of the description in the center and characteristics or details about that topic surrounding it.
- **Comparison chart:** Using a Venn diagram, T-chart, double-bubble diagram, or other organizer that shows comparisons, students record the similarities and differences between two topics.

- **Sequence chart:** Students create a visual representation of the order of certain events by connecting them with arrows.
- **Causation chart:** Students create a diagram that shows the causes and effects of a situation or event.
- **Free-flowing web:** Students show the connections between various topics and subtopics by writing each topic or subtopic in a circle and drawing lines between them.

Anticipation Guides

Before presenting new content, the teacher can have students respond to a series of statements that relate to upcoming information. After students respond to the statements, the teacher leads the class in a discussion about how students responded. This activates students' prior knowledge about a topic and helps them consider issues and ideas associated with new content. To plan for this strategy, teachers should write down statements about the content that they'll present to students and questions or prompts to present during discussion.

Word Splashes

The teacher uses this strategy to help students preview vocabulary terms and concepts associated with new content. The teacher prepares a number of words and descriptions of those words associated with the new content and presents them to students. Students try to sort the terms into categories that make sense to them. The teacher then allows students to share their categories and sorting strategies and leads the class in a discussion of how the terms and concepts relate to each other and to students' prior knowledge and individual interests.

Figure 6.2 can help guide students' use of this strategy.

Vocabulary Card Template

Term: ____________________	**Term:** ____________________
Description: ____________________	**Description:** ____________________
____________________	____________________
____________________	____________________
____________________	____________________

Source: Marzano Research, 2016.

Figure 6.2: Vocabulary card template.

Visit **go.SolutionTree.com/instruction** *for a free reproducible version of this figure.*

Preassessments

The teacher administers a preassessment to students before presenting new content. This strategy exposes students to the most important information in an upcoming presentation, and the teacher can use preassessment results to gain an understanding of which students have a lot of prior knowledge about upcoming content and which do not. Preassessments used as preview activities should involve going over each question and allowing students to identify what they are confused and need to learn more about.

Figure 6.3 (page 122) can help students reflect on their results of the preassessment.

Preassessment Reflection Worksheet

Name: ____________________ Date: __________

Text: ____________________

Use this worksheet to keep track of what you weren't sure about during the pretest and record the information you need to learn about that question during the unit.

Question:
My answer on the pretest:
I am confused or need to learn more about:

Source: Marzano Research, 2016.

Figure 6.3: Preassessment reflection worksheet.

Visit **go.SolutionTree.com/instruction** *for a free reproducible version of this figure.*

Monitoring Element 15

Specific student responses and behaviors allow the teacher to determine whether this element is being implemented effectively and producing the desired effects.

- Students can explain the links they are making with their prior knowledge.
- Students engage in brief summarizing activities.
- Students can make predictions about what they expect.

Use this list to monitor student responses to element 15.

To monitor your own use of this element, use the scale in figure 6.4 in combination with the reproducible "Tracking Teacher Actions: Previewing Strategies" (page 164). As with other proficiency scales, level 3 or higher is the goal.

4 Innovating	I adapt behaviors and create new strategies for unique student needs and situations.
3 Applying	I engage students in learning activities that require them to preview and link new knowledge to what has been addressed, and I monitor the extent to which students are making linkages.
2 Developing	I engage students in learning activities that require them to preview and link new knowledge to what has been addressed, but I do not monitor the effect on students.
1 Beginning	I use the strategies and behaviors associated with this element incorrectly or with parts missing.
0 Not Using	I am unaware of strategies and behaviors associated with this element.

Figure 6.4: Self-rating scale for element 15—Previewing strategies.

The following examples describe what each level of the scale might look like in the classroom.

- **Not Using (0):** A teacher begins a lesson without asking students to first think about the new content.
- **Beginning (1):** A teacher previews new content before beginning a lesson but does not ask students to think about how the new information relates to previously learned information.

- **Developing (2):** A teacher previews new content and asks students to think about how it relates to previously learned information but does nothing to determine if students are activating their prior knowledge.
- **Applying (3):** A teacher previews new content and asks students to explain how it relates to previously learned information. He assesses what students already know about the new content, including any confusion and misconceptions, and adjusts his instruction accordingly.
- **Innovating (4):** A teacher uses various strategies to preview new information. When she notices that some students are having difficulty overcoming misconceptions about upcoming content, she gives a short pretest on the coming lesson. She then uses the results of the pretest to make note of specific students who will need some extra help making linkages with what they already know.

Element 16: Highlighting Critical Information

An effective teacher identifies important information to which students should pay particular attention. Research has shown that when important information is presented visually or dramatically, students can recall 57–77 percent of the information one year later (as opposed to only 53 percent for verbal presentation) (Nuthall, 1999; Nuthall & Alton-Lee, 1995). It is important to choose learning activities and presentation methods that best suit the information you're presenting (Marzano, 2007).

There are eleven strategies within this element.

1. Repeating the most important content
2. Asking questions that focus on critical information
3. Using visual activities
4. Using narrative activities
5. Using tone of voice, gestures, and body position
6. Using pause time
7. Identifying critical-input experiences
8. Using explicit instruction to convey critical content
9. Using dramatic instruction to convey critical content
10. Providing advance organizers to cue critical content
11. Using what students already know to cue critical content

The following sections will explore each strategy to provide you with guidelines to effectively implement this element. Read through each before creating a plan for your classroom. Teachers may use the strategies individually or in combination. Remember, these are not merely activities to be checked off; they are methods of creating a practice that combines your art with the science of highlighting critical information. Reflect on your use of each strategy by filling out the "Strategy Reflection Log" on page 331.

Repeating the Most Important Content

One way to highlight critical information is for the teacher to continually repeat the information that is important to the lesson or unit when opportunities present themselves. Repeating not only identifies which information is critical, but helps students remember that information for later recall.

The use of repetition may vary based on its instructional purposes, class needs, and the type of information being repeated. The following are ways to implement repetition effectively.

- **Use the appropriate interval of repetition:** Repeating information in quick succession (without pauses) can grab students' attention and alert them to the importance of the information; however, repetition that is too rapid can cause students to become bored and tune out the teacher. Repeating information with a pause between each statement gives students time to digest and consider between each repetition, which allows them to listen to each successive statement with increasingly greater comprehension.

- **Use the appropriate style of delivery:** For information that is important to remember with precision (for example, the alphabet or a mathematical formula), the teacher should use a constant tone, cadence, and body language. This can create associations in the students' minds that will help them recall the information in detail. For information that is important to understand conceptually (for example, a physical process or the events of a narrative), the teacher should use varied tone, cadence, and body language. This can discourage rote memorization and instead propel the student to a deeper understanding of the content.
- **Revisit information:** Repetition does not have to be restricted to the moment when information is first introduced. Repeating information throughout the lesson, or even throughout the day, can emphasize its importance and promote quick recall.
- **Ask students to repeat the information:** Asking students to repeat the information back to the teacher or to each other compels them to pay close attention to the information being conveyed. Asking them to rephrase the information when they repeat it can also promote comprehension. Additionally, warning students ahead of time that they will be asked to repeat certain information will prompt them to pay closer attention during the lesson.
- **Repeat a student's answer:** Repeating a student's answer (or repeating only the correct information from the answer) can emphasize the information. Repeating information when a student volunteers it can also subtly convey to the class that the information is important in its own right, and not merely because it came from the teacher.
- **Highlight related information:** Repeating certain pieces of information together can highlight and strengthen connections between them. For example, repeating the capital of each state along with the name of the state (Denver, Colorado; or Indianapolis, Indiana) can help students remember which capital goes with which state.

Asking Questions That Focus on Critical Information

Questioning is a common method of highlighting critical information. Beyond merely reminding students of previous information, questions prompt students to understand the importance of information by highlighting connections to current content. These connections demonstrate the critical nature of important information.

There are multiple ways to question students about a given content area. The following suggestions provide several methods for highlighting the critical nature of important information.

- **Ask narrow questions:** Narrow questions are not to be confused with simple questions. Narrow questions are those that focus on a specific component, category, or property of information and highlight the importance of that information. For example, instead of asking students how to complete a perfect square polynomial, ask students to "describe the steps necessary to complete a perfect square polynomial." Emphasizing the procedural nature of completing the square reinforces that it is an important skill to master.
- **Ask multipart questions:** Multipart questions are those that require several steps to be completed or that contain several smaller questions that students need to address. Multipart questions emphasize the importance of the underlying skills or content knowledge necessary to answer the question. For example, asking students to calculate the surface area of different classroom objects can highlight the importance of multiplication skills and taking accurate measurements.

- **Ask students to explain why information is important:** Asking students to explain the importance of information not only emphasizes the information itself but also trains students in identifying other similar critical information. For example, asking students why the water cycle is important can prompt them to identify other important environmental processes.
- **Ask students to relate current information to previous content:** Asking students to connect current content to past content can help underscore the critical nature of the information being presented. These types of questions prompt students to examine the central themes or foundational nature of certain pieces of critical information. For example, asking students how the current discussion of World War II relates to a previous lesson on the Treaty of Versailles can illustrate the important social and economic factors of world politics.

Using Visual Activities

Visual activities or presentations of content can greatly enhance student learning. Using storyboards, graphic organizers, and pictures to highlight critical information can help students create mental pictures of the information and promote comprehension and recall. For example, illustrating a sentence with a storyboard can help students identify the parts of the sentence, such as the subject, verb, and object. (See chapter 3, page 41, for examples of graphic organizers.)

Using Narrative Activities

Stories are a powerful way to introduce new content. Teachers can use stories to anchor information in students' memory and signal to students that certain information is important. The narrative structure of a story is also particularly useful for highlighting important relationships between different events or pieces of information.

The following are suggestions for using narratives to highlight critical content.

- **Personalize content:** Some subjects and processes can be hard for students to comprehend, but a story can personalize content in a way that makes it easier to assimilate. For example, students may have trouble grasping the water cycle, but telling a story about a water droplet who journeys from the Pacific Ocean to fall as a snowflake in London provides an approachable context for framing the processes of evaporation and precipitation.
- **Bring historical events to life:** A history lesson may come across as dry and uninteresting to students who have difficulty connecting it to their daily lives. A story, however, can communicate historical events in a way that makes them relevant to the lived experiences of students. For example, a unit on the American Civil War may quickly become a jumble of dates and strange names, but having students read excerpts from historical fiction about the siege of Atlanta can bring the history to life.
- **Familiarize students with other cultures:** Many students have little contact with other cultures in their daily lives. The details of life in other cultures can be difficult to visualize, but stories can help students relate to them. For example, a story about a Mexican family visiting their relatives in the cemetery can ground an unfamiliar holiday like the Day of the Dead in the familiar framework of a family get-together.
- **Have students tell a story in their own words:** Not all stories need to come from the teacher. Rephrasing concepts in their own language can help students understand difficult content, and stories are a great way to do this. For example, having students write or storyboard a narrative about a caterpillar who is becoming a butterfly can help them understand the stages of a butterfly's life cycle.

Using Tone of Voice, Gestures, and Body Position

Nonverbal communication is extremely important in the classroom. Students' level of interest in the content can be strongly influenced by the level of interest that the teacher displays. Tone of voice, gestures, and body position are all important when presenting content, though the teacher should be aware that overuse may lessen their effect.

Table 6.1 describes the features of nonverbal communication.

Table 6.1: Positive and Negative Nonverbal Communication

	Positive Nonverbal Communication (Displays interest, excitement, and confidence)	Negative Nonverbal Communication (Displays disinterest, boredom, and insecurity)
Tone of voice	• Lively • Varied pitch and volume • Pausing or slowing down for emphasis	• Monotone
Gestures	• Intentional gestures that emphasize or coordinate with speech • Animated facial expressions • Smiling	• Fidgeting, playing with hair, tapping pencil, and so on • Blank facial expression
Body position	• Standing up straight, open posture • Head up, making eye contact	• Slouching, leaning on something • Looking down, avoiding eye contact • Crossing arms over body

Using Pause Time

Pausing during the presentation of new content can signal its importance. This creates a sense of anticipation about what will occur next. The use of pause time when presenting information is also useful for making sure that students have sufficient opportunity to take in and process the content. Used in this manner, pause time gives students time to organize their thoughts and prepare questions. Table 6.2 suggests effective uses for pause time.

Table 6.2: Using Pause Time

Situation	Description
After introducing information that seems simple or inconsequential but is actually very important	Pausing here ensures that students do not overlook the importance of the information being presented.
After introducing information that presents a new viewpoint or sheds new light on previously learned information	Pausing here not only signals the presence of important information but can also prompt students to re-evaluate their understanding of previous information.
After introducing information that is surprising in light of previously learned information	Pausing here prompts students to more deeply consider the current content as well as re-examine their overall understanding of the unit or section.
After a student arrives at an important conclusion during his or her response	Sometimes students expect critical new information to come only from the teacher. Pausing here signals to the rest of the class that the information given by their fellow student was important.

Situation	Description
After introducing an abundance of information	Pausing here gives students time to digest and organize the new information.
After introducing information that is confusing or difficult	Pausing here allows students time to parse the information and allows the teacher time to gauge student reactions and judge whether further explanation is necessary.
After introducing information that is controversial	Pausing here allows time for students to formulate and re-evaluate opinions about the topic.
To allow students to respond or elaborate to the information	Pausing for student input signals to the students that the information, as well as their own understanding and opinions, are important.

Source: Marzano Research, 2016.

Identifying Critical-Input Experiences

Critical-input experiences introduce important new content to students and are vital to enhancing student learning. It is vital that a teacher recognize which activities that have been designed for students are the most important. Visual, dramatic, and narrative activities in particular help students visualize, understand, and store new content effectively for later recall. Choosing two to three well-structured input experiences per learning goal and identifying them clearly not only provides focus for the teacher but also signals to students that the information being presented is critical to their understanding of the content.

Identifying critical-input experiences is vital not only for the teacher but for the student as well. Signaling the presence of a critical-input experience before it begins can help prepare students to more effectively absorb, store, and understand the information. The following are suggestions for preparing students for critical-input experiences.

- **Use nonlinguistic cues:** Before beginning a critical-input experience, cue students that the following activity will present critical information. This may be done by simply telling them that the information will be important, but cues can be nonlinguistic as well. For example, a teacher might insert a linked image into a presentation that plays a particular sound, such as the sound of a trumpet or a drumroll, when clicked. When teachers use them regularly, nonlinguistic cues can quickly alert students to pay special attention to the information about to be presented.
- **Ask students to summarize what they already know:** Before beginning a critical-input experience, ask students to summarize the information they already know about the new content. This can be general knowledge or information learned from previous lessons. Have them organize that knowledge into categories or processes, paying special attention to gaps or areas of uncertainty. Summarizing what they already know not only helps students review previously learned information but also prepares them to quickly identify and categorize critical new information.
- **Ask preview questions about the upcoming content:** Before beginning a critical-input experience, pose a few questions to students about the content before presenting it. Make students aware that you don't expect them to know the answers yet but they should give the questions careful consideration during the input experience. Inferential questions, which require students to go beyond what they already know, are especially useful. Questioning students beforehand stimulates curiosity and prepares them to identify key information during the critical-input experience.

Using Explicit Instruction to Convey Critical Content

Explicit instruction is one of the most powerful and essential means of introducing critical content. It is especially important if students seem to be struggling with the content area or when the information itself is foundational or leaves no room for errors. Teachers should use plain, clear language to identify and convey critical content and should pace the delivery of content so that students have plenty of time to process the information. Consider the following explicit instruction guidelines (Marzano Research, 2016). Teachers can consult them while planning for instruction and during the explicit instruction of critical content.

Before presenting critical information:

- **Organize the information**—Make sure that the information is broken into manageable chunks. If possible, plan to begin with something students already know and then connect it to the new information.
- **Get the class's attention**—Make sure students are calm, undistracted, and focused. Answer any questions or deal with any outstanding issues before beginning.
- **Identify the information as critical**—Clearly and explicitly cue the upcoming information as critical. Identify why it is important.

While presenting critical information:

- **Speak clearly and plainly**—Speak clearly and loudly. Paraphrase difficult words, phrases, or concepts with easy-to-understand language. If applicable, model a skill or process for the class.
- **Move at a slower pace**—Take the content one chunk at a time. With new and complicated information, students need time to process and assimilate one step before moving on to the next.
- **Monitor class engagement**—Continuously check to make sure that students are focused and attentive. Look for signs that students are distracted or struggling with the material and adjust your clarity and pace appropriately.
- **Don't be afraid to repeat**—Repeating or revisiting material helps cement it in students' minds. Re-explaining information in a new way can also help struggling students understand difficult content.

After presenting critical information:

- **Check for comprehension**—Check to see whether students appear to have absorbed and understood the material. Ask them to repeat or explain the new information. Identify and revisit areas they may be struggling with.
- **Ask for questions**—Solicit questions from students. Some students may not be sure of what they need to ask or of how to phrase the question, so give them plenty of time. Try prompting them with questions of your own.

Using Dramatic Instruction to Convey Critical Content

The teacher asks students to participate in a dramatic activity that conveys the critical content. Dramatic activities can range from skits and role playing to hand gestures and other body movements. It is important that the teacher asks students to link dramatic instruction to the critical content being conveyed. Dramatic instruction should also include all students, as merely observing the dramatic activity does not convey the critical information as effectively as participating.

A handout like figure 6.5 can help guide students' use of this strategy.

Dramatic Instruction Handout

Name: ______________________________ Date: ______________

Unit: ______________________________

Dramatic activity: ______________________________

Today the teacher asked the class to:

This activity taught us about:

During the activity, it was my job to:

My job demonstrated what we're learning by showing:

This activity helped me to understand:

Source: Marzano Research, 2016.

Figure 6.5: Dramatic instruction handout.

Visit **go.SolutionTree.com/instruction** *for a free reproducible version of this figure.*

Providing Advance Organizers to Cue Critical Content

The teacher designs advance organizers that identify and preview critical content for students. Advance organizers can be anything from a simple verbal cue to a classroom chart to a descriptive metaphor for the content. The purpose of an advance organizer is to provide students with a clear identification of upcoming critical information and how that information fits into the larger unit or content area.

Figure 6.6 (page 130) provides directions for creating a simple advance organizer.

Using What Students Already Know to Cue Critical Content

The teacher uses what students already know to identify and explain critical content. As students learn new information, they situate it within and connect it to their understanding of previous content. The teacher should first assess students' current understanding of basic vocabulary and facts as well as their proficiency in key skills or processes. The teacher can then identify and highlight ways in which information students already possess relates to upcoming critical content. Visit **go.SolutionTree.com/instruction** for the reproducible "Relationship Card Activity" to help students identify relationships between information they already know and critical content.

Monitoring Element 16

Specific student responses and behaviors allow the teacher to determine whether this element is being implemented effectively and producing the desired effects.

- Students can describe the level of importance of specific information.
- Students can explain why specific content is important to know.
- Students visibly adjust their level of attention when teachers present important content.

Use this list to monitor student responses to element 16.

Advance Organizer

To create a simple advance organizer using a blank sheet of paper, follow these steps.

1. Fold the paper in half.

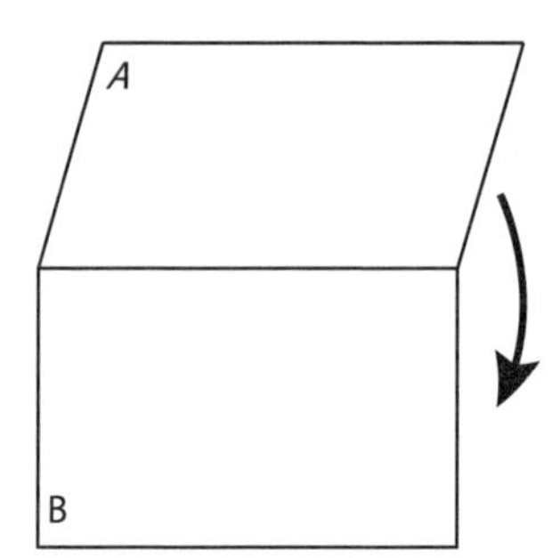

2. On the inside top half of the organizer (section A), draw a picture that represents the critical content.

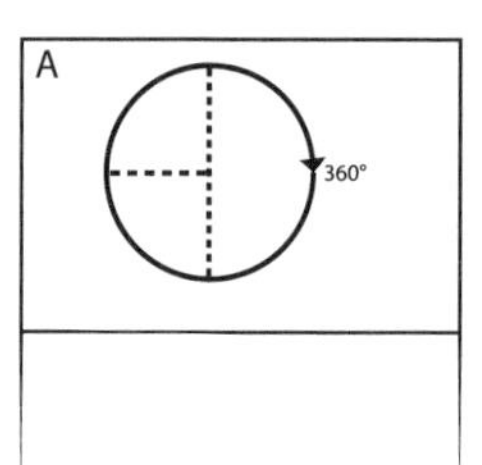

3. On the inside bottom half of the organizer (section B), write a short description of the critical content. Be sure to use key terms and concepts from the content.

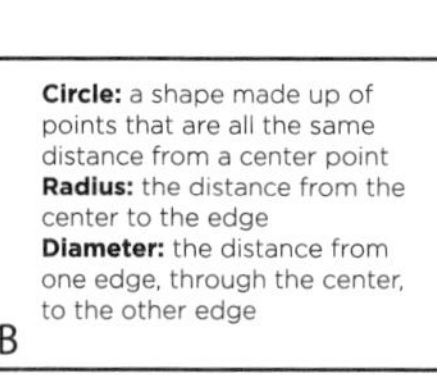

4. On the front of the organizer (section C), write a short word or phrase to label the critical content.

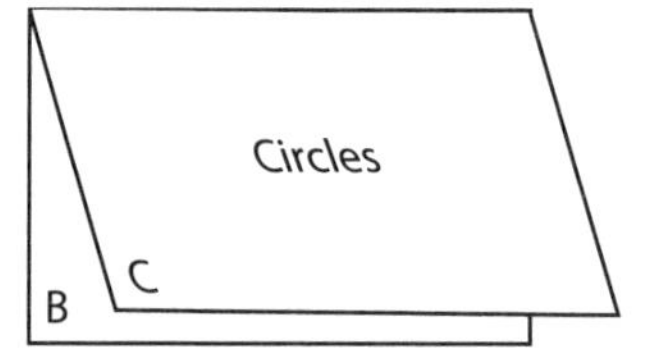

5. On the back of the organizer (section D), list a few key terms or phrases that are important to remember from the critical content.

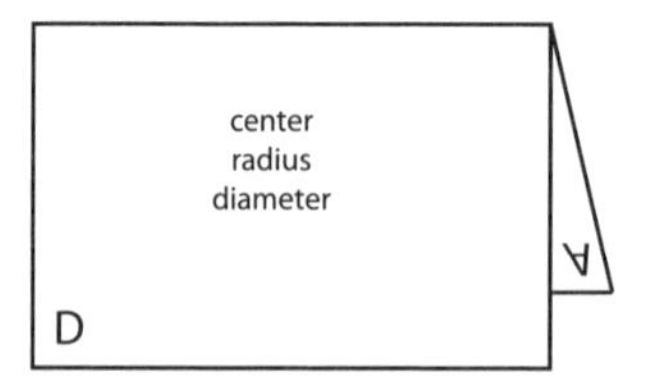

Fill out a similar organizer for each chunk of critical content within a unit, then display them in order somewhere visible to students. As you move through the unit, open and close the organizers as appropriate so that students are always aware of the critical content they are currently learning and how it relates to other content within the unit.

Source: Marzano Research, 2016.

Figure 6.6: Directions for simple advance organizer.

Visit **go.SolutionTree.com/instruction** *for a free reproducible version of this figure.*

To monitor your own use of this element, use the scale in figure 6.7 in combination with the reproducible "Tracking Teacher Actions: Highlighting Critical Information" (page 165). As with other proficiency scales, level 3 or higher is the goal.

4 Innovating	I adapt behaviors and create new strategies for unique student needs and situations.
3 Applying	I signal to students which content is critical versus noncritical, and I monitor the extent to which students are attending to critical information.
2 Developing	I signal to students which content is critical versus noncritical, but I do not monitor the effect on students.
1 Beginning	I use the strategies and behaviors associated with this element incorrectly or with parts missing.
0 Not Using	I am unaware of strategies and behaviors associated with this element.

Figure 6.7: Self-rating scale for element 16—Highlighting critical information.

The following examples describe what each level of the scale might look like in the classroom.

- **Not Using (0):** A teacher places the same amount of emphasis on all the content he presents, regardless of its importance.
- **Beginning (1):** A teacher highlights some information, but there is no strong relationship between the importance of information and how much it is highlighted.
- **Developing (2):** A teacher highlights critical information directly, using repetition and tone of voice, but is not sure how to tell if she is helping students pay more attention to certain content or remember it better.
- **Applying (3):** A teacher highlights critical information directly and with nonlinguistic cues. He is able to see that students respond by visibly adjusting their level of engagement. The assessment results that he tracks over time show that students are recalling the content more than before.
- **Innovating (4):** A teacher uses various strategies to highlight critical information. When responses to her questions reveal that some students are having trouble recognizing the importance of certain new information, she designs an advance organizer to preview upcoming critical content and show how content relates to what they already know.

Element 17: Reviewing Content

The teacher engages students in a brief review of content that highlights critical information. Research has shown that students require about four exposures to new information before it becomes integrated into their knowledge base. These exposures should be spaced closely together (one to two days apart; Marzano, 2018; Nuthall, 1999; Rovee-Collier, 1995). One way that students integrate new information into their knowledge base is by linking it to information already there (Marzano, 2007).

There are eight strategies within this element.

1. Cumulative review
2. Cloze activity
3. Summary
4. Presented problem
5. Demonstration
6. Brief practice test or exercise
7. Questioning
8. Give one, get one

The following sections will explore each strategy to provide you with guidelines to effectively implement this element. Read through each before creating a plan for your classroom. Teachers may use the strategies individually or in combination. Remember, these are not merely activities to be checked off; they are methods of creating a practice that combines your art with the science of reviewing content. Reflect on your use of each strategy by filling out the "Strategy Reflection Log" on page 331.

Cumulative Review

The most powerful form of review is cumulative review. The teacher not only reviews content from the current unit but helps students relate it to learning or content from previous units. For example, the teacher might have students review the process of evaporation from a unit on the water cycle, and then identify how the same process is present in the current lesson on the regulation of body temperature by warm-blooded animals. Cumulative review also involves students identifying misconceptions they held previously and creating new generalizations. Following is the four-step process for cumulative review.

1. After each unit or set of lessons on the same topic, have students record the key content regarding that topic.
2. After the next unit or set of lessons, students again record the key content. In addition, have students identify misconceptions they are now aware of based on the new content and create generalizations based on the new and old content.
3. Repeat step 2 with each new unit or set of lessons.
4. Periodically have students list their generalizations from previous units or sets of lessons and create one or more overarching generalizations.

Cloze Activity

Using a cloze activity, the teacher presents previously learned information to students with pieces missing and asks them to fill them in. For example, consider the following sample cloze activities.

- Ancient Egyptian civilization is perhaps most famous for building __________, which were used as tombs for their __________.
- The three __________ that our bodies need for energy are carbohydrates, fats, and __________.
- The bald __________ is the national animal of the United States. It has a __________ of over six feet and white __________ on its head.
- South America is one of the seven __________. The northern part has the __________ rainforest, which is the largest in the world. South America also contains the Andes __________ as well as __________ countries.
- Fill in the mathematical operator: 4 __________ 6 = 24
- Our strategy for taking a test has three steps: (1) Read all the questions. (2) Fill in your answers. (3) __________.
- Chantelle is baking a cake. She has preheated the oven and mixed the dry ingredients. Next, she should __________.

Summary

To review previously learned content, students briefly discuss what information they remember or found important using short summaries. Teachers can either create summaries for students to review or ask students to prepare their own summaries. The latter option requires teaching students how to create succinct, personalized records of the information they have learned from a new lesson. Teachers should have students consider the main ideas, important details, and key vocabulary for the lesson or unit.

Presented Problem

In this strategy, the teacher presents students with a problem that requires them to use previously learned information in order to solve it. For example, the teacher might ask students to solve a mathematics problem involving exponents that requires them to review previously learned multiplication and division skills.

A worksheet like figure 6.8 can help guide students' use of this strategy.

Presented Problem Worksheet

Name: ______________________________ Date: ______________

Problem: ______________________________

Describe the problem:
What do you already know that will help you solve this problem:
Answer:
What are some new ideas you have about what you learned previously:

Source: Marzano Research, 2016.

Figure 6.8: Presented problem worksheet.

Visit **go.SolutionTree.com/instruction** *for a free reproducible version of this figure.*

Demonstration

The teacher asks students to demonstrate a skill or process that requires them to use previously learned information or a previously learned procedure. For example, a teacher might have students demonstrate how to find the distance between two points on a graph in order to review the distance formula.

A planning guide like figure 6.9 can help you plan for the use of this strategy.

Planning Guide for Student Demonstrations

Class: ______________________________

Unit topic: ______________________________

Skills and processes in this unit:

I plan to ask my students to:

This will require the following procedures and information from previous units:

Common mistakes students might make:

When we are done, I will emphasize:

Source: Marzano Research, 2016.

Figure 6.9: Planning guide for student demonstrations.

Visit **go.SolutionTree.com/instruction** *for a free reproducible version of this figure.*

Brief Practice Test or Exercise

The teacher asks students to complete an exercise that prompts them to remember and apply previously learned information. For example, a teacher might ask students to draw a diagram of a cell or take a short mathematics quiz that incorporates content from previous units. After the test or exercise, students should review any information they remembered or applied incorrectly.

A planning guide like figure 6.10 can help you plan for the use of this strategy.

Planning Guide for Practice Tests or Exercises

Class: ______________________________

Unit topic: ______________________________

Key content (including vocabulary and processes) that students need to remember or understand:

I will use the following types of problems or exercises to target this content:

I will use the following activity to have students discuss the reviewed content after the test:

Source: Marzano Research, 2016.

Figure 6.10: Planning guide for practice tests or exercises.

Visit **go.SolutionTree.com/instruction** *for a free reproducible version of this figure.*

Questioning

The teacher asks questions that require students to recall, recognize, or apply previously learned information. These questions might also ask students to make inferences or decisions based on the previously learned information.

A planning guide like figure 6.11 can help you plan for the use of this strategy.

Planning Guide for Questioning

Class: ______________________________

Unit topic: ______________________________

Questions that require students to recall or recognize basic details or execute simple procedures:

Questions that require students to explain or exemplify generalizations and principles:

Questions that require students to apply content in new ways:

Source: Marzano Research, 2016.

Figure 6.11: Planning guide for questioning.

Visit **go.SolutionTree.com/instruction** *for a free reproducible version of this figure.*

Give One, Get One

After locating information on a specific topic in their academic notebooks (see page 57), students stand up and move to find a partner, carrying their notebooks with them. The pair compares what each student has recorded in his or her academic notebook. Students each share at least one piece of information they recorded that the other student did not. Based on this information, students add to or revise the entries in their notebooks. As time allows, students can find a different partner and repeat the process. The teacher leads a discussion afterward in which students share new information they collected or how they revised their notebooks to make them more accurate or complete. Consider using the following discussion questions.

- Did you learn any new information from your partner that you added to your notebook?
- What new information did you add to your notebook?
- Did you correct any information in your notebook based on your partner's suggestions?
- What misconceptions did you correct?
- Did you and your partner have any disagreements or differing opinions?
- How did you resolve your disagreements?
- How did talking to your partner change how you think about the content?
- How will you use the new or corrected information going forward?

Monitoring Element 17

Specific student responses and behaviors allow the teacher to determine whether this element is being implemented effectively and producing the desired effects.

- Students can describe their previous understanding of content.
- Students are rethinking what they have previously learned.
- Students ask questions about what they have previously learned.

Use this list to monitor student responses to element 17.

To monitor your own use of this element, use the scale in figure 6.12 in combination with the reproducible "Tracking Teacher Actions: Reviewing Content" (page 166). As with other proficiency scales, level 3 or higher is the goal.

4 Innovating	I adapt behaviors and create new strategies for unique student needs and situations.
3 Applying	I engage students in a brief review of content that highlights the critical information, and I monitor the extent to which students can recall and describe previous content.
2 Developing	I engage students in a brief review of content that highlights the critical information, but I do not monitor the effect on students.
1 Beginning	I use the strategies and behaviors associated with this element incorrectly or with parts missing.
0 Not Using	I am unaware of strategies and behaviors associated with this element.

Figure 6.12: Self-rating scale for element 17—Reviewing content.

The following examples describe what each level of the scale might look like in the classroom.

- **Not Using (0):** A teacher continually presents new content.
- **Beginning (1):** A teacher mentions content from previous lessons when it is related to the current lesson, but he doesn't deliberately plan for this or focus on the critical information.

- **Developing (2):** A teacher uses quick activities at the beginning of each class to review critical information from the previous day, but she does not know if this is helping students recall more content in the long run.
- **Applying (3):** A teacher regularly engages students in a brief review of previously learned content as a way to introduce new content. He monitors students' assessment results but does not see the gains he expects. He adds cumulative reviews to his routine and is able to see the impact reflected in students' scores.
- **Innovating (4):** A teacher uses various strategies to engage students in a brief review of content that highlights critical information. When some students appear to have difficulty solving problems in the current unit, she administers a brief practice test covering prerequisite knowledge from earlier units to identify which skills they need to review and then presents them with problems that help them practice those skills.

Element 18: Revising Knowledge

Using this strategy, the teacher engages students in a revision of previous knowledge about content they addressed in previous lessons. Research has shown that when students initially learn about an idea or concept, their knowledge about it is partial and fuzzy. To complete and sharpen their knowledge, students need to add information and correct errors in their understanding (Hofstetter, Sticht, & Hofstetter, 1999; Schwanenflugel, Stahl, & McFalls, 1997; Stahl, 1999).

There are seven strategies within this element.

1. Academic notebook entries
2. Academic notebook review
3. Peer feedback
4. Assignment revision
5. The five basic processes
6. Visual symbols
7. Writing tools

The following sections will explore each strategy to provide you with guidelines to effectively implement this element. Read through each before creating a plan for your classroom. Teachers may use the strategies individually or in combination. Remember, these are not merely activities to be checked off; they are methods of creating a practice that combines your art with the science of revising knowledge. Reflect on your use of each strategy by filling out the "Strategy Reflection Log" on page 331.

Academic Notebook Entries

The teacher asks students to make new entries in their academic notebooks after a critical-input experience, after group work or processing, or after reviewing and correcting homework. Over the course of a unit, and during related units, students re-examine their notebooks to correct inaccuracies or incomplete information. Students should write five details about what they learning, a summary of what they learned, and any questions they have.

Academic Notebook Review

Students use their academic notebooks to identify important vocabulary terms, big ideas and concepts, generalizations, and other information they should study for an exam or quiz. Students can also use their academic notebooks to generate questions such as the following (Marzano Research, 2016).

- What type of information does this entry describe? A skill or process? A fact or set of facts? An event?
- If this entry is describing a skill or process, what are the steps of that skill or process?

- What are the key concepts described in this entry?
- What vocabulary terms are associated with this entry?
- Are there any terms, phrases, or concepts that appear frequently in this entry?
- Are there any terms, phrases, or concepts in this entry that also appear in other entries?
- Did my teacher frequently repeat any of this information or spend more time than usual going over any of this information?
- How does the information in this entry relate to a broader topic?
- Can I rephrase, summarize, or explain the information in this entry in a different way?
- How would I represent this information visually?
- Is there anything in this entry that I am confused about or that I have questions about?

Peer Feedback

Students trade academic notebooks and respond in writing to each other's entries. Students should ask questions about the content, quality, and thoroughness of their peers' entries, and make suggestions for improvement. They should also look for ways to improve the entries in their own notebooks.

A worksheet like figure 6.13 can help guide students' use of this strategy.

Academic Notebook Entry Peer Feedback Worksheet

Name of reviewer: ______________________ Date: ______________

Name of notebook author: ______________________ Topic: ______________

1. Is the information in this entry portrayed clearly and concisely?
2. What is the most important information in this entry?
3. Is the information in this entry organized well? (Is key information identified as important? Are any charts or drawings used appropriately?) If not, how could it be reorganized?
4. What information in this entry is inaccurate or incomplete?
5. What questions do you have about this entry?
6. What could your peer do to improve this or other notebook entries?
7. What information or structures from your peer's academic notebook could you use to improve your own academic notebook?

Source: Marzano Research, 2016.

Figure 6.13: Worksheet for peer feedback of academic notebook entries.

Visit **go.SolutionTree.com/instruction** *for a free reproducible version of this figure.*

Assignment Revision

Using this strategy, the teacher invites students to revise assignments. When returning the assignment to students, the teacher can offer students the opportunity to revise their assignments according to the feedback given and resubmit them to try to obtain a higher score. Students who choose not to resubmit the assignment can simply accept their initial score, but students who resubmit a revised assignment should have their score for the revised assignment recorded. Visit **go.SolutionTree.com/instruction** for the reproducible "Student Revision Guide" that students can use when revising an assignment.

The Five Basic Processes

The teacher directs students in using the five basic processes to revise their knowledge of the content. The five basic processes are (Marzano Research, 2016):

1. **Reviewing prior understanding of the content**—Students should look over their assignments, quizzes, tests, and notes. How well do they think they understood the information?
2. **Identifying and correcting mistakes**—They should look for facts they got wrong, incomplete ideas, ideas that don't make sense, or conclusions that don't have enough support, and fix them.
3. **Identifying gaps in knowledge and filling them in**—Is there anything missing from their prior knowledge of the information? They should fill in any gaps in their notes.
4. **Deciding where to amend prior knowledge**—What new information have they discovered about the topic since they first learned about it? Is there anything they can add to their overall understanding of the topic?
5. **Explaining the reasoning behind the revisions**—Why did they make the changes they did? Is their understanding of the topic more complete and coherent than it was before revising it? How?

Visual Symbols

Teachers direct students in the use of visual symbols to revise their knowledge of the content. Visual symbols are shorthand ways of highlighting information and changes in understanding when revising academic notes.

See figure 6.14 for examples of visual symbols.

Symbol	Meaning
X	This symbol is used when the student realizes that a section of notes contains incorrect information.
→	This symbol is used to indicate that a particular section of notes is linked to another nonadjacent section of notes on the same page.
○ ☆	These symbols are used to highlight information that is important.
New Add ^	This symbol is used to note that new information has been added to a specific section of notes.

Figure 6.14: Examples of visual symbols for revising notes.

Writing Tools

The teacher directs students to revise their knowledge through the use of writing tools. This does not mean that students revise pre-existing work, but rather that students use a variety of writing tools to revise and deepen their understanding of the content. These tools involve exercises such as summarizing, concluding, quick-writes, sentence stems, and student-generated assessments. Following are examples of writing tools.

- **Summarizing:** Summarizing involves students writing short descriptions of the main idea and key details of a topic. For revision purposes, multiple summaries should be written as students progress through the material. This not only produces a record showing the evolution of students' understanding of the material, but also provides opportunities for students to return to their summaries in order to identify and correct gaps and misconceptions.

- **Concluding:** Concluding involves students writing short conclusions (similar to the conclusion of an essay) based on the details they have learned about the material. Concluding is different from summarizing in that it focuses less on recapping the material and more on explaining the meaning of the content or making generalizations, inferences, or connections.
- **Quick-writes:** Quick-writes involve students writing in response to a short open-ended prompt given by the teacher within a limited amount of time. For example, the following prompt might be presented to students to begin a quick-write: How is this information different from something we've learned previously? Quick-writes can not only promote writing fluency but also give students practice in quickly organizing and expressing their understanding of a topic. Quick-writes can be retained and revised as students learn additional information about a topic.
- **Sentence stems:** Sentence stems are sentence starter templates the teacher provides to students (for example, "I learned that __________" or "I used to think __________, but now I think __________"). Sentence stems can help students who have trouble starting or organizing their thoughts about a topic. Teachers can use them in conjunction with other writing tools and may also reveal gaps in students' knowledge or understanding of the content.
- **Student-generated assessments:** Using student-generated assessments involves students designing their own assessments (such as a test or writing project) for the relevant content. Having students generate and execute their own plans for assessing their knowledge of a content area is a useful way to help them examine prior learning. Writing assessments after the revision of prior knowledge can also help students form a clear picture of how their understanding has evolved over the course of the unit.

Monitoring Element 18

Specific student responses and behaviors allow the teacher to determine whether this element is being implemented effectively and producing the desired effects.

- Students make corrections in what they have previously learned.
- Students can explain previous misconceptions they had about the content.
- Students appear pleased with the increase in their understanding.

Use this list to monitor student responses to element 18.

To monitor your own use of this element, use the scale in figure 6.15 in combination with the reproducible "Tracking Teacher Actions: Revising Knowledge" (page 167). As with other proficiency scales, level 3 or higher is the goal.

4 Innovating	I adapt behaviors and create new strategies for unique student needs and situations.
3 Applying	I engage students in revision of previous content, and I monitor the extent to which these revisions deepen students' understanding.
2 Developing	I engage students in revision of previous content, but I do not monitor the effect on students.
1 Beginning	I use the strategies and behaviors associated with this element incorrectly or with parts missing.
0 Not Using	I am unaware of strategies and behaviors associated with this element.

Figure 6.15: Self-rating scale for element 18—Revising knowledge.

The following examples describe what each level of the scale might look like in the classroom.

- **Not Using (0):** A teacher focuses only on students' understanding of content that has just been presented.
- **Beginning (1):** A teacher informally asks students to look over past academic notebook entries about the content but doesn't provide the structure students need to identify and correct errors.
- **Developing (2):** A teacher guides students through the process of correcting previous misconceptions in their knowledge using the five basic processes. He asks the class to review their original notes from a lesson and prompts students to look at their notes through the lens of each of the five processes. Students write down their corrections, but the teacher has no way of monitoring them.
- **Applying (3):** A teacher helps students review and revise their prior knowledge of content. After they make changes in their academic notebooks, she has them complete and turn in a reflection worksheet on which they explain the changes they made and how the process impacted their understanding.
- **Innovating (4):** A teacher uses various strategies to help students review and revise their past understanding of content. When she notices that some students are having difficulty identifying errors in their academic notebooks, she teaches them to use visual tools to review and revise their own notebook entries and implements a peer feedback process as an extra layer of support.

Element 19: Reflecting on Learning

The effective teacher engages students in activities that help them reflect on their learning and the learning process. Research has shown that asking students to identify and record what they are confused about enhances their learning. Reflection data are also useful for diagnosing errors or gaps in students' knowledge (Butler & Winne, 1995; Cross, 1998; Marzano, 2018).

There are five strategies in this element.

1. Reflective journals
2. Think logs
3. Exit slips
4. Knowledge comparisons
5. Two-column notes

The following sections will explore each strategy to provide you with guidelines to effectively implement this element. Read through each before creating a plan for your classroom. Teachers may use the strategies individually or in combination. Remember, these are not merely activities to be checked off; they are methods of creating a practice that combines your art with the science of reflecting on learning. Reflect on your use of each strategy by filling out the "Strategy Reflection Log" on page 331.

Reflective Journals

Students use a portion of their academic notebooks to respond to reflection questions. Questions might prompt students to reflect on what predictions they made about the day's lesson that were correct or incorrect, what information in the lesson was easy or difficult to understand, how well they understand the major material the class is studying, how well they think they did during the day, or what they think they could have done better during the day. Reflective journals are not intended to be complete, finished products; instead, they are living documents that give students the freedom to change, revise, and restructure their understanding. Students can use the following questions to create a journal entry (Marzano Research, 2016).

- What information, process, or other content did you learn about today?
- How do you feel about what you learned today? What parts were easy? What parts were hard?
- What did you do well today?
- What could you have done better today?

Think Logs

Using this strategy, students reflect on specific cognitive skills (for example, classification, the ability to draw inferences, decision making, creative thinking, or self-regulation) that were emphasized during a lesson. Prompts might include asking students how they would explain classification to a friend, asking them to describe an inference they drew during the day, or asking them how comfortable (or uncomfortable) they are with the decision-making process. Table 6.3 provides examples of cognitive skills.

Table 6.3: Examples of Cognitive Skills

Cognitive Skill	Description
Generating conclusions	Combining segments of known information to form a new idea
Identifying logical errors	Looking at an argument or idea to see if it makes logical sense
Presenting and supporting claims	Giving evidence to support a claim or conclusion
Navigating digital sources	Finding relevant and reliable information from electronic sources
Using problem solving	Overcoming an obstacle or other limiting situation to accomplish a goal
Using decision making	Using specific criteria in order to select the best choice from among a group of alternatives that at first appear to be equal
Experimenting	Coming up with and testing explanations for something that has been observed
Investigating	Looking for any sort of confusions or contradictions in an idea or event and then looking for ways to resolve them
Identifying basic relationships between ideas	Studying how one idea is related to another
Generating and manipulating mental images	Forming a mental picture of information in order to understand it better

Exit Slips

Using this strategy, at the end of a lesson, students respond to specific reflective questions on an exit slip that they fill out before leaving the room. Exit slip questions might include the following.

- What are the main ideas of today's lesson?
- What parts of the lesson do you feel most sure about?
- What parts of the lesson do you feel least sure about?
- Do you have specific questions about today's lesson?
- With which aspects of today's classwork were you most successful?
- With which aspects of today's classwork were you least successful?
- What could you do differently to improve your work?
- What could you do differently to improve your learning?

Knowledge Comparisons

Students compare their current level of knowledge on a topic, or level of competence with a procedure, to their previous levels of knowledge or competence. Students can use diagrams or flowcharts to show the progression of their knowledge gain. For example, students might create a chart showing the increase in the number of vocabulary terms they have learned.

A chart like figure 6.16 can help guide students' use of this strategy.

Knowledge Comparison Chart

Name: ____________________

Topic: ____________________

Date	What I know	How I learned it	How I can improve

Summary and notes:

Source: Marzano Research, 2016.

Figure 6.16: Knowledge comparison chart.

Visit **go.SolutionTree.com/instruction** *for a free reproducible version of this figure.*

Two-Column Notes

Students use two-column notes as an extended reflection activity at the end of a lesson. In the left-hand column, students record facts or other information that they found interesting from the lesson. In the right-hand column, they record their reactions, questions, and extended ideas related to the facts or information in the left-hand column.

Monitoring Element 19

Specific student responses and behaviors allow the teacher to determine whether this element is being implemented effectively and producing the desired effects.

- Students can describe what they are clear about and what they are confused about.
- Students can describe their levels of effort and the relationship of their effort to their learning.
- Students can describe what they might do to improve their learning.

Use this list to monitor student responses to element 19.

To monitor your own use of this element, use the scale in figure 6.17 in combination with the reproducible "Tracking Teacher Actions: Reflecting on Learning" (page 168). As with other proficiency scales, level 3 or higher is the goal.

4 Innovating	I adapt behaviors and create new strategies for unique student needs and situations.
3 Applying	I engage students in reflecting on their own learning and the learning process, and I monitor the extent to which students self-assess their understanding and effort.
2 Developing	I engage students in reflecting on their own learning and the learning process, but I do not monitor the effect on students.
1 Beginning	I use the strategies and behaviors associated with this element incorrectly or with parts missing.
0 Not Using	I am unaware of strategies and behaviors associated with this element.

Figure 6.17: Self-rating scale for element 19—Reflecting on learning.

The following examples describe what each level of the scale might look like in the classroom.

- **Not Using (0):** A teacher moves from one lesson to the next without asking students to think about what they have learned.
- **Beginning (1):** A teacher asks students to think about the information they have just learned at the conclusion of a lesson but does not provide specific guidance.
- **Developing (2):** A teacher poses specific questions to students to prompt them to think about what they have learned and explore the learning process. However, he does not record or monitor their answers.
- **Applying (3):** A teacher poses specific questions to students to prompt them to think about what they have learned and explore the learning process. He asks students to record their thoughts, and regularly reviews these journals with them to evaluate their progress and help them adjust their approach to learning.
- **Innovating (4):** A teacher uses various strategies to engage students in reflection on their own learning and the learning process. When she notices that a particular student is having difficulty improving his learning in a specific content area, she leads him in an examination of his past efforts in other content areas to identify the practices that led to subsequent improvement.

Element 20: Assigning Purposeful Homework

An effective teacher designs homework to help students deepen their knowledge of informational content or practice a skill, strategy, or process. Research has shown that homework increases student achievement (Bloom, 1984; Cooper, 1989; Cooper, Robinson, & Patall, 2006; Fraser, Walberg, Welch, & Hattie, 1987; Graue, Weinstein, & Walberg, 1983; Hattie, 1992; Paschal, Weinstein, & Walberg, 1984; Walberg, 1999). Homework should have a clear purpose and be structured to ensure a high rate of completion. It should not be a burden to parents or students (Marzano, 2007).

There are four strategies in this element.

1. Homework preview
2. Homework to deepen knowledge
3. Homework to practice a process or skill
4. Parent-assessed homework

The following sections will explore each strategy to provide you with guidelines to effectively implement this element. Read through each before creating a plan for your classroom. Teachers may use the strategies individually or in combination. Remember, these are not merely activities to be checked off; they are methods of creating a practice that combines your art with the science of assigning purposeful homework. Reflect on your use of each strategy by filling out the "Strategy Reflection Log" on page 331.

Homework Preview

The teacher asks students to read a passage of text or view media that introduces a concept or idea they will study in class. He or she might ask students to keep a list of their questions, observations, or connections as they read or view the content. In class, the teacher might have students share their lists and discuss each other's ideas. Teachers can have students consider the following questions in their journal (Marzano Research, 2016).

- What do you think are the most important things to remember about this new information?
- What parts of this new information did you find the most interesting?
- How does this new information relate to what you already know?
- What questions do you have about this new information?

Homework to Deepen Knowledge

Using this strategy, the teacher asks students to complete an assignment that helps them compare, contrast, or classify specific aspects of the content. The teacher might also have students create analogies or metaphors involving specific aspects of the content. If using this homework strategy, the teacher should ensure that students have a thorough understanding of the concepts they are working with. See figure 6.18 to help guide your use of this strategy.

Categorization Exercise

Name: ______________________________ Date: ______________

Topic: ______________________________

Write down six facts about this topic that you learned in class.

1. ______________________________
2. ______________________________
3. ______________________________
4. ______________________________
5. ______________________________
6. ______________________________

In the boxes below, separate the facts into two categories. The facts in each category should be similar to each other or have something in common. Below each box, describe how you categorized the facts or describe what they have in common.

______________________________ ______________________________

______________________________ ______________________________

______________________________ ______________________________

Finally, describe how the facts in each box are different from the facts in the other box:

Source: Marzano Research, 2016.

Figure 6.18: Categorization exercise.

Visit **go.SolutionTree.com/instruction** *for a free reproducible version of this figure.*

Homework to Practice a Process or Skill

The teacher asks students who have independently performed a process or skill in class to practice it at home in order to increase their fluency, speed, and accuracy. For example, the teacher might have students practice the process of solving quadratic equations or ask them to use the scientific method to investigate something outside of class.

A worksheet like figure 6.19 can help guide students' use of this strategy.

Student Reflection for Practicing a Process or Skill at Home

Name: ______________________________ Date: ______________

Class: ______________________________

Describe the process or skill you were practicing:

How long did you practice the process or perform the skill, and how well do you think you performed it?

In what ways could you improve your performance of the process or skill?

What would you need to do to get better at performing the process or skill?

Source: Marzano Research, 2016.

Figure 6.19: Worksheet for practicing at home.

Visit **go.SolutionTree.com/instruction** *for a free reproducible version of this figure.*

Parent-Assessed Homework

To assist students with homework, parents or family members can ask reflective questions or listen to students give an oral summary of material they read. To help students develop fluency with skills or procedures, parents might also time them in executing a specific skill or process. Parents should act as supporters, not teachers, when assisting with homework, and should have a clear idea of their role and what is expected of them. Visit **go.SolutionTree.com/instruction** for the reproducible "Homework Tips for Parents and Guardians" for a tip sheet to send home with students.

Monitoring Element 20

Specific student responses and behaviors allow the teacher to determine whether this element is being implemented effectively and producing the desired effects.

- Students understand the purpose of homework.
- Students are better prepared for new learning after completing homework.
- Students' understanding is deepened after being assigned homework.
- Students' speed, accuracy, or fluency increases after completing homework.
- Students report that completing homework has helped them learn.

Use this list to monitor student responses to element 20.

To monitor your own use of this element, use the scale in figure 6.20 (page 146) in combination with the reproducible "Tracking Teacher Actions: Assigning Purposeful Homework" (page 169). As with other proficiency scales, level 3 or higher is the goal.

The following examples describe what each level of the scale might look like in the classroom.

- **Not Using (0):** A teacher assigns no homework even though situations arise in which it could be used effectively.
- **Beginning (1):** A teacher assigns homework as a matter of course. Sometimes that homework amounts to busywork.
- **Developing (2):** A teacher assigns purposeful homework targeted at deepening students' knowledge or providing practice with a skill, strategy, or process, though she is unsure whether

4 Innovating	I adapt behaviors and create new strategies for unique student needs and situations.
3 Applying	When appropriate (as opposed to routinely), I assign homework that is designed to deepen knowledge of information or provide practice with a skill, strategy, or process, and I monitor the extent to which students understand the homework.
2 Developing	When appropriate (as opposed to routinely), I assign homework that is designed to deepen knowledge of information or provide practice with a skill, strategy, or process, but I do not monitor the effect on students.
1 Beginning	I use the strategies and behaviors associated with this element incorrectly or with parts missing.
0 Not Using	I am unaware of strategies and behaviors associated with this element.

Figure 6.20: Self-rating scale for element 20—Assigning purposeful homework.

her students understand the relevance of the homework or how effective the homework is in terms of deepening their understanding.

- **Applying (3):** A teacher assigns purposeful homework targeted at deepening students' knowledge or providing practice with a skill, strategy, or process. He solicits questions from students about the homework and addresses their concerns before sending them home. When students turn in the homework, he goes over it with them to determine how well it enhanced their learning.
- **Innovating (4):** A teacher assigns various types of purposeful homework targeted at deepening students' knowledge or providing practice with a skill, strategy, or process. When some students question the importance of the homework, she is able to explain its purpose and identify its relevance to the class's learning goals. She also makes adaptations to homework assignments for specific students who are having difficulty with the content.

Element 21: Elaborating on Information

The effective teacher asks questions or engages students in activities that require elaborative inferences that go beyond what was explicitly taught. Research has shown that questioning is associated with student achievement gains (Guzzetti et al., 1993; Hamaker, 1986; Redfield & Rousseau, 1981; Walberg, 1999; Wise & Okey, 1983). Teachers should use questions in sequences, beginning with questions about details and moving to questions that require students to synthesize and integrate information to formulate and defend claims (Marzano & Simms, 2014).

There are three strategies in this element.

1. General inferential questions
2. Elaborative interrogation
3. Questioning sequences

The following sections will explore each strategy to provide you with guidelines to effectively implement this element. Read through each before creating a plan for your classroom. Teachers may use the strategies individually or in combination. Remember, these are not merely activities to be checked off; they are methods of creating a practice that combines your art with the science of elaborating on information. Reflect on your use of each strategy by filling out the "Strategy Reflection Log" on page 331.

General Inferential Questions

The teacher uses two kinds of general inferential questions: (1) default questions and (2) reasoned inference questions. Default questions ask students to use their background knowledge to answer questions. In short, students default to what they already know to come up with an answer. Reasoned inference questions require students to reason and draw conclusions or make predictions about information. The teacher should present explicit information that the students use as the premise from which they draw conclusions. Consider the following thirteen question types to generate default questions.

1. **People:** What time period is associated with this person? What places are associated with this person? What events are associated with this person? What accomplishments are associated with this person?
2. **Organizations and groups:** What beliefs are associated with this organization or group? What locations are associated with this organization or group? What time period is associated with this organization or group? What events are associated with this organization or group?
3. **Intellectual or artistic products:** What person is associated with this product? What time period is associated with this product? What event is associated with this product? What causes or consequences are associated with this product? What places are associated with this product? What values are associated with this product?
4. **Naturally occurring objects or animals:** What events are associated with this object or animal? What people are associated with this object or animal? What time period is associated with this object or animal? What locations are associated with this object or animal? What system is this object or animal a part of? What color, number or quantity, or dimension is associated with this object or animal?
5. **Naturally occurring places:** What events are associated with this place? What people are associated with this place? What time period is associated with this place? What location is associated with this place?
6. **Manmade objects:** What locations are associated with this object? How is this object used? What larger entity is this object part of? What is the process for making this object? What does this object look like? What value is associated with this object? What dangers are associated with this object?
7. **Manmade places:** What events are associated with this place? What people are associated with this place? What location is associated with this place? What actions are performed at this place? What larger entity is this place part of? How is this place acquired or sold? What value is associated with this place? What dangers are associated with this place?
8. **Events:** What people are associated with this event? What time period or date is associated with this event? What places are associated with this event? What causes or consequences are associated with this event? What happened during this event? What equipment was used during this event? What problems did this event cause or solve?
9. **Natural phenomena:** What places are associated with this phenomenon? What time is associated with this phenomenon? What causes or consequences are associated with this phenomenon? What happened or happens during this phenomenon?
10. **Physical actions:** What process is associated with this physical action? What locations are associated with this physical action? What purpose is associated with this physical action? What causes or consequences are associated with this physical action?
11. **Mental actions:** What process is associated with this mental action? What purpose is associated with this mental action? What causes or consequences are associated with this mental action?

12. **Feelings, conditions, or states:** What actions are associated with this feeling, condition, or state? What causes or consequences are associated with this feeling, condition, or state? What places are associated with this feeling, condition, or state? What values are associated with this feeling, condition, or state? How does something or someone arrive at this feeling, condition, or state? What dangers are associated with this feeling, condition, or state?
13. **Human constructs (ways of organizing the world):** What concept does the human construct refer to? What measurement, quantity, or quality is associated with the human construct? In what way does the human construct help organize the world?

To stimulate reasoned inferences, a teacher must first identify premises to provide to students. A premise is something that we know to be true or assume to be true. Typically, we state premises as generalizations. The premise or premises a teacher selects are driven by what he or she wants to emphasize in a given lesson. To identify the premises to use, a teacher might ask him- or herself, "What generalizations have we addressed that I want to reinforce?" Once premises have been selected the teacher can use the following three steps.

1. Provide the premise or premises to students using stems such as these.
    a. Let's assume that the following is true.
    b. We know that these things are true.
    c. Before, we learned that the following is true.
2. Ask students to determine what they conclude based on the premises using prompts such as these.
    a. What do we know has to be true because the premises are true?
    b. What do we know has to happen?
    c. What can you predict has to occur?
3. Ask students to explain their reasoned inferences using prompts such as these.
    a. Explain why you are sure of that.
    b. Explain the reasoning behind your conclusions.
    c. Explain the logic underlying your conclusions.

Elaborative Interrogation

The teacher probes a student's answer by using elaborative interrogation and asking questions that prompt the student to reflect on the nature of and justifications for his or her response. The teacher might ask, "Why do you believe that to be true?" in order to stimulate a student to provide evidence to support his or her conclusion. Based on the student's response, the teacher asks the student to generate an if-then statement. After the student generates an if-then statement, the teacher asks if he or she might think differently about the original conclusion.

Consider the following examples of elaborative interrogation questions (Marzano Research, 2016).

Questions that require students to provide evidence to support their conclusions:

- Why do you believe that to be true?
- What makes you think that?
- How do you know that is correct?
- What evidence do you have for that conclusion?

Questions that help students make if-then generalizations about content:

- Based on what you've said, what would be an if-then statement that would be true?
- You've said that __________ is true. What else must be true then?
- If __________ happened, what else would have to happen?

Questions that require students to reconsider their original answer:

- Now that you've made an if-then statement, does the way you think about your answer change? How?
- What is another conclusion that you might have come to?
- Do you see things differently now? How?

Questioning Sequences

Using this strategy, the teacher asks a sequence of detail questions, category questions, elaboration questions, and evidence questions to promote deep understanding and cognition. Detail questions identify and build a base of factual information that students can subsequently use to answer deeper and more complex questions. Category questions prompt students to generate lists of examples and identify important characteristics of a category. Elaboration questions encourage students to use these lists to form claims and conclusions. Evidence questions engage students in argumentation and evaluation as they find evidence to support their claims and revise their conclusions to exclude misconceptions or errors in reasoning. Table 6.4 provides an outline of each question phase and options for questioning.

Table 6.4: Questioning Sequence

Question Phase	Options
Detail phase	Ask questions about important details, such as people; organizations or groups; intellectual or artistic products; naturally occurring objects or animals; naturally occurring places; manmade objects; manmade places; events; natural phenomena; physical actions; mental actions; feelings, conditions, or states; and human constructs.
Category phase	• Ask students to identify examples within a category. • Ask students to describe the general characteristics of a category. • Ask students to make comparisons within and across categories.
Elaboration phase	• Ask students to explain reasons for characteristics. • Ask students to describe the effects of specific characteristics. • Ask students to predict what might occur under certain conditions.
Evidence phase	• Ask students to identify sources that support their elaborations. • Ask students to explain the reasoning they used to construct their elaborations. • Ask students to qualify or restrict some of their conclusions. • Ask students to find errors in the reasoning used to construct their elaborations. • Ask students to examine their elaborations from different perspectives.

Source: Marzano Research, 2016.

Monitoring Element 21

Specific student responses and behaviors allow the teacher to determine whether this element is being implemented effectively and producing the desired effects.

- Students volunteer answers to inferential questions.
- Students provide explanations for their answers.
- Students describe the teacher's questions as challenging but helpful.

Use this list to monitor student responses to element 21.

To monitor your own use of this element, use the scale in figure 6.21 in combination with the reproducible "Tracking Teacher Actions: Elaborating on Information" (page 170). As with other proficiency scales, level 3 or higher is the goal.

4 Innovating	I adapt behaviors and create new strategies for unique student needs and situations.
3 Applying	I ask students to elaborate on information, and I monitor the extent to which my actions affect students' responses.
2 Developing	I ask students to elaborate on information, but I do not monitor the effect on students.
1 Beginning	I use the strategies and behaviors associated with this element incorrectly or with parts missing.
0 Not Using	I am unaware of strategies and behaviors associated with this element.

Figure 6.21: Self-rating scale for element 21—Elaborating on information.

The following examples describe what each level of the scale might look like in the classroom.

- **Not Using (0):** A teacher asks many questions during instruction, but they are almost all simple questions that only require students to recall isolated pieces of information.
- **Beginning (1):** A teacher asks students to provide support for their answers but does not ask questions that lend themselves to requiring support.
- **Developing (2):** A teacher asks questions that require students to categorize information and elaborate on their answers, and encourages them to make inferences, but doesn't try to determine how these questions enhance students' understanding of the content.
- **Applying (3):** A teacher asks questions that require students to categorize information and elaborate on their answers. He uses various strategies that encourage students to make inferences and takes note of when students build reasoned conclusions from previous information. His monitoring allows him to see that students are increasingly elaborating on information without being prompted.
- **Innovating (4):** A teacher asks questions that require students to categorize information and elaborate on their answers. She uses various strategies that encourage students to make reasoned inferences based on their analyses of the information. For students who exhibit difficulty defending conclusions, she applies a series of detail questions, category questions, elaboration questions, and evidence questions to help them clarify their reasoning.

Element 22: Organizing Students to Interact

An effective teacher organizes students to interact in a thoughtful way that facilitates collaboration. Research has shown that cooperative learning is associated with improved student achievement (Bowen, 2000; Haas, 2005; Hall, 1989; Johnson, Maruyama, Nelson, & Skon, 1981; Lipsey & Wilson, 1993; Lou et al., 1996; Walberg, 1999). Learning in groups helps students process information because it exposes students to multiple perspectives about new knowledge (McVee, Dunsmore, & Gavelek, 2005).

There are sixteen strategies in this element.

1. Group for active processing
2. Group norms creation
3. Fishbowl demonstration
4. Job cards
5. Predetermined buddies to help form ad hoc groups
6. Contingency plan for ungrouped students
7. Group using preassessment information

8. Pair-check
9. Think-pair-share and think-pair-square
10. Student tournaments
11. Inside-outside circle
12. Cooperative learning
13. Peer-response groups
14. Peer tutoring
15. Structured grouping
16. Group reflecting on learning

The following sections will explore each strategy to provide you with guidelines to effectively implement this element. Read through each before creating a plan for your classroom. Teachers may use the strategies individually or in combination. Remember, these are not merely activities to be checked off; they are methods of creating a practice that combines your art with the science of organizing students to interact. Reflect on your use of each strategy by filling out the "Strategy Reflection Log" on page 331.

Group for Active Processing

In this strategy, the teacher assigns students to groups of two to five members for processing new information. Groups can have a specific purpose (ad hoc groups) or serve long-term partnerships. In either case, groups should have operating rules of behavior and interaction. The teacher might place students in groups randomly, group them based on current levels of understanding, or even mix students who appear to understand something quite well with those who don't. When students process new information in groups, they are exposed to the ways other students process information, some of which might enhance their own understanding.

Following are tips for grouping students to process new content.

- **Organize groups appropriately:** Consider the content you will be presenting or the purpose for which you are grouping students before putting them in groups. For difficult content, consider grouping students who might have trouble understanding the content with students who are likely to understand it more easily. For a problem-solving activity, consider grouping students with partners with whom they have worked well in the past.
- **Allow students to process information collectively:** This strategy does not have to wait until after the teacher presents the content. Try grouping students at the beginning of the lesson so they can process information collectively throughout. Pause during the presentation of new content and prompt students to discuss, ask each other questions, and formulate questions to ask the whole class.
- **Ask students to present what they have learned:** Formalize the discussion process by having students and groups perform specific tasks that involve sharing knowledge. Ask each student to summarize his or her understanding of the content for the group and then have each group compile a collective summary. Groups can also work together to create a nonlinguistic representation, such as a diagram or demonstration, of the content. Allow each group to present to the whole class, then lead a whole-class discussion on the similarities and differences in the groups' findings.

Group Norms Creation

In order to ensure that student groups (especially long-term groups) function smoothly, the teacher asks students to create a list of norms (collective attitudes and behaviors) to govern the group's functioning. Norms provide a set of expectations regarding students' behavior within a group. For example, a group might have the norm "We listen attentively when others are talking," which conveys that students expect each other to be respectful and avoid side conversations. To help groups create a set of norms, the teacher might give each group member several index cards and ask students to write down the norms that are most important to them. Students can then aggregate and classify the norms to create a list of the beliefs and attitudes that will help guide the behavior of group members.

Using a contract, such as the one in figure 6.22, can help guide students' creation of group norms.

Group Interaction Contract

Group members: ______________________________

Questions to consider when creating norms:

- How will we decide who speaks and when?
- If we think of something to say while someone else is speaking, what will we do?
- How can we make sure that we disagree respectfully?
- If we need to make a decision as a group, what will our process be?
- How can we encourage everyone to participate?

Our norms:

1. ______________________________
2. ______________________________
3. ______________________________
4. ______________________________
5. ______________________________

Member signatures: ____________________ Date: ____________________

Source: Marzano Research, 2016.

Figure 6.22: Group interaction contract.

Visit **go.SolutionTree.com/instruction** *for a free reproducible version of this figure.*

Fishbowl Demonstration

The teacher gives students a visual representation of what effective group work looks like by asking students to form a circle ("fishbowl") around a group that demonstrates what effective group work looks like. The demonstration group might model behaviors such as paraphrasing, pausing, clarifying, questioning, brainstorming, and using respectful language.

A handout like figure 6.23 can help guide students' use of this strategy.

Job Cards

The teacher uses job cards to designate specific roles that students are to take within their groups. Examples of different jobs include facilitator, summarizer, questioner, and note taker. This strategy can also help equalize participation when students work in groups.

Figure 6.24 offers some sample job cards.

Predetermined Buddies to Help Form Ad Hoc Groups

In this strategy, the teacher gives students a blank chart showing a clock (with twelve blanks, one for each hour), the seasons (with four blanks), or another theme-based graphic with blanks. See figure 6.25 (page 154). Before enacting this strategy, the teacher provides time for students to find a partner for each blank and fill the partner's name in on their chart. For example, if Maddie and John agree to be summer partners, Maddie signs the summer blank on John's chart and John signs the summer blank on Maddie's chart. When

Fishbowl Group Observation Handout

During the fishbowl demonstration, place a tally mark under each group member's column every time he or she exhibits an effective group behavior.

Behaviors	Member 1:	Member 2:	Member 3:	Member 4:	Member 5:
Using respectful language					
Demonstrating active listening					
Pausing to let another group member speak					
Asking a question					
Paraphrasing another group member					
Clarifying another group member's statement					
Offering a new idea					
Other:					

Source: Marzano Research, 2016.

Figure 6.23: Fishbowl group observation handout.

Visit **go.SolutionTree.com/instruction** *for a free reproducible version of this figure.*

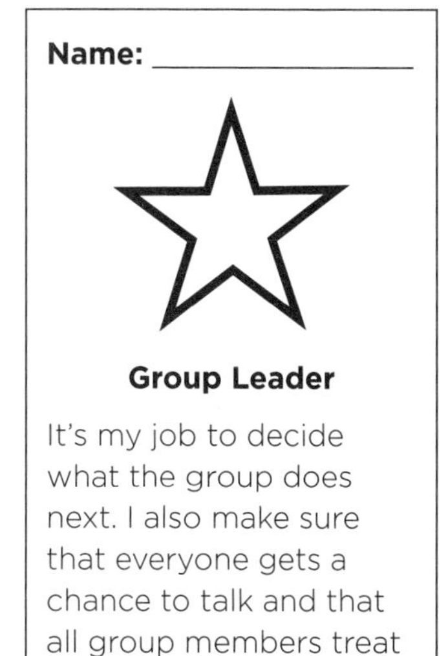

Name: ____________

Group Leader

It's my job to decide what the group does next. I also make sure that everyone gets a chance to talk and that all group members treat one another with respect.

Name: ____________

Group Note Taker

It's my job to write down all the important ideas my group comes up with.

Name: ____________

Group Questioner

It's my job to think up important questions to ask the group about our topic.

Name: ____________

Group Summarizer

It's my job to gather everybody's ideas together into one big idea that can be explained in a simple way.

Source: Marzano Research, 2016.

Figure 6.24: Sample job cards.

Visit **go.SolutionTree.com/instruction** *for a free reproducible version of this figure.*

the teacher wants to form quick, ad hoc groups, he or she asks students to find their summer (or, for example, two o'clock) buddies, and students quickly pair up.

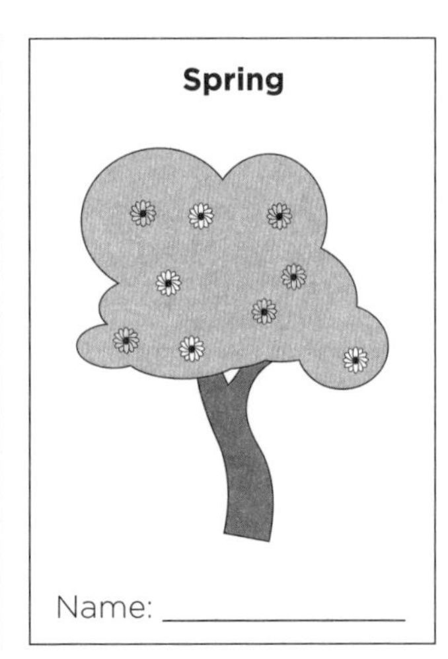

Source: Marzano Research, 2016.

Figure 6.25: Buddy chart.

Contingency Plan for Ungrouped Students

For students who don't have a group, the teacher can designate a meeting spot and can then help those students pair up or join existing groups. In every class, there will sometimes be students who are left out of initial group formation simply because there is an odd number of students or the movement associated with forming groups makes it difficult to see available spots. However, teachers will want to avoid a situation in which the same students are consistently left out. Some students have difficulty forming relationships, and this can make them reluctant to pair up with others when asked to find a partner for group activities. Teachers can help remedy this by creating relationship-building opportunities so students will be more comfortable with their classmates and less intimidated when asked to find a partner. Assign students to pairs and have them practice forming relationships with each other. Make sure that students pair up with a new partner every time, and ask them to engage in some of the following prompts.

- **Introductions:** Have students introduce themselves, encouraging them to smile and shake hands. Ask them to take turns saying their name and where they are from. Model an introduction in front of the class with a volunteer.
- **Sharing:** Have students tell a fun fact or interesting anecdote about themselves. If they can't think of anything, try prompting them with questions such as "What is your favorite thing about school?" or "What do you like to do to have fun?"
- **Compliments:** Have students give a compliment to their partner. Encourage them to avoid physical characteristics, though this may not be possible in a class of new students who are unfamiliar with each other. If necessary, start off by addressing a few of the more shy or isolated students in the class and saying something complimentary about each one.
- **Storytelling:** Have students tell each other a story. The story can be about themselves or even be completely fabricated. The point is to acclimate students to speaking at length to one another. Encourage participation by telling the class a story of your own.
- **Questions:** Have students take turns asking their partners questions. Make sure that they only ask one question at a time and that they give the other person plenty of time to answer. Walk

around the class and suggest questions if necessary. Encourage pairs of students to pursue areas of interest with further questions to stimulate conversation.

Group Using Preassessment Information

After administering a preassessment, the teacher can use the information gained about individual students' prior knowledge to assign students to groups. In some cases, the teacher might want to mix students with high prior knowledge and students with low prior knowledge together. In other cases, the teacher might want to differentiate by grouping students with high prior knowledge together and creating separate groups of students with medium and low prior knowledge.

Figure 6.26 shows students assigned to categories based on their assessment scores, simplifying the process of creating homogeneous or heterogeneous groups. Teachers can subdivide the large-group categories in the figure to create smaller groups.

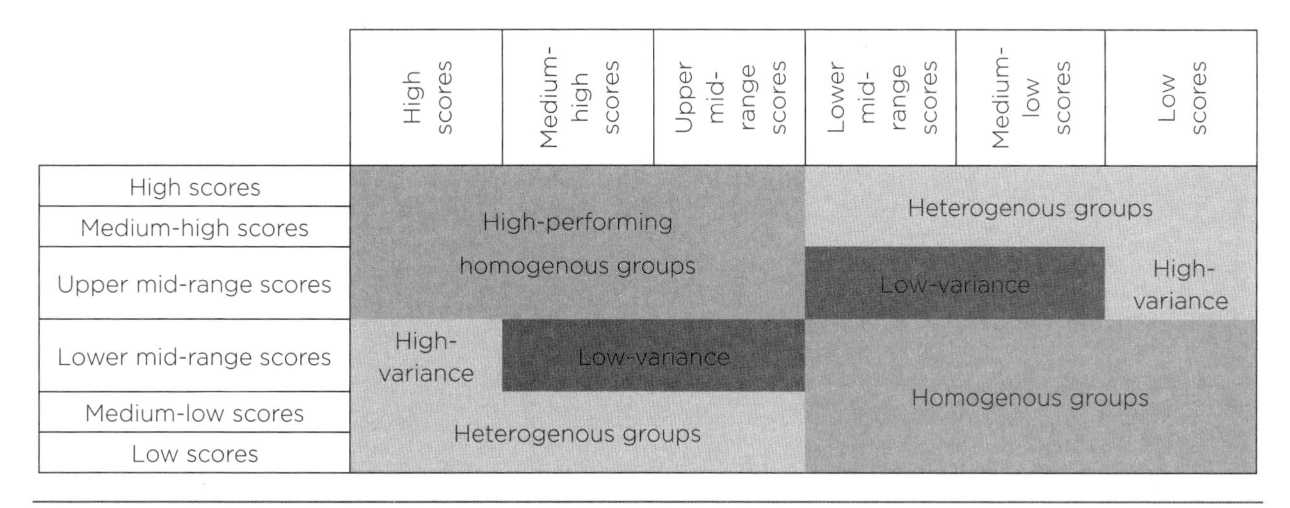

Figure 6.26: Sample grouping table.

Pair-Check

Spencer Kagan and Miguel Kagan (2009) originally developed pair-check. In this strategy, within groups of four, students form pairs (two pairs per group) and designate who will be partner A and who will be partner B. Using a set of exercises, problems, or questions, partner A works on the first exercise, problem, or question while partner B coaches when necessary and praises partner A's work when complete. For the second exercise, problem, or question, the partners reverse roles. Then, the pair checks their answers with the other pair in their group. The goal is for all four group members to reach consensus about each solution. If solutions do not match, group members discuss and coach each other until they reach a common solution. They repeat the process, with consensus achieved after every two exercises, problems, or questions. Following are tips for using this strategy.

- **Pair students appropriately:** In pair-check, students will work closely with their partner and some tasks or problems may prove challenging. Effective teamwork is a major objective, so make sure to group students appropriately. Be aware not only of students' levels of ability in the content area but also of their communication and social interaction skills. Grouping a quiet student with an outgoing student might draw the quiet student into greater participation, for instance, but if pairs are too unbalanced one student may simply take over the activity.
- **Ask students to think out loud:** A key component of pair-check is its focus on the process of problem solving. Ask the students working on the problem to think aloud as they work. This

allows their coaching partners to observe their strategy and provide helpful suggestions and encouragement. If necessary, model thinking aloud by narrating your own thought process as you solve a couple of problems in front of the class.

- **Instruct students on coaching one another:** Make sure that when students are in the coaching role, they do not simply suggest possible answers. The point of the activity is to provide encouragement and suggestions while collaborating in the problem-solving process. Model this behavior in front of the class with a volunteer before having pairs work on their own.
- **Monitor student pairs:** While students are working in pairs, walk around the class and monitor their interactions. Be careful not to interrupt the brainstorming process, but give hints when pairs appear to be truly stuck. Try to focus suggestions on the coaching partner rather than the student working the problem. For example, try directing the coach's attention to a certain step in the process that is causing his or her partner difficulty. When possible, provide assistance in such a way that students are encouraged to communicate with each other rather than directly with you.

Think-Pair-Share and Think-Pair-Square

Frank Lyman (1981) originally developed think-pair-share. After grouping students in pairs, the teacher presents a problem. Students think about the problem individually for a predetermined amount of time. Then, students each share their thoughts, ideas, and possible solutions with their partners. Pairs discuss and come to a consensus about their solution. The teacher then asks pairs to share what they decided with the class. In a variation (think-pair-square), pairs confer with another pair (making a group of four) and come to a consensus in that group as well before sharing with the whole class.

A handout like figure 6.27 can help guide students' use of this strategy.

Think-Pair-Share Activity Handout

Name: ______________________ Partner name: ______________________

Think!

My Answer	My Partner's Answer

Pair!

Our Answer

Share!

Source: Marzano Research, 2016.

Figure 6.27: Think-pair-share activity handout.

Visit **go.SolutionTree.com/instruction** *for a free reproducible version of this figure.*

Student Tournaments

Using student tournaments, the teacher organizes students into teams to compete in various academic games. The teacher might keep track of each team's points over the course of a unit and provide a tangible reward, such as a gold coin or certificate, or recognition to the top one or two teams. Teachers should remix team members after each unit to ensure that students have the opportunity to work with a variety of peers.

A scoring chart like that in figure 6.28 can guide students' use of this strategy.

Student Tournament Scoring Chart

Class: ____________________ Dates: ________ through ________

Unit: ____________________

Date	Game	Points				
		Team 1	Team 2	Team 3	Team 4	Team 5
Totals						

Winning team: ____________________

Promised reward: ____________________

Source: Marzano Research, 2016.

Figure 6.28: Student tournament scoring chart.

Visit **go.SolutionTree.com/instruction** *for a free reproducible version of this figure.*

Inside-Outside Circle

Spencer Kagan and Miguel Kagan (2009) originally developed the inside-outside circle. Students form two concentric circles with an equal number of students in each circle. Students forming the inner circle stand facing outward, and students forming the outward circle stand facing inward (so that each person in the inner circle faces a person in the outer circle). The teacher asks a question or presents a problem, and students discuss their thoughts, answers, and solutions with the person facing them. On a signal from the teacher, each person in the inner circle takes one step to the left, so that everyone now faces a new partner. Partners again compare answers and solutions, after which the teacher asks individuals to share answers or solutions with the group. The teacher might also ask students to share what they discussed with their partners and how it changed (or didn't change) their thinking.

A handout like figure 6.29 (page 158) can help guide students' use of this strategy.

Cooperative Learning

The teacher appropriately structures and governs the use of cooperative learning during cognitively complex tasks. This involves four tasks.

1. Designing structures for group and individual accountability
2. Providing ongoing coaching of students' interpersonal and group skills

Inside-Outside Circle Activity Handout

Name: ______________________________ Date: ______________

Discussion question: ______________________________

____

____

____

____

____

____

As you speak with your partners, keep the following questions in mind:

- How is my partner's perspective different than mine?
- How is my partner's perspective similar to mine?
- What new issue or point of view is my partner presenting that I hadn't thought of?
- Does my partner's perspective raise any new questions?
- Does anything my partner is saying cause me to rethink my own perspective?

Use the following space to take notes about your partners' perspectives:

Partner 1:

Partner 2:

Partner 3:

Source: Marzano Research, 2016.

Figure 6.29: Inside-outside circle activity handout.

Visit **go.SolutionTree.com/instruction** *for a free reproducible version of this figure.*

3. Specifying clear roles and responsibilities for all group members
4. Using a variety of grouping criteria and grouping structures that make sense in the larger scheme of classroom activities and instructional segments

A chart like figure 6.30 can help guide students' use of this strategy.

Cooperative Learning Feedback Chart

Group: ______________________ Date: ______________

Project or unit: ______________________

Group members: ______________________

Criteria	Comments
All group members participated equally in group activities.	
The group demonstrated successful interpersonal skills (cooperation, time management, conflict resolution, and so on).	
The group distributed tasks and responsibilities evenly.	
The group completed all progress-check activities and documents on time.	
All group members contributed to the final presentation, demonstration, or product.	
The group demonstrated understanding of the material.	
Other comments:	

Source: Marzano Research, 2016.

Figure 6.30: Cooperative learning feedback chart.

Visit **go.SolutionTree.com/instruction** *for a free reproducible version of this figure.*

Peer-Response Groups

Students work with peers to give and receive feedback on their cognitively complex tasks. To ensure equal participation and consistent feedback, the teacher assigns roles to students and uses scoring scales or checklists to ensure similar standards for each member of the group. When giving feedback, students should consider the aspects of their partner's work that most interested and confused them and offer suggestions for improvement and future work (Marzano Research, 2016).

Peer Tutoring

Advanced students volunteer to help students who need just a little assistance to move up to competence or proficiency on a four-point scale. Advanced students should probably not tutor severely struggling students (who need intensive help from the teacher); rather, the teacher pairs advanced students with students who need only a small amount of help or guidance to achieve competence or proficiency.

A handout like figure 6.31 (page 160) can help guide students' use of this strategy.

Peer Tutor Handout

Name: ______________________________ Date: ______________

Peer name: __________________________ Unit or topic: ______________

While you work with your peer, think about and discuss each of the following questions. Fill out the answers together and give this sheet to your peer at the conclusion of your tutoring session.

As you begin, take some time to look over your peer's work or let your peer explain his or her understanding of a topic. Focus on getting a complete picture of what your peer knows. Be sure to give your peer plenty of time to think and speak.

Explain your overall impression of your peer's work:

Identify some things that your peer has done well:

What area does your peer think he or she is having difficulty in?

Now that you have reviewed your peer's work or understanding of a topic, break down the topic into smaller bits. If it is a skill or process, break it down into steps. If it is a concept your peer is having difficulty understanding, break it down into smaller pieces or categories of information. If your peer is executing a specific step of a skill or process incorrectly, ask him or her to explain why he or she is doing it that way. If he or she is having difficulty understanding a specific part of a broader concept, ask him or her to explain what he or she knows about that part. You and your peer may find it useful to write out a list or make a diagram during this step.

Are there any gaps in your peer's understanding of the topic? If so, explain.

Are there any misconceptions in your peer's understanding of the topic? If so, explain.

Explain your own understanding of the area or areas of the topic in which your peer is having difficulty.

What suggestions might you offer for ways in which your peer might improve his or her work or understanding of the topic?

Do you have any additional comments for your peer?

Source: Marzano Research, 2016.

Figure 6.31: Peer tutor handout.

Visit **go.SolutionTree.com/instruction** *for a free reproducible version of this figure.*

Structured Grouping

The teacher designs and implements structured group activities that feature both individual and group accountability. Individual group members carry out specific tasks and responsibilities while working together on the final product. Structured group activities deepen and extend students' understanding of a topic rather than introduce new content.

A handout like figure 6.32 can help ensure accountability during this strategy.

Accountability Handout for Working in Groups

Name: ______________________________ Date: ______________

Group: ____

Fill out this section individually.

My group has been assigned the following task: ______________________________

____

My role within the group is ______________________________.

This means that it is my job to ______________________________.

In order to complete my task for this specific assignment, I will need to:

My task is necessary to complete the group assignment because:

If I encounter a problem while working on my task, I will:

Fill out this section by discussing the questions with your group.

As a group, in order to complete our task, we will need to:

The members of our group have been assigned the following roles:

If any member of our group has difficulty with his or her role, we will:

If our entire group has difficulty completing our task, we will:

Source: Marzano Research, 2016.

Figure 6.32: Accountability handout for working in groups.

Visit **go.SolutionTree.com/instruction** *for a free reproducible version of this figure.*

Group Reflecting on Learning

The teacher organizes students into groups to reflect on their learning progress, on activities they have participated in with their peers, or on a piece of work they have produced. Groups can be as small as two students, but the teacher should make a plan so that groups can be formed quickly and regularly. The reflection process should guide students in sharing their reflections, encouraging each other, and identifying ways to grow in their learning.

A worksheet like figure 6.33 (page 162) can help guide students' use of this strategy.

Group Reflection Worksheet

Name: ______________________________ Date: ______________

Group: ______________________________

Consider these questions during group reflection. Your answers should reflect your own thoughts and your group's input.

How do I think my learning is going so far?

Are there any areas I do really well in?

What is it about how I approach those areas that helps me to be successful?

Are there any areas in which I am not doing as well as I would like?

Why do I think I struggle in those areas that I don't do so well in?

How do the other members of my group approach those areas that I have trouble with?

Is there anything I can do differently that might help me to be more successful?

The next time I start to have trouble, I will:

Source: Marzano Research, 2016.

Figure 6.33: Group reflection worksheet.

Visit **go.SolutionTree.com/instruction** *for a free reproducible version of this figure.*

Monitoring Element 22

Specific student responses and behaviors allow the teacher to determine whether this element is being implemented effectively and producing the desired effects.

- Students move into groups quickly and with purpose.
- Students treat each other with respect.
- Students interact in a manner that deepens their understanding.
- Students work efficiently in groups.

Use this list to monitor student responses to element 22.

To monitor your own use of this element, use the scale in figure 6.34 in combination with the reproducible "Tracking Teacher Actions: Organizing Students to Interact" (page 171). As with other proficiency scales, level 3 or higher is the goal.

4 Innovating	I adapt behaviors and create new strategies for unique student needs and situations.
3 Applying	I organize students to interact in a thoughtful way that facilitates collaboration, and I monitor the extent to which students collaborate.
2 Developing	I organize students to interact in a thoughtful way that facilitates collaboration, but I do not monitor the effect on students.
1 Beginning	I use the strategies and behaviors associated with this element incorrectly or with parts missing.
0 Not Using	I am unaware of strategies and behaviors associated with this element.

Figure 6.34: Self-rating scale for element 22—Organizing students to interact.

The following examples describe what each level of the scale might look like in the classroom.

- **Not Using (0):** A teacher does not organize students into groups to help them process content.
- **Beginning (1):** A teacher organizes students for group activities but provides little direction for group behavior.
- **Developing (2):** A teacher groups students with care and provides detailed guidance for group activities but is not sure if students are benefitting from the experience.
- **Applying (3):** A teacher groups students with care and provides detailed guidance for group activities. He monitors and provides aid to groups as well as individual students during the activities and is able to see students growing in their understanding of the content.
- **Innovating (4):** A teacher uses various strategies to successfully organize students to interact in group activities. When some students still seem to be having difficulty with the content, she restructures the activity so that they interact productively with other students who can provide them with helpful new perspectives on the material.

Action Steps

Use the "Tracking Teacher Actions" reproducibles that follow (pages 164–171) to monitor your implementation of each element in this chapter.

Additionally, visit the appendix (page 329) for the reproducible "Tracking Progress Over Time" (page 330), which helps teachers set goals related to their proficiency with each element and track their progress toward these goals over the course of a unit, semester, or year. Also, the "Strategy Reflection Log" (page 331) in the appendix provides a space to write down your thoughts and reflect on the implementation process for specific strategies related to each element. Finally, visit **go.SolutionTree.com/instruction** for both student surveys and teacher surveys, the results of which provide feedback about your proficiency with each element.

Tracking Teacher Actions: Previewing Strategies

The teacher can use this form to plan his or her usage of strategies related to the element of previewing strategies.

Check Strategies You Intend to Use	Strategies	Description of Instructional Plan
	Informational Hooks	
	Bell Ringers	
	What Do You Think You Know?	
	Overt Linkages	
	Preview Questions	
	Brief Teacher Summaries	
	Skimming	
	Teacher-Prepared Notes	
	K-W-L Strategy	
	Advance Organizers	
	Anticipation Guides	
	Word Splashes	
	Preassessments	
	Other:	
	Other:	

Source: Adapted from Marzano Research. (2016). Marzano compendium of instructional strategies. *Centennial, CO: Author.*

Tracking Teacher Actions: Highlighting Critical Information

The teacher can use this form to plan his or her usage of strategies related to the element of highlighting critical information.

Check Strategies You Intend to Use	Strategies	Description of Instructional Plan
	Repeating the Most Important Content	
	Asking Questions That Focus on Critical Information	
	Using Visual Activities	
	Using Narrative Activities	
	Using Tone of Voice, Gestures, and Body Position	
	Using Pause Time	
	Identifying Critical-Input Experiences	
	Using Explicit Instruction to Convey Critical Content	
	Using Dramatic Instruction to Convey Critical Content	
	Providing Advance Organizers to Cue Critical Content	
	Using What Students Already Know to Cue Critical Content	
	Other:	
	Other:	

Source: Adapted from Marzano Research. (2016). Marzano compendium of instructional strategies. *Centennial, CO: Author.*

Tracking Teacher Actions: Reviewing Content

The teacher can use this form to plan his or her usage of strategies related to the element of reviewing content.

Check Strategies You Intend to Use	Strategies	Description of Instructional Plan
	Cumulative Review	
	Cloze Activity	
	Summary	
	Presented Problem	
	Demonstration	
	Brief Practice Test or Exercise	
	Questioning	
	Give One, Get One	
	Other:	
	Other:	

Source: Adapted from Marzano Research. (2016). Marzano compendium of instructional strategies. *Centennial, CO: Author.*

Tracking Teacher Actions: Revising Knowledge

The teacher can use this form to plan his or her usage of strategies related to the element of revising knowledge.

Check Strategies You Intend to Use	Strategies	Description of Instructional Plan
	Academic Notebook Entries	
	Academic Notebook Review	
	Peer Feedback	
	Assignment Revision	
	The Five Basic Processes	
	Visual Symbols	
	Writing Tools	
	Other:	
	Other:	

Source: Adapted from Marzano Research. (2016). Marzano compendium of instructional strategies. *Centennial, CO: Author.*

Tracking Teacher Actions: Reflecting on Learning

The teacher can use this form to plan his or her usage of strategies related to the element of reflecting on learning.

Check Strategies You Intend to Use	Strategies	Description of Instructional Plan
	Reflective Journals	
	Think Logs	
	Exit Slips	
	Knowledge Comparisons	
	Two-Column Notes	
	Other:	
	Other:	

Source: Adapted from Marzano Research. (2016). Marzano compendium of instructional strategies. *Centennial, CO: Author.*

Tracking Teacher Actions: Assigning Purposeful Homework

The teacher can use this form to plan his or her usage of strategies related to the element of assigning purposeful homework.

Check Strategies You Intend to Use	Strategies	Description of Instructional Plan
	Homework Preview	
	Homework to Deepen Knowledge	
	Homework to Practice a Process or Skill	
	Parent-Assessed Homework	
	Other:	
	Other:	

Source: Adapted from Marzano Research. (2016). Marzano compendium of instructional strategies. *Centennial, CO: Author.*

Tracking Teacher Actions: Elaborating on Information

The teacher can use this form to plan his or her usage of strategies related to the element of elaborating on information.

Check Strategies You Intend to Use	Strategies	Description of Instructional Plan
	General Inferential Questions	
	Elaborative Interrogation	
	Questioning Sequences	
	Other:	
	Other:	

Source: Adapted from Marzano Research. (2016). Marzano compendium of instructional strategies. *Centennial, CO: Author.*

Tracking Teacher Actions: Organizing Students to Interact

The teacher can use this form to plan his or her usage of strategies related to the element of organizing students to interact.

Check Strategies You Intend to Use	Strategies	Description of Instructional Plan
	Group for Active Processing	
	Group Norms Creation	
	Fishbowl Demonstration	
	Job Cards	
	Predetermined Buddies To Help Form Ad Hoc Groups	
	Contingency Plan for Ungrouped Students	
	Group Using Preassessment Information	
	Pair-Check	
	Think-Pair-Share and Think-Pair-Square	
	Student Tournaments	
	Inside-Outside Circle	
	Cooperative Learning	
	Peer-Response Groups	
	Peer Tutoring	
	Structured Grouping	
	Group Reflecting on Learning	
	Other:	
	Other:	

Source: Adapted from Marzano Research. (2016). Marzano compendium of instructional strategies. *Centennial, CO: Author.*

PART III

Context

CHAPTER 7

Using Engagement Strategies

Engagement is a critical component of deepening students' knowledge. Effective engagement strategies often encourage students to interact with the content in purposeful but unexpected ways and allow students to personally respond to the information presented to them. Teachers should notice when students seem disinterested and employ strategies to enhance students' motivation to learn.

The goal of this design area is for students to be paying attention, energized, intrigued, and inspired. Teachers are able to meet this goal by answering the question, What engagement strategies will I use to help students pay attention, be energized, be intrigued, and be inspired? The ten elements and associated strategies in this chapter help the teacher do just that.

Element 23: Noticing and Reacting When Students Are Not Engaged

An effective teacher scans the room, making note of when students are not engaged and taking overt action to re-engage them. Research has shown that engagement increases student achievement (Bloom, 1976; Frederick, 1980; Lysakowski & Walberg, 1982; Walberg, 1982). Different indicators of engagement include students' on-task behavior, positive emotions toward learning, personal investment in learning, and level of attention to instructional activities (Reeve, 2006).

There are five strategies within this element.

1. Monitoring individual student engagement
2. Monitoring overall class engagement
3. Using self-reported student engagement data
4. Re-engaging individual students
5. Boosting overall class energy levels

The following sections will explore each strategy to provide you with guidelines to effectively implement this element. Read through each before creating a plan for your classroom. Teachers may use the strategies individually or in combination. Remember, these are not merely activities to be checked off; they are methods of creating a practice that combines your art with the science of noticing and reacting when students are not engaged. Reflect on your use of each strategy by filling out the "Strategy Reflection Log" on page 331.

Monitoring Individual Student Engagement

Teachers can scan the room and identify specific students who appear to be disengaged to ensure high levels of classroom engagement. The teacher can do this during whole-class or small-group instruction as well as during individual seatwork. Once a student is identified, the teacher should use specific interventions to re-engage the student. For example, if a teacher notices a student gazing out the window for extended periods of time during whole-class instruction, the teacher might decide to physically move him- or herself between the unfocused student and the window as a means to draw the student's attention back to the lesson being taught. Teachers can look for these signs of individual student engagement (Marzano Research, 2016).

During whole-class instruction:

- Note-taking
- Making direct eye contact or following the teacher with his or her eyes
- Reacting to content being presented (for example, laughing or looking surprised)
- Following directions (for example, raising hand or moving when requested)
- Asking questions or presenting comments related to content
- Responding to questions when called upon

During small-group instruction:

- Interacting with other students
- Maintaining appropriate volume levels
- Referring to text or instructions while working
- Taking notes while working
- When queried, identifying the work their group has accomplished

During seatwork:

- Working quietly
- Keeping eyes focused on work at hand
- Writing in text or on handouts
- Not interacting (talking, laughing, exchanging looks) with or being distracted by other students

Monitoring Overall Class Engagement

To ensure class engagement, the teacher monitors levels of engagement exhibited by the class as a whole. When monitoring class engagement, a teacher can assess the degree to which the entirety of the class seems to be interested in the work at hand. For example, in a class with low engagement, when the teacher asks a question, students may not volunteer to answer the question (with the exception of a few of the same students). In a class with high engagement, students seem authentically interested in the material and eager to deepen their knowledge about the content. Teachers can look for the following indicators of high and low engagement (Marzano Research, 2016).

High levels of overall engagement:

- Students are alert and attentive.
- Different students volunteer to answer questions when asked.
- Class discussion is fruitful and needs little guidance.
- Students can explain what they find interesting about the content.
- Students can work independently or as a group and stay on task.
- Students respond to cues (laughing at jokes, following directions, and so on).

Low levels of overall engagement:

- The majority of students seem bored or disengaged.
- Some students are disruptive or act out and successfully distract other students.
- Students regularly incorrectly answer questions about content addressed during class.
- The teacher spends the majority of his or her time dealing with problematic students rather than teaching.

Using Self-Reported Student Engagement Data

The teacher periodically asks students to signal their level of engagement. The teacher could ask students to self-report their engagement levels informally throughout a class or unit by asking students to raise their hands if they feel their energy levels dropping or create a system to let students consistently report their engagement. For example, each student might have three cards: (1) a white card that signifies high engagement, (2) a gray card that signifies medium engagement, and (3) a black card that signifies that the student needs help. The teacher can poll the class by having students hold up the card that best represents their engagement level.

Following are other examples of student engagement measurement tools.

- The teacher asks students to rank their current engagement during class. Students signal high engagement with a thumbs-up, low engagement with a thumbs-down, and medium engagement with an open hand parallel to the floor. The teacher can also ask students to rank their current interest in the material by holding up five fingers to indicate that they are very interested in the material and one finger indicating no interest in the material at all. Teachers can use this tool at the end of the unit to determine the interest level a class had in specific material.
- The teacher provides a scale, like the following, that ranks engagement: (0) not engaged at all, (1) hardly engaged, (2) moderately engaged, (3) engaged, or (4) highly engaged. The teacher can use this scale to assess students' engagement during class or their overall interest in the material being taught. The teacher might also include this scale at the end of assessments throughout or at the end of a unit and ask students to use it to rate their interest level in the material covered.
- If a teacher wants to provide an anonymous way for students to identify their engagement levels, the teacher can pass out index cards to the class and ask them to write down the answers to two questions: (1) How engaged are you right now? and (2) What can I do to make class more engaging? The teacher then collects the responses and reviews the answers, taking into consideration students' suggestions.
- The teacher creates some sort of visual cue that students can use to signal that they are beginning to disengage during class. For example, the teacher might provide a "speedometer" made out of paper at every seat that students can use to represent their engagement level. If the teacher notices a student move the needle on his or her speedometer to zero, the teacher uses specific strategies to re-engage the student.

Re-Engaging Individual Students

Once a teacher identifies a student who is not engaged or reacting to the content being presented, the teacher should take action to re-engage the student. There are a variety of actions that teachers can take to re-engage students who are not paying attention. For example, if a teacher notices that a student is doodling rather than taking notes, the teacher can call on that specific student and ask him or her for input related to the content being taught.

The following are other tactics tailored to re-engage individual students.

- **Remove the distraction:** If a student is disengaged because of a specific person, object, or situation, the teacher identifies and removes the distraction. For example, if a teacher notices that something outside the classroom is distracting a student, the teacher can close the window blinds or shut the classroom door. If a student is texting on his or her cell phone or a neighbor is distracting him or her, the teacher can confiscate the cell phone or physically separate the two students.
- **Directly call on the student:** If a student appears to be bored or not paying attention, the teacher can directly call on the student for his or her input on the content. Alternatively, the teacher can simply say the student's name to subtly let that student know that he or she is aware of the lapse in attention.
- **Ask the student:** If a student seems particularly disengaged during class, the teacher might choose to query the student about his or her engagement levels either after class or during a class transition. For example, as the lesson switches from direct instruction to small-group work, the teacher might pull the student aside, explain that he or she noticed the student's low level of energy, and ask why this is the case.

Boosting Overall Class Energy Levels

If a teacher notices that the energy levels in the classroom are low or that more than a few students are disengaged, the teacher can use specific activities to re-engage a group of students or the entire class. For example, a teacher might notice halfway through a lecture that a group of students in the back of the classroom does not seem engaged. The teacher might pause his or her lecture and ask all students to pull out their journals and write a few comments and questions about the content thus far. After giving a few minutes of working time, the teacher might choose a student from the initially disengaged group to share what he or she has written.

Following are other re-engagement tactics for groups of students.

- **Incorporate movement:** If energy levels in the class seem low, the teacher can ask all the students in the class to stand up and stretch for a few minutes. This will break up the content and allow students to burn off extra pent-up physical energy which, when built up, can sometimes cause anxiousness.
- **Take a break:** The teacher announces to the class that he or she recognizes that the class's energy seems low. The teacher then asks whether or not a quick break from the material (no more than five minutes) would be helpful, but the teacher only grants this break with the understanding that the students will come back and focus on the material at hand.
- **Incorporate student participation:** If student engagement seems low, the teacher can find ways to get students to participate. For example, rather than calling on students to respond to questions, the teacher might use a ball or other object to determine who answers a given question. The teacher then throws the ball to a student and has that student pass the item to a student of his or her choice.
- **Adapt the lesson:** If a teacher notices that students seem to be bored by the content, he or she may want to find a way to tailor the lesson to be more engaging. For example, if students seem to have low energy during a direct instruction lesson, the teacher might ask students to get into

small groups and discuss the content that was just presented. The teacher can then go around to groups, identify areas of confusion, and correct misconceptions.

- **Incorporate competition:** If energy levels seem low, the teacher can use the prospect of an academic game to help students focus. For example, if the teacher senses the class seems to have low energy, the teacher might hint that at the end of the period, the class is going to play a trivia game that relies on knowledge of the content being presented.
- **Increase enthusiasm:** If the teacher senses that the class is bored, he or she may make an active choice to become especially enthusiastic about the content being presented. By modeling enthusiasm with hand gestures, body language, and tone of voice, some students may find the material to be more engaging.

Monitoring Element 23

Specific student responses and behaviors allow the teacher to determine whether this element is being implemented effectively and producing the desired effects.

- Students appear aware of the fact that the teacher is taking note of their engagement levels.
- Students try to increase their engagement levels when appropriate.
- When asked, students explain that the teacher expects high engagement levels.

Use this list to monitor student responses to element 23.

To monitor your own use of this element, use the scale in figure 7.1 in combination with the reproducible "Tracking Teacher Actions: Noticing and Reacting When Students Are Not Engaged" (page 224). As with other proficiency scales, level 3 or higher is the goal.

4 Innovating	I adapt behaviors and create new strategies for unique student needs and situations.
3 Applying	I notice and react when students are not engaged, and I monitor the extent to which my actions affect students' engagement.
2 Developing	I notice and react when students are not engaged, but I do not monitor the effect on students.
1 Beginning	I use the strategies and behaviors associated with this element incorrectly or with parts missing.
0 Not Using	I am unaware of strategies and behaviors associated with this element.

Figure 7.1: Self-rating scale for element 23—Noticing and reacting when students are not engaged.

The following examples describe what each level of the scale might look like in the classroom.

- **Not Using (0):** A teacher is so focused on getting through a lesson that he or she does not pay attention to the interest level of the class and, as such, does not notice when students are not paying attention to the material being presented.
- **Beginning (1):** A teacher may notice when students are not interested or engaged in the materials but does not take action to re-engage the students. Rather, the teacher focuses on students who are paying attention.

- **Developing (2):** A teacher notices when students are not engaged and uses specific strategies to re-engage them. However, the teacher does not keep track of which activities successfully re-engage students in the material and which are less effective.
- **Applying (3):** A teacher notices when students are not engaged and, depending on the situation, effectively uses specific strategies to re-engage either individual students or boost the energy level of the entire class. The teacher also keeps track of the effects of a given strategy and how successful it is in the short term (immediately re-engaging a student) and the long term (after a chunk of time has passed during class).
- **Innovating (4):** A teacher notices when energy levels of a class seem to be declining and pre-emptively uses re-engagement strategies to boost energy levels before students are completely disengaged. The teacher often uses a combination of strategies that simultaneously boost the energy levels of the entire class and specific students who appear to be less interested than others.

Element 24: Increasing Response Rates

An effective teacher uses response-rate techniques to maintain student engagement. Research has shown that mild pressure has a positive influence on students' learning (Becker, 1988; Marzano, 2018; Skinner, Fletcher, & Hennington, 1996). Mild pressure prompts students to focus their attention on the source of the pressure. Increasing the rate at which students respond during questioning is one way to apply mild pressure in the classroom (Good & Brophy, 2003).

There are nine strategies within this element.

1. Random names
2. Hand signals
3. Response cards
4. Response chaining
5. Paired response
6. Choral response
7. Wait time
8. Elaborative interrogation
9. Multiple types of questions

The following sections will explore each strategy to provide you with guidelines to effectively implement this element. Read through each before creating a plan for your classroom. Teachers may use the strategies individually or in combination. Remember, these are not merely activities to be checked off; they are methods of creating a practice that combines your art with the science of increasing response rates. Reflect on your use of each strategy by filling out the "Strategy Reflection Log" on page 331.

Random Names

In this strategy, the teacher writes each student's name on a separate slip of paper or popsicle stick and keeps them in a jar or other container. After asking a question, the teacher selects a name at random from the jar and calls on that student to answer. The teacher should put the selected name back into the jar once the student has answered so that every student always has the same odds of being chosen.

Calling on students at random creates mild pressure. This mild pressure is beneficial for increasing student engagement; however, to avoid causing stress or putting too much pressure on students, the teacher must make sure that students feel comfortable being called on even when they do not know the answer. When first implementing the random names strategy, be sure to explain to students that they have the following options when their name is drawn.

- **Respond to the question:** If students know the answer or feel comfortable taking their best guess, they can respond to the question. If they know some of the answer, but not all of it, they can give a partial response.

- **Ask for help:** If students are called on but do not know the answer, they can ask for help from the teacher or another student. This might come in the form of a hint, a restatement of the question, or several incremental questions. The teacher might also work through the question or problem with students to help them reach the answer.
- **Opt out temporarily:** If students are called on and do not know the answer, they can ask the teacher to come back to them later. The teacher moves on to another student or another question, giving the first student a longer time to think about the question. The teacher must make sure to remember to follow up and give the student a chance to answer again later.

Hand Signals

In this strategy, students respond nonverbally to a question that has a limited number of possible responses. For example, students use a thumbs-up to indicate they understand the content being addressed, a thumbs-down to indicate they do not understand, and a thumbs-sideways to indicate they understand some of the content but are also confused about some of the content. Students can also use hand signals to indicate responses to multiple-choice questions: one finger indicates that response A is correct, two fingers indicate response B, three fingers indicate response C, and four fingers indicate response D.

Figure 7.2 provides one example of the use of hand signals.

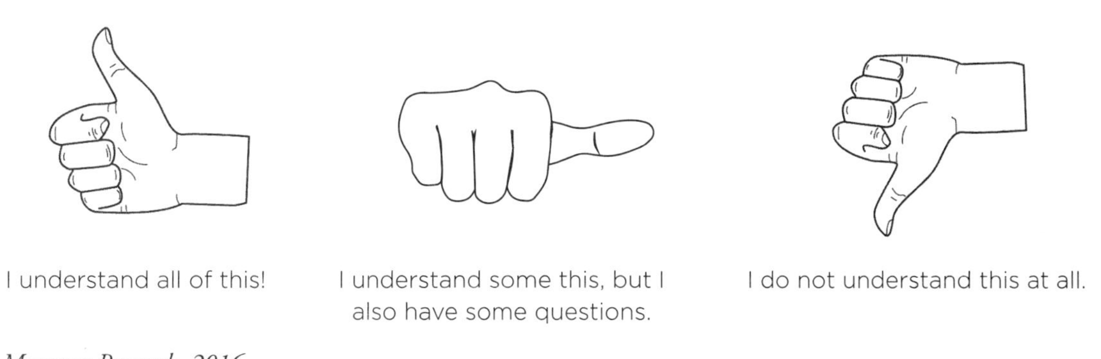

I understand all of this!

I understand some this, but I also have some questions.

I do not understand this at all.

Source: Marzano Research, 2016.

Figure 7.2: Signaling your level of understanding.

Visit **go.SolutionTree.com/instruction** *for a free reproducible version of this figure.*

Response Cards

In this strategy, students write their answers on small (for example, 12 × 12–inch) whiteboards or chalkboards and reveal them to the teacher simultaneously. This strategy works best with questions that have brief answers with little or no variability in the correct answer. For example, questions that require students to write down vocabulary words or the answer to a short mathematics problem would work well with response cards. Consider creating your own response cards.

- **Individual whiteboards:** Creating a set of small whiteboards for the classroom is often cheaper than purchasing them and is fairly easy. Visit a hardware store and look for white shower board, melamine, or tileboard. This comes in large sheets, which you can ask store employees to cut into 12 × 12–inch squares. Colorful electrical tape works well to cover the edges. Dry-erase markers can be purchased at most office supply stores, or a teacher might include this item on the student supply list. To keep students from getting marker on their hands, provide or ask students to bring items to use as erasers, such as dryer sheets, old socks, or small pieces of cloth.

- **Multiple-choice cards:** If you plan to ask multiple-choice questions, you can use simple paper response cards. Cut a sheet of construction paper or cardstock into quarters and write each letter option (A, B, C, D) on one of the sections. Alternatively, use index cards. Make sure to use a marker when writing the letters, as pen will be difficult to read from a distance. Create enough sets of four cards so that each student will have his or her own set.

Response Chaining

After a student responds to a question, the teacher can ask a second student to explain why the initial answer was correct, partially correct, or incorrect. The teacher might also ask the second student to paraphrase the initial answer before responding. The teacher can call on a third student to respond to the second student's response.

Use a tracking sheet like in figure 7.3 to guide your use of this strategy.

Question or Content	Number of Students in Chain						
	1	2	3	4	5	6	7
	1	2	3	4	5	6	7

Source: Marzano Research, 2016.

Figure 7.3: Tracking sheet for response chaining.

Visit **go.SolutionTree.com/instruction** *for a free reproducible version of this figure.*

Paired Response

Students confer in pairs to answer a question. The teacher then calls on a pair. One student can verbalize the answer for the pair, or both can contribute.

Figure 7.4 provides prompts that students can use to have productive paired response conversations.

Choral Response

Using choral response, the teacher presents target information in a clear and concise statement and asks the class to repeat the information as a group. The goal is to form an *imprint* of important information. For example, the teacher would say, "The organ system that allows blood to move throughout the body is called the cardiovascular system. What is it called?" The class would then respond, "The cardiovascular system." The key is to consider one to three elements of target content for the choral response and have clear and concise phrasing. Consider the following four steps (Marzano Research, 2016).

1. Present or remind students of the target content ("The circulatory system pumps blood").
2. Prompt a choral response ("What system pumps blood?").
3. Wait for students to respond ("The circulatory system").
4. Repeat the target content ("That's right, blood is pumped by the circulatory system").

Wait Time

The purpose of this strategy is for the teacher to give students time to think and compose their answers after asking a question. The teacher therefore pauses for at least three seconds after posing a question. The teacher also allows for a pause of at least three seconds if a student stops speaking in the middle of an answer and teaches students to allow a three-second pause between student answers.

Paired Response Prompts

Print, cut apart, and distribute copies of these cards to help students have productive paired response conversations.

Clarifying	**Paraphrasing**
If you are unsure about what your partner is saying, ask: "Can you clarify what you meant by that?" or "Can you rephrase that to help me understand better?"	**To let your partner know that you listened and understood, say:** "So what you're saying is . . ." and then restate their point in your own words.
Extending	**Disagreeing**
If you need more details from your partner, ask: "Can you say more about that?" **If you would like to add more to what your partner said, say:** "I agree, and I'd like to add to that by saying . . ." and then add your thoughts.	**If you disagree with your partner, say:** "I disagree with you because . . ." and then give the reasons why you disagree. If you want to offer an opposing idea, say: "I see why you might say that, but I think . . ." and then add your idea.

Source: Marzano Research, 2016.

Figure 7.4: Paired response prompts.

Visit **go.SolutionTree.com/instruction** *for a free reproducible version of this figure.*

Teachers often feel awkward standing in silence for a few seconds when giving wait time, especially if they are new to the strategy. The following list gives examples of what a teacher might do to occupy him- or herself during wait time and reduce awkwardness.

- Count the number of seconds.
- Make eye contact with students around the room.
- Move from one place in the room to another.
- Take several deep breaths.
- Scan the classroom for student engagement.
- Think of three good answers to the question.
- Think of a clue or hint to give if a student answers incorrectly.

Elaborative Interrogation

After a student answers a question, the teacher probes the answer by asking, "How do you know that to be true?" or "Why is that so?" The teacher might also ask the student to provide evidence to support his or her conclusions. To ensure that elaborative interrogation increases response rates, multiple students must be involved in each answer. One way to do this is to have students work in pairs or threes as the teacher moves through the elaborative interrogation process.

Following are examples of elaborative interrogation questions.

- How do you know that to be true?
- Why is that so?
- What evidence supports that answer?
- How did you arrive at that answer?
- Can you say more about that?
- Can you explain why you think that?
- Can you explain your reasoning?
- What information did you consider to decide on that answer?
- What aspects of our discussion influenced your answer?
- How might your answer change if __________?
- Based on your answer, what can you say about __________?

Multiple Types of Questions

The teacher uses a combination of types of questions such as the following. Using multiple types of questions both engages the class and allows for different cognitive processes to play a role in learning.

- **Retrieval questions:** These require students to recognize, recall, and execute knowledge that was directly taught. For example, Which organs in the human body remove waste and toxins from the blood?
- **Analytical questions:** These require students to take information apart and determine how the parts relate to the whole. For example, How did Charles Darwin's observations of finches in the Galapagos help lead to his theory of evolution?
- **Predictive questions:** These require students to form conjectures and hypotheses about what will happen next in a narrative or sequence of information or actions. For example, What do you think will happen if Macbeth kills the king?
- **Interpretive questions:** These require students to make and defend inferences about the intentions of an author. For example, What does Harper Lee imply through Atticus Finch's description of mockingbirds?
- **Evaluative questions:** These require students to use criteria to make judgments and assessments of something. For example, What is the most efficient way to do subtraction in your head?

To ensure that multiple types of questions increase response rates, multiple students must be involved in each answer. One way to do this is to organize students into pairs or threes and assign different question types to each group.

Monitoring Element 24

Specific student responses and behaviors allow the teacher to determine whether this element is being implemented effectively and producing the desired effects.

- Multiple students respond or the entire class responds to questions.
- Students pay attention to the answers other students provide.
- Students can describe the thinking that led to specific answers.
- Students are aware that the teacher expects all students to answer questions.

Use this list to monitor student responses to element 24.

To monitor your own use of this element, use the scale in figure 7.5 in combination with the reproducible "Tracking Teacher Actions: Increasing Response Rates" (page 225). As with other proficiency scales, level 3 or higher is the goal.

4 Innovating	I adapt behaviors and create new strategies for unique student needs and situations.
3 Applying	I use response-rate techniques to maintain student engagement, and I monitor the extent to which the techniques keep students engaged.
2 Developing	I use response-rate techniques to maintain student engagement in questions, but I do not monitor the effect on students.
1 Beginning	I use the strategies and behaviors associated with this element incorrectly or with parts missing.
0 Not Using	I am unaware of strategies and behaviors associated with this element.

Figure 7.5: Self-rating scale for element 24—Increasing response rates.

The following examples describe what each level of the scale might look like in the classroom.

- **Not Using (0):** A teacher lectures on the content for long stretches of time without pausing to ask students questions.
- **Beginning (1):** A teacher asks questions during teacher-led instruction, but he only calls on students who volunteer.
- **Developing (2):** A teacher uses response-rate techniques to give all students in her class frequent opportunities to respond. However, she makes little effort to determine if the strategies are having a measurable impact on student engagement.
- **Applying (3):** While using strategies to increase response rates, a teacher notes several indicators of engagement, such as students' level of attention and how prepared they are to answer a question when called on. When he first starts using the strategies, students seem caught off guard and take a few moments to answer the questions that he asks. After a few weeks of consistent use, though, he notices that students seem to be preparing their answers before he calls on them.
- **Innovating (4):** A teacher is using and monitoring strategies to increase response rates, and she notices that one student seems frustrated. This student is used to volunteering to answer questions and therefore having many chances to share what he thinks with the class. Now that this teacher is using a wider variety of response strategies, he has fewer individual chances to speak. To remedy this, the teacher works out a system with this student in which he writes down his answers to questions that other students answered verbally.

Element 25: Using Physical Movement

An effective teacher uses physical movement to maintain student engagement. Research has shown that increased physical activity is associated with higher energy levels (Dwyer, Blizzard, & Dean, 1996; Dwyer, Sallis, Blizzard, Lazarus, & Dean, 2001). Higher energy, in turn, allows students to pay more attention to what is happening in class. Additionally, physical movement increases blood flow to the brain, which facilitates thinking and learning (Jensen, 2005).

There are six strategies within this element.

1. Stand up and stretch
2. Vote with your feet
3. Corners activities
4. Stand and be counted
5. Body representations
6. Drama-related activities

The following sections will explore each strategy to provide you with guidelines to effectively implement this element. Read through each before creating a plan for your classroom. Teachers may use the strategies individually or in combination. Remember, these are not merely activities to be checked off; they are methods of creating a practice that combines your art with the science of using physical movement. Reflect on your use of each strategy by filling out the "Strategy Reflection Log" on page 331.

Stand Up and Stretch

Periodically, the teacher can ask students to stand up and stretch. This activity is especially useful when students need to change their focus, concentration, or level of engagement, because it causes more blood and oxygen to flow to the brain. The teacher can also instruct students to stretch in their seats if they feel tired or unfocused during class. Following are examples of stretches that teachers can use in class.

- **Side stretch:** Stand with feet slightly more than hip-width apart. Raise one arm above head, and place other hand on the hip. Lean torso toward the side where the hand is on the hip.
- **Hamstring stretch:** Stand with feet about six inches apart. Bend forward and reach arms down toward toes. Make sure head and neck are relaxed; look down toward toes or back through legs.
- **Quad stretch:** Place one hand on desk for balance. Stand on one leg and bend other leg at knee to raise the foot behind the body. Use hand to grasp top of foot or ankle and pull gently up and forward to increase stretch. Be sure to stand up straight throughout; do not bend at waist or hips.
- **Whole-body stretch:** Stand with feet hip-width apart. Raise both arms above head. Stand on tiptoes and try to touch the ceiling.
- **Lunge:** Stand with feet hip-width apart. Take a medium to large step forward with one foot. Forward leg should bend at the knee, keeping the shin vertical, while the back leg stays straight. Keep the torso upright and place hands on hips or raise arms above head.
- **Triceps stretch:** Raise one arm above head. Bend arm at elbow so that the hand touches the back of the same shoulder. Use the opposite hand to grasp the elbow and gently push back to increase the stretch.
- **Deltoid stretch:** With arm straight at shoulder level, reach across body so that the upper arm touches the chest. Use opposite hand to grasp forearm and pull toward body to increase the stretch.
- **Neck stretch:** Stand or sit with good posture (back straight, not supported by chair). Tilt head slowly to each side. Nod head forward as if touching chin to chest.

Vote With Your Feet

The teacher posts a sign in each corner of the room identifying responses to a true-or-false or multiple-choice question or reactions to answers to a question (incorrect, partially correct, totally correct). For example, if the question is multiple choice, the teacher would post signs reading A, B, C, and D in various parts of the room. Choices might also be statements of various opinions or perspectives on a topic. Students move to the corner that has the sign with the answer they think is correct. Before discussing the correct answer, the teacher asks one student under each option to explain why he or she believes that answer is correct.

Following are example discussion questions.

- Why did you choose this answer?
- What evidence do you have that your choice is right?

- Under what circumstances might you choose a different answer?
- Why do you think or how did you determine that the other options are incorrect?
- (If not choosing is an option) Why are you unsure of the answer?
- (If using a vote-discuss-revote sequence) Why did you change your mind?

Corners Activities

The teacher splits the class into four groups, which then rotate to each of the four corners of the classroom to examine four different questions related to key content. The teacher assigns a recorder to stay in each corner to summarize students' comments about that corner's question. At the end, each recorder reads the summary from that corner. Visit **go.SolutionTree.com/instruction** for the reproducible "Corners Activity Procedure" for student instructions.

Stand and Be Counted

After a lesson, students stand up based on their self-assessment of how well they understood the key ideas and concepts presented in the lesson. The teacher presents a self-assessment scale, gives students a moment to think, and then prompts students at each level of the scale to stand. For example, a teacher might present a 1–4 scale in which 1 indicates "I didn't understand any of the concepts presented in this lesson," 2 indicates "I need help understanding many of the ideas and concepts presented today," 3 indicates "I understand most of the ideas and concepts presented today," and 4 indicates "I clearly understand all the concepts presented in this lesson." After giving students time to reflect and rate themselves, the teacher would say, "Okay, stand up if you gave yourself a one on the scale." When students stand for a particular level, the teacher makes note of how many there are, asks them to sit back down, and then prompts students at the next level of the scale to stand up.

Body Representations

With this strategy, students create body representations in which they act out important content or critical aspects of a topic.

Following are examples of body representations.

- **Cause-and-effect chain:** Represent a chain of events that cause one another by assigning each event in the chain to one student. Students then line up in order and state their events. To further symbolize the causal relationship, students might hold hands and pass a gentle squeeze down the line as they say their individual events. Alternatively, students could pass a ball or other object down the line.
- **Mathematical operations:** Create a gesture or physical symbol that students learning and practicing various mathematical operations can use. For example, students could symbolize multiplication by crossing the arms in an X above one's head, division by drawing a slash in the air, and so on.
- **Vocabulary terms:** The teacher designates gestures or movements that correspond with key vocabulary terms for a lesson or unit. These might be related fairly literally to the definition of the word—for example, the word *obliterate* could be associated with a gesture that looks like erasing or wiping away to remind students of its meaning. Gestures could also convey other information about the word; for example, a teacher might create gestures that denote the parts of speech and use them when introducing new terms.

- **Key people:** Design movements that go along with key people or historical figures. For example, the gesture for Betsy Ross could be placing one's right hand over the heart as if saying the Pledge of Allegiance to remind students that she sewed the first American flag.
- **Geographical locations:** Have students move around the classroom as if on a map when explaining where events took place. For example, a teacher could define cardinal directions (north, south, east, west) and important locations within the classroom and take students on a miniaturized version of Lewis and Clark's journey.

Drama-Related Activities

In a drama-related activity, students act out an event they're studying, taking the roles of various participants in the event. This works especially well with historical situations, current events, and events in literature. Use figure 7.6 to plan for this strategy.

Drama-Related Activity Planning Guide

Class: ______________________________

Topic of lesson or unit: ______________________________

Key pieces of content:

An event that students can act out:

Details of this event—time period, location, people involved, causes, effects, and so on:

How will students choose or be assigned roles?

How will I ensure they have enough background knowledge to act out the event accurately?

How will I debrief the re-enactment afterward to ensure learning?

Source: Marzano Research, 2016.

Figure 7.6: Planning guide for drama-related activity.

Visit **go.SolutionTree.com/instruction** *for a free reproducible version of this figure.*

Monitoring Element 25

Specific student responses and behaviors allow the teacher to determine whether this element is being implemented effectively and producing the desired effects.

- Students actively engage in the strategies.
- Students' energy levels appear to increase.
- Students can explain how the physical movement keeps their interest and helps them learn.

Use this list to monitor student responses to element 25.

To monitor your own use of this element, use the scale in figure 7.7 in combination with the reproducible "Tracking Teacher Actions: Using Physical Movement" (page 226). As with other proficiency scales, level 3 or higher is the goal.

4 Innovating	I adapt behaviors and create new strategies for unique student needs and situations.
3 Applying	I use physical movement to maintain student engagement, and I monitor the extent to which these activities enhance student engagement.
2 Developing	I use physical movement to maintain student engagement, but I do not monitor the effect on students.
1 Beginning	I use the strategies and behaviors associated with this element incorrectly or with parts missing.
0 Not Using	I am unaware of strategies and behaviors associated with this element.

Figure 7.7: Self-rating scale for element 25—Using physical movement.

The following examples describe what each level of the scale might look like in the classroom.

- **Not Using (0):** A teacher structures her lessons in such a way that students remain in their seats throughout the class period.
- **Beginning (1):** A teacher uses physical movement strategies sporadically when it crosses his mind to do so.
- **Developing (2):** A teacher uses physical movement with her students at the beginning of class and during breaks between lessons, but she does not monitor students' engagement levels during instruction.
- **Applying (3):** A teacher pays attention to his class's level of engagement during lessons. When he notices that students seem to be tired, bored, or lacking energy, he uses physical movement strategies to re-engage them.
- **Innovating (4):** A teacher has planned to use physical movement in her classes; in particular, she likes to incorporate body representations into her lessons as she finds that it increases student engagement and helps students remember the content better. In some of her classes, however, the body representations she usually uses are ineffective—some students have difficulty participating because of physical differences or because they feel uncomfortable with activities that require physical contact with others. In these classes, she invents new ways to physically represent content that work for all students.

Element 26: Maintaining a Lively Pace

An effective teacher uses pacing techniques to maintain students' engagement. Research has shown that instructional pace affects students' ability to pay attention to classroom activities (Emmer & Gerwels, 2006). To maintain a lively pace, a teacher must transition smoothly and quickly from one instructional activity to the next. Interruptions, lulls in activity, and slow transitions waste time and make it hard for students to stay engaged (Arlin, 1979; Smith, 1985).

There are four strategies within this element.

1. Instructional segments
2. Pace modulation
3. Parking lot
4. Motivational hooks

The following sections will explore each strategy to provide you with guidelines to effectively implement this element. Read through each before creating a plan for your classroom. Teachers may use the strategies individually or in combination. Remember, these are not merely activities to be checked off; they are methods of creating a practice that combines your art with the science of maintaining a lively pace. Reflect on your use of each strategy by filling out the "Strategy Reflection Log" on page 331.

Instructional Segments

The teacher ensures that each of the following aspects of management and instruction are well planned and occur in a brisk, but not hurried, fashion.

- **Administrative tasks:** These include handing in assignments, distributing materials, and storing materials after an activity.
- **Presentation of new content:** This requires the teacher to switch back and forth between presenting new content in small chunks and allowing time for students to process newly presented chunks of information.
- **Practicing and deepening understanding of key knowledge and skills:** These activities involve students in practicing processes, examining similarities and differences, and examining errors in reasoning to come to a deeper understanding of the content.
- **Application of knowledge to new situations:** Through complex reasoning processes, this requires students to interact with the content using problem-solving, decision-making, investigation, experimental-inquiry, systems analysis, and hypothesis-testing processes.
- **Getting organized into groups:** This involves students knowing where to look to find out what group they are in, where to meet with their groups, and where to find supplies.
- **Seatwork:** This requires students to complete work or activities independently. Students should know which activities they are allowed to engage in once they have completed their seatwork, such as helping other students, beginning to work on more advanced content, beginning to work on an activity that addresses the content from another perspective, or studying a topic of their own choice.
- **Transitions:** These require students to end one activity and begin the next. The teacher must signal the end of the previous activity, announce the next activity (including when it will start, how long it will take, and when it will end), and cue students to move quickly to the next activity.

Establishing procedures for each of these activities can help students understand what is expected during different parts of a lesson. To help students conduct common activities and transitions efficiently, teachers can and should pre-emptively teach procedures for those instructional segments. To set students up for success, teachers should:

- **Identify events that require procedures**—This list might include events such as turning in homework, going to the restroom, lining up for recess, completing individual seatwork, asking for help, transitioning between various activities, and so on.
- **Identify a goal or desired outcome for each event**—This step helps define what successful execution of the procedure will look like. For example, the goal of asking for help might be to get one's questions answered quickly without disrupting other students.
- **Write a series of steps for each event**—Each procedure should provide enough detail that students know exactly what to do but not so much that the procedure becomes impossible to remember. For example, the procedure for going to the restroom might consist of the following five steps: (1) raise your hand and, when the teacher calls on you, ask to use the restroom;

(2) if granted permission, go to the sign-out sheet by the door; (3) write down your name and the time you are leaving; (4) take the hall pass and go quickly and directly to the bathroom; (5) upon your return, replace the hall pass and write the time of your return on the sign-out sheet.

- **Have students practice the procedures until they can do them independently**—Typically, this involves the teacher demonstrating the procedure first, then guiding students through it, then watching them complete the steps on their own to ensure proficiency.

Pace Modulation

The teacher speeds up or slows down the pace of the lesson to meet the engagement needs of students. Following are ways to adjust pacing.

- **Processing time:** To slow down the pace of content delivery, give students more processing time between chunks. To speed up the pace, give less processing time.
- **Group interaction:** Providing more opportunities for students to interact with partners and groups will slow the pace of a class, while fewer group activities will speed it up.
- **Individual responses:** Using mostly individual response strategies will increase pacing.
- **Formative assessment:** If students seem either bored or overwhelmed, using quick informal assessment strategies can help determine what students already know and what can therefore be skipped to speed up the pace; or what students are missing or confused about that needs to be revisited to slow the pace.
- **Types of lessons:** A fast-paced lesson might consist of a brief period of direct instruction and several practicing and deepening or knowledge application lessons. A lesson with a slower pace will spend the majority of the time on direct instruction.
- **Pace of speech:** Simply talk more quickly or more slowly to adjust the lesson's pace.
- **Presentation of content:** Slow down the pace by writing most of the content on the board; speed up the class by only presenting it orally.
- **Visual aids:** Using visual aids such as pictures and graphic organizers to reinforce content slows down the pace, while using few or no visual aids speeds it up.

Parking Lot

If the teacher or students get stuck or bogged down on the answer to a specific question or a specific issue, the teacher writes the issue in a space on the board called the *parking lot*. The teacher and students come back to the issue the next day after everyone has had time to think about it and gather information about it. Another version of the parking lot creates space for tangentially related or off-topic questions. If a student thinks of a question but realizes that it's not appropriate to ask at the time, he or she can write it on a sticky note and post it in the parking lot.

Motivational Hooks

By using motivational hooks, the teacher uses anecdotes, video clips, audio clips, newspaper headlines, and other short attention-grabbing media to spark students' attention. The teacher might also present unusual information or personal stories related to the lesson topic. Consider the following questions for planning motivational hooks (Marzano Research, 2016).

- What content am I presenting?
- What is the most interesting aspect of that content?
- What anecdotes or personal stories can I tell about the content?

- What video clips related to the content can I show?
- What audio clips related to the content can I play?
- What unusual information about this content can I present?
- What other attention-grabbing media (even unrelated to the content) can I use to pique students' interest?

Monitoring Element 26

Specific student responses and behaviors allow the teacher to determine whether this element is being implemented effectively and producing the desired effects.

- Students quickly adapt to changes in classroom activities and re-engage in the content.
- Students report that the pace of the class is neither too fast nor too slow.

Use this list to monitor student responses to element 26.

To monitor your own use of this element, use the scale in figure 7.8 in combination with the reproducible "Tracking Teacher Actions: Maintaining a Lively Pace" (page 227). As with other proficiency scales, level 3 or higher is the goal.

4 Innovating	I adapt behaviors and create new strategies for unique student needs and situations.
3 Applying	I use pacing techniques to maintain students' engagement, and I monitor the extent to which these techniques keep students engaged.
2 Developing	I use pacing techniques to maintain students' engagement, but I do not monitor the effect on students.
1 Beginning	I use the strategies and behaviors associated with this element incorrectly or with parts missing.
0 Not Using	I am unaware of strategies and behaviors associated with this element.

Figure 7.8: Self-rating scale for element 26—Maintaining a lively pace.

The following examples describe what each level of the scale might look like in the classroom.

- **Not Using (0):** A teacher presents all content at the same pace. He also neglects to use consistent transition procedures with his students, leading to a great deal of wasted time.
- **Beginning (1):** A teacher tries to maintain a lively instructional pace but ends up rushing through the content and confusing her students.
- **Developing (2):** A teacher moves faster through the content when students become bored and slows down when they get confused. This seems beneficial, but she doesn't have any proof beyond a general intuition.
- **Applying (3):** A teacher maintains a quick pace in his classroom without overwhelming students by teaching efficient transitions and keeping a list of questions to revisit later. He knows that his students are more engaged based on the results of surveys that he administers periodically.
- **Innovating (4):** A teacher maintains an appropriate pace during instruction and monitors the effect on student engagement. He realizes that while his pacing is working for the majority of students in his class, there are a few students who get bored more easily than the rest. To help

keep these students engaged, he uses an interesting content-related fact or real-life application to introduce each instructional segment.

Element 27: Demonstrating Intensity and Enthusiasm

An effective teacher communicates the importance or relevance of specific content to students and views the topics he or she teaches as interesting, meaningful, and important. Research has shown that a teacher's intensity and enthusiasm is positively associated with students' energy, engagement, and achievement (Armento, 1978; Bettencourt, Gillett, Gall, & Hull, 1983; Coats & Smidchens, 1966; Land, 1980; Marzano, 2018; Mastin, 1963; McConnell, 1977; Rosenshine, 1970; Williams & Ware, 1976, 1977; Wyckoff, 1973). Intensity involves directly stating the importance of content to students. Enthusiasm involves viewing a topic as interesting, meaningful, and important and communicating those views to students while studying the topic (Good & Brophy, 2003).

There are eight strategies in this element.

1. Direct statements about the importance of content
2. Explicit connections
3. Nonlinguistic representations
4. Personal stories
5. Verbal and nonverbal signals
6. Humor
7. Quotations
8. Movie and film clips

The following sections will explore each strategy to provide you with guidelines to effectively implement this element. Read through each before creating a plan for your classroom. Teachers may use the strategies individually or in combination. Remember, these are not merely activities to be checked off; they are methods of creating a practice that combines your art with the science of demonstrating intensity and enthusiasm. Reflect on your use of each strategy by filling out the "Strategy Reflection Log" on page 331.

Direct Statements About the Importance of Content

Students frequently become more engaged during class if they understand the relevance of the lesson as it applies to their own lives. To help students understand why they are learning the content, the teacher can incorporate direct statements about the importance of specific content into his or her lessons. Often, these statements depend on real-world examples of content knowledge from outside of the classroom. For example, before a unit on geometry, a teacher might explain how geometry plays a role in various professions such as fashion design and architecture. Consider the following questions when trying to get students to understand the relevance of a lesson.

- What careers use this content?
- How do those careers use this content?
- What college subjects require this content?
- Which college courses require this content?
- What previous knowledge does this content rely on?
- What later learning does this content enable?

Explicit Connections

A teacher may draw explicit connections between content and the real world in order to make the content more exciting or relevant for students. When making explicit connections, the teacher may choose to relate the content to a student's life or to current events. Creating explicit connections between content and students' interests requires a teacher to know a little bit about each student's interests, hobbies, or previous life experiences. For example, when teaching about organic molecules, a science teacher might relate consumption of carbohydrates, proteins, and fats to sports and discuss ways a student's diet can maximize his or her athletic performance (like eating extra carbohydrates two days before a marathon). However, this would be most effective in boosting engagement if multiple student athletes are present in class. When connecting content to a current event, a teacher should assess students' familiarity with local, national, or global events and the degree to which they find specific events relevant to their lives. Students could answer the following questions in regard to such a lesson (Marzano Research, 2016).

- What do I think I know about the content?
- What do I hope to know about the content after the unit?
- Which of my interests relate to this content?
- How might this content relate to my life?
- How might this content relate to the real world?

Nonlinguistic Representations

Nonlinguistic representations commonly take the form of graphic organizers, pictographs, flow charts, or diagrams. A teacher can use these visual elements to increase students' interest in the material and help them visualize connections or patterns in the content they might not have recognized previously. Nonlinguistic representations also provide a teacher with an opportunity to model his or her own interest in the content and to make relevant real-world connections. For example, during a mathematics lesson on triangulation, a teacher could provide images of navigational tools and maps that ancient mariners might have used to plot courses in open water, then explain why he or she finds these tools to be fascinating.

Following are methods for nonlinguistic representation.

- **The actual object:** If a term is concrete and easy to depict, simply sketch a picture of it.
- **A symbol for the term:** If a term is abstract, sketch a symbol that represents the term.
- **An example of the term:** If a term is abstract, sketch an example of the term.
- **A cartoon with a character using the term:** If a term is abstract, use speech bubbles to show how a character in a cartoon might use the term.
- **A graphic for the term:** If a term is abstract, sketch a graphic that depicts the meaning of the term.

Personal Stories

The teacher tells personal stories about the content to make it more accessible to students. The teacher might recall and retell his or her own reactions to the content, identify content that was difficult to understand at first, or explain why content provided important personal insights. The teacher might also invite students to tell stories about their personal connections to content. For example, a teacher might talk about his or her feelings upon finishing reading the short story "The Lottery" by Shirley Jackson and relate the story to other instances that have evoked similar feelings. Teachers can consider the following questions when planning for this strategy (Marzano Research, 2016).

- When did you first learn the content?
- Was the content easy or difficult for you to learn? Why?
- What memories do you associate with the content?
- What images do you associate with the content?
- What people do you associate with the content?

- What feelings do you associate with the content?
- When have you used the content in your life?

Verbal and Nonverbal Signals

The teacher uses verbal signals such as the volume and tone of voice, verbal emphasis on specific words or phrases, pausing to build anticipation and excitement, and the rate of speech to communicate intensity and enthusiasm to students. The teacher can also communicate intensity and enthusiasm nonverbally by smiling, gesturing, making eye contact, and moving around the room while teaching. Consider the following verbal and nonverbal signals (Marzano Research, 2016).

Verbal Signals

Verbal signals include:

- Variation of the volume of the voice
- Variation of the speed of speaking
- Variation of the pitch and tone of the voice
- Pausing to build anticipation
- Emphasis on specific words and phrases
- Repetition of specific words and phrases

Nonverbal Signals

Facial expression and body language can cue nonverbal signals.

Facial expression:

- Direct eye contact with students
- Raised eyebrows
- Widely opened eyes
- Smiling

Body language:

- Clapping, thumbs up, high fives, and other signs of approval
- Movement around the classroom
- Keeping body faced toward students
- Large arm gestures and motions

Humor

Depending on a teacher's personality and instructional style, he or she might show a funny political cartoon or video, direct jokes at him- or herself, use silly quotes or voices, or point out absurdities in a textbook, film, or article to demonstrate enthusiasm for a topic. To avoid unnecessary theatrics, teachers should take care to use humor appropriately, strategically, and in moderation. For example, when teaching grammar, a teacher might find humorous examples of misspelled words or instances when incorrect grammar changes the meaning of phrases. The teacher would present these examples before or after the lesson as a way to emphasize the importance of the content while simultaneously creating a lighthearted classroom atmosphere.

Consider the following when using humor.

- **Students' age and maturity:** When incorporating humor into the classroom, teachers should take into account students' ages and maturity levels to determine whether certain humorous examples are appropriate.
- **Students' background knowledge:** Use of humor will not boost students' engagement if the students do not have the proper background knowledge to understand the joke.
- **Inappropriate humor:** Teachers should avoid all humor that relies on biased speech (for example, racism, sexism, or ableism) as the punchline. Teachers should also avoid sexually explicit

references when using humor. If a teacher chooses to incorporate humorous videos or cartoons into a lesson, the teacher should take care to screen the media before showing them to students.

- **Role modeling:** When using self-directed humor, teachers should consider whether or not they would want their students mimicking the behavior or directing that type of humor toward others. Furthermore, when using humor with an individual student, teachers should consider how the humor or responses from the class might affect the student.
- **Reaction to students' inappropriate humor:** If a teacher overhears students using hurtful humor, he or she should intervene and explicitly outline why the students' comments are disrespectful or inappropriate. If the students' behavior stems from the teacher's humor used in the classroom, he or she should address his or her comments to the class as needed.

Quotations

The teacher uses quotations to add context to the content being presented. For quotations that are relevant to content, teachers might search for quotations by relevant historical figures or about the topic being taught. The teacher may also choose to incorporate quotations related to specific qualities or dispositions he or she wants students to have such as determination, inspiration, curiosity, or respect. For example, before an assessment on the American Civil War, the teacher might present a quote by Abraham Lincoln that she finds either inspiring or relevant to the content on the test.

There are many websites on the internet that provide libraries of quotations that teachers can search or browse by subject or author. A few such websites follow.

- www.quotationspage.com
- www.quotegarden.com
- www.brainyquote.com
- www.thinkexist.com
- www.wikiquote.com
- www.searchquotes.com

Movie and Film Clips

Teachers can use video clips of movies, documentaries, and news stories to help students gain new perspectives on content and connect content to real-world events and situations. For example, when teaching *The Odyssey*, an English instructor might play clips from *O Brother, Where Art Thou?* at the beginning of the unit and have students jot down their thoughts. After finishing *The Odyssey*, the teacher could play the same clips (or the entirety of the film) and facilitate a class discussion about how the movie relates to different parts of Homer's epic poem. Additionally, students could also make their own movies and broadcasts that connect the content to their lives.

Figure 7.9 provides a template for a permission request form.

Monitoring Element 27

Specific student responses and behaviors allow the teacher to determine whether this element is being implemented effectively and producing the desired effects.

- Students say the teacher likes the content and likes teaching.
- Students' attention levels increase in response to the teacher's interest and enthusiasm.

Use this list to monitor student responses to element 27.

To monitor your own use of this element, use the scale in figure 7.10 in combination with the reproducible "Tracking Teacher Actions: Demonstrating Intensity and Enthusiasm" (page 228). As with other proficiency scales, level 3 or higher is the goal.

Permission Request Form

Dear parent or guardian,

Teachers are required to obtain permission from parents before screening movies to students. For this unit, I would like to show the film ________________________________, which is rated _____. Proper discretion will be used when screening the film to students to ensure that the content is appropriate for the age and maturity levels of students. I would like to show this film because it relates to our lesson on ____.

If you have any questions about the content of the film, do not hesitate to ask.

Thank you for your cooperation.

Sincerely,

Teacher name: ____________________________

Class: ____________________________________

— —

Student name: ____

Class section: ______________________________ Movie: ______________________________

__ Yes, my son or daughter has my permission to view the film.

__ No, my son or daughter does not have my permission to view the film.*

Parent signature: __________________________

Parent name: ______________________________

Students who do not receive permission to watch a film will be provided with alternative academic activities.

Source: Marzano Research, 2016.

Figure 7.9: Permission request form template.

Visit **go.SolutionTree.com/instruction** *for a free reproducible version of this figure.*

4 Innovating	I adapt behaviors and create new strategies for unique student needs and situations.
3 Applying	I demonstrate intensity and enthusiasm, and I monitor the extent to which students' engagement increases.
2 Developing	I demonstrate intensity and enthusiasm, but I do not monitor the effect on students.
1 Beginning	I use the strategies and behaviors associated with this element incorrectly or with parts missing.
0 Not Using	I am unaware of strategies and behaviors associated with this element.

Figure 7.10: Self-rating scale for element 27—Demonstrating intensity and enthusiasm.

The following examples describe what each level of the scale might look like in the classroom.

- **Not Using (0):** A teacher appears bored by the content he teaches. When speaking about the content, he does not change his intonation or add interesting elements to the presentation.
- **Beginning (1):** A teacher can explain the relevance of the content being taught, but only when students prompt her. She incorporates movie and film clips into her lesson but does not tie them back into the content being taught.
- **Developing (2):** A teacher exhibits enthusiasm for her subject area but does so without paying attention to how her show of excitement affects her students.
- **Applying (3):** A teacher uses a variety of strategies to show his enthusiasm for the content he is teaching. Furthermore, by assessing student engagement before, during, and after specific strategies, he is able to see that the incorporation of humor, personal stories, and direct statements about the importance of content into lessons makes students more enthusiastic about the material being taught.
- **Innovating (4):** A teacher fluently uses various strategies to show her intensity and enthusiasm for the material being taught. When a specific student queries the relevance of content, she tailors explanations of the importance of the content to that student using humor, prior knowledge about the student, and her own previous experiences learning the content.

Element 28: Presenting Unusual Information

An effective teacher uses unusual or intriguing information about the content in a manner that enhances student engagement. Research has shown that missing or unknown information captures students' attention (Jensen, 2005; Kirsch, 1999). Teachers can use unusual information that is unrelated to the content to capture students' attention at the beginning of a lesson (Marzano, 2007). Unusual information related to the content can increase students' engagement during a lesson (Jonas, 2004).

There are six strategies within this element.

1. Teacher-presented information
2. Webquests
3. Fast facts
4. Believe it or not
5. History files
6. Guest speakers and first-hand consultants

The following sections will explore each strategy to provide you with guidelines to effectively implement this element. Read through each before creating a plan for your classroom. Teachers may use the strategies individually or in combination. Remember, these are not merely activities to be checked off; they are methods of creating a practice that combines your art with the science of presenting unusual information. Reflect on your use of each strategy by filling out the "Strategy Reflection Log" on page 331.

Teacher-Presented Information

The teacher can present unusual or intriguing information to capture students' attention. Facts related to the content are preferred, but any unusual information can attract students' attention and help them feel interested in what the teacher is about to say. When planning this strategy, teachers should jot down the most interesting aspects of the content, think of ways to capture students' attention at the start of the lesson, and consider information to re-engage students who get bored or lose interest.

Webquests

Students explore the internet and find a range of obscure but interesting facts and ideas associated with the content being studied. Typically, webquests involve a teacher-designed learning path. That is, students visit specific links or websites provided by the teacher to answer a set of questions. Older students may use a more open-ended approach, but teachers of any age group should be careful to ensure that students stay on task when using the internet.

A webquest, as it will be presented to students, typically has six components.

1. **Introduction:** Explains general information about the webquest and its purpose or sets up an imaginary situation as a frame for the webquest to capture students' interest
2. **Task:** Presents the ultimate goal of the webquest
3. **Sources:** Lists links to online resources where students can find the information needed to complete the task
4. **Process:** Describes a clear set of steps that students should follow to complete the task
5. **Guidance:** Provides students with a structure, such as a set of questions or a graphic organizer, for organizing the information they find
6. **Conclusion:** Concludes the webquest by reminding students what they have learned and prompting them to reflect or make connections to other knowledge

Fast Facts

Students quickly share the most unusual (but factual) information they have discovered about a particular topic. To use this strategy, the teacher must provide time for students to research information about the topic being addressed. An engaging activity is for students to write down the facts and details they find, circle the most interesting fact, and summarize the fact into a short headline (Marzano Research, 2016).

Believe It or Not

Students create an electronic database of unusual or little-known information about the content they are studying. This can be preserved from one year to the next, with each class reading previous contributions, correcting misconceptions where appropriate, and adding their own unusual information.

When creating the database of unusual information, teachers should make sure that each entry includes the following information.

- Content area
- Topic
- Piece of unusual information
- Space to add supplemental information

When students submit interesting information, their submissions should consist of the content area, the topic, and the piece of unusual information. For example, a student might submit the following entry.

Content area: Science
Topic: Reptiles
Did you know? The black mamba snake can move at fourteen miles per hour!

When students are looking through the database, they can add supplemental information to an entry if they find a fact that they know more about. If students discover a misconception or mistake in the database, they can correct it.

History Files

Students research different historical perceptions in the content areas they are studying. For example, medical facts have changed a great deal since the time of Hippocrates, and comparing one fact (such as the role of blood in the body) throughout history can yield new insights for students.

Following are sample topics.

- Attitudes toward indigenous cultures
- Child labor
- Children's education
- Dinosaurs
- Diseases
- Intelligence
- International relations
- Leadership
- Marriage
- Nature and the environment
- Nutrition
- Psychology
- The role of technology
- The shape of the Earth
- The solar system
- Space exploration
- Treatment of animals
- Use of controlled substances
- Women's rights

Guest Speakers and First-Hand Consultants

Students learn about real-world applications of the content by listening to guests share experiences from their careers. Guest speakers add novelty to the class routine but also provide a realistic view of how the learning taking place in the classroom can benefit the students outside the school walls.

A worksheet like figure 7.11 can help students prepare for a guest speaker.

Get Ready for a Guest Speaker

A guest speaker will be visiting our class on (date) ________________.

Our guest speaker's name is ________________.

This person is going to help us learn more about the topic of ________________, which we've been discussing in class.

Our guest speaker knows a lot about this topic because ________________.

To prepare for the speaker's visit, please respond to the following prompts.

What I already know about this topic:

What I still want to know about this topic:

Three or more questions I could ask our guest speaker:

Source: Marzano Research, 2016.

Figure 7.11: Worksheet to get ready for a guest speaker.

Visit **go.SolutionTree.com/instruction** *for a free reproducible version of this figure.*

Monitoring Element 28

Specific student responses and behaviors allow the teacher to determine whether this element is being implemented effectively and producing the desired effects.

- Student engagement levels increase with the presentation of unusual information.
- Students can explain how the unusual information makes the content more interesting.
- Students ask questions about the unusual information that is presented.

Use this list to monitor student responses to element 28.

To monitor your own use of this element, use the scale in figure 7.12 in combination with the reproducible "Tracking Teacher Actions: Presenting Unusual Information" (page 229). As with other proficiency scales, level 3 or higher is the goal.

4 Innovating	I adapt behaviors and create new strategies for unique student needs and situations.
3 Applying	I use unusual or intriguing information to capture students' attention, and I monitor the extent to which this information enhances engagement.
2 Developing	I use unusual or intriguing information to capture students' attention, but I do not monitor the effect on students.
1 Beginning	I use the strategies and behaviors associated with this element incorrectly or with parts missing.
0 Not Using	I am unaware of strategies and behaviors associated with this element.

Figure 7.12: Self-rating scale for element 28—Presenting unusual information.

The following examples describe what each level of the scale might look like in the classroom.

- **Not Using (0):** A teacher knows interesting facts about the content but doesn't share them with her class because they are not strictly relevant to what students need to know.
- **Beginning (1):** A teacher sometimes begins lessons with an unusual piece of information but does not select information that is related to the content of the lesson.
- **Developing (2):** A teacher uses intriguing information at the beginning of lessons and throughout her presentations of content. However, she does so without noting whether student engagement has been affected.
- **Applying (3):** A teacher presents unusual information at the start of class to grab students' attention. When he notices his students getting bored or losing interest during the course of the lesson, he re-engages them by introducing an intriguing fact or story.
- **Innovating (4):** A teacher uses unusual information to spark students' attention at the beginning of a lesson and to increase waning engagement levels throughout class. Occasionally, however, he will find that a particular lesson does not hold students' attention, even with the unexpected facts he presents. In these cases, he has students briefly research the topic using their iPads independently or in small groups to find their own unusual information and present it to the class.

Element 29: Using Friendly Controversy

An effective teacher uses friendly controversy techniques to maintain student engagement. Research has shown that mild controversy and mild competition have a positive influence on students' learning (Cahill, Prins, Weber, & McGaugh, 1994; Jensen, 2005). Mild controversy involves asking students to express their opinions on an issue and then resolve discrepancies between individuals' perspectives (Good & Brophy, 2003). Mild competition involves competing in the spirit of fun, without embarrassment or consequences for losing (Epstein & Harackiewicz, 1992; Moriarity, Douglas, Punch, & Hattie, 1995; Reeve & Deci, 1996).

There are nine strategies within this element.

1. Friendly controversy
2. Class vote
3. Seminars
4. Expert opinions
5. Opposite point of view
6. Diagrams comparing perspectives
7. Lincoln-Douglas debate
8. Town-hall meeting
9. Legal model

The following sections will explore each strategy to provide you with guidelines to effectively implement this element. Read through each before creating a plan for your classroom. Teachers may use the strategies individually or in combination. Remember, these are not merely activities to be checked off; they are methods of creating a practice that combines your art with the science of using friendly controversy. Reflect on your use of each strategy by filling out the "Strategy Reflection Log" on page 331.

Friendly Controversy

Students explain and defend their positions on topics about which they disagree. The teacher asks students to follow specific guidelines when engaging in friendly controversy. Guidelines ensure that students feel free to disagree with others but do so respectfully and allow for everyone to express their opinions. Provide students with the guidelines for using friendly controversy (Marzano Research, 2016).

- You may criticize ideas but not people.
- When you state your opinion, try to provide evidence or reasons for it.
- Even if you are anxious to say something, give others the chance to finish speaking.
- As others speak, listen with the intent to understand why they think their opinion is accurate, rather than just waiting for your turn to talk.
- Speak calmly and respectfully. Avoid raising your voice or using a rude tone.
- Ask questions if you do not understand another person's point.
- Disagree using respectful language and explain why you disagree.
- Be willing to take responsibility for your interactions.

Class Vote

Students vote on a particular issue. Before and after the vote, students discuss the merits of various positions. The teacher might ask students to vote again after the final discussion. To incorporate movement, the teacher might ask students to stand on a particular side of the classroom to represent their initial vote. Undecided students stand in the middle of the room. After each side presents arguments for its point of view, students have the opportunity to switch sides, and the teacher asks undecided students to make a decision.

A tracking sheet, like figure 7.13, can help students keep track of the votes.

Class Vote Tracking Sheet

Topic of vote: ______________________________

Initial Vote

Options				
Number of Votes				

Record important points raised during class discussion of the topic.

Final Vote

Options				
Number of Votes				

What changed between the two votes? Why?

Source: Marzano Research, 2016.

Figure 7.13: Class vote tracking sheet.

Visit **go.SolutionTree.com/instruction** *for a free reproducible version of this figure.*

Seminars

In groups, students explore a text, video, or other resource that expresses highly opinionated perspectives about a key issue or topic related to the curriculum content. Groups contain three to five members with specific roles, such as moderator, recorder, time keeper, synthesizer, and group representative. After discussion in small groups, the whole class joins together to discuss. All groups might explore the same resource, or each group might investigate a different perspective on the same topic.

Figure 7.14 provides examples of job cards you might use for this strategy.

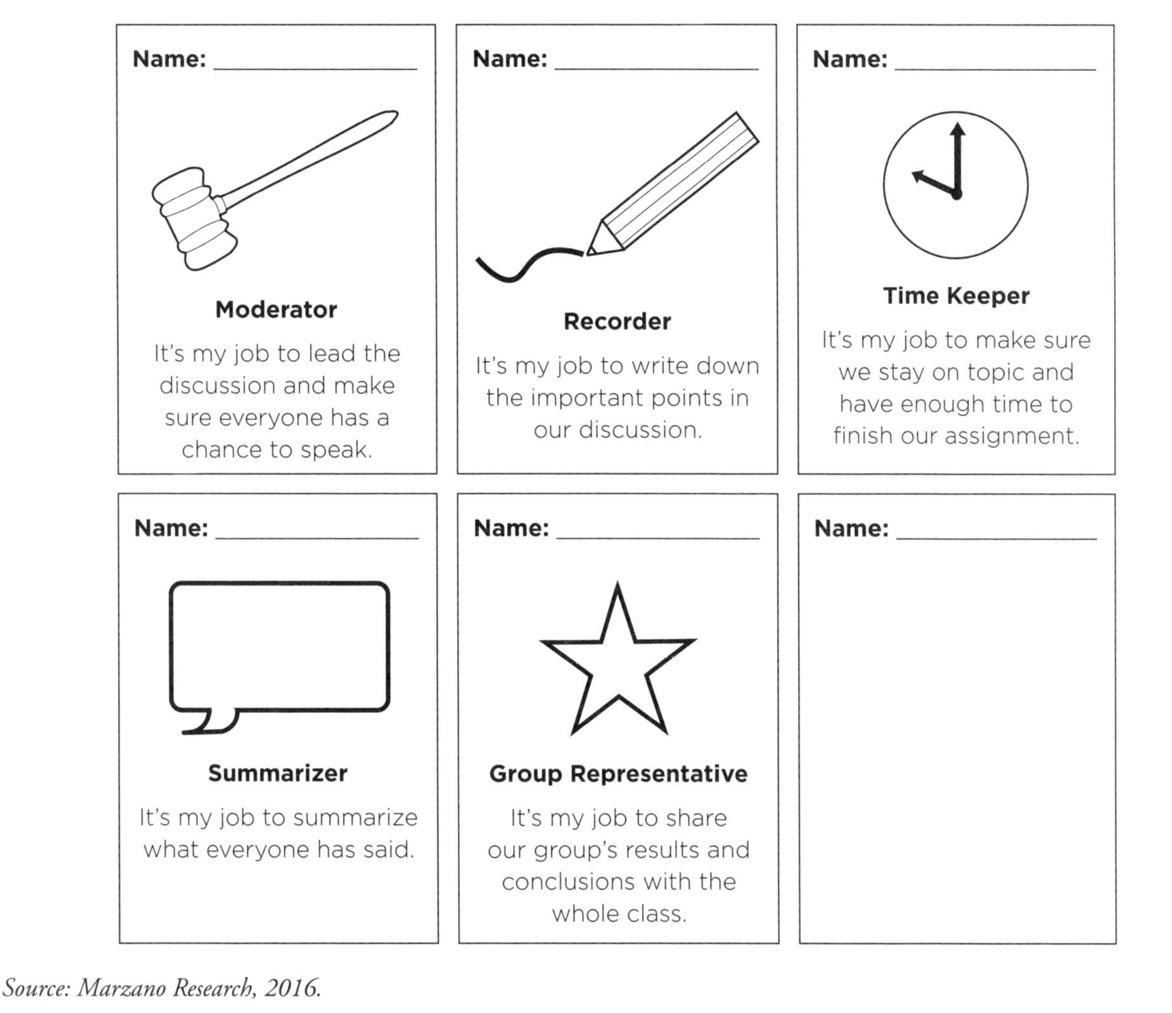

Source: Marzano Research, 2016.

Figure 7.14: Seminar job cards.

Visit **go.SolutionTree.com/instruction** *for a free reproducible version of this figure.*

Expert Opinions

Students research the opinions of experts who hold contrasting perspectives and points of view about a particular issue or topic. The teacher might use this strategy in a cooperative jigsaw where students each research a particular researcher or thought leader and then report back to the whole group about what they discovered. The class then discusses the merits of the various perspectives and the validity (or lack thereof) of a particular thinker's ideas, positions, and evidence. Have students consider people who are experts on the topic, select one to research in depth and explain why they chose their expert, and record the person's ideas, opinions, and positions on the topic. Students should be careful to include sources for their information as well.

Opposite Point of View

Students defend the opposite point of view from the one they agree with or support. This can help students with overly dogmatic or rigid attitudes explore the nuances of a particular topic or issue and can reinforce the process of providing evidence to support a claim. They can consider what they believe about the topic, write down a point of view different from their own, and jot reasons and evidence that support that point of view.

Diagrams Comparing Perspectives

Students can use a Venn diagram to compare various points of view. The diagram can highlight similarities and differences between two or three ideas. Visit **go.SolutionTree.com/instruction** for the reproducible "Diagramming Perspectives" for a Venn diagram you can use for this strategy.

Lincoln-Douglas Debate

Students practice assuming affirmative or negative positions on an issue and giving supporting evidence for their position. The teacher chooses two teams to debate opposing sides of a specific policy or issue. One side argues in favor of the policy or issue (affirmative team), and the other side argues against it (negative team). Each side gets the opportunity to make an opening argument, cross-examine the opposing side, and present a rebuttal. After the debate, each team evaluates its performance as a group, and students self-evaluate their own performance as a member of the team.

A worksheet like figure 7.15 can help guide students' use of this strategy.

Town-Hall Meeting

Diana E. Hess (2009) originally developed this strategy in her book *Controversy in the Classroom: The Democratic Power of Discussion*. To help students see a complex issue from multiple perspectives, the teacher facilitates a discussion among several parties with varying perspectives, as might be seen in a local town-hall meeting. First, designate specific roles that students assume during a town-hall meeting. Roles can be based on the people or groups most likely to have strong opinions about an issue or most likely to be affected by a new policy or change in existing policy. Then assign students to each group and consider how to structure the discussion. The students participate in an open discussion while the teacher mediates. Students stay in character for their respective roles and argue from that point of view for the duration of the discussion. The students then participate in a debriefing in which they evaluate their own performances and the discussion as a whole.

Legal Model

Hess (2009) also developed the legal model, in which students critically examine how Supreme Court decisions affect policy. They form their opinions and arguments based on textual evidence from past Supreme Court cases. Each student completes a "ticket" or outline of the essential arguments that each Supreme Court justice made in the case being studied. Students must complete their tickets in order to participate in the discussion and may use them throughout the discussion as a reference guide. The teacher leads a discussion of the case being studied. Using questions that focus on the facts, opinions, and ideas of the case, the teacher helps students articulate their arguments based on the textual evidence they have read. At the end, students participate in a debriefing to evaluate their individual and group performance. When planning for this strategy, consider the following questions (Marzano Research, 2016).

- How does this case relate to the content students are learning?
- What are the facts of this case?
- What are the opinions involved in this case?
- What are the important ideas exemplified by this case?
- What aspects of the case will I ask students to focus on during discussion?

Debate Reflection Guide

Name: ______________________ Date: ______________

Topic: ______________________

Complete this section by discussing the prompts and questions with your team.

Summarize your team's argument.

Summarize the other team's argument.

How well did your team prepare for the debate?

How well did your team respond to and refute the other team's points?

What was the best thing your team did?

What is something your team could do better next time?

Complete this section on your own.

What was your role on the team?

How well did you prepare for your role?

How well did you execute your role?

What was the best thing you did?

What is something you could do better next time?

How well did your team work together as a whole?

Source: Marzano Research, 2016.

Figure 7.15: Debate reflection guide.

Visit **go.SolutionTree.com/instruction** *for a free reproducible version of this figure.*

Monitoring Element 29

Specific student responses and behaviors allow the teacher to determine whether this element is being implemented effectively and producing the desired effects.

- Students readily engage in the friendly controversy activities.
- Students describe friendly controversy activities as *stimulating*, *fun*, and *interesting*.
- Students can explain how the friendly controversy activities help them better understand the content.

Use this list to monitor student responses to element 29.

To monitor your own use of this element, use the scale in figure 7.16 in combination with the reproducible "Tracking Teacher Actions: Using Friendly Controversy" (page 230). As with other proficiency scales, level 3 or higher is the goal.

4 Innovating	I adapt behaviors and create new strategies for unique student needs and situations.
3 Applying	I use friendly controversy techniques to maintain student engagement, and I monitor the effect on students' engagement.
2 Developing	I use friendly controversy techniques to maintain student engagement, but I do not monitor the effect on students.
1 Beginning	I use the strategies and behaviors associated with this element incorrectly or with parts missing.
0 Not Using	I am unaware of strategies and behaviors associated with this element.

Figure 7.16: Self-rating scale for element 29—Using friendly controversy.

The following examples describe what each level of the scale might look like in the classroom.

- **Not Using (0):** A teacher avoids controversy in her classroom because she is afraid it will lead to conflict.
- **Beginning (1):** A teacher allows students to express their differing opinions on various topics, but he does not provide any structured activities to encourage deeper interactions.
- **Developing (2):** A teacher frequently has her students engage in structured debates and other perspective-taking activities, but she does not specifically do anything to track whether or not these activities are having their intended effect.
- **Applying (3):** A teacher uses friendly controversy in his classroom and monitors signs of student engagement to make sure the strategies are having the desired effect.
- **Innovating (4):** A teacher uses structured controversy activities and encourages informal debates during class discussions. It becomes clear, however, that some students disengage during informal debates because they do not feel comfortable participating in these less structured interactions. In order to engage all students, the teacher provides added structure for these students by calling on them specifically to give them a chance to speak and by displaying useful sentence stems on the board to help them phrase their points.

Element 30: Using Academic Games

An effective teacher uses academic games and inconsequential competition to maintain student engagement. Research has shown that games and puzzles are associated with increased attention (Jensen, 2005; Kirsch, 1999). The principle of clozentropy postulates that games and puzzles hold students' attention because of an innate human desire to fill in missing information (Broadhurst & Darnell, 1965; Darnell, 1970, 1972; Ebbinghaus, 1987; Taylor, 1953; Weiner, 1967). Another theory states that humans pay attention to games and puzzles because we seek to decrease the discrepancy between what we predict will happen and what actually happens (Weiner, 1967).

There are eight strategies within this element.

1. What Is the Question?
2. Name That Category
3. Talk a Mile a Minute
4. Classroom Feud
5. Which One Doesn't Belong?
6. Inconsequential competition
7. Questions into games
8. Vocabulary review games

The following sections will explore each strategy to provide you with guidelines to effectively implement this element. Read through each before creating a plan for your classroom. Teachers may use the strategies individually or in combination. Remember, these are not merely activities to be checked off; they are methods of creating a practice that combines your art with the science of using academic games. Reflect on your use of each strategy by filling out the "Strategy Reflection Log" on page 331.

What Is the Question?

In this strategy, the teacher creates and displays a matrix with content-based categories across the top and point values (generally 100, 200, 300, 400, and 500) down the side. This can be done using a bulletin board, an overhead transparency, or PowerPoint. The teacher also creates clues (words, pictures, or a combination of the two) and puts one in each matrix cell, with more difficult clues corresponding to higher point values.

A student or team selects a category and point value. The teacher reveals the corresponding clue. The student answering must state a question for which the clue would be the answer. The teacher decides if a student's question represents an adequate understanding of the concept or term. If the student answers correctly, his or her team gets the points for the question and the same student or team picks the next category and level. If the student answers incorrectly, a student on the other team gets a chance to answer. If that student answers correctly, that team gets the points and the next pick; if incorrect, no points are awarded and the original team picks next.

Figure 7.17 provides a sample board for this strategy.

	Angles	The Coordinate Plane	Polygons and Area	Triangle Relationships	Quadrilaterals
100	These types of angles add up to 90°, forming a right angle.	?	?	?	?
200	?	?	?	?	?
300	?	?	?	?	?
400	?	?	?	?	?
500	?	?	?	?	?

Figure 7.17: Sample board for What Is the Question?

Name That Category

Using this strategy, the teacher creates a game board that looks like a pyramid divided into sections with various categories and point values. The teacher organizes students into teams with one clue giver and one or more guessers. Teams sit so that clue givers face the game board and guessers face the opposite direction. The teacher reveals one category on the game board (the rest remain covered). The clue giver must list words that fit in that category until teammates correctly identify the category name. As soon as one team has correctly identified the first category, the teacher reveals the next one.

Figure 7.18 (page 208) provides a sample board for this strategy.

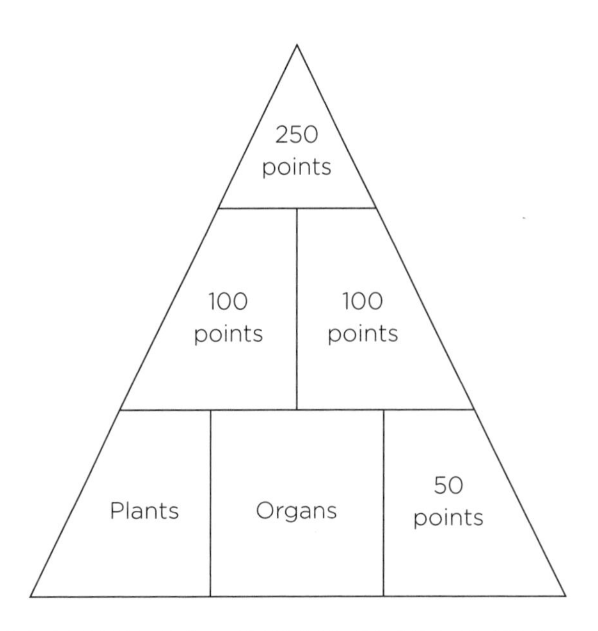

Figure 7.18: Sample board for Name That Category.

Talk a Mile a Minute

The teacher prepares a set of cards, each with a category and list of items that fit in that category (for example, the shapes category card might have *square*, *circle*, *rectangle*, *triangle*, *right triangle*, *oval*, and *diamond* listed as words). The teacher organizes students into teams, and each team designates one team member as the talker. The teacher gives a card to each team. The talker tries to get his or her team to say each of the words by quickly describing them. The talker cannot use any of the words in the category title or any rhyming words. The talker keeps talking until the team members identify all of the terms on the card. If team members are having trouble with a particular term, the talker can skip it and come back to it later. The first few teams to identify all the terms receive points. Afterward, the teacher might lead a discussion of which words were hard to guess and how the successful talkers represented those words.

Figure 7.19 provides a sample card for this strategy.

Reptiles	
Sea turtle	Boa constrictor
Tortoise	Chameleon
Crocodile	Gecko
Alligator	Gila monster
Rattlesnake	

Figure 7.19: Sample card for Talk a Mile a Minute.

A student might help his or her teammate guess the term *boa constrictor* by saying, "This animal has scales, does not have legs, and kills its prey by squeezing it."

Classroom Feud

In Classroom Feud, the teacher constructs at least one question for every student in the class. Questions can be multiple choice, fill in the blank, or short answer. The teacher organizes students into teams, and they take turns being the responder for their team. The teacher presents a question to a responder who has fifteen seconds to confer with team members and identify the team's answer. The responder tells the team's answer to the teacher. If correct, that team receives a point. If incorrect, the opposing team has the opportunity to answer. That team's most recent responder acts as responder for his or her group and has fifteen seconds to confer and answer the question. If correct, that team receives a point. If incorrect, no point is awarded. When every student on both teams has functioned as the responder, the team with the most points wins. Visit **go.SolutionTree.com/instruction** for the reproducible "Classroom Feud Rules and Procedures."

Which One Doesn't Belong?

In this strategy, the teacher creates word groups containing three terms that are similar and one term that is different. Students work independently or in groups. The teacher displays one word group at a time. Students have a set amount of time to pick out the term that does not belong and write down why they think that term is different. This game can be formal (keeping track of points) or informal (the teacher pauses during a lesson to offer four words to the class and ask them to identify which one doesn't belong).

Following are examples of word sets for this strategy. The word that does not belong is italicized. The explanation of why it is considered different appears in parentheses.

- big, blue, sad, *quickly* (The first three words are adjectives, while the last is an adverb.)
- snowflake, *chapter*, barnyard, everyday (All are compound words except one.)
- assonance, consonance, alliteration, *allegory* (The first three are poetic techniques related to sound.)
- centimeter, inch, *gram*, meter (Three measure length while the other measures weight.)
- *toys*, food, water, shelter (Toys are not a requirement for life.)
- electrical energy, *chemical energy*, sound, thermal energy (All are types of kinetic energy except chemical energy, which is potential.)
- dog, horse, *lion*, sheep (Three are domestic animals; one is wild.)
- legislative, executive, *autocratic*, judicial (Three describe the branches of U.S. government, but autocratic does not.)

Inconsequential Competition

The teacher can use any type of inconsequential competition (including academic games like those previously described) to increase student engagement. The teacher should clearly delineate roles in student groups and change group membership systematically (for example, after each unit) so that students with a high degree of content mastery are regularly paired with those who have lower content mastery. In this way, all students can experience winning and losing. The teacher might consider giving a tangible reward to the top two or more teams at the end of a unit. Teachers can use this strategy to review vocabulary terms, spelling words, literary terms and elements, historical facts, and dates. It can also highlight different perspectives and points of view, key content, competing theories and hypotheses, and different approaches to mathematical problem solving. When planning for inconsequential competition, consider key terms and concepts to create games around, structured games to use around the content, and opportunities for impromptu games during the lesson or unit (Marzano Research, 2016).

Questions Into Games

The teacher turns questions into impromptu games by forming students into four equally sized groups before asking a series of questions during a lesson. Each group can name itself, if desired. After the teacher asks a question, group members talk together for one minute and record their answer on a response card. On the teacher's signal, each group holds up its answer. The teacher keeps a record of the groups that gave the correct answer. After the series of questions, the teacher acknowledges the team with the highest point total.

Provide students with a worksheet like figure 7.20 to use with this strategy.

Tracking Sheet for Questions Into Games

Tally the points each team receives for correct answers in the following boxes.

Team 1: ______________________ (name)	Team 2: ______________________ (name)
Team 3: ______________________ (name)	Team 4: ______________________ (name)

Students on Team 1:

Students on Team 2:

Students on Team 3:

Students on Team 4:

Source: Marzano Research, 2016.

Figure 7.20: Tracking sheet for questions into games.

Visit **go.SolutionTree.com/instruction** *for a free reproducible version of this figure.*

Vocabulary Review Games

The teacher can also use games to review vocabulary with students. Games are an important element of a vocabulary program, as they help students solidify and apply their understanding of terms. One resource for further game structures is the book *Vocabulary Games for the Classroom* by Lindsay Carleton and Robert J. Marzano (2010), which contains thirteen games for vocabulary development. Teachers can also find many vocabulary games online.

Figure 7.21 describes some games from *Vocabulary Games for the Classroom* (Carleton & Marzano, 2010).

Game	Description
Word Harvest	A relay game for lower-elementary grade levels in which students race to "harvest" and categorize vocabulary terms from a word wall
Name It!	A relay game for lower-elementary grade levels in which students choose pictures from a bucket and try to describe them in one word
Puzzle Stories	A game for upper-elementary grade levels in which students rush to assemble puzzles and write narratives based on the revealed image
Two of Kind	A Memory-inspired game for lower- and upper-elementary grade levels in which students match homonyms (for example, flower and flour)
Opposites Attract	A Memory-inspired game for lower- and upper-elementary grade levels in which students match antonyms (for example, multiply and divide)
Magic Letter, Magic Word	A game for lower- and upper-elementary grade levels in which students complete a fill-in-the-blank clue using the first letter of the word as a hint
Definition, Shmefinition	A Balderdash-inspired game for upper-elementary through high school grade levels in which students create dictionary definitions for unknown terms and guess which definition is correct

Figure 7.21: Sample vocabulary games.

Monitoring Element 30

Specific student responses and behaviors allow the teacher to determine whether this element is being implemented effectively and producing the desired effects.

- Students engage in the academic games enthusiastically.
- Students can describe the content the games focus on.
- Students can explain how the games enhanced their understanding of the content.

Use this list to monitor student responses to element 30.

To monitor your own use of this element, use the scale in figure 7.22 in combination with the reproducible "Tracking Teacher Actions: Using Academic Games" (page 231). As with other proficiency scales, level 3 or higher is the goal.

4 Innovating	I adapt behaviors and create new strategies for unique student needs and situations.
3 Applying	I use academic games and inconsequential competition to maintain student engagement, and I monitor the extent to which students focus on the academic content of the game.
2 Developing	I use academic games and inconsequential competition to maintain student engagement, but I do not monitor the effect on students.
1 Beginning	I use the strategies and behaviors associated with this element incorrectly or with parts missing.
0 Not Using	I am unaware of strategies and behaviors associated with this element.

Figure 7.22: Self-rating scale for element 30—Using academic games.

The following examples describe what each level of the scale might look like in the classroom.

- **Not Using (0):** A teacher worries that his students will be too competitive and so avoids using academic games altogether.
- **Beginning (1):** A teacher uses academic games to help her students review content before an assessment, but she often awards bonus points to the winners, which she uses to raise their grades.
- **Developing (2):** A teacher uses academic games with the intent of increasing student engagement and helping students practice and deepen their knowledge, but she does not try to monitor these outcomes.
- **Applying (3):** A teacher has students play games with the content as a way to help them maintain attention during class and retain the content better. He notices that he has to stop lessons to re-engage students less often, and assessment results indicate that the games are helping students remember the content as well.
- **Innovating (4):** A teacher uses inconsequential competition and monitors student outcomes for increased engagement. She notices that, after several iterations of the same game, some students seem to lose interest. To combat this, she finds new game structures online and rotates through the options to create variety.

Element 31: Providing Opportunities for Students to Talk About Themselves

An effective teacher provides students with opportunities to relate what is being addressed in class to their personal interests. Research has shown that students pay more attention to information that is personally meaningful to them (Csikszentmihalyi, 1990; McCaslin et al., 2006; McCombs, 2001; Roeser, Peck, & Nasir, 2006). If students perceive that information is relevant to their personal goals and self-images, they will take greater interest in it (Marzano, 2007; McCombs, 2001).

There are four strategies within this element.

1. Interest surveys
2. Student learning profiles
3. Life connections
4. Informal linkages during class discussion

The following sections will explore each strategy to provide you with guidelines to effectively implement this element. Read through each before creating a plan for your classroom. Teachers may use the strategies individually or in combination. Remember, these are not merely activities to be checked off; they are methods of creating a practice that combines your art with the science of providing opportunities for students to talk about themselves. Reflect on your use of each strategy by filling out the "Strategy Reflection Log" on page 331.

Interest Surveys

At the beginning of the school year or the beginning of a unit, a teacher should take time to reach out to students and get to know them better. One highly practical method for gathering information about students is an interest survey. These surveys can cover a range of topics such as interests, goals, personal or family history, existing knowledge about the content area, or expectations and desires for class. The teacher might administer an interest survey on the first day of class, then review the survey throughout the year as needed.

When creating a student interest survey, teachers should consider the grade level and subject area they teach and customize their surveys accordingly. To ensure that interest surveys are not overwhelming, teachers should not include more than ten items. Teachers can choose questions from the following list, which is sorted into categories: general education, specific classes, extracurricular activities, and students' personal backgrounds. Visit **go.SolutionTree.com/instruction** for reproducible versions of these questions.

Questions related to general education:

- What is your favorite class? Why?
- What is your least favorite class? Why?
- What class do you find to be the easiest? Why?
- What class do you find to be the most difficult? Why?
- What class do you find to be the most interesting? Why?
- What is a subject you are curious about or would like to learn more about?
- When you encounter a challenge at school, how do you address it?
- What is one aspect of school you find to be challenging?
- What is one aspect of school you find to be rewarding?
- What is one aspect of school you find to be easy?
- What characteristics have your favorite teachers all shared?
- What can a teacher do to ensure that you remain engaged during class?

- What is an activity or assignment from a previous class that you found to be interesting or meaningful? Why?
- What is an activity or assignment from a previous class that you thought you did a good job on? Why?
- What careers seem interesting to you?
- What careers do you think you would be successful in?

Class-specific questions:

- What do you expect to learn in this class?
- What is an area related to this class that you are excited to learn about?
- What do you think you already know about this subject or this unit?
- Why do you think the content in this class is important?
- How do you think this subject relates to your own life?
- What have you previously learned that you think may contribute to your understanding of the content in this class?

Questions related to extracurricular activities:

- When you are not at school, how do you spend your time?
- What is a hobby of yours? Why do you enjoy it?
- Do you belong to any clubs? If so, which ones?
- Do you belong to any sports teams? If so, which ones?
- Do you have a part-time job? If so, what is it, and how often do you work?
- What are things that you are responsible for out of school? How do these responsibilities make you feel?

Questions related to personal background:

- List the members of your immediate family and briefly describe each individual.
- Who would you consider your friends?
- How would you describe yourself?
- How would your friends describe you?
- How would your previous teachers describe you?
- What is your favorite book? Why?
- What is your favorite movie? Why?
- What is your favorite television show? Why?
- What is your favorite sports team? Why?
- If you could travel anywhere in the world, where would you go? Why?
- If you had the chance to have a conversation with anyone (dead or alive), who would it be, and why?
- If you had one wish, how would you use it?
- If you won the lottery, what would you do with the money?
- What is something you think you are good at?
- What is something that you want to get better at?
- What is your favorite type of music, or who is your favorite musical artist? Why?
- What is your favorite food?
- Explain a time you felt proud of your accomplishments.
- Explain a time when hard work has paid off.
- Do you consider yourself introverted or extroverted? (Note: a teacher may need to explain the difference between introversion and extroversion to students before including this item on an interest survey.)
- What is something you consider yourself very knowledgeable about?
- What is an interest that you have that is not related to school?

Student Learning Profiles

The teacher uses student learning profiles to collect self-reported information from students about their preferred learning activities and styles (such as visual, auditory, kinesthetic, analytical, or practical), the circumstances and conditions under which they learn best, and ways in which they prefer to express themselves (for example, writing, oral communication, physical expression, artistic media, and others). The teacher might create student learning profiles using formal inventories or informal discussions and surveys. After a teacher has gathered data using student learning profiles, he or she should use the information to inform his or her interactions with students.

Following are questions you might use to create student learning profiles.

- When learning new material, I prefer to: (a) get a handout with the information on it, (b) have it explained to me by the teacher, or (c) try it out myself.
- When studying, I'm most successful if I: (a) create visual outlines, flashcards, charts, or graphs of the material covered so far, (b) have someone verbally quiz me or repeat my notes out loud, or (c) do something active (like pacing back and forth) while studying.
- What is your preferred type of assignment? (Note: A teacher may choose to tailor this question to provide options for summative assessments, such as giving students a choice between an essay, oral exam, physical expression, or creative project.)
- Do you prefer to work alone, in a pair, in a small group, or in a large group? (However, teachers may also prompt students to explain why they hold these preferences.)
- What sort of activities do you think best help you learn?
- Describe your ideal classroom to learn in.
- Under what circumstances do you find it difficult to focus or learn?

Life Connections

Effective teachers intentionally plan breaks during instructional time so that students can identify and discuss links between the content they're studying and their own personal experiences, hobbies, and interests. Students can look for and explain similarities and differences between their interests and experiences and the content being studied. Students might also complete analogies comparing aspects of their experiences and interests to elements of the content. Lastly, students can create nonlinguistic representations (such as graphic organizers, pictographs, or figures) that express relationships between the content they're studying and their personal interests and experiences.

Provide students with a worksheet like figure 7.23 to guide their use of this strategy.

Informal Linkages During Class Discussion

To create informal linkages between the content and students' lives, teachers should become familiar with students' interests and personal experiences. Identifying why an upcoming unit is important to students' lives will be key to their engagement. As the class discusses certain topics, the teacher can relate the content to his or her existing knowledge about students. However, teachers can also refer to a previously complied list of students' interests if necessary. Once the teacher establishes the link between the content and a student, the teacher should verbally note it. For example, a teacher might say, "Robert, you're interested in astronomy, aren't you? What do you think about the information we just read and the new information about Pluto?" during a science unit on the solar system. Consider the following sentence stem to plan for informal linkages.

"I can relate the content to my student, __________, because of his or her interest in __________. These two things relate because ____."

Life Connections

Name: ______________________________

Class: ______________________________

In class, we are studying:

This content relates to my life because:

My hobby, interest, or personal experience this content reminds me of is:

This content reminds me of this hobby, interest, or personal experience because:

The content is similar to my hobby, interest, or personal experience because:

The content is different from my hobby, interest, or personal experience because:

Use the space below to draw the relationship between your hobby, interest, or personal experience and the content being taught.

Source: Marzano Research, 2016.

Figure 7.23: Worksheet for life connections.

Visit **go.SolutionTree.com/instruction** *for a free reproducible version of this figure.*

Monitoring Element 31

Specific student responses and behaviors allow the teacher to determine whether this element is being implemented effectively and producing the desired effects.

- Students engage in activities that help them make connections between their personal interests and the content.
- Students can explain how making connections between content and their personal interests makes class more interesting and enhances their content knowledge.
- Students describe class as being relevant to them personally.

Use this list to monitor student responses to element 31.

To monitor your own use of this element, use the scale in figure 7.24 in combination with the reproducible "Tracking Teacher Actions: Providing Opportunities for Students to Talk About Themselves" (page 232). As with other proficiency scales, level 3 or higher is the goal.

4 Innovating	I adapt behaviors and create new strategies for unique student needs and situations.
3 Applying	I provide opportunities for students to talk about themselves, and I monitor the extent to which my actions affect students' engagement.
2 Developing	I provide opportunities for students to talk about themselves, but I do not monitor the effect on students.
1 Beginning	I use the strategies and behaviors associated with this element incorrectly or with parts missing.
0 Not Using	I am unaware of strategies and behaviors associated with this element.

Figure 7.24: Self-rating scale for element 31—Providing opportunities for students to talk about themselves.

The following examples describe what each level of the scale might look like in the classroom.

- **Not Using (0):** The teacher is only vaguely aware of students' lives outside of school. The teacher does not provide opportunities for students to relate content to their personal interests.
- **Beginning (1):** The teacher administers student interest surveys and student learning profiles at the beginning of the year. However, the teacher does not use the data gathered to relate the content to students' lives.
- **Developing (2):** When appropriate, the teacher provides opportunities for students to make linkages between the content being taught and their lives. However, the teacher does not try to determine if making these linkages helps students remember the content.
- **Applying (3):** The teacher uses interest surveys to better understand students' personal lives and keeps a running list of relevant information about students. The teacher then uses the information on this list to create informal linkages during class discussion and let students comment on those linkages. The teacher notices that, since she has been using these strategies together, students seem more engaged in the material.
- **Innovating (4):** The teacher identifies students who seem to be disengaged from the material and asks them to fill out more in-depth interest surveys. Using the data gathered from the additional surveys, the teacher creates informal linkages during class discussion or, when needed, meets with students to relate content being taught to their personal interests and have them comment on the linkages.

Element 32: Motivating and Inspiring Students

An effective teacher encourages students to self-reflect, set personally relevant goals, and connect to something greater than themselves. Research has shown that motivation increases students' enthusiasm, effort, persistence, and academic performance and reduces the risk of substance abuse and dropping out of school (Csikszentmihalyi & Nakamura, 1989; Hardré & Reeve, 2003; Larson, 2000; National Research Council & Institute of Medicine, 2004; Ormrod, 2014). Intrinsic motivation—motivation that comes from within a person—often has greater and longer-lasting effects than those of external motivation—motivation that is awarded to an individual from someone or something else (Deci, Koestner, & Ryan, 2001). In order to intrinsically motivate students, teachers can trigger students' emotional response systems using inspiration to encourage personal growth and connection to something greater than self (Scott & Marzano, 2014).

There are eight strategies within this element.

1. Academic goal setting
2. Growth mindset cultivation
3. Possible selves activities
4. Personal projects
5. Altruism projects
6. Gratitude journals
7. Mindfulness practice
8. Inspirational media

The following sections will explore each strategy to provide you with guidelines to effectively implement this element. Read through each before creating a plan for your classroom. Teachers may use the strategies individually or in combination. Remember, these are not merely activities to be checked off; they are methods of creating a practice that combines your art with the science of motivating and inspiring students. Reflect on your use of each strategy by filling out the "Strategy Reflection Log" on page 331.

Academic Goal Setting

The teacher helps students identify long-term academic goals to be accomplished over the course of a unit, semester, or year. The teacher then works with students to help them identify specific actions and smaller, short-term goals that, if completed, will help them accomplish their long-term goals. For example, a teacher might set long-term goals with students at the beginning of the semester. In order to do this, the teacher asks students to identify individual goals as well as three or four actionable steps that they can take to achieve such goals. The teacher reviews students' plans, then sets aside one class period to meet with students briefly to review their goals, ensure their goals are realistic, and discuss their actionable steps and short-term goals.

Provide students with a worksheet like figure 7.25 for use with this strategy.

Academic Goal-Setting Worksheet

Name: ______________________________

Long-term academic goal: ______________________________

Complete by: ______________________________

Related short-term goals:

1. ______________________________

Complete by: ______________________________

2. ______________________________

Complete by: ______________________________

3. ______________________________

Complete by: ______________________________

Actions I can take to accomplish this goal:

1. ______________________________
2. ______________________________
3. ______________________________

Source: Marzano Research, 2016.

Figure 7.25: Worksheet for academic goal setting.

Visit **go.SolutionTree.com/instruction** *for a free reproducible version of this figure.*

Growth Mindset Cultivation

The concept of the growth mindset, which Carol Dweck (2006) champions, refers to the idea that what we think of as intelligence is actually a learnable skill. In other words, people with growth mindsets believe that they can increase their intelligence or abilities through hard work. On the other hand, those with a fixed mindset feel that intelligence is innate and cannot be changed, regardless of effort. Within the classroom, it is important for a teacher to inspire growth mindsets in students, as students with growth mindsets are more likely to develop new skills and remain optimistic about challenging tasks, while students with fixed mindsets tend to choose activities that play to their existing strengths and are more likely to give up when faced with a challenging problem.

When addressing the concept of growth mindsets with students, a teacher can use the following six steps to help students understand the differences between growth and fixed mindsets and to help them apply this knowledge to their own lives.

1. **Define *growth mindset* and *fixed mindset*:** A teacher can use the following definitions. A growth mindset is the belief that with hard work, one can increase his or her abilities, intelligence, or skills;

a fixed mindset is the belief that work cannot affect one's abilities, intelligence, or skills—people are born with a specific set of abilities that does not change.

2. **Provide examples of a growth mindset and examples of a fixed mindset:** For example, a student with a fixed mindset would say, "There are some subjects in school that I am good at, and some that I am not good at." A student with a growth mindset would say, "There are some subjects in school I try harder at than others."
3. **Explain how individuals may have a growth mindset in one area of their life but a fixed mindset in a different area:** For example, a student may have a fixed mindset in terms of his or her ability with mathematics; that is, the student believes that no matter how much work he or she puts in, he or she will always be bad at math. This same student, however, may have a growth mindset when it comes to athletic abilities and recognize that when he or she practices a sport, his or her abilities increase.
4. **Ask students to reflect on areas in which they have growth mindsets and areas in which they have fixed mindsets:** The teacher could ask students to engage in a writing exercise in which students consider various abilities and intelligences and assess the degree to which they feel their mindsets are growth oriented or fixed. The teacher could also identify various areas (for example, mathematics, writing, athletics, time management, social skills, and so on) and ask students to determine whether they have growth or fixed mindsets in these areas. Finally, a teacher might also use an assessment, such as those found at https://mindsetworks.com/assess, to help students assess their mindsets.
5. **Ask students to experiment with changing their mindsets from fixed to growth oriented:** In order to have students change their mindsets, a teacher should ask students to examine their beliefs and the thoughts they hold about themselves. Once students identify thoughts that are characteristic of fixed mindsets, ask them to experiment with changing their inner narrative to one that reflects a growth mindset. For example, a student who has a fixed mindset when it comes to athletic abilities might think, "I'm bad at sports and always have been." That student, when thinking such thoughts, might try to alter the dialogue: "I don't practice enough when I play sports, which is why I often think that I'm bad at them."
6. **Explain to students that mindsets can change:** A teacher can explain to students the idea of *neuroplasticity*—that the brain changes and adapts in response to an individual's experience. As such, the brain modifies itself based on an individual's needs. The teacher can provide instances of this phenomenon to students. For example, the teacher might explain that in a study comparing the brains of taxi drivers and bus drivers, the taxi drivers had larger hippocampi (the part of the brain responsible for spatial recognition and representation), as they have to navigate entire cities based on passengers' needs, while bus drivers repeatedly drive the same route and do not exercise that part of the brain as much. The teacher can also find examples of individuals who worked hard in order to develop unlikely skills and abilities.

Possible Selves Activities

A teacher can use possible selves activities to help students imagine what they could develop into later in life. Without such considerations, students may not be cognizant of the full range of possibilities available to them nor recognize that certain possible selves could be achieved that previously seemed off-limits or unattainable. Once students have an idea of the range of directions their lives could take, they may be more able and motivated to develop skills and acquire knowledge necessary to achieve specific goals. For example, a student may decide that she wants to become an astronaut after a possible selves activity, though previously she had never considered this as a possibility. This student may dislike mathematics, but really enjoy science classes. After recognizing the possibility of becoming an astronaut, the student researches the education, background, knowledge, and skills necessary to enter the space program. With this knowledge, the student may begin to try harder at mathematics, as she recognizes that competence with mathematics is a skill required of astronauts.

Table 7.1 describes possible selves activities.

Table 7.1: Possible Selves Activities

Activity	Description
Accomplishment introductions	Students introduce themselves in a way that indicates something they would like to accomplish someday. For example, students might think of a person who has accomplished something similar to their goal and then introduce themselves using their first name and the last name of the person they thought of. If a student named Jake wanted to be a star football quarterback someday, he might introduce himself as Jake Manning (in recognition of Peyton Manning, the former star football quarterback for the Denver Broncos). If a student named Christina wanted to be a writer someday, she might introduce herself as Christina Rowling (in recognition of J. K. Rowling, author of the Harry Potter series).
Life images	Students find pictures of individuals doing various activities related to school, work, family, lifestyle, community service, health, or hobbies. For example, students might search in magazines or online for pictures of people engaging in specific fitness activities that they are interested in or enjoy. Doing this helps students see that they too can engage in a variety of activities and having a picture serves as a visual reminder.
Timelines	Students create timelines for their futures. Ask them to think about what they would like to do or accomplish in the future (imagining as far into the future as possible). Have students think specifically about important choices they may have to make, roadblocks they might encounter, or circumstances that might affect their future goals. Teachers can guide this work by helping students understand what typically takes place after high school, including school or career choices, opportunities to move away from home, increased responsibilities, and so on.
Possible selves research	Students find information about what is required to become their possible selves. For example, a student who wants to become a restaurant owner and chef might research how to operate a successful business, which type of cuisine he or she would like to focus on, and how to get started (for example, by attending a culinary school or by starting with a food truck and eventually moving into a restaurant space). A student who wants to become a teacher might research what education is required, which schools are the best, and what jobs or volunteer opportunities might be available to get an idea of what it's like to work with kids.
Informational interviews	Students contact adults in their communities who have accomplished goals similar to those of the students. For example, a student who wants to run her own business someday might use a list of women-owned businesses to find individuals who can advise her about her journey. A student who wants to become a nurse might reach out to a local hospital or doctor's office to ask for an interview or the opportunity to job shadow for a few hours.

Personal Projects

The teacher can use personal projects—projects that require students to select a personally relevant goal and work toward it—to encourage students' desire for personal growth. In order for personal projects to be successful, however, students must select topics they are truly interested in and excited about. Personal projects are often related to broader life or long-term goals rather than academic content. The teacher should have students consider the following seven questions at various stages of the personal project to help students remain focused throughout their project. Visit **go.SolutionTree.com/instruction** for a reproducible version of these questions.

1. What do I want to accomplish?
2. Who else has accomplished the same goal, and who will support me?
3. What skills and resources will I need to accomplish my goal?
4. What will I have to change in order to achieve my goal?
5. What is my plan for achieving my goal, and how hard will I have to work?
6. What small step can I take right now?
7. How have I been doing? What have I learned about myself?

To further motivate a class, the teacher can choose his or her own personal project and model appropriate behaviors, such as researching, setting smaller goals, and re-evaluating timelines.

Altruism Projects

Altruism projects encourage students to connect to something greater than themselves. The teacher should have students brainstorm aspects of their community that they are interested in getting involved with. Once the class has a list, the teacher can either group students interested in similar things together or have the whole class decide on one topic from the list to address. The class or groups brainstorm potential ways to help and create action plans with specific steps for setting their altruism projects in motion. The teacher should provide help but take care not to lead the project, as this takes ownership away from the students. The teacher may also want to reach out to parents for their assistance if specific altruism projects require time or resources outside of class for execution.

Following are sample altruism projects.

- Collect appropriate donations (clothes, household goods, books, food, toys, and so on) and give them to a charity of the students' choosing.
- Create care packages for families in need during the holidays or for troops stationed abroad.
- Start a letter-writing campaign to a local politician or national organization.
- Tutor younger students, the elderly, or English learners.
- Read to K–2 students or the elderly.
- Hold a bake sale or other fundraising event for a charity of the students' choosing.
- Clean up a local park or outdoor space.
- Hold an event (dance, 5K race, and so on) and donate the proceeds to a charity of the students' choosing.
- Coordinate with local shops and stores to have them provide, match, or donate supplies for a community project.
- Host a food packaging event in which students solicit donations, bag the food items, and distribute them to those in need.
- Go to an animal shelter and help take care of the animals and the facilities.
- Participate in a day of service organized by another organization or group.

Gratitude Journals

The teacher can use gratitude journals to help students feel connected to something greater than themselves. When introducing gratitude journals, the teacher should first model the behavior by listing a few things that he or she is grateful for and recording them somewhere visible in the room or in his or her own personal gratitude journal. Students then brainstorm a few things they are grateful for individually, in small groups, or as a class and record their items in their own gratitude journals. Students might explain why they are grateful for an item or items on their list and brainstorm ways to show their gratitude. Students can add new entries to their gratitude journals daily or weekly. At the end of the week, month, unit, or semester, the teacher can lead students in a review of their gratitude journals and facilitate a discussion about how their entries have changed and how students feel about the practice.

Mindfulness Practice

Mindfulness is the practice of being aware of one's thoughts, feelings, and internal and external worlds. The practice of mindfulness has been linked to positive increases in attention, behavior, academic performance, and physical health. Furthermore, a teacher can encourage mindfulness in students by engaging them in various activities that take up relatively little time but can facilitate great gains for students. For example, a teacher might ask students at the beginning of each class period to write down their intention for the class at the top of their notes. Students might write such intentions as "Today, I want to challenge myself to stay engaged all class," "I'm going to be less critical of my mistakes," or "I'm going to turn something negative into a positive." The teacher may sporadically ask students to recall their intention. A teacher, if sensing that students seem restless, may also engage students in deep breathing, quick guided meditation, or other soothing practices to help them refocus their thoughts.

Table 7.2 describes mindfulness activities for students. These strategies appeared in *Mindfulness for Teachers: Simple Skills for Peace and Productivity in the Classroom* (Jennings, 2015).

Table 7.2: Mindfulness Activities

Activity	Description
Setting intentions	Students set an intention every morning, such as "I want to challenge myself today" or "I intend to make something positive out of something negative." Throughout the day, ask students to recall their intention and assess the degree to which they have been honoring it.
Three breaths	This strategy is helpful when students are anxious or need a break. Students can take three deep breaths with their hands resting on their stomachs so that they can feel their abdomen fill with air.
Mindful walking	During transition periods, teachers can instruct students to pay particular attention to the way they walk. Students can focus on the way their feet hit the ground, with the heel, then ball of the foot, then the toes making contact with the floor. Teachers can also have the class take breaks to take a brief walk outside the classroom.
Mindful listening	During transition times, teachers may also engage students in listening activities. It may be helpful to have a specific chime or bell used exclusively for this activity. To begin, teachers announce, "We're going to do a listening activity that will help our minds relax and become more focused. First, let's all sit up nice and tall in our seats with our hands folded in our laps (or on the desk). In a few minutes, I'm going to ring this chime and we're going to listen to the sound until it disappears. I find that I can focus my attention on my hearing best when I close my eyes. You can try that, but if you aren't comfortable closing your eyes, you can lower your gaze to your hands." After the students seem collected, the teacher rings the bell. Once the ringing has stopped, the teacher begins class.

Source: Jennings, 2015.

Inspirational Media

Inspiration occurs when a person sees evidence that one of his or her ideals—a belief that represents how an individual would like the world to be—is true. Inspirational media can take many forms, including movies, books, quotes, internet clips, newspaper articles, anecdotes, stories, and pictures. A teacher can expose students to an inspirational story and then have students discuss why the example was powerful. A teacher can also have students discuss their own ideals and ways in which the media reinforces specific ideals as true or false. For example, if a student holds the ideal that underdogs can win and then sees an underdog win in a tangible way, that student will become inspired. This student might explain that this is inspiring to him because the student considers himself an underdog in certain areas of life and he rarely sees evidence that the underdog can win.

A worksheet like figure 7.26 can guide students' use of this strategy.

Inspirational Media Worksheet

Name: ______________________________

Today we experienced an inspirational . . . (circle one)

story movie book picture video quote

My description or summary:

It made me feel:

I felt this way because:

One ideal it represented is:

This ideal is important to me because:

Source: Marzano Research, 2016.

Figure 7.26: Worksheet for inspirational media.

Visit **go.SolutionTree.com/instruction** *for a free reproducible version of this figure.*

Monitoring Element 32

Specific student responses and behaviors allow the teacher to determine whether this element is being implemented effectively and producing the desired effects.

- Students set long-term goals and identify steps they must take to accomplish them.
- Students engage with community members in meaningful ways.
- Students work on projects of their own design that are meaningful to them.
- Students describe the class as *motivating* or *inspiring*.

Use this list to monitor student responses to element 32.

To monitor your own use of this element, use the scale in figure 7.27 in combination with the reproducible "Tracking Teacher Actions: Motivating and Inspiring Students" (page 233). As with other proficiency scales, level 3 or higher is the goal.

4 Innovating	I adapt behaviors and create new strategies for unique student needs and situations.
3 Applying	I use activities designed to motivate and inspire students, and I monitor the extent to which my actions affect students.
2 Developing	I use activities designed to motivate and inspire students, but I do not monitor the effect on students.
1 Beginning	I use the strategies and behaviors associated with this element incorrectly or with parts missing.
0 Not Using	I am unaware of strategies and behaviors associated with this element.

Figure 7.27: Self-rating scale for element 32—Motivating and inspiring students.

The following examples describe what each level of the scale might look like in the classroom.

- **Not Using (0):** A teacher does not engage students in personally relevant goal-setting activities or reflective practices. He occasionally creates long-term projects, but students have no input in designing the projects or setting goals.
- **Beginning (1):** A teacher engages students in motivating and inspiring activities but provides little guidance. She asks students to complete personal projects but does not support students in setting short-term goals, nor does she provide time for students to work on their projects. As a result, students feel lost and overwhelmed.
- **Developing (2):** A teacher conducts lessons in which he teaches students strategies for mindfulness as they relate to their efforts in class. However, he does not monitor students' behavior afterward to see if they continue to use the strategies successfully.
- **Applying (3):** A teacher engages students in long-term projects of their own design. He helps students set personally relevant long-term goals and create plans for achieving those goals. He monitors students' progress toward their goals and helps them re-evaluate their short-term goals as necessary to complete their long-term goals.
- **Innovating (4):** A teacher combines multiple strategies that encourage both personal growth and a connection to something greater than self. She asks students to complete altruism projects, but several students display a lack of self-efficacy, saying that they are "too young to make a difference." Before starting the projects, the teacher uses inspirational media that show other students of their age making an impact on their community. Throughout the project, the teacher has students write weekly entries in their gratitude journals that relate to their progress on their altruism projects, focusing particularly on the impacts they have made in others' lives.

Action Steps

Use the "Tracking Teacher Actions" reproducibles that follow (pages 224–233) to monitor your implementation of each element in this chapter.

Additionally, visit the appendix (page 329) for the reproducible "Tracking Progress Over Time" (page 330), which helps teachers set goals related to their proficiency with each element and track their progress toward these goals over the course of a unit, semester, or year. Also, the "Strategy Reflection Log" (page 331) in the appendix provides a space to write down your thoughts and reflect on the implementation process for specific strategies related to each element. Finally, visit **go.SolutionTree.com/instruction** for both student surveys and teacher surveys, the results of which provide feedback about your proficiency with each element.

Tracking Teacher Actions: Noticing and Reacting When Students Are Not Engaged

The teacher can use this form to plan his or her usage of strategies related to the element of noticing and reacting when students are not engaged.

Check Strategies You Intend to Use	Strategies	Description of Instructional Plan
	Monitoring Individual Student Engagement	
	Monitoring Overall Class Engagement	
	Using Self-Reported Student Engagement Data	
	Re-Engaging Individual Students	
	Boosting Overall Class Energy Levels	
	Other:	
	Other:	

Source: Adapted from Marzano Research. (2016). Marzano compendium of instructional strategies. *Centennial, CO: Author.*

Tracking Teacher Actions: Increasing Response Rates

The teacher can use this form to plan his or her usage of strategies related to the element of increasing response rates.

Check Strategies You Intend to Use	Strategies	Description of Instructional Plan
	Random Names	
	Hand Signals	
	Response Cards	
	Response Chaining	
	Paired Response	
	Choral Response	
	Wait Time	
	Elaborative Interrogation	
	Multiple Types of Questions	
	Other:	
	Other:	

Source: Adapted from Marzano Research. (2016). Marzano compendium of instructional strategies. *Centennial, CO: Author.*

Tracking Teacher Actions: Using Physical Movement

The teacher can use this form to plan his or her usage of strategies related to the element of using physical movement.

Check Strategies You Intend to Use	Strategies	Description of Instructional Plan
	Stand Up and Stretch	
	Vote With Your Feet	
	Corners Activities	
	Stand and Be Counted	
	Body Representations	
	Drama-Related Activities	
	Other:	
	Other:	

Source: Adapted from Marzano Research. (2016). Marzano compendium of instructional strategies. *Centennial, CO: Author.*

Tracking Teacher Actions: Maintaining a Lively Pace

The teacher can use this form to plan his or her usage of strategies related to the element of maintaining a lively pace.

Check Strategies You Intend to Use	Strategies	Description of Instructional Plan
	Instructional Segments	
	Pace Modulation	
	Parking Lot	
	Motivational Hooks	
	Other:	
	Other:	

Source: Adapted from Marzano Research. (2016). Marzano compendium of instructional strategies. *Centennial, CO: Author.*

Tracking Teacher Actions: Demonstrating Intensity and Enthusiasm

The teacher can use this form to plan his or her usage of strategies related to the element of demonstrating intensity and enthusiasm.

Check Strategies You Intend to Use	Strategies	Description of Instructional Plan
	Direct Statements About the Importance of Content	
	Explicit Connections	
	Nonlinguistic Representations	
	Personal Stories	
	Verbal and Nonverbal Signals	
	Humor	
	Quotations	
	Movie and Film Clips	
	Other:	
	Other:	

Source: Adapted from Marzano Research. (2016). Marzano compendium of instructional strategies. *Centennial, CO: Author.*

Tracking Teacher Actions: Presenting Unusual Information

The teacher can use this form to plan his or her usage of strategies related to the element of presenting unusual information.

Check Strategies You Intend to Use	Strategies	Description of Instructional Plan
	Teacher-Presented Information	
	Webquests	
	Fast Facts	
	Believe It or Not	
	History Files	
	Guest Speakers and First-Hand Consultants	
	Other:	
	Other:	

Source: Adapted from Marzano Research. (2016). Marzano compendium of instructional strategies. *Centennial, CO: Author.*

Tracking Teacher Actions: Using Friendly Controversy

The teacher can use this form to plan his or her usage of strategies related to the element of using friendly controversy.

Check Strategies You Intend to Use	Strategies	Description of Instructional Plan
	Friendly Controversy	
	Class Vote	
	Seminars	
	Expert Opinions	
	Opposite Point of View	
	Diagrams Comparing Perspectives	
	Lincoln-Douglas Debate	
	Town-Hall Meeting	
	Legal Model	
	Other:	
	Other:	

Source: Adapted from Marzano Research. (2016). Marzano compendium of instructional strategies. *Centennial, CO: Author.*

Tracking Teacher Actions: Using Academic Games

The teacher can use this form to plan his or her usage of strategies related to the element of using academic games.

Check Strategies You Intend to Use	Strategies	Description of Instructional Plan
	What Is the Question?	
	Name That Category	
	Talk a Mile a Minute	
	Classroom Feud	
	Which One Doesn't Belong?	
	Inconsequential Competition	
	Questions Into Games	
	Vocabulary Review Games	
	Other:	
	Other:	

Source: Adapted from Marzano Research. (2016). Marzano compendium of instructional strategies. *Centennial, CO: Author.*

Tracking Teacher Actions: Providing Opportunities for Students to Talk About Themselves

The teacher can use this form to plan his or her usage of strategies related to the element of providing opportunities for students to talk about themselves.

Check Strategies You Intend to Use	Strategies	Description of Instructional Plan
	Interest Surveys	
	Student Learning Profiles	
	Life Connections	
	Informal Linkages During Class Discussion	
	Other:	
	Other:	

Source: Adapted from Marzano Research. (2016). Marzano compendium of instructional strategies. *Centennial, CO: Author.*

Tracking Teacher Actions: Motivating and Inspiring Students

The teacher can use this form to plan his or her usage of strategies related to the element of motivating and inspiring students.

Check Strategies You Intend to Use	Strategies	Description of Instructional Plan
	Academic Goal Setting	
	Growth Mindset Cultivation	
	Possible Selves Activities	
	Personal Projects	
	Altruism Projects	
	Gratitude Journals	
	Mindfulness Practice	
	Inspirational Media	
	Other:	
	Other:	

Source: Adapted from Marzano Research. (2016). Marzano compendium of instructional strategies. *Centennial, CO: Author.*

CHAPTER 8

Implementing Rules and Procedures

Part of a mental set conducive to learning is the perception that the classroom environment is orderly and safe. The teacher fosters such a perception through well-articulated rules and procedures. Rules and procedures are a facet of classroom management that provide the framework for student behavior and practices throughout the school year. An effective teacher should clearly define all established rules and procedures and help prevent behavior that might interfere with students' learning. In addition, good classroom management also considers students' needs and how certain routines might encourage, or discourage, students' learning habits. In this set of strategies, rules refer to general expectations or standards for the classroom, while procedures more specifically delineate how students are to behave or perform certain tasks.

The goal of this design area is for students to understand and follow rules and procedures. Teachers are able to meet this goal by answering the question, What strategies will I use to help students understand and follow rules and procedures? The five elements and associated strategies in this chapter help the teacher do just that.

Element 33: Establishing Rules and Procedures

An effective teacher establishes rules and procedures in the very beginning of the year and revises them throughout the year as needed. Research shows that establishing rules and procedures results in a decrease in disruptive behavior (Marzano, 2003). Rules are general expectations (such as "Keep the classroom orderly"), while procedures apply to specific behaviors (such as "Hang up your coat and backpack when you arrive") (Emmer, Evertson, & Worsham, 2003; Evertson, Emmer, & Worsham, 2003). Teachers should establish rules and procedures at the beginning of the year (Anderson, Evertson, & Emmer, 1980; Eisenhart, 1977; Emmer, Evertson, & Anderson, 1980; Emmer, Sanford, Clements, & Martin, 1982; Emmer, Sanford, Evertson, Clements, & Martin, 1981; Evertson & Emmer, 1982; Evertson, Emmer, Sanford, & Clements, 1983; Evertson & Weinstein, 2006; Moskowitz & Hayman, 1976; Sanford & Evertson, 1981).

There are thirteen strategies within this element.

1. Using a small set of rules and procedures
2. Explaining rules and procedures to students
3. Generating rules and procedures with students
4. Modifying rules and procedures with students
5. Reviewing rules and procedures with students
6. Using the language of responsibility and statements of school beliefs
7. Posting rules around the room

8. Writing a class pledge or classroom constitution
9. Using posters and graphics
10. Establishing gestures and symbols
11. Modeling with vignettes and role playing
12. Holding classroom meetings
13. Implementing student self-assessment

The following sections will explore each strategy to provide you with guidelines to effectively implement this element. Read through each before creating a plan for your classroom. Teachers may use the strategies individually or in combination. Remember, these are not merely activities to be checked off; they are methods of creating a practice that combines your art with the science of establishing rules and procedures. Reflect on your use of each strategy by filling out the "Strategy Reflection Log" on page 331.

Using a Small Set of Rules and Procedures

Classroom rules and procedures are fundamental to building a productive learning community. However, students are more likely to understand and adhere to rules if a teacher prioritizes rules and procedures by restricting them to five to eight per class. Generally, a teacher should begin the year by establishing general classroom rules, then work toward procedures for more specific areas such as the beginning and end of the school day or period, transitions, and the efficient use of materials and equipment.

Table 8.1 provides examples of topics for rules and procedures.

Table 8.1: Examples of Topics for Rules and Procedures

Event or Activity	Elementary Examples	Secondary Examples
General classroom behavior	• Being polite and helpful when dealing with others • Respecting the property of others • Listening when others are talking • Keeping hands and feet to oneself	• Bringing material to class • Being in assigned seats at the beginning of class • Respecting and being polite to others • Talking or not talking at specific times • Respecting other people's property
Beginning and ending the period or school day	• Beginning the school day with specific social activities (for example, acknowledging birthdays or important events in students' lives) • Beginning the day with the Pledge of Allegiance • Doing administrative activities (for example, taking attendance or collecting lunch money) • Ending the day by cleaning the room and completing individual tasks • Ending the day by putting away materials	• Taking attendance at the beginning of the period • Addressing students who missed the work from the previous day because of absence • Dealing with students who are tardy at the beginning of the period • Ending the period with clear expectations for homework
Transitions and interruptions	• Leaving the room • Returning to the room • Use of the bathroom • Use of the library and resource room • Use of the cafeteria • Use of the playground • Fire and disaster drills • Classroom helpers	• Leaving the room • Returning to the room • Fire and disaster drills • Split lunch period

Event or Activity	Elementary Examples	Secondary Examples
Use of materials and equipment	• Distributing materials • Collecting materials • Storage of common materials • The teacher's desk and storage areas • Students' desks and storage areas • Use of the drinking fountain, sink, and pencil sharpener	• Distributing materials • Collecting materials • Storage of common materials
Seatwork and teacher-led activities	• Student attention during presentations • Student participation • Talking among students • Obtaining help • Staying in one's seat • Behavior when work has been completed	• Student attention during presentations • Student participation • Talking among students • Obtaining help • Staying in one's seat • Behavior when work has been completed
Group work	• Movement in and out of the group • Expected behaviors of students in the group • Expected behaviors of students not in the group • Group communication with the teacher	• Movement in and out of the group • Group leadership and roles in the group • Relationship of the group to the rest of the class or other groups in the class • Group communication with the teacher

Explaining Rules and Procedures to Students

At the beginning of the school year or term, as a teacher presents the rules he or she has established for the classroom, the teacher can also take time to explain each rule and why he or she chose them. Because rules often can be quite general, the teacher's explanation should focus on exemplifying situations in which a rule applies and describing specific behaviors that demonstrate adherence to the rules. The teacher and students might make rules more explicit by creating procedures (how-to steps) for them. These how-to steps are often referred to as *standard operating procedures*, or SOPs. When presenting rules and procedures to students, the teacher should also explain the reasons why each one is important.

There are two basic formats for SOPs: (1) procedural lists and (2) flow charts. Procedural lists and flow charts should always be constructed with input from students and revised as they are used. A procedural list articulates simple sequential steps. They often ensure safety or compliance (for example, non-negotiable procedures such as bus routines), when multiple solutions aren't necessary (for example, hand washing), as a list of actionable items (for example, what to bring to class), or when there is a need for reminders. The following steps can help classrooms design a procedural list: (1) determine the sequence of steps, (2) create an easy-to-understand visual display to post in the classroom (using pictures or symbols if needed), and (3) ensure comprehension and compliance with regular practice and monitoring. To illustrate, consider the following four-step procedural list of SOPs for safely carrying an iPad.

1. Grip the iPad on either side with two hands.
2. Put your thumbs to the back and fingers to the front.
3. Hold the iPad chest-high in front of you.
4. Always pay attention while walking.

Flow charts are useful when there are multiple solutions to a problem (for example, common classroom computer issues), when there are multiple choices that do not have to go in a certain order (for example, during learning center activities), when you can apply if-then statements (for example, if you are finished, then . . .), or when you can use yes-or-no questions (for example, Are you stuck?). The following five steps can help classrooms design a flow chart.

1. Begin with a title or question that guides the reader to the next steps.
2. Use yes-or-no prompts to create multiple pathways or outcomes.
3. Develop internal loops as needed to define accountability steps (for example, Do you have evidence of mastery?).
4. Create closure or a *begin again* step.
5. Ensure comprehension and compliance with regular practice and monitoring.

Generating Rules and Procedures With Students

Teachers do not have to generate rules and procedures; they can devote class time to designing rules and procedures from the ground up. In other words, the teacher shifts responsibility to the entire class for crafting the classroom rules and the specific procedures associated with them. While this takes more time, generating rules and procedures as a class can increase student ownership of the classroom.

Following are the six steps for generating rules and procedures with students.

1. Facilitate a whole-class discussion about the characteristics of a class that facilitates learning.
2. Assemble small groups of students and ask them to create initial lists of suggestions for rules. Provide examples of previous classes' rules if necessary.
3. Combine the rule suggestions from all the small groups into one list and post it somewhere in the classroom.
4. Facilitate another whole-class discussion about the aggregated list of rules. Groups who suggested a rule can explain why they think it is important, and students can discuss the benefits of each one.
5. Have the class vote on each rule and add the rules that obtain a majority (or consensus, depending on the teacher's preferences) to the class's final list of rules.
6. Facilitate a whole-class discussion about the final list of rules and address students' questions or concerns. Students might design procedures for rules that need further clarification.

Modifying Rules and Procedures With Students

One way to involve students in the process of creating rules and procedures is to present general rules to the class and ask students to operationalize them by coming up with specific behaviors or procedures for each rule. List the student-generated procedures underneath the general rule and post them prominently in the classroom for future reference. A second approach is to present students with general rules and specific procedures but then invite them to modify those rules and procedures as they see fit. Teachers might organize students into small groups and ask them to suggest changes. Groups can list their suggestions on the board, and the class would discuss all the suggestions. Teachers would add suggested changes that gain consensus to the original set of rules and procedures. Consider the following questions when creating rules and procedures with students (Marzano Research, 2016).

- What does the classroom look like when this rule is being followed?
- What are individual student behaviors associated with this rule?
- What are the steps students must take to follow this rule?
- What modifications, if any, would you suggest to make this rule easier for students to follow?
- What modifications, if any, would you suggest to make this rule more effective?
- Why is this rule necessary?

Reviewing Rules and Procedures With Students

Even when rules and procedures are well designed initially, the class must review and adapt them as time goes by. Periodic reviews of rules and procedures can prove extraordinarily useful in promoting students' ownership of their behavior. If students seem to systematically violate or ignore rules and procedures, the teacher calls the lapse to students' attention and reviews and models the rule or procedure as necessary. The teacher might also ask for suggestions about how to get behavior back on track. If students need clarification on a rule or procedure, the teacher can lead a discussion about the need for the rule—on occasion, this discussion might lead to a rule or procedure being changed or dropped altogether. For example, consider a classroom that requires students to raise their hands and obtain permission from the teacher to get up during seatwork. Over time, the teacher and students recognize that this procedure simply does not work well—at times, the teacher is occupied and does not notice a student's raised hand for quite a while. Additionally, students assert that they can be trusted to leave their seats without disrupting the class. After the discussion, the teacher and students agree to suspend the rule.

Following are the six process steps for leading a review of rules and procedures with students.

1. Discern a rule that students regularly violate or disregard. For example, a teacher might realize that students forget to turn in homework at the end of the class period on their way out the door.
2. Talk with the class about students consistently breaking the rule, why they created the rule in the first place, and its role in keeping the classroom safe or efficient. For example, at the beginning of a class period, the teacher might read the rule aloud ("On their way out of the classroom, students should drop their homework off in the designated folder by the classroom door") and identify how students are breaking the rule ("Some of you are forgetting to turn in your homework"). The teacher then reiterates why the rule is important ("Your homework helps me determine what you understand and what we need to work on more closely").
3. After explaining why the rule was initially created and why the rule is not functioning currently, facilitate a class discussion with students about how they feel about the rule. For example, once the teacher finishes her explanation of the rule about turning in homework at the end of class, the teacher might ask students for their opinions. Some students might agree with the rule as it stands; some students might ask the teacher to remind students before they leave to turn in homework, because they find it difficult to remember; and other students might ask the teacher to consider revising the collection method for homework altogether.
4. The teacher takes into consideration the comments and suggestions given during the discussion. At this point, the teacher might ask the class to vote on whether they would like to keep or change the rule, present her own suggestion for how the rule or procedure should be revised, or resume regular instruction and make a decision later about rule revision.
5. Before implementing changes, regardless of whether the class voted or the teacher revised it himself or herself, the teacher should take time going over the revision of the rule with the class. This may include modeling the new behavior or comparing and contrasting changes between the new and old rule. For example, the teacher may decide that she will stand by the door and directly collect homework from students as they exit the classroom. The teacher explains the revision to students and asks students to help model the behavior.
6. After explaining the new rule or procedure, the teacher should ask students if they need further clarification. In some instances, the teacher may want to ask what actions they can take to ensure a rule or procedure is followed. For example, the teacher might ask students their feelings about

the new rule and how she can streamline the process to make it more efficient. Students might suggest that the teacher remind them at the end of class that she will be collecting homework so that students will remember to keep homework out when packing up at the end of class.

Using the Language of Responsibility and Statements of School Beliefs

Establishing a language of responsibility is important in helping students develop responsibility for their own behavior—if they have no language to talk about responsibility, they have few tools with which to explore the concept. To create a language of responsibility in the classroom, the teacher can lead a discussion about concepts like freedom, equality, responsibility, threats, opinions, and rights. After introducing, defining, and discussing these and other relevant terms, the teacher should use the terms consistently to describe and discuss classroom behavior. The teacher can then facilitate a discussion about how the key concepts apply to students during school hours and relate them to rules and procedures.

Figure 8.1 provides sample definitions of concepts.

Concept	Merriam-Webster's Definition	Elementary Definition	Secondary Definition
Freedom	The quality or state of being free; as absence of necessity, coercion, or constraint in choice or action; liberation from slavery or restraint or from the power of another; the quality of being frank, open, or outspoken	Freedom means that I should be allowed to do the things I want to do.	Freedom is a concept in which individuals are allowed to do or say what they want without being stopped or judged by others.
Equality	The quality or state of being equal (regarding or affecting all objects in the same way); the quality or state of having the same rights, social status, and so on	Equality means that everyone treats one another the same.	Equality is a concept that dictates that all individuals receive the same treatment and are not discriminated against, regardless of race, appearance, gender, religious beliefs, sexual orientation, and so on.
Responsibility	The state of being the person who caused something to happen; a duty or task that you are required or expected to do; something that you should do because it is morally right, legally required, and so on	Responsibility means doing the right thing because you want to or have to or knowing how your actions make or made other things happen.	Responsibility is being able to understand how you contributed to an event and being able to decide what you should or should not do based on whether it is morally right or wrong.
Threat	A statement saying you will be harmed if you do not do what someone wants you to do; someone or something that could cause trouble, harm, or so on; the possibility that something bad or harmful could happen	A threat is when someone says they'll hurt you if you don't do what they want you to do.	A threat is when someone or something creates a possibility of harm to yourself, your freedom, people you care about, your environment, and so on.

Concept	Merriam-Webster's Definition	Elementary Definition	Secondary Definition
Opinion	A belief, judgment, or way of thinking about something; what someone thinks about a particular thing	An opinion is something you believe—such as whether a food is good or bad or which superhero is best—that other people might not agree with.	An opinion is a subjective statement with which others may agree or disagree.
Right	Behavior that is morally good or correct; something that a person is or should be morally or legally allowed to have, get, or do	A right is something that I am always allowed to have or do.	Rights are baseline things (actions) that everyone automatically has permission to do or have, as dictated by society.

Figure 8.1: Sample definitions of concepts.

Posting Rules Around the Room

Posting rules around the classroom can be helpful as both a visual reminder for students and as a way for teachers to hold students accountable for their behavior. Teachers should post general classroom rules in a prominent location where students can frequently and easily see them, whereas they can post rules and procedures for specific areas or activities near their relevant locations. For example, a teacher might post the general classroom rules by the doorway leading into the classroom, whereas the teacher would post the rules related to appropriate computer use by the classroom computers.

Figure 8.2 provides examples of rules and procedures for specific classroom areas.

Computer use	• Keep food and drink away from the computer. • Get permission from the teacher before using the computer. • Follow the teacher's directions for using the computer; do not use the computer for personal needs. • Ask before printing. • Remember to log off after you are done.
Art center	• Leave the art center the way you found it. • Be considerate in your use of resources and supplies at the art center. • If materials are not working or are missing, let the teacher know. • Only touch your own art.
Library	• Put books back where and in the order you found them. • Write your name in the ledger when you check out a book. • Be quiet when reading and respect others who are reading. • Be respectful of the books and take care to keep them in good condition.
Outside the classroom	• To leave the classroom, you must have a hall or bathroom pass. • Walk in a single-file and orderly line when walking in the halls as a class. • When in the hallway, be quiet and take care not to disturb other classes. • Stay with the group when moving as a class.
Personal cubby area	• Put your jacket and backpack in your cubby at the beginning of the day. • Keep your cubby organized. • Only touch your own cubby. • Only go into your cubby at the beginning of the day, at lunch, and at the end of the day.

Figure 8.2: Examples of rules and procedures for specific classroom areas.

Writing a Class Pledge or Classroom Constitution

A class pledge or constitution serves as a way to help students buy into and take responsibility for the classroom rules and procedures. It is an informal contract—when students sign it, they are promising to follow the rules that the teacher and the class have set. Students should be directly involved in writing the class pledge or constitution based on the classroom rules and procedures. This document describes what the ideal classroom looks like and what behaviors are necessary to achieve that ideal. All students sign the final copy, and the teacher displays it in the classroom.

Following are examples of class pledges and classroom constitutions.

- When we care about each other in our classroom, we share what we have, listen carefully, help each other learn, work hard, and have fun together. We understand that everyone makes mistakes, that we stand up for ourselves and others, and that when someone asks us to stop, we stop. This is who we are even when no one is watching.
- I pledge today to do my best, in reading, mathematics, and all of the rest. I promise to obey the rules in my class and in my school. I'll respect myself and others too. I'll expect the best in all I do. I am here to learn all I can, to try my best and be all I am.
- I promise that when I'm in our classroom, I will be the best that I can be. I will be a good student and a good friend and treat others the way that I want to be treated. I will do my part to keep school safe, smart, and fun.

Using Posters and Graphics

Using posters and graphics to display rules, procedures, and character traits helps students better remember them while simultaneously decorating the classroom. These posters and graphics emphasize the importance of specific rules and procedures or specific character traits important to proper classroom functioning (integrity, emotional control, and so on). For example, if a teacher's signal for students to be quiet and pay attention is to raise his or her hand in the air, a graphic to emphasize this procedure could be a drawing of a hand with the class's five steps for good listening written on each finger. Students can also create these posters and graphics as a class activity, which adds another element of buy-in and responsibility for appropriate behavior.

There are numerous websites on the internet that provide free resources for teachers including free posters and graphics to hang in a classroom. Teachers can also search Pinterest for ideas of how to display rules and procedures visually around the room. The following list contains a few websites that offer free printable posters and graphics. Visit **go.SolutionTree.com/instruction** to access live links to the following websites.

- **We Are Teachers:** www.weareteachers.com/lessons-resources/classroom-printables
- **Kids Know It Network:** www.kidsknowit.com/free-educational-posters/free-classroom-posters.php
- **Freeology:** www.freeology.com/quote-posters
- **Technology Rocks. Seriously.:** www.technologyrocksseriously.com/p/school-signs.html
- **Edgalaxy:** www.edgalaxy.com/classroom-posters-charts

Establishing Gestures and Symbols

Within the classroom, there are some messages that teachers or students need to communicate frequently, such as "quiet down" or "I need help with this assignment." It is often more efficient to use gestures and symbols to communicate these messages. Teacher and students can collaborate to establish gestures or symbols that communicate common messages. For example, a raised hand might indicate a need for quiet or attention, turning the lights off and on could signal that group work has become too noisy, a raised book or pencil could show that a student needs help from the teacher, and teachers might use words or phrases, such as *groups*, to send students to preassigned work areas.

Figure 8.3 provides examples of hand gestures and symbols to use in classrooms.

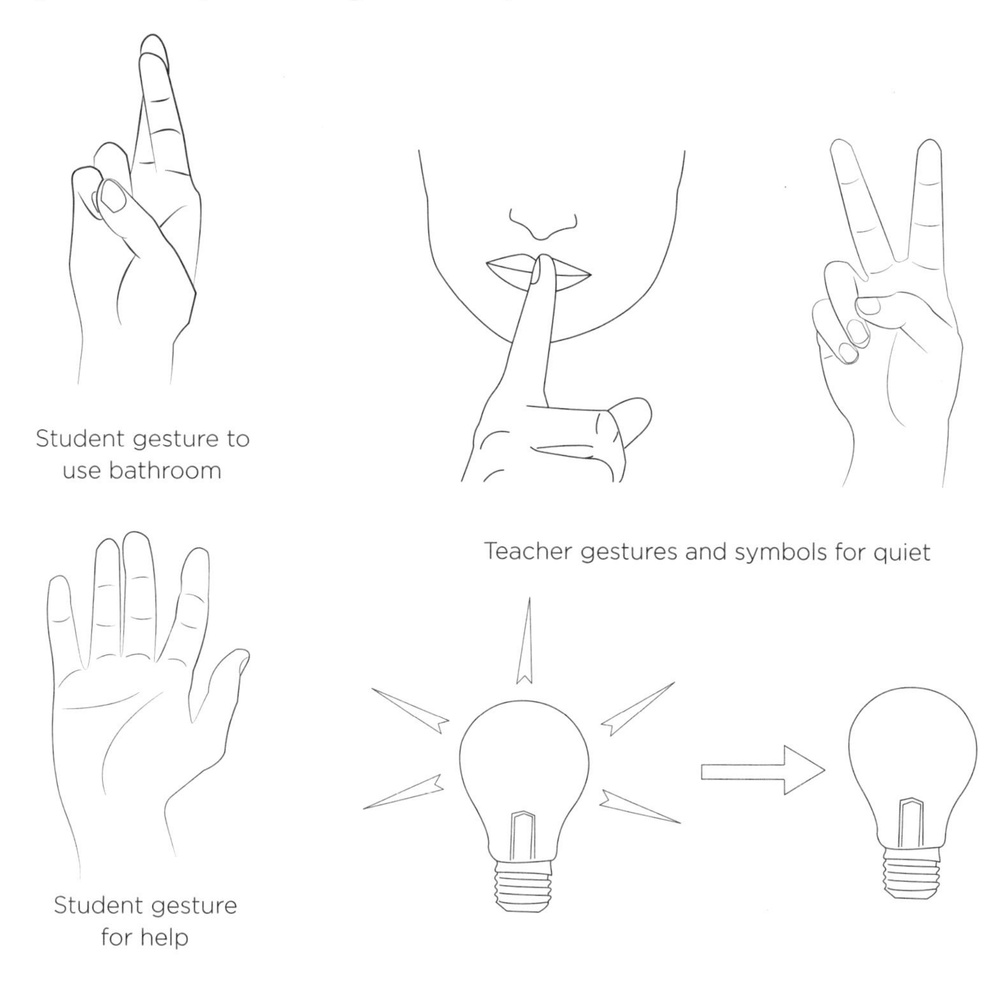

Source: Marzano Research, 2016.

Figure 8.3: Gestures and symbols for the classroom.

Visit **go.SolutionTree.com/instruction** *for a free reproducible version of this figure.*

Modeling With Vignettes and Role Playing

Students need a clear understanding of what the teacher means when he or she says that rules and procedures help create a focused, respectful atmosphere for learning. A fun way to show examples and nonexamples of appropriate behavior is to have students model them through role playing. A teacher might divide the class into small groups and assign two groups to each classroom rule or procedure. One group would create a skit that demonstrates a nonexample of a rule or procedure—that is, students would intentionally act out breaking the rule, often in a humorous manner. The second group would act out correct adherence to the rule. Students can also write short stories or vignettes that exemplify classroom rules and procedures if a less theatrical version of this strategy is desired.

Table 8.2 (page 244) defines expectations for classroom behaviors.

Table 8.2: Classroom Behaviors

Behavior	Looks Like	Sounds Like
Walking in the hallway	Walking at a responsible speed, not touching other students, not stopping in the middle of the hallway and blocking the flow of students	Quiet or talking at a conversational volume
Engaging in individual seatwork	Sitting in their assigned seat, keeping hands to themselves, keeping eyes on their own work	No students talking unless they are speaking with the instructor
Talking with a classmate	Showing good listening skills, responding to teacher cues to return to work when signaled	Using a quiet but conversational tone, not escalating voices, using appropriate language and discussing appropriate topics
Going to the bathroom	Raising hand to ask teacher for hall or bathroom pass, waiting for an appropriate pause in the content (if possible), being prompt in returning to the classroom	Asking to go to the restroom after being called upon, being quiet in the hallway, re-entering the classroom quietly
Responding to a question	Raising hand when wanting to respond, waiting to be called on	Not calling out, responding to the question once the teacher calls on the student, answering at an appropriate volume and with an appropriate tone
Asking the teacher a question	Raising hand when wanting to speak, using eye contact to signal to the teacher, choosing appropriate times to ask questions, waiting an appropriate amount of time to see if the question will be answered later in lesson	Speaking at a volume appropriate for the situation (for example, a student asking a teacher a question during a test would speak at a different volume than a student asking a question during class discussion), not calling out
Listening to a lesson	Following the teacher with their eyes, holding pencil and taking notes as needed, raising hand to ask questions or add comments as appropriate, ignoring distractions	Listening quietly unless called on

Holding Classroom Meetings

Classroom meetings are a time for students and the teacher to discuss how the classroom is functioning and identify how it might run more smoothly. In these meetings, the teacher and students bring up issues relative to classroom management, including rules and procedures. Students might verbally raise issues for discussion during this time, or if students do not feel comfortable volunteering issues, then the teacher might ask students to suggest issues beforehand or submit them in a suggestion box for discussion during classroom meetings. For example, a teacher might call a classroom meeting upon noticing that students are not adhering to specific rules and procedures or after a specific incident (for example, a physical or verbal altercation between multiple students might warrant a classroom meeting). The teacher leads the meeting and ensures it is orderly and respectful but also lets all students have a chance to voice their questions, comments, and concerns.

Setting clear guidelines for classroom meetings is crucial if the meetings are to be effective. Teachers may want to consider the following questions when creating guidelines for classroom meetings.

- Do I regularly schedule classroom meetings or call them in reaction to a specific event? For example, a teacher might decide that classroom meetings will be held every other Friday for the final fifteen minutes of class.
- What is an appropriate length for a class meeting? Should I cap this time or let the discussion go on for as long as feels appropriate? For example, a teacher might decide that if a classroom

meeting feels as though it is cut off, he or she will recap the conversation at the beginning of the following class period and allow an additional ten minutes of discussion, focusing on voices who may not have had a chance to speak during the previous meeting.

- Can students call a class meeting? If so, what is the process for this? For example, a teacher might decide that students can call a classroom meeting if they feel it is particularly necessary. If this is the case, the student should individually meet with the teacher, express his or her concerns, and explain why this warrants a classroom meeting over other avenues of remediation.
- What is the format of the classroom meeting? Is it an open discussion or should I moderate the conversation? For example, a teacher might decide that the format of a classroom meeting will be an open discussion; however, if the discussion becomes ineffective, disrespectful, or chaotic, he or she will moderate the discussion by choosing who speaks and for how long.
- How can I create a respectful atmosphere that makes students feel safe when sharing? How does this translate into specific speaking guidelines for class meetings? For example, a teacher might decide that students who are disrespectful or accusatory of their fellow students will be removed from the discussion. Such students get one strike, but if they have to be reminded multiple times, they will be asked to listen respectfully and allow others to speak.
- To what degree is student participation mandatory? For example, a teacher might decide that students can choose to only listen and not participate in classroom meetings.
- How should I arrange the class to ensure the most successful classroom meetings? For example, a teacher might decide to have students arrange their desks in a circle so that all students and the teacher can see each other's faces.
- How can I ensure that classroom meetings stay on topic and focus on policies and issues rather than specific individuals? For example, a teacher might decide that he or she will guide students back to the topic at hand if they get off topic. A teacher might also make a rule that students will not refer to specific other students or their actions to make points, particularly if such a callout is in a negative light.

Implementing Student Self-Assessment

To implement student self-assessment, the teacher periodically asks students to assess their own level of adherence to classroom rules and procedures. To do so, the teacher simply presents students with rules or procedures and asks them to rate their adherence to those rules and procedures on a scale of 0 (not adhering) to 4 (exemplary adherence). A teacher might choose to have students assess their own behavior relative to general classroom rules or the rules and procedures for a specific activity, such as working in groups. Students should be given the opportunity to self-assess on a fairly regular basis so that they can see their own progress. For general classroom rules and procedures, this might occur once a week or every other week. For specific activities, this might occur after each instance of the activity or after every third instance, depending on how frequently students engage in that activity.

Provide students with a rating sheet like figure 8.4 (page 246) for their self-assessments.

Student Self-Assessment Rating Sheet

Name: ____________________

Rule or procedure: ____________________

Date	0 Not Adhering	1 Occasionally Adhering	2 Adhering More Often Than Not	3 Adhering Most of the Time	4 Exemplary Adherence

Source: Marzano Research, 2016.

Figure 8.4: Rating sheet for student self-assessment.

Visit **go.SolutionTree.com/instruction** *for a free reproducible version of this figure.*

Monitoring Element 33

Specific student responses and behaviors allow the teacher to determine whether this element is being implemented effectively and producing the desired effects.

- Students can describe established rules and procedures.
- Students describe the classroom as an orderly place.
- Students regulate their own behavior.

Use this list to monitor student responses to element 33.

To monitor your own use of this element, use the scale in figure 8.5 in combination with the reproducible "Tracking Teacher Actions: Establishing Rules and Procedures" (page 274). As with other proficiency scales, level 3 or higher is the goal.

4 Innovating	I adapt behaviors and create new strategies for unique student needs and situations.
3 Applying	I establish rules and procedures, and I monitor the extent to which my actions affect students' behavior.
2 Developing	I establish rules and procedures, but I do not monitor the effect on students.
1 Beginning	I use the strategies and behaviors associated with this element incorrectly or with parts missing.
0 Not Using	I am unaware of strategies and behaviors associated with this element.

Figure 8.5: Self-rating scale for element 33—Establishing rules and procedures.

The following examples describe what each level of the scale might look like in the classroom.

- **Not Using (0):** The teacher has rules and procedures in mind for the classroom but assumes students will know them as a matter of common sense and doesn't take time to explicitly or properly explain them to students.

- **Beginning (1):** The teacher posts rules and procedures around the classroom but does not point them out to students and misses opportunities to refer to them.
- **Developing (2):** The teacher establishes rules and procedures and invites students to modify them in order to encourage student ownership of the classroom. However, the teacher doesn't focus on monitoring whether this helps improve student behavior.
- **Applying (3):** The teacher uses classroom meetings to identify rules and procedures that should be modified, then modifies them with students. Based on her records of behavior management responses, the teacher is able to see how the changes to the existing rules and procedures help the classroom function more smoothly.
- **Innovating (4):** The teacher effectively uses a variety of strategies to establish, explain, and remind students of rules and procedures. The teacher also reaches out to individual students who repeatedly break rules and procedures. He works with them to establish verbal and nonverbal cues that let them know they are breaking the rules or create special rules and procedures to help them better self-manage their behavior.

Element 34: Organizing the Physical Layout of the Classroom

An effective teacher organizes the physical layout of the classroom to facilitate movement and focus on learning. Research has identified four important aspects of room organization: (1) learning centers, technology, and equipment; (2) decorations; (3) materials; and (4) student and teacher desks (Marzano, Gaddy, Foseid, Foseid, & Marzano, 2005). The physical arrangement of the classroom should be compatible with planned instructional activities (Brophy, 2006; Weinstein, 1977).

There are twelve strategies within this element.

1. Designing classroom décor
2. Displaying student work
3. Considering classroom materials
4. Placing the teacher's desk
5. Placing student desks
6. Planning areas for whole-group instruction
7. Planning areas for group work
8. Planning learning centers
9. Considering computers and technology equipment
10. Considering lab equipment and supplies
11. Planning classroom libraries
12. Involving students in the design process

The following sections will explore each strategy to provide you with guidelines to effectively implement this element. Read through each before creating a plan for your classroom. Teachers may use the strategies individually or in combination. Remember, these are not merely activities to be checked off; they are methods of creating a practice that combines your art with the science of organizing the physical layout of the classroom. Reflect on your use of each strategy by filling out the "Strategy Reflection Log" on page 331.

Designing Classroom Décor

When considering the classroom décor, a teacher should aim to create a welcoming and functional learning environment. The teacher can post pictures and posters and create homey touches (such as curtains) or use themes relevant to the season or upcoming events to make the classroom feel friendly. The teacher should also align the classroom décor with learning goals and instructional priorities, so that it enforces the value and relevance of what students are learning. To this end, the teacher may leave empty spaces on the walls at the beginning of the year and post student work later on. Bulletin boards might display learning goals, classroom rules and procedures, assignments, school announcements, or school spirit paraphernalia, and calendars might display daily schedules or assignment timelines. Other learning resources on the walls could include the alphabet (in elementary classrooms), poems, vocabulary lists, historical timelines, information on current topics of study, the correct format for assignments (headings, page numbers, and so on), or exemplars and prototypes for assignments. In general, the emphasis in classroom decoration and use of wall space should be on functionality. Visit **go.SolutionTree.com/instruction** for the reproducible "Considerations for Classroom Décor" for questions and checklists to use with elementary and secondary classrooms.

Displaying Student Work

It is important for students to see themselves represented in the classroom and to benefit from examples of effective student work and other relevant visual artifacts. As such, a teacher should consider how to display students' work in the classroom and how such displays reinforce learning. A teacher can either post the same assignment from all students or post particularly noteworthy assignments from individual students. If a teacher chooses the latter, he or she should regularly switch out displayed student work when possible to give more students the opportunity to have their work posted. Furthermore, the teacher should be able to explain why he or she thought any posted work is exemplary.

Following are suggestions for displaying student work.

- Regularly consider the student work posted around the room and whether or not it has become outdated. The teacher may want to update student work if several weeks have passed since the end of a unit or if the work is unrelated to the current instructional unit.
- Display student work using clear 8 ½ × 11–inch pockets into which students slide their exemplary assignments or compositions. This allows students to identify work that they are proud of and post it for others to see.
- In some cases, it is appropriate to display an assignment or project from every student. When this is the case, make sure that every student is represented in the display and have students find their work on the walls.
- Especially in middle and high school, display only exemplary work as a type of reward for students who do well on a particular assignment. This has the benefit of providing the class with examples of quality work. However, the teacher should take care to vary the students whose work is posted, as displaying students' work should boost students' academic confidence, not make other students feel inadequate.
- When changing the student work displayed in the classroom, make note of the changes to the class. During this time, the teacher can explain why he or she felt that the posted work warranted being displayed.

Considering Classroom Materials

When a teacher monitors his or her learning materials and ensures that they are accessible and organized, he or she facilitates a classroom environment that runs smoothly and efficiently. The teacher should consider the placement and organization of various classroom materials as well as the frequency of their use. As such, teachers can place frequently used materials (such as pens, pencils, and a pencil sharpener) in a location that allows for easy access. Additionally, they should organize and label them in such a way that students can find what they need quickly and independently. Materials that students use less frequently may be stored in a less accessible space and brought out for students when necessary (such as bandages and first-aid equipment). The teacher should also plan ahead to consider the classroom materials needed for specific lessons and units and take care to acquire them in a prompt manner to ensure their availability at the proper times. Visit **go.SolutionTree.com/instruction** for the reproducible "Classroom Materials Checklist."

Placing the Teacher's Desk

When placing his or her desk in the classroom, a teacher should consider how he or she plans to use the desk during class time and when he or she is alone. Ideally, a teacher's desk should allow the teacher to monitor the class during seatwork and easily access it during whole-group instruction. Often, a teacher will either place his or her desk in the front or the back of the room. When a teacher's desk is in the front of the room, it allows the teacher to easily make direct eye contact with students during independent seatwork, while placing a teacher's desk in the back of the room allows the teacher to monitor the class without students knowing which part of the room is being observed. Regardless of its position, the teacher should be able to see and hear all parts of the classroom when seated, and the desk should be in an accessible location.

A teacher can use the following questions to assess the placement of his or her desk.

- Does my desk impede the flow of traffic?
- What do I primarily use my desk for?
- How do I use my desk during whole-group instruction?
- How do I use my desk during individual seatwork?
- How do I use my desk when I am not teaching a class?
- Should I place my desk at the front of the room or at the back of the room?
- Can I easily see all students from my desk, regardless of the type of instruction occurring?

Placing Student Desks

The organization of student desks and chairs can either inhibit or facilitate student learning. When considering the placement of student desks, the teacher should consider how students may use them during whole-class, small-group, and individual instruction. The arrangement of students' desks should allow students to hear directions, watch instruction, access necessary materials, and move quickly and safely around the classroom. A teacher should also be able to see and make eye contact with all students from various locations in the classroom. If needed, a teacher might also use seating charts that ensure that students stay on task and are not distracted by their neighbors.

A teacher can use the following questions to assess the placement of student desks.

- Are there enough desks and chairs for my students?
- Can each student see and hear me, regardless of where I am in the classroom?
- Is there a clear traffic pattern around the desks in the classroom?
- Can students easily access materials from their desks?
- How easily can students break up into pairs or small groups?
- How do students use their desks during whole-class instruction? Does the seating arrangement facilitate this?
- How do students use their desks during small-group instruction? Does the seating arrangement facilitate this?
- How do students use their desks during individual seatwork? Does the seating arrangement facilitate this?
- Does the seating arrangement encourage or deter off-task behavior?
- Do I need a seating chart? If so, are there specific students who should not be close to one another?

Planning Areas for Whole-Group Instruction

When designing a classroom's layout, a teacher should consider how the class interacts with the space during whole-group instruction. A teacher may consider the ease of access to materials frequently used during whole-group instruction, the teacher's ability to instruct and monitor the class, and students' ability to hear the teacher and see the board. First, the teacher must decide where whole-group instruction will take place, and this is generally informed by the placement of the black- or whiteboard or projector (which teachers often have little control over). After deciding where the whole-group instruction will take place, the teacher can consider the layout of the desks, the placement of materials, and how both facilitate easeful learning and an orderly classroom.

A teacher can use the following questions to assess the effectiveness of the classroom's physical layout for whole-group instruction.

- What do I need for whole-group instruction (black- or whiteboard, projector, interactive whiteboard, and so on)? How do these needs inform the design of the area for whole-group instruction?
- How easily can students transition from whole-group instruction to group work or individual seatwork?
- During whole-group instruction, can I see all of my students? Can all of my students see me?
- During whole-group instruction, can all of my students easily hear my directions?
- How easily can students access necessary materials during whole-group instruction?
- Can I easily move around the room during whole-group instruction?
- Does the area for whole-group instruction encourage the participation of all students?

Planning Areas for Group Work

To facilitate differentiated instruction and productive interaction among students, the classroom should include areas for small-group instruction in addition to the area for whole-class instruction. The teacher should consider where small groups of students can meet and how easy this is considering the placement of students' desks. The teacher may also want to create a space where he or she can meet with a small group of students while the rest of the class completes individual seatwork; this is often accomplished by placing a table off to the side of the classroom or through the use of learning centers or labs. In all cases, areas for small-group instruction should provide easy access to related materials (for example, chart paper and markers) and be out of the way so as not to block traffic patterns.

A teacher can use the following questions to assess the classroom's physical layout in relation to group work.

- Where can small groups of students meet for group work?
- How easily can students transition from whole-group instruction to group work or individual seatwork?
- During group work, can I see all of my students? Can all of my students see me?
- During group work, can all of my students easily hear my directions?
- How easily can students access necessary materials during group work?
- Can I easily move through the classroom to check on individual groups of students?
- Does the classroom layout encourage focused work from various groups?
- Is there a place where I can meet with small groups of students during individual seatwork?
- Are there any locations in which I do not want students to congregate during group work?

Planning Learning Centers

When designing the physical layout of the classroom, a teacher should consider the location of learning centers, if necessary. This is most often a concern for elementary school teachers; typically, the teacher will want to place learning centers away from major traffic patterns. Teachers should be able to easily monitor a learning center from all parts of the room. It should be close to books, resources, and other materials that may be required to complete tasks at the center. Furthermore, the learning centers should be isolated enough that students can work within the learning centers and focus on the task at hand without being distracted by other students.

A teacher can use the following questions when setting up learning centers in the classroom.

- How will students use the learning centers?
- How many learning centers are needed?
- How are the learning centers affected by the primary patterns of movement around the class?
- Should some centers be close to particular books, materials, or other resources?
- Can I monitor students in learning centers, regardless of where I am in the room?
- Will the placement of the learning centers help students focus on the task at hand?

Considering Computers and Technology Equipment

In most classrooms, computers and technology are integral parts of the learning environment. Most classrooms have an overhead projector or interactive whiteboard for whole-class instruction. Many classrooms have their own computer or computer stations to which students have access. When designing the physical layout of a classroom, the teacher should consider the various technologies in his or her classroom, their purposes, and how students make use of them. A teacher can then use these considerations to inform the placement of computers and technology equipment. For example, a teacher who regularly uses an overhead projector might place it so he or she can easily access it for whole-class instruction, while the same teacher might place the classroom printer off to the side of the room, as she uses it less frequently.

A teacher can use the following questions when setting up computers and technology equipment.

- How does technology play a role in instruction (for example, overhead projectors and computer access)?
- Does each student have a clear line of sight to the projector or computer display?
- Are computers and technology equipment physically close to their accessories?
- Do computers and technology equipment in the classroom disrupt traffic patterns when they are in use or when they are stored?
- Are computers and technology equipment in a location where I can monitor students' use of them?
- Do I have guidelines posted about appropriate use of computer and technology equipment?
- Are computers and technology equipment close to an adequate power source?
- Do the computers and technology equipment in my classroom distract students?

Considering Lab Equipment and Supplies

Though this may not be relevant to all educators, most science teachers will have to consider effective storage and use of lab equipment and supplies. When making these decisions, the teacher should consider student safety, protection for the equipment, and ease of access and use for students. In particular, some lab equipment and supplies—such as living and preserved animal and plant specimens, chemicals, glassware, and so on—require special considerations, especially concerning safety. Furthermore, many science classrooms are designed as a laboratory, which limits the teacher in terms of the locations of specialized equipment and spaces for instruction. If this is the case, the teacher should create a separate lecture area so that students are not near the laboratory equipment unnecessarily, if possible.

A teacher can use the following questions when setting up lab equipment and supplies.

- How and with what frequency will students use specific lab equipment and supplies?
- Do certain materials and equipment require special placement for safety reasons (for example, chemicals or lab equipment)?
- Are certain materials and equipment permanent fixtures? If so, how does this affect my classroom design?
- How do I store my lab equipment and supplies? Does this protect both students and the equipment?
- How accessible are lab equipment and supplies?
- Do I have a separate space for instruction so that students are not near lab equipment unnecessarily?
- Have I considered the lab equipment and supplies needed for specific units or lessons? Do I order supplies in a timely manner?
- In case of an emergency, does this layout impede or facilitate proper safety protocols?
- Do I have rules and guidelines posted around the classroom that encourage safe use of lab equipment and supplies?

Planning Classroom Libraries

The purpose of classroom libraries is to support student learning; therefore, they should be accessible to students. The teacher should place libraries where they will provide support for individual, small-group, and whole-group learning activities. Students should be able to easily access the classroom library, but bookshelves should not cause traffic jams or create blind spots where students can be out of view of the teacher. The teacher can also consider the contents of his or her classroom library, the way in which the books are organized, and systems for ensuring that books are returned to the bookshelves.

When building a classroom library, teachers should consider what the library already has and how they can build on the existing library. This may include seeking out books on specific topics or in specific genres. Furthermore, teachers should keep in mind students' ages and reading levels as well as the appropriateness of content. Teachers do not need to go out and purchase brand-new books. Rather, they can add to a classroom library on a relatively low budget using the following resources.

- Thrift stores
- Garage and estate sales
- Library sales
- Ebay (www.ebay.com)
- Book Outlet (http://bookoutlet.com)
- Donations from parents and community members

Following are four steps for cataloging and organizing books in your classroom.

1. Ensure that your name is in every book. Write or stamp your name and school on one of the first or last few pages of each book as well as along the side of pages if possible.
2. Consider how to organize the classroom library. You may choose to organize books by author, topic, genre, or reading level.

3. Once you decide on an organization structure, sort books in the library. This may take several tries if you are organizing by topic, genre, or reading level, as there may be some books that defy classification initially. It may help to label books based on their classifications to facilitate ease of reshelving books.
4. Place the books in the library. Create a key that explains the library's system of organization clearly or post an explanation near the bookshelves.

Consider how students will access books in the library using the following questions.

- Will students be allowed to bring books home? If yes, for how long?
- How will students check out books?
- What sort of system will be in place to keep track of which student has which book?
- How will students return books?
- Will students be responsible for reshelving books they have checked out, or will this be a classroom job?
- What is the proper way to handle books? What happens if students are not respectful of the books in the library?
- What will be my policy if a student keeps a book for too long? What if a student loses a book?
- How will I teach students how to use the classroom library?
- What visual resources will I provide to help students access books in the library correctly?

Involving Students in the Design Process

Although many teachers arrange the classroom before students arrive for the first day of class, asking students to be involved in the design process can help them feel invested and comfortable as they work in and move around the classroom. The teacher may informally poll students to solicit their feedback about the classroom décor and the organization of the room or formally survey them. If a teacher does choose to involve students in the design process, he or she should use their input to make changes—a teacher who asks for student input but then ignores it may make students feel as though he or she does not care about their opinions.

A teacher can involve students in the design process of the classroom in the following ways.

- Ask students to complete the "Student Survey for Organizing the Physical Layout of the Classroom" (visit **go.SolutionTree.com/instruction** to download a copy of this survey). Use the results to inform changes to the physical layout of the classroom. A teacher can also review the results, identify patterns in the responses, and ask the class directly about their answers.
- Facilitate a class discussion on the physical layout of the classroom. Solicit positive and negative comments from students as well as changes they would make to the classroom. Use this discussion to inform changes to the physical layout of the classroom.
- Informally ask students about the physical layout of the classroom before class starts or during transitions. A teacher could focus these questions to address specific elements of the classroom. For example, a teacher might ask a few students before the period starts, "I'm thinking about rearranging the desks in the classroom. How do you think I should do it?"
- Create a list of possible changes to the classroom layout and run each one by the class. Take comments and suggestions from students. Consider these comments to create a new list of modifications to the classroom layout. Have the class vote on each of the changes.
- Ask students to bring in or create their own decorations for the classroom. Post these decorations and acknowledge the students who brought them in.

Monitoring Element 34

Specific student responses and behaviors allow the teacher to determine whether this element is being implemented effectively and producing the desired effects.

- Students move easily about the classroom.
- Students make use of materials and learning centers.
- Students access and use examples of their work the teacher has displayed.
- Students access and use the information on bulletin boards.
- Students can easily focus on instruction.

Use this list to monitor student responses to element 34.

To monitor your own use of this element, use the scale in figure 8.6 in combination with the reproducible "Tracking Teacher Actions: Organizing the Physical Layout of the Classroom" (page 275). As with other proficiency scales, level 3 or higher is the goal.

4 Innovating	I adapt behaviors and create new strategies for unique student needs and situations.
3 Applying	I organize the physical layout of the classroom, and I monitor the extent to which my actions affect students' behavior.
2 Developing	I organize the physical layout of the classroom, but I do not monitor the effect on students.
1 Beginning	I use the strategies and behaviors associated with this element incorrectly or with parts missing.
0 Not Using	I am unaware of strategies and behaviors associated with this element.

Figure 8.6: Self-rating scale for element 34—Organizing the physical layout of the classroom.

The following examples describe what each level of the scale might look like in the classroom.

- **Not Using (0):** A teacher hasn't put much thought into the physical layout of her classroom, and, as such, the classroom often is counterproductive to learning. For example, the teacher finds it difficult to transition between whole-class instruction and group work because of the arrangement of the desks.
- **Beginning (1):** A teacher recognizes that décor is important and hangs up classroom decorations as well as students' work. However, the teacher rarely changes these decorations, so they are often outdated and unrelated to the content she's teaching.
- **Developing (2):** A teacher realizes that she does a lot of group-work activities with her class, so she reorganizes the rows of desks into clusters of four. This eliminates students' need to move when starting group work, but the teacher is not sure how it has affected overall classroom behavior.
- **Applying (3):** A teacher tries various arrangements for students' desks including small clusters, one large circle, and traditional rows. The teacher tries each for a few weeks, monitors how students' behavior is affected, and weighs the pros and cons of each. The teacher uses this experiment to inform her preference for student desk arrangement.
- **Innovating (4):** A teacher involves groups of students in the design process by identifying areas that need improvement and letting them independently create solutions. For example, the teacher recognizes that the classroom library and the arrangement of student desks are not effective. The teacher divides the class into two groups and has one group focus on the classroom

library and one group focus on the arrangement of student desks. The students collaborate, make changes to the existing models, then explain the reasoning behind their changes to the group.

Element 35: Demonstrating Withitness

An effective teacher is alert and aware of what is occurring in the classroom at all times. Research has shown that teacher withitness (being aware of what is going on in the classroom at all times) is associated with a decrease in classroom disruptions (Brophy, 1996; Kounin, 1983; Marzano, 2003). Appropriate teacher reactions to positive or negative behavior are also associated with a decrease in classroom disruptions (Marzano, 2003).

There are four strategies within this element.

1. Being proactive
2. Occupying the whole room physically and visually
3. Noticing potential problems
4. Using a series of graduated actions

The following sections will explore each strategy to provide you with guidelines to effectively implement this element. Read through each before creating a plan for your classroom. Teachers may use the strategies individually or in combination. Remember, these are not merely activities to be checked off; they are methods of creating a practice that combines your art with the science of demonstrating withitness. Reflect on your use of each strategy by filling out the "Strategy Reflection Log" on page 331.

Being Proactive

Teachers can resolve many behavioral issues with careful planning and proactive steps. To become proactive, a teacher is aware of what could potentially go wrong or cause disruption in class and pre-emptively takes actions to avoid such scenarios. For example, a proactive teacher might confer privately with potentially disruptive students to review classroom expectations, create contingency plans for various behavior scenarios that might arise throughout the day, or seek out information regarding incidents that have occurred outside of class that may affect student behavior. A proactive teacher might also create prearranged cues that signal inappropriate behavior. For example, the teacher might make a small mark on a notepad on the student's desk or tap twice on the desktop if the student's behavior is becoming disruptive or unacceptable.

Table 8.3 provides examples of proactive behaviors for types of potentially disruptive students.

Table 8.3: Examples of Proactive Behaviors

Type of Student	Indicators	Proactive Teacher Behavior
Passive	Avoidant of social interactions for fear of having a negative interaction or being dominated by others; afraid of criticism, ridicule, or rejection	Create a safe and inclusive classroom environment; encourage assertiveness and positive self-talk; reward and celebrate even the smallest of successes; withhold criticisms.
Aggressive	Interrupts during class; lashes out; intimidates other students physically or verbally; rude or disrespectful to teacher; experiences relatively few successes	Describe the student's behavior; reward or apply consequences consistently when behavior is or is not appropriate; encourage extracurricular involvement; give the student additional responsibilities so he or she can experience success.

continued →

Type of Student	Indicators	Proactive Teacher Behavior
Perfectionist	Holds him- or herself to unnecessarily high standards; motivated by fear of embarrassment rather than intellectual curiosity; unwilling to participate if there is a chance of failure	Talk with student about expectations and try to help student create realistic expectations; encourage student to make mistakes; show acceptance; have student tutor other students; create time limits for the amount of time the student can spend on an assignment.
Socially inept	Has few or no friends; seems unaware of how his or her actions affect others; seems unaware of subtle social cues or struggles to keep up natural conversations; appears anxious when interacting with others; considers him- or herself a loner	Talk to the student about social cues and ways in which he or she may miss them; make suggestions regarding hygiene, dress, mannerisms, and posture; spend time interacting with the student modeling appropriate behavior and showing that he or she is a valuable member of class.
Attention difficulties	Inattentive; distracted easily by unusual events; difficult to re-engage or get on task; late or incomplete work; difficulty with organization, remembering, or listening	Talk with necessary individuals about getting student tested or creating an individualized learning plan; create signals to let the student know when he or she is being disruptive or needs to refocus; teach basic concentration, study, and thinking skills; assign a peer tutor.

Occupying the Whole Room Physically and Visually

The teacher is aware of what occurs in the classroom and notes the behavior of individual and groups of students. The teacher makes eye contact regularly with students to let them know he or she is aware of their actions and is monitoring the classroom. Furthermore, the teacher spends time in each quadrant of the room on a regular basis and physically moves through the classroom during instruction and individual seatwork.

Figure 8.7 can help you plan for the use of this strategy.

Planning Guide for Occupying the Whole Room Physically and Visually

Class period: ______________________________

Whole Class Instruction

I plan to physically occupy the following spaces:

I plan to make eye contact with, become physically proximate to, or pay particular attention to the following students:

Questions to ask myself during whole-class instruction:

- Am I in a place where I can make eye contact with all of my students?
- If students are being disruptive, is there a way for me to physically move closer to those students without interrupting the lesson?
- Is there a way for me to move around my classroom without interrupting the lesson?

Small-Group Work

I plan to physically occupy the following spaces:

I plan to make eye contact with, become physically proximate to, or pay particular attention to the following students:

Questions to ask myself during small-group work:

- Have I physically moved between groups to ensure they're on task?
- Have I occupied each of the quadrants of the classroom?
- Have I been making eye contact with students to let them know I'm aware of their actions?

Individual Seatwork

I plan to physically occupy the following spaces:

I plan to make eye contact with, become physically proximate to, or pay particular attention to the following students:

Questions to ask myself during individual seatwork:

- Have I physically moved through each of the quadrants of the classroom containing students?
- If a student is being disruptive or seems restless, have I physically moved to be in the proximity of that student?
- Have I been scanning the room with my eyes to let students know I'm aware of their actions?

Source: Marzano Research, 2016.

Figure 8.7: Planning guide for occupying the whole room physically and visually.

Visit **go.SolutionTree.com/instruction** *for a free reproducible version of this figure.*

Noticing Potential Problems

Teachers should be alert throughout lessons so that they can identify and pre-emptively address situations that could develop into larger disruptive behaviors. Teachers can watch for small groups of students huddled together talking intensely; one or more students not engaging in a class activity for an extended period of time; students in a specific area looking at each other and smiling; members of the class looking at a specific location and smiling; students giggling or smiling whenever the teacher looks at or walks near a particular part of the room; or whispering, giggling, or unusual noises when the teacher's back is to the class. Teachers can then take appropriate actions to defuse the potentially disruptive behavior before it escalates.

Table 8.4 provides examples of problems and teacher actions.

Table 8.4: Sample Problems and Teacher Actions

Problem	Teacher Actions
Disengaged students	The teacher might move physically closer to, make eye contact with, or verbally cue the students to stay on task.
Students talking with one another during a lesson	The teacher could move closer to or verbally call on the students. If the behavior continues, the teacher might directly ask the students to stay on task or separate the group physically.

continued →

Problem	Teacher Actions
Students making eye contact across the room	The teacher could physically place him- or herself between the students making eye contact. Alternatively, the teacher could verbally call on one or more of the students to show the teacher is aware they are disengaged.
Students whispering, giggling, or making unusual noises when the teacher's back is turned	The teacher could make an effort to face the class or engage the class in a brief break activity so students can refocus. The teacher might also ask the class directly about the disruption.
Students disengaging because of an outside distraction	The teacher might acknowledge the outside distraction, then ask students to re-engage in the material. The teacher should also attempt to remove the distraction if possible (such as pulling down blinds or closing the classroom door).
Students all looking toward one area of the classroom	The teacher could physically move toward that quadrant of the classroom to assess whether the students are being distracted by a student or something physically in the classroom. Depending on whether the behavior continues, the teacher might directly ask students about the disruption.
Students not focusing during small-group work	The teacher might move nearer to the small group and engage the group in a questioning sequence. If the group seems unprepared, the teacher can tell the initially distracted group he or she will return to check their answers and can move on to another group.

Using a Series of Graduated Actions

A teacher who uses a series of graduated actions assesses each disruptive behavior in class and tailors his or her reactions to the disruption at hand. If the distraction persists, the teacher can continue to escalate his or her reactions. For example, when noticing disruptive behavior, the teacher makes eye contact with those students involved in the incident or who exhibit the behavior. If the problem persists, the teacher might stand right next to the offending student or students and use nonverbal cues to communicate that they need to stop their inappropriate behavior and join in what the class is doing. If the behavior still persists, the teacher could talk to the offending students quietly and privately and request (not demand), in a positive way, that they re-engage with what the class is doing and reiterate that their participation is welcome and needed. Finally, if the behavior does not stop, the teacher would stop the class and calmly and politely state the consequences that will ensue if the students continue their current behavior, while communicating that the students have a decision to make.

A plan like figure 8.8 can guide your use of this strategy.

Monitoring Element 35

Specific student responses and behaviors allow the teacher to determine whether this element is being implemented effectively and producing the desired effects.

- Students recognize that the teacher is aware of their behavior.
- Students describe the teacher as aware of what is going on.
- Students extinguish potentially disruptive behaviors quickly and efficiently.

Use this list to monitor student responses to element 35.

To monitor your own use of this element, use the scale in figure 8.9 in combination with the reproducible "Tracking Teacher Actions: Demonstrating Withitness" (page 276). As with other proficiency scales, level 3 or higher is the goal.

Plan for Graduated Actions

If students are engaging in disruptive behavior, the teacher will react in the following way.

- The teacher will first make eye contact with the student or students to signal the teacher is aware of the disruptive behavior.
- If the disruption continues, the teacher will move toward the student or students and use nonverbal cues to communicate the behavior is unacceptable.
- If the disruption still continues, the teacher will quietly talk to the student or students to ask them to stop and let them know their participation is needed.
- If the disruption still continues, the teacher will stop class, confront the offending behavior, and explain the consequences if the behavior does not stop.

Potential consequences include:

1. ______________________________

2. ______________________________

3. ______________________________

4. ______________________________

I understand how my teacher plans to react to disruptive behavior and the potential consequences that could result from continued disruptive behavior.

Student name: ______________________ Date: ______________

Source: Marzano Research, 2016.

Figure 8.8: Plan for graduated actions.

Visit **go.SolutionTree.com/instruction** *for a free reproducible version of this figure.*

4 Innovating	I adapt behaviors and create new strategies for unique student needs and situations.
3 Applying	I demonstrate withitness, and I monitor the extent to which my actions affect students' behavior.
2 Developing	I demonstrate withitness, but I do not monitor the effect on students.
1 Beginning	I use the strategies and behaviors associated with this element incorrectly or with parts missing.
0 Not Using	I am unaware of strategies and behaviors associated with this element.

Figure 8.9: Self-rating scale for element 35—Demonstrating withitness.

The following examples describe what each level of the scale might look like in the classroom.

- **Not Using (0):** The teacher is unaware of when students are distracted and does not take steps to stop the behavior from distracting the entire class.
- **Beginning (1):** The teacher recognizes when students are engaging or about to engage in disruptive behavior but does not react to the situation.
- **Developing (2):** The teacher actively moves through the various quadrants of the classroom, letting his students know that he is aware of everything going on in the room, but he does not follow through to ensure that his level of awareness is extinguishing disruptive behavior.

- **Applying (3):** The teacher exhibits withitness by noticing potential problems and being proactive to stop disruptive behaviors before they start. The teacher has identified specific students who often exhibit disruptive behavior and has sought out private meetings with them to better understand what actions the teacher can take to ensure they stay on task. Since those meetings and acting upon those conversations, the teacher notices that the students exhibit less disruptive behavior than before and classes tend to run smoother.
- **Innovating (4):** The teacher makes the entire class aware of the graduated actions she will take when a student is being distracting to the class. However, the teacher has also identified aggressive and socially inept students in her class for whom her regular strategies have not worked well. She has worked privately with them to create graduated action plans specific to their needs.

Element 36: Acknowledging Adherence to Rules and Procedures

An effective teacher consistently and fairly acknowledges adherence to rules and procedures. Research has shown that recognizing adherence to rules and procedures is associated with a decrease in classroom disruptions (Stage & Quiroz, 1997). Tangible recognition and group contingency are also associated with decreases in classroom disruptions (Marzano, 2003).

There are eight strategies within this element.

1. Verbal affirmation
2. Nonverbal affirmation
3. Tangible recognition
4. Token economies
5. Daily recognition form
6. Color-coded behavior
7. Certificates
8. Phone calls, emails, and notes

The following sections will explore each strategy to provide you with guidelines to effectively implement this element. Read through each before creating a plan for your classroom. Teachers may use the strategies individually or in combination. Remember, these are not merely activities to be checked off; they are methods of creating a practice that combines your art with the science of acknowledging adherence to rules and procedures. Reflect on your use of each strategy by filling out the "Strategy Reflection Log" on page 331.

Verbal Affirmation

An effective teacher uses short verbal affirmations such as "thank you," "good job," "that's great," or "very good." The teacher might also have short conversations or write notes to students to acknowledge their adherence to rules and procedures. The teacher would describe what the student did that constituted adhering to a rule or procedure and how the behavior contributed to the proper functioning of the class. For example, a teacher might say, "Thank you for pushing in your chair when you got up. You're helping keep our classroom clean and safe." This aspect of verbal affirmations is essential to helping students behave well habitually. The teacher might also contrast the student's current behavior with past behavior that failed to adhere to a rule or procedure.

Three steps for verbally acknowledging positive behavior include the following (Marzano Research, 2016).

1. Notice a positive behavior (for example, a student helping another pick up dropped materials).
2. Approach the student and describe the behavior, either while they are performing the behavior or immediately after ("You helped your classmate pick up her papers.").
3. Make a statement that recognizes the positive value of the behavior ("That was very nice and helpful!").

Consider using the following sentence stems with students. Use positive adjectives like *attentive, caring, considerate, cooperative, determined, hardworking, helpful, friendly, generous, honest, patient, persistent, respectful,* and *responsible.*

- "Thank you for __________."
- "I see that you __________. That tells me that you __________ [positive trait or behavioral expectation]."
- "It's very __________ of you to __________."
- "I know everyone appreciates it when you __________."
- "Everyone, notice how __________ is __________. That is demonstrating __________."

Nonverbal Affirmation

The teacher uses a smile, a wink, a nod of the head, a thumbs-up sign, an OK sign (thumb and forefinger loop), a pantomimed tip of the hat, a pat on the back, or a high five to acknowledge students' adherence to rules and procedures. For example, when the class lines up for recess quickly and quietly, the teacher might high-five each student on the way out of the room.

Figure 8.10 provides examples of nonverbal affirmations.

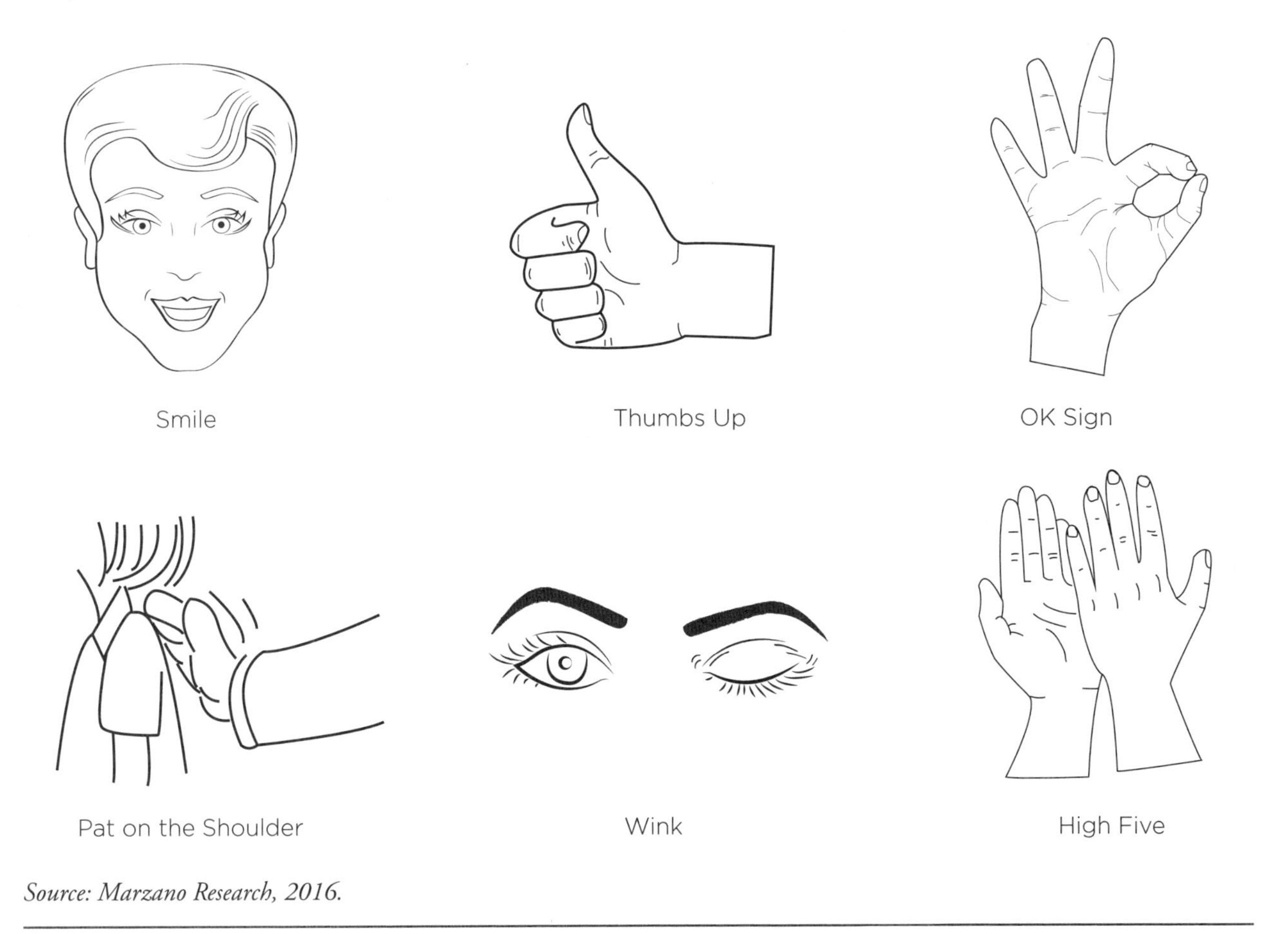

Source: Marzano Research, 2016.

Figure 8.10: Examples of nonverbal affirmations.

Visit **go.SolutionTree.com/instruction** *for a free reproducible version of this figure.*

Tangible Recognition

Teachers can use privileges, activities, or items as rewards for positive behavior. For example, a teacher could reward students who stayed focused during independent work time by allowing them a few minutes to talk to friends at the end of class. Any use of tangible recognition should be accompanied by a thorough class discussion of the rationale behind the system to ensure it is not perceived as a type of bribe or form of coercion.

Following are examples of tangible recognition.

- **Friday Fun Club:** Usually appropriate for the elementary level, with Friday Fun Club, students who have earned membership in the club get to play a fun, educational game for the last hour of school on Friday.
- **Reward field trips:** Usually appropriate for the secondary level, reward field trips also work well in lower grades. Students who have no or few discipline referrals are allowed to go on a special field trip.
- **Public recognition:** Teachers might display a class poster with the names of students who have met a certain standard of excellence, or students might post thank-you messages to each other or to teachers on a common bulletin board.
- **Lunch in the classroom:** A well-behaved student or group of students gets to eat lunch in the classroom with the teacher.
- **Snack parties:** Students who exhibit exemplary behavior over a certain period of time (for example, one month) get to attend a popcorn, pizza, ice cream, or other snack party during lunch, recess, or after school.
- **Attire rewards:** Students earn the privilege of wearing typically off-limits clothing such as pajamas or hats to school. At schools where students are required to wear uniforms, students could earn a free-dress day.
- **Citizen of the Month:** The teacher selects one student each month to be recognized for going above and beyond behavioral expectations. The student is then recognized in front of the class. The teacher might describe to the class what the student did to earn recognition or use a bulletin board to post the student's picture and a written description of their behavior.

Token Economies

The teacher uses a system in which students receive tokens, chits, or points when they meet expectations. They can then exchange these tokens, chits, or points for privileges, activities, or items. For example, a teacher might hand out a plastic poker chip for behaviors such as raising one's hand to ask a question. Students could then purchase rewards, such as a no homework pass, when they have accumulated enough chips.

Figure 8.11 offers an example token economy reward chart.

Reward	Cost (points, tokens, tickets, and so on)
Raffle ticket	One
Pencils and erasers	Five
Teacher's chair privileges	Ten
Group work with a friend	Fifteen
Show-and-tell time	Twenty
Snack in class	Twenty-five
Whole-class reward	Thirty
School T-shirt	Fifty

Figure 8.11: Example of a token economy reward chart.

Daily Recognition Form

The teacher awards each student a starting score at the beginning of class (for example, twenty points) for a prearranged set of expectations (for example, four points for punctuality, four points for preparation, four points for on-task behavior, four points for respectfulness, and four points for work completion). If a student fails to meet a particular expectation, some or all of the points associated with that expectation are taken away. In other words, if a student meets all expectations throughout the day, his ending score would be twenty points. A student who comes to class without a pencil and paper might lose some of her points in the preparation category. The teacher can use a tracking sheet placed on each student's desk to keep track of points throughout the day or class period. At the end of the period or day, students tally their total points, and the teacher records daily totals in a ledger. Students who achieve certain point levels earn privileges, activities, or items.

Figure 8.12 provides a template for a daily recognition form.

Template for a Daily Recognition Form

Name: ______________________ Date: ______________

Expectations	Starting Points	Points Taken Away	Ending Points
Totals			

Source: Marzano Research, 2016.

Figure 8.12: Template for a daily recognition form.

Visit **go.SolutionTree.com/instruction** *for a free reproducible version of this figure.*

Color-Coded Behavior

In this strategy, the teacher gives each student three cards (red card = unacceptable behavior, yellow card = acceptable behavior with room for improvement, green card = exceptional adherence to rules and procedures) to keep on his or her desktop. All students begin the day or period with the green card on top. If a student's behavior warrants it, the teacher changes the exposed card to indicate the level of behavior being exhibited. For example, a student who speaks out of turn once or twice might have his color changed to yellow. If he continues to call out repeatedly, the teacher would switch his card to red. Students whose behavior has warranted a change to yellow or red may work to have the green card reinstated by displaying appropriate behavior. Many elementary teachers use a variation of this strategy involving a poster that shows a color (red, yellow, or green) for each student. Students each begin the day on green, and the teacher asks them to change their color if their behavior warrants it.

Certificates

Teachers can use reward certificates to increase parental involvement and awareness of behavior at school. For example, a student who helps another student with her work could receive a certificate as a special recognition of his helpfulness. Teachers can personalize blank certificates with a student's name and the reason for the reward, while preprinted certificates that correspond to specific desired behaviors can quickly reward positive behavior.

Figure 8.13 provides examples of reward certificates.

Source: Marzano Research, 2016.

Figure 8.13: Sample reward certificates.

Visit **go.SolutionTree.com/instruction** *for a free reproducible version of this figure.*

Phone Calls, Emails, and Notes

Effective teachers make phone calls and send emails or notes to a student's parents or guardians to recognize positive behavior. This affirmation can do wonders for the self-confidence and future behavior of students, and it can be very uplifting for a teacher to hear the sense of pride in a family member's voice. Particularly for students who have frequent behavior issues at school, a teacher or family member's acknowledgment of even one good day can make a huge impact. The teacher might make a goal of one positive phone call every afternoon. The teacher can also compose individual or group emails and notes to the parents or guardians of students who behaved appropriately during a particular week. All communication should be specific about how a student's behavior reinforced a positive classroom environment and climate. For example, a teacher could send an email to a student's parents telling them that she did an excellent job as the facilitator of a group discussion.

A sheet like figure 8.14 can help you track contact with students' parents or guardians.

Home Contract Log for Positive Behavior			
Student Name	**Date of Contact**	**Phone Call, Email, or Note**	**Behavior**
		PC E N	
		PC E N	

Source: Marzano Research, 2016.

Figure 8.14: Home contact log for positive behavior.

Visit **go.SolutionTree.com/instruction** *for a free reproducible version of this figure.*

Monitoring Element 36

Specific student responses and behaviors allow the teacher to determine whether this element is being implemented effectively and producing the desired effects.

- Students appear appreciative of the teacher's acknowledgment.
- Students describe the teacher as aware of their good behavior.
- Students regularly adhere to rules and procedures.

Use this list to monitor student responses to element 36.

To monitor your own use of this element, use the scale in figure 8.15 in combination with the reproducible "Tracking Teacher Actions: Acknowledging Adherence to Rules and Procedures" (page 277). As with other proficiency scales, level 3 or higher is the goal.

4 Innovating	I adapt behaviors and create new strategies for unique student needs and situations.
3 Applying	I acknowledge adherence to rules and procedures consistently and fairly, and I monitor the extent to which my actions affect students' behavior.
2 Developing	I acknowledge adherence to rules and procedures consistently and fairly, but I do not monitor the effect on students.
1 Beginning	I use the strategies and behaviors associated with this element incorrectly or with parts missing.
0 Not Using	I am unaware of strategies and behaviors associated with this element.

Figure 8.15: Self-rating scale for element 36—Acknowledging adherence to rules and procedures.

The following examples describe what each level of the scale might look like in the classroom.

- **Not Using (0):** A teacher only comments on students' behavior when they are breaking the rules and ignores opportunities to acknowledge adherence to rules and procedures.
- **Beginning (1):** A teacher occasionally thanks her students for being courteous or working quietly, but she often forgets to do so and does not use any tangible rewards or other forms of recognition.
- **Developing (2):** A teacher acknowledges his class's good behavior with strategies such as verbal praise and certificates for individual students. His efforts are deliberate, but he does not spend time trying to determine if the strategies are having a measurable impact.
- **Applying (3):** A teacher regularly acknowledges and rewards students for following the rules, using a variety of strategies. She also makes sure the strategies are having their desired effect by taking note of instances of misbehavior and looking for patterns. She is able to see that misbehavior has decreased in her classroom as she has become more skilled with this element.

- **Innovating (4):** A teacher uses various strategies to acknowledge when students are behaving appropriately. One of his students, however, is not responding as well to the strategies as others and continues to misbehave. In response, the teacher modifies his implementation of the token economy to provide extra support to this student.

Element 37: Acknowledging Lack of Adherence to Rules and Procedures

An effective teacher consistently and fairly applies consequences when students do not follow rules and procedures. Research has shown that recognizing adherence to rules and procedures is associated with a decrease in classroom disruptions (Stage & Quiroz, 1997). Tangible recognition and group contingency also decrease the number of classroom disruptions (Marzano, 2003).

There are nine strategies within this element.

1. Verbal cues
2. Pregnant pause
3. Nonverbal cues
4. Time-out
5. Overcorrection
6. Interdependent group contingency
7. Home contingency
8. High-intensity situation plan
9. Overall disciplinary plan

The following sections will explore each strategy to provide you with guidelines to effectively implement this element. Read through each before creating a plan for your classroom. Teachers may use the strategies individually or in combination. Remember, these are not merely activities to be checked off; they are methods of creating a practice that combines your art with the science of acknowledging lack of adherence to rules and procedures. Reflect on your use of each strategy by filling out the "Strategy Reflection Log" on page 331.

Verbal Cues

Using verbal cues, a teacher says a student's name, quietly reminds a student that he or she is not following a rule or procedure, quietly states the expected appropriate behavior, or simply tells a student to stop the current behavior. The teacher might also use comments such as, "Bill, think about what you are doing right now" or "Mariah, is what you are doing helping you focus your attention?" Consider using the following sentence stems (Marzano Research, 2016).

- __________ (*say student name*), please stop __________ (*describe behavior*).
- __________ (*say student name*), when you __________ (*describe behavior*), it __________ (*describe effect on others*). Could you __________ (*suggest appropriate behavior*) instead?
- __________ (*say student name*), you are not __________ (*state rule or expectation*) right now. Can you try that again?
- __________ (*say student name*), is what you are doing right now helping you __________ (*describe expected task or behavior*)?
- __________ (*say student name*), how do you think __________ (*describe behavior*) affects your classmates and their ability to learn?
- __________ (*say student name*), if you continue to __________ (*describe behavior*), you will __________ (*describe consequence*). What should you be doing instead?
- __________ (*say student name*), __________ (*describe behavior*) goes against __________ (*describe value or expectation*). That's not acceptable in our classroom.

Pregnant Pause

When using a pregnant pause, the teacher stops teaching in response to recurring disruptive behavior, creating an uncomfortable silence that will direct the attention in the room toward the misbehaving student.

This can be a powerful motivator for a student to adjust his or her behavior. For example, if a student is talking to his neighbor during teacher-led instruction, the teacher might stop speaking until the student realizes the class is waiting on him. However, if the student's goal in misbehaving was to attract attention, this strategy can backfire. The teacher should be prepared to verbally confront the student in front of the group if necessary.

Following are four steps for using a pregnant pause.

1. Notice a student behaving inappropriately during instruction.
2. Stop teaching and look at the student.
3. Wait for the misbehaving student to notice the pregnant pause.
4. Assess the student's reaction. If the student responds to the attention by ceasing the inappropriate behavior, resume teaching. If the student is encouraged by the attention and continues misbehaving, use another more direct strategy (such as a verbal cue) to convey that the behavior needs to stop.

Nonverbal Cues

The teacher uses eye contact, proximity, subtle gestures (such as shaking the head "no," putting a finger on the lips, tapping a student's desk, giving a thumbs-down, or raising eyebrows) to signal to students that their behavior is inappropriate. For example, if a student is being disruptive during silent reading time, the teacher might make eye contact with that student, raise his eyebrows in a disapproving manner, and shake his head "no."

Figure 8.16 provides examples of nonverbal cues.

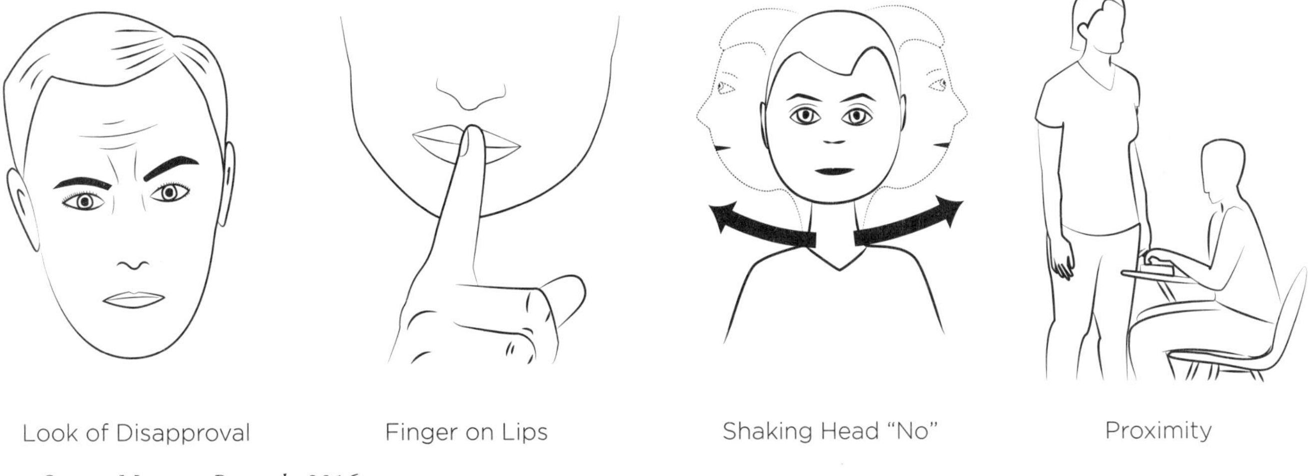

Source: Marzano Research, 2016.

Figure 8.16: Examples of nonverbal cues.

Visit **go.SolutionTree.com/instruction** *for a free reproducible version of this figure.*

Time-Out

In this strategy, the teacher asks an offending student to go to a designated place (inside or outside the classroom) until the student is ready to resume regular classroom activities. The teacher might use a graduated process for sending students to time-out: (1) warning; (2) time-out inside the classroom, where the student can continue to attend to the academic activities that are occurring; and (3) time-out outside the classroom. To illustrate, imagine a student who gets up and wanders the room, bothering other students. After the first one or two times this happens, the teacher might give her a warning. If the behavior continues, the student is placed in a time-out chair away from other students but still within the classroom. If an in-class time-out fails to change the student's behavior, she is given a time-out outside the classroom. If the student leaves the classroom for a time-out, the teacher must ensure that the student is still supervised. Finally, the student should develop a concrete action plan specifying what she will do differently upon returning to the classroom. This action plan can ask students to identify why they received a time-out, why they behaved a certain way, their plan for next time, how they will behave when returning to class, and ways for the teacher to help.

Overcorrection

In this strategy, the teacher requires a student who has behaved destructively to make things better than they were before the student acted to destroy them. For example, if a student destroyed class property, the student would need to repair what was destroyed and then improve additional class property. If a student interrupted the class's opportunity to learn, the student would need to learn the material independently and then assist the rest of the class in learning the material. An important step in this strategy is closely monitoring students while they complete overcorrection tasks.

Table 8.5 provides examples of overcorrection consequences.

Table 8.5: Examples of Overcorrection Consequences

Inappropriate Behavior	Overcorrection Consequence
Drawing on a desk	Cleaning every desk
Running in the hallway	Walking up and down the hallway several times
Throwing food at lunch	Cleaning the whole cafeteria
Disrupting instruction	Teaching the content to other students
Using rude language toward a classmate	Writing an apology letter to every classmate
Speaking out of turn	Practicing the correct procedure repeatedly

Interdependent Group Contingency

With interdependent group contingency, the teacher gives the entire class positive consequences only if every student in the class meets a certain behavioral standard. This type of group contingency reinforces positive group behavior and extinguishes negative group behaviors, but teachers should use it carefully, especially at the secondary level where students have a well-developed sense of fairness. Combat this perception by pre-emptively explaining to students that during the learning process, a class succeeds and fails as a team.

Following are examples of interdependent group contingencies.

- **Marble jar:** Usually used at the elementary level, the teacher adds a marble to a jar for good class behavior and removes a marble from the jar for inappropriate class behavior. When the jar is full, the class earns a tangible reward or privilege.
- **Tally marks:** The teacher puts a tally mark on the board when the class behaves appropriately. Alternatively, the teacher might give a tally mark to individual groups or teams that display appropriate behavior. When either the class or an individual team has received a previously agreed-on number of tally marks, the students earn a tangible reward or privilege.
- **Countdown:** The teacher and students identify a certain number of "slips in protocol" considered acceptable during a specific time interval (such as a class period or day). The teacher makes a mark on the board every time a student fails to follow the target behavior. If fewer marks are tallied than the prearranged number, the whole class retains a privilege or earns a reward.
- **Group grades:** The teacher and students agree that every student in a group will be assigned the group's grade as his or her individual grade. When using this strategy, the teacher should ensure that each member of the group contributes equally to the final outcome or product.

- **Mystery motivator:** The teacher writes down a reward, places it in a sealed envelope, and displays the envelope at the front of the classroom. The teacher then identifies a number of points the class must earn and the time frame in which they must earn them to receive the reward. The class earns a point for each instance of positive behavior and loses a point for each instance of inappropriate behavior. If, at the end of the specified time frame, the class has reached the required number of points, the teacher reveals the reward that the class will receive.

Home Contingency

In this strategy, the teacher meets with the student and parents or guardians to identify and discuss the student's use of inappropriate behavior in class. This helps the student perceive that his or her teacher and parents or guardians are unified in their attempt to help the student control his or her classroom behavior. With input from the teacher and parents or guardians, the student should identify positive and negative consequences associated with his or her behavior in class. The teacher and parents or guardians can then implement the consequences the student identifies in the classroom and at home. For example, the student might be allowed to play a video game after school if he behaved in class but have that privilege taken away if he misbehaves. The teacher should communicate with the student's parents or guardians about the student's daily behavior.

Figure 8.17 can help guide your use of this strategy.

Home Contingency Log

Student name: ____________________

Parent or guardian: ____________________

Phone number: ____________________

Email address: ____________________

Target behavior standard: ____________________

Reward if met: ____________________

Consequence if not met: ____________________

Date	Behavioral Notes	Reward or Consequence?	Home Contacted

Source: Marzano Research, 2016.

Figure 8.17: Home contingency log.

Visit **go.SolutionTree.com/instruction** *for a free reproducible version of this figure.*

High-Intensity Situation Plan

Although effective classroom and behavior management strategies can prevent many situations from escalating, most—if not all—teachers will eventually face a situation in which a student becomes out of control. Planning for these situations can prevent emotional reactions on the part of the teacher and allow the teacher to handle the situation efficiently and effectively. The basic outline of a plan for high-intensity situations should include the following four considerations: (1) assessing the severity of the situation, (2) remaining calm, (3) actively listening to the student's concerns, and (4) removing the student from the situation once he or she has regained some control.

Following are seven steps for defusing high-intensity situations from *Managing the Inner World of Teaching* (Marzano & Marzano, 2015).

1. **Know your students' tendencies:** In many cases, previous instances of aggressive behavior are the best predictors of future incidents. Thus, it is important for teachers to be aware of students who have exhibited aggressive behavior in the past. However, don't use past incidents to justify labeling specific students as troublemakers. Instead, help students who have experienced angry outbursts in the past feel welcome and valued in class by giving them a bit of extra attention. Planning for positive interactions on a systematic basis can be extremely effective in reducing the possibility or frequency of future incidents.
2. **Recognize that the student is out of control:** Whenever possible, teachers should know their students well enough to be able to tell when a student has reached his or her breaking point. For some students, this might manifest as yelling or wild gestures. Others, however, might become very quiet or draw inward before erupting. It is particularly important to be aware of incidents that have the potential to provoke students, such as a recent fight or argument with another teacher or student.
3. **Put physical distance between yourself and the student, and avoid threatening behavior:** When a student is extremely agitated and might act out physically, give the student enough physical space so that he or she doesn't feel threatened or provoked. Avoid using gestures or mannerisms that might be interpreted as aggressive, such as pointing your finger, raising your voice, squinting your eyes, furrowing your brows, moving toward the student, standing too close to the student, or hovering over the student. Rather, speak directly to the student in a calm and respectful voice. Look directly at the student without staring and keep your expressions as neutral as possible. Try to put distance between the student and other students in the class, especially if the student is lashing out at a peer. You might accomplish this by placing yourself between the aggressive student and the rest of the class or by asking the class to move to a specific location, such as one corner of the classroom.
4. **Calm yourself:** When a student lashes out or acts aggressively, it is natural to feel as if the student's outburst is a personal attack. To counteract these feelings and allow yourself to interact with the student in a calm and positive way, repeat positive affirmations to yourself, such as "This is not a personal attack on me; this student must be experiencing a great deal of pain and hurt to act in this way" or "This is just one moment in time. Help it to pass quickly without letting it harm anyone, including the student. Don't make things worse."
5. **Listen attentively:** Listen attentively to the student without agreeing or disagreeing with what he or she is saying. Use active listening skills, such as making eye contact and paraphrasing, to let the student know he or she is being heard. Keep your posture, expression, gestures, and tone of voice as neutral as possible as you focus on what the student is saying. When the student finishes speaking, respond with phrases such as "I think I understand how you feel" or "I understand what you're thinking." Then ask, "What else is bothering you?" Repeat this process until the student isn't able to think of anything else to say. At this point, the student will also likely be calmer due to feeling heard and understood.
6. **Remove the student from the situation:** Once the student is calmer, use a simple, repeated request designed to remove the student from the situation (for example, "Billy, I'd like you to go with me out to the hallway to get things back to normal. Will you please do that with me now?"). Repeat your request calmly but persistently until the student complies.

7. **Set up a plan to avoid future outbursts:** About a day or so after the incident, connect with the student and communicate that you wish to re-establish the relationship and do not bear a grudge against the student for what happened. Talk about the incident, including why it occurred, and let the student know you hear and understand his or her thoughts and feelings. Create an action plan for future situations to ensure that the student will communicate with you before things escalate out of control.

Overall Disciplinary Plan

Using this strategy, the teacher creates an overall plan for dealing with disciplinary situations. It might include developing relationships with students, exhibiting withitness, articulating positive and negative consequences for behavior, and creating guidelines for dealing with high-intensity situations.

- **Developing relationships with students:** Seek to improve relationships with all students, especially those who tend to be disruptive in class.
- **Exhibiting withitness:** List typical responses to student misbehavior. Analyze the list and determine which responses are effective and which are not.
- **Articulating positive and negative consequences for behavior:** Make sure that students can describe appropriate and inappropriate behavior. Meet with students to point out specific behaviors that need to be curtailed. Help students develop explicit plans to curtail inappropriate behavior and refine the plan as needed. Isolate offending students from the class until they make a commitment to appropriate behavior.
- **Creating guidelines for dealing with high-intensity situations:** Develop an action plan for responding to high-intensity situations. Know when to involve administrators to help avoid or deal with high-intensity situations.

Figure 8.18 can help you create an overall disciplinary plan.

Overall Disciplinary Plan

Developing Relationships With Students	Exhibiting Withitness	Articulating Positive and Negative Consequences for Behavior	Creating Guidelines for Dealing With High-Intensity Situations
Strategies and Plan:	Effective Strategies: Ineffective Strategies:	Positive Consequences: Negative Consequences: Plan for Communicating to Students:	Response Plan: Administrators to Involve:

Source: Marzano Research, 2016.

Figure 8.18: Template for overall disciplinary plan.

Visit **go.SolutionTree.com/instruction** *for a free reproducible version of this figure.*

Monitoring Element 37

Specific student responses and behaviors allow the teacher to determine whether this element is being implemented effectively and producing the desired effects.

- Students cease inappropriate behavior following the teacher cues.
- Students accept consequences for their behavior as a natural part of the way the class is conducted.
- Students describe the teacher as *fair* relative to the consequences for not following rules and procedures.

Use this list to monitor student responses to element 37.

To monitor your own use of this element, use the scale in figure 8.19 in combination with the reproducible "Tracking Teacher Actions: Acknowledging Lack of Adherence to Rules and Procedures" (page 278). As with other proficiency scales, level 3 or higher is the goal.

4 Innovating	I adapt behaviors and create new strategies for unique student needs and situations.
3 Applying	I apply consequences for not following rules and procedures consistently and fairly, and I monitor the extent to which rules and procedures are followed.
2 Developing	I apply consequences for not following rules and procedures consistently and fairly, but I do not monitor the effect on students.
1 Beginning	I use the strategies and behaviors associated with this element incorrectly or with parts missing.
0 Not Using	I am unaware of strategies and behaviors associated with this element.

Figure 8.19: Self-rating scale for element 37—Acknowledging lack of adherence to rules and procedures.

The following examples describe what each level of the scale might look like in the classroom.

- **Not Using (0):** A teacher ignores students who are misbehaving, hoping they will stop of their own accord.
- **Beginning (1):** A teacher sometimes uses verbal cues when students are behaving disruptively, but he often waits until the behavior is out of control instead of acknowledging it pre-emptively.
- **Developing (2):** A teacher uses strategies such as verbal cues and time-outs to manage her students' lack of adherence to rules and procedures and usually addresses incidents before they become problematic. She is becoming more confident in her classroom management abilities but isn't sure if the strategies are preventing further instances of misbehavior.
- **Applying (3):** A teacher uses a variety of strategies to respond promptly and appropriately to varying degrees of misbehavior. By examining the number of times she has to use the more extreme responses such as office referrals and home contingencies, she is able to see that strategies such as verbal cues and pregnant pauses are helping prevent instances of misbehavior from escalating.
- **Innovating (4):** A teacher uses various strategies to respond to inappropriate behavior. However, a few of his students continue to have trouble with the procedures for transitioning between activities. To emphasize this problem area, he designs an interdependent group contingency around how long it takes the class to complete transitions.

Action Steps

Use the "Tracking Teacher Actions" reproducibles that follow (pages 274–278) to monitor your implementation of each element in this chapter.

Additionally, visit the appendix (page 329) for the reproducible "Tracking Progress Over Time" (page 330), which helps teachers set goals related to their proficiency with each element and track their progress toward these goals over the course of a unit, semester, or year. Also, the "Strategy Reflection Log" (page 331) in the appendix provides a space to write down your thoughts and reflect on the implementation process for specific strategies related to each element. Finally, visit **go.SolutionTree.com/instruction** for both student surveys and teacher surveys, the results of which provide feedback about your proficiency with each element.

Tracking Teacher Actions: Establishing Rules and Procedures

The teacher can use this form to plan his or her usage of strategies related to the element of establishing rules and procedures.

Check Strategies You Intend to Use	Strategies	Description of Instructional Plan
	Using a Small Set of Rules and Procedures	
	Explaining Rules and Procedures to Students	
	Generating Rules and Procedures With Students	
	Modifying Rules and Procedures With Students	
	Reviewing Rules and Procedures With Students	
	Using the Language of Responsibility and Statements of School Beliefs	
	Posting Rules Around the Room	
	Writing a Class Pledge or Classroom Constitution	
	Using Posters and Graphics	
	Establishing Gestures and Symbols	
	Modeling With Vignettes and Role Playing	
	Holding Classroom Meetings	
	Implementing Student Self-Assessment	
	Other:	
	Other:	

Source: Adapted from Marzano Research. (2016). Marzano compendium of instructional strategies. *Centennial, CO: Author.*

Tracking Teacher Actions: Organizing the Physical Layout of the Classroom

The teacher can use this form to plan his or her usage of strategies related to the element of organizing the physical layout of the classroom.

Check Strategies You Intend to Use	Strategies	Description of Instructional Plan
	Designing Classroom Décor	
	Displaying Student Work	
	Considering Classroom Materials	
	Placing the Teacher's Desk	
	Placing Student Desks	
	Planning Areas for Whole-Group Instruction	
	Planning Areas for Group Work	
	Planning Learning Centers	
	Considering Computers and Technology Equipment	
	Considering Lab Equipment and Supplies	
	Planning Classroom Libraries	
	Involving Students in the Design Process	
	Other:	
	Other:	

Source: Adapted from Marzano Research. (2016). Marzano compendium of instructional strategies. *Centennial, CO: Author.*

Tracking Teacher Actions: Demonstrating Withitness

The teacher can use this form to plan his or her usage of strategies related to the element of demonstrating withitness.

Check Strategies You Intend to Use	Strategies	Description of Instructional Plan
	Being Proactive	
	Occupying the Whole Room Physically and Visually	
	Noticing Potential Problems	
	Using a Series of Graduated Actions	
	Other:	
	Other:	

Source: Adapted from Marzano Research. (2016). Marzano compendium of instructional strategies. *Centennial, CO: Author.*

Tracking Teacher Actions: Acknowledging Adherence to Rules and Procedures

The teacher can use this form to plan his or her usage of strategies related to the element of acknowledging adherence to rules and procedures.

Check Strategies You Intend to Use	Strategies	Description of Instructional Plan
	Verbal Affirmation	
	Nonverbal Affirmation	
	Tangible Recognition	
	Token Economies	
	Daily Recognition Form	
	Color-Coded Behavior	
	Certificates	
	Phone Calls, Emails, and Notes	
	Other:	
	Other:	

Source: Adapted from Marzano Research. (2016). Marzano compendium of instructional strategies. *Centennial, CO: Author.*

Tracking Teacher Actions: Acknowledging Lack of Adherence to Rules and Procedures

The teacher can use this form to plan his or her usage of strategies related to the element of acknowledging lack of adherence to rules and procedures.

Check Strategies You Intend to Use	Strategies	Description of Instructional Plan
	Verbal Cues	
	Pregnant Pause	
	Nonverbal Cues	
	Time-Out	
	Overcorrection	
	Interdependent Group Contingency	
	Home Contingency	
	High-Intensity Situation Plan	
	Overall Disciplinary Plan	
	Other:	
	Other:	

Source: Adapted from Marzano Research. (2016). Marzano compendium of instructional strategies. *Centennial, CO: Author.*

CHAPTER 9

Building Relationships

CONTEXT

Important aspects of a mental context conducive to learning are a sense of being welcome and that teachers and peers value basic human needs. When teachers satisfy these needs, a student feels relaxed and comfortable. Teachers can help students feel this way by focusing on teacher-to-student relationships and student-to-student relationships.

The goal of this design area is for students to feel welcome, accepted, and valued. Teachers are able to meet this goal by answering the question, What strategies will I use to help students feel welcome, accepted, and valued? The three elements and associated strategies in this chapter help the teacher do just that.

Element 38: Using Verbal and Nonverbal Behaviors That Indicate Affection for Students

When appropriate, an effective teacher uses verbal and nonverbal behaviors that indicate affection for students. Research has shown that teacher behaviors such as gestures, smiles, and encouraging remarks are associated with gains in student achievement and other positive outcomes (Harris & Rosenthal, 1985; Marzano, 2018). Teachers who smile, joke, and show enthusiasm positively affect student engagement and enthusiasm (Anderman & Wolters, 2006; Bettencourt et al., 1983; Gettinger & Kohler, 2006; Moskowitz & Hayman, 1976; Perry, Turner, & Meyer, 2006; Rosenshine & Furst, 1973).

There are nine strategies within this element.

1. Greeting students at the classroom door
2. Holding informal conferences
3. Attending after-school functions
4. Greeting students by name outside of school
5. Giving students special responsibilities or leadership roles in the classroom
6. Scheduling interaction
7. Creating a photo bulletin board
8. Using physical behaviors
9. Using humor

The following sections will explore each strategy to provide you with guidelines to effectively implement this element. Read through each before creating a plan for your classroom. Teachers may use the strategies individually or in combination. Remember, these are not merely activities to be checked off; they are methods of creating a practice that combines your art with the science of using verbal and nonverbal behaviors that indicate affection for students. Reflect on your use of each strategy by filling out the "Strategy Reflection Log" on page 331.

Greeting Students at the Classroom Door

At the beginning of a period, the teacher makes an effort to greet students at the door. The teacher uses each student's first name when they enter to show that the teacher values them and is aware of when they are or are not there. The teacher might also ask students how they are feeling and make positive comments about their learning or achievements. For example, the day after a student is absent, as the student walks in the classroom, the teacher might say, "We missed you yesterday!" to acknowledge the student was not in class. The teacher might then encourage the student to find a time to meet with the teacher to go over what he or she missed while out.

Following are English greetings to use in the classroom.

- "G'day"
- "Good morning"
- "Good afternoon"
- "Greetings"
- "Hey"
- "How are you doing?"
- "Howdy"
- "How's it going?"
- "How was your weekend?"
- "What's up?"

Following are non-English greetings to use in the classroom.

- "As-salāmu alaykum" (pronounced ahl sah-LAHM ah-LAY-koom; Arabic)
- "Nĭ hău" (pronounced NEE-HAOW; Chinese)
- "Dobrý den" (pronounced DOH-bree dehn; Czech)
- "Hallo" (pronounced HAH-lo; Dutch)
- "Bonjour" (pronounced bohn-ZHOOR; French)
- "Guten tag" (pronounced GOO-ten tahg; German)
- "Geia sou" (pronounced YAH-soo; Greek)
- "Aloha" (pronounced ah-LOH-hah; Hawaiian)
- "Shalom" (pronounced shah-LOHM; Hebrew)
- "Namaste" (pronounced nah-mah-STAY; Hindi)
- "Szia" (pronounced ZEE-yah; Hungarian)
- "Dia duit" (pronounced DEE-ah GHWIT; Irish Gaelic)
- "Ciao" (pronounced CHOW; Italian)
- "Konnichi ha" (pronounced kon-NEE-chee-wa; Japanese)
- "Annyeong" (pronounced AHN-YONG; Korean)
- "Salve" (pronounced sal-way; Latin)
- "Buna ziua" (pronounced BOO-nuh ZEE-wah; Romanian)
- "Privet" (pronounced PREE-vyet; Russian)
- "Zdravo" (pronounced ZDRAH-voh; Serbian, Croatian, Bosnian)
- "Hola" (pronounced OH-la; Spanish)
- "Hujambo" (pronounced fu-JAM-bo; Swahili)
- "Hej" (pronounced HEY; Swedish)
- "Sawatdi" (pronounced sah-waht-DEE; Thai)
- "Merhaba" (pronounced MEHR-hah-bah; Turkish)
- "Xin chào" (pronounced sin-CHOW; Vietnamese)
- "Sawubona" (pronounced sah-woo-BOH-nah; Zulu)

Following are affectionate nonverbal gestures to use in the classroom.

- Shaking hands
- Waving
- High-fiving
- Making eye contact in a friendly way
- Patting the student on the back
- Smiling at the student

- Pointing at the student in a nonthreatening way
- Winking
- Saluting

Holding Informal Conferences

Informal conferences, unlike more formal academic conferences, allow teachers to chat with students without students projecting expectations onto the meeting. During informal conferences, a teacher might give compliments, ask for student opinions, mention student successes, and pass on positive comments from other teachers. In order to schedule informal conferences, teachers can plan a time in-between classes, before or after school, or during lunch or other breaks to check in. Alternatively, informal conferences can be spur-of-the-moment and fairly short. For example, a teacher might stop a student on the way out of class and say something along the lines of "Kara, what did you think of the homework assignment last night?" or "Josh, I was so impressed by your performance in the school musical yesterday—you ought to be really proud of that!"

When addressing students during an informal conference, teachers can bring up or ask students about their thoughts on or feelings toward one or more of the following topics.

- School, local, state, national, or international news events (for example, a recent school election or the discovery of water on Mars)
- Pop culture (for example, a celebrity couple having a baby or a famous actress's charity event)
- School-level or professional sports (for example, the school winning the state track championships or the local professional football team losing its game)
- New movies or books (for example, a new movie about a superhero or the release of the sequel to a young adult novel)
- Developments in a television show (for example, a plot twist in a popular television show or the elimination of a contestant on a reality show)
- Recommendations (for example, for restaurants, stores, books, movies, music, and so on)
- Weekend plans (for example, what the student did the previous weekend or plans for the upcoming weekend)
- Academic compliments (for example, on a recently completed project or a compliment from another teacher)
- Nonacademic compliments (for example, for being a cheerful presence in class)
- Extracurricular activities (for example, the student's performance on the debate team or in the school orchestra)
- Schoolwide events (for example, spirit week, homecoming, or end-of-year exams)
- Family (for example, inquiring about a brother or sister)
- Activities during vacation (for example, ask the student how he or she spent vacation)
- Class (for example, ask the student how he or she thinks the class is going)
- School (for example, ask the student what changes he or she would make to the school if he or she were the principal)
- Goals (for example, ask the student what he or she hopes to accomplish during this year in an academic or nonacademic sense)
- Dreams (for example, ideal careers, vacations, or homes)
- Hypothetical situations (for example, prompt the student with a hypothetical question like "If you had the choice of a superpower, what would it be?" or "If you had to eat only one type of food for the rest of your life, what would it be?")
- Food (for example, ask a student what his or her favorite candy or snack is or ask a student for a recipe)

- Jokes (for example, find an age-appropriate joke and share it with the student)
- Pets (for example, ask students about their pets and inquire about them at a later date)
- Academic history (for example, ask the student about previous teachers or schools attended)
- Accomplishments (for example, ask the student about his or her proudest accomplishments to date)

Attending After-School Functions

The teacher shows affection for and interest in students, particularly students who may feel alienated, by attending their after-school activities. If attending, the teacher should let the student know ahead of time and then make an effort to connect with the student at the event, if possible. While this takes time from the teacher's life outside work, it can be helpful in future interactions with the student. Furthermore, the teacher can also make an effort to go to popular school events such as sports games, band and orchestra concerts, or school plays and musicals, even if the teacher does not have specific students in mind to reach out to. Attending such events often shows that a teacher cares about the school community as a whole and provides an opportunity to connect with previous, current, or potential students as well as their parents and other faculty members. Teachers can display a chart in the classroom that allows students to fill in the event, date and time, and location of after-school functions.

Greeting Students by Name Outside of School

During the school day, it is crucial that teachers build relationships with students to facilitate a safe and productive learning environment. However, it is also likely that teachers will run into students or their parents outside of school hours in neighborhood venues such as the grocery store, movie theater, or shopping mall. When this occurs, teachers should make sure to greet students by name and interact in a friendly demeanor. This interaction need not be lengthy and can be as simple as saying, "Hi, Emily. It's good to see you. Have a good day!"

Following are tips for appropriate out-of-school communication with students.

- When encountering a student or a student's family outside of school, engage in a short and friendly conversation.
- If a student approaches you outside of school, even if you are in a hurry, take the time to acknowledge the student and be polite.
- If you cannot remember the name of a student during an interaction outside of school, you should smile at the student and respond as social conventions dictate, though not try to call the student by name.
- When possible, you can also incorporate background knowledge about the student (academic, extracurricular, or personal) into the conversation to let the student know that you are invested in his or her well-being.
- Keep out-of-school communication with students brief. While out-of-school communication can be a great way to show a student you care, be sure to consider the appropriateness of the interaction.
- Consider your own social media presence and avoid connecting with students via social media websites.
- Review and adhere to your school's guidelines related to out-of-school communication with students.

Giving Students Special Responsibilities or Leadership Roles in the Classroom

One way to indicate affection for students is to assign them specific tasks or responsibilities in the classroom. Specific tasks or responsibilities for students might include being a line leader on the way to lunch, taking care of a class pet, handing out materials, or collecting assignments. Furthermore, if a student's previous actions have warranted it, the teacher might give the student a leadership role in the classroom, which can further demonstrate the teacher both cares for and trusts the student. For example, a teacher could ask a student to lead a project or be responsible for completing a specific task in the classroom or on a field trip.

Responsibilities are special assignments that a student is responsible for. Teachers can use the following suggestions to identify relevant responsibilities to assign to students.

- Handing out materials
- Collecting assignments
- Alphabetizing papers, materials, notebooks, or other items
- Sweeping the floor
- Wiping down the chalkboard or whiteboard at the end of the day
- Taking attendance
- Watering the classroom plants
- Feeding the classroom pet
- Delivering a message to the office
- Escorting a student to the nurse's office
- Researching information (if a question comes up in class, ask a specific student to find the answer to the question and report back tomorrow)
- Telling the teacher when a certain amount of time has passed or cueing the teacher when a certain amount of time is left in the class
- Turning on and off electronics in the classroom; adjusting the volume, brightness, or other settings for specific electronics in the classroom
- Opening and closing the blinds
- Making a decision that affects the whole class (for example, if the teacher asks whether the class should move into individual seatwork or small-group work, the student asked gets to decide)

Leadership roles either indicate a leadership position for a specific project or over a longer period of time. For example, a classroom responsibility might be to water the plants, but if a teacher assigns a specific student to be responsible for watering the plant for a week independently, then the responsibility shifts into a leadership role.

- **Material or supply chief:** Keeps the classroom materials and supplies in order
- **Spill control:** Cleans up in the event of a spill
- **Animal caretaker:** Takes care of the classroom pet
- **Plant caretaker:** Takes care of and waters the plants in the classroom
- **Recycling inspector:** Reminds students to recycle and makes sure the bins aren't too full
- **Librarian:** Ensures the classroom library is orderly
- **Clean-up chief:** Oversees clean-up processes and makes sure that all the tasks get completed
- **Teacher's helper:** Does little tasks for the teacher as needed
- **Project leader:** Communicates with the teacher during projects
- **Note taker:** Takes notes during class for absent students

- **Attendance taker:** Takes attendance at the beginning of class or during a field trip to make sure all students are accounted for
- **Computer helper:** Makes sure all computers are turned off or students are logged off at the end of the day
- **Electrician:** Makes sure lights are off when the classroom is empty
- **Daily reporter:** Checks the weather and date each day and posts it somewhere in the room

Scheduling Interaction

An effective teacher creates a schedule (listing the date, student, and topic of conversation) that ensures regular interaction with each student by selecting a few students each day to seek out and talk to. The teacher might interact with students in the lunchroom, during breaks between classes, or right after school. During these personalized encounters, the teacher can talk about academic or nonacademic things, so long as the teacher makes the student feel as though he or she is on the teacher's radar. For example, a teacher might divide the students in his or her class into about ten pairs or small groups, then reach out to the students in one group or pair each day. At the end of two weeks, the teacher begins the cycle again to ensure regular interactions with all students.

Creating a Photo Bulletin Board

A bulletin board can display students' photos, personal goals, hobbies, interests, and other fun facts (see figure 9.1). The content of a photo bulletin board can change from time to time based on the unit or can highlight students who have performed well on assignments, shown dramatic improvement on a learning goal, or enacted classroom values outside of class. The teacher can also coordinate the photo bulletin board with student interest surveys to help students in the class get to know one another. For example, the teacher could ask students to bring in photographs of themselves and to complete a personal survey. The teacher would attach students' photographs to their surveys and post them at the beginning of the year so that students can get to know each other.

Photo Bulletin Board

[Place Photo Here]

Name: ________________________________

In this picture, I am: ________________________________

This photo is important to me because: ________________________________

Source: Marzano Research, 2016.

Figure 9.1: Template for photo bulletin board.

Visit **go.SolutionTree.com/instruction** *for a free reproducible version of this figure.*

Using Physical Behaviors

The teacher monitors his or her physical behaviors and gestures to ensure that they signal affection and encouragement for students. For example, a teacher might use smiles and high fives to communicate affection for students, while patting a student on the back or putting a hand on a student's shoulder could be used to communicate interest or concern for a student. While talking to a student, the teacher makes eye contact, stands close to the student (enough to communicate concern or interest without invading their personal space), or looks interested in what they have to say.

As always, when using physical behaviors to indicate affection, teachers should be aware of how their actions affect students and use their discretion to ensure that behaviors remain appropriate.

- **Smiling:** Smiling is a universal symbol of happiness and indicates a pleasant mindset. When teachers encounter students and want to show that they care for them, even just a smile in acknowledgment of their presence can go a long way toward building amicable classroom relationships.
- **Making eye contact:** When talking with students, teachers can hold eye contact to demonstrate engagement in the conversation. However, teachers should monitor the length of time they hold eye contact with students to ensure that it does not verge on the brink of staring.
- **Mirroring actions of students:** Mirroring, also called *isopraxism*, is a subconscious way that humans and other animals show a connection to one another. Teachers can subtly mirror students' physical gestures, such as by crossing their legs when a student does.
- **Standing close to students:** Teachers can stand in the physical proximity of students to show their interest in and affection for students. Not only does being near a student open up opportunities for interaction between a student and a teacher, but it also shows a fondness for and comfort around that student.
- **Leaning forward while sitting:** If a teacher is sitting down and talking to a student or small group of students, the teacher can indicate interest in what is being said by leaning forward in his or her chair toward the speaker.
- **Shaking hands:** Shaking hands is often a sign of respect. Teachers may shake students' hands as a greeting or goodbye in and out of class or ask to shake students' hands after they turn in an assessment to indicate that the teacher trusts the students.
- **Giving high fives:** High fives are an energetic way to show students that you appreciate them or their actions. High fives can be given as a reward when students do a good job on something or to acknowledge students' presence in a fun way.
- **Patting students on the back:** Teachers can pat students on the back to show their appreciation. Pats on the back can also be a sympathetic gesture for teachers to use with students who seem upset.
- **Nodding:** While students are speaking, teachers can use head nods to indicate agreement or that they are listening to what students are saying. Teachers can also use head nods to acknowledge the presence of a student, particularly if the environment is loud or if the student and teacher are just passing by one another.
- **Waving:** If a student is outside of a comfortable speaking range, a teacher can wave to show that he or she sees the student. Depending on the situation, the teacher can use a wave as a brief acknowledgment of the student or follow up by going over and starting a conversation.
- **Applauding:** By clapping his or her hands, a teacher can show that he or she thinks that students are doing a good job. The teacher should also model intensity and enthusiasm during this gesture and may accompany the action with verbal recognition, such as by saying "Bravo!" or "Yes, well done!"

Using Humor

Humor is a great way for a teacher to build relationships with students. When using humor in the classroom, the teacher can use playful banter or self-directed humor. The teacher might also use historical and popular sayings to make a point or incorporate cartoons, jokes, puns, and plays on words into instruction. The teacher can also tease students in a lighthearted manner; however, if a teacher does tease students, he or she must consider what is being said, how it might affect the student, and the degree to which it is appropriate. For example, a teacher may tease a student if the student is actively being silly and seems to want attention, whereas the same teacher might not tease a student if the student is reserved and generally shies away from being the center of attention.

Following are ways to incorporate humor into the classroom.

- **Playful banter:** Teachers and students can exchange playful banter, where both parties engage in lighthearted teasing. Teachers should be careful of which students they engage in banter with, be aware of when playful banter has gone on for too long, and monitor whether the tone of the banter becomes serious or mean-spirited. Teachers should also monitor exchanges between students to ensure the tone and content is appropriate for a classroom setting—if students cannot use playful banter appropriately among themselves, teachers should avoid modeling this behavior.
- **Self-directed humor:** Perhaps one of the easiest ways to incorporate humor into the classroom is to use self-directed humor. Teachers can do this by pointing out when they do something silly or when they make a mistake. This strategy is particularly powerful for perfectionist students, as it models to students not to take themselves too seriously.
- **Cartoons:** Teachers can place cartoons on assessments, PowerPoints, and handouts, or project them on the board at the beginning or end of class. Teachers should find cartoons that are relevant to the content being taught. Alternatively, to make cartoons into an activity, teachers can ask students to create their own humorous cartoons or captions for cartoons.
- **Puns and plays on words:** Puns and plays on words are fun ways to manipulate language in humorous ways and can be incorporated into one-on-one interactions with students or into a lesson itself. However, puns and plays on words will not be successful if students are not aware of the basis of joke. Teachers should consider age level and the difficulty of the joke before sharing a pun or play on words.
- **Jokes:** Similar to puns and plays on words, teachers can tell jokes to students at any point in a lesson or during one-on-one interactions. Jokes can be content-related, though teachers can use jokes unrelated to content being taught as well. Alternatively, teachers can also ask students to bring in their own jokes. Jokes should always be screened for appropriateness before being shared.
- **Assignments:** One fun way to make assignments more enjoyable is to incorporate humor into them. For example, a teacher may create a writing assignment on a humorous topic or add funny, nonserious questions or answers to worksheets or assessments.
- **Classroom decorations:** When decorating their classroom, teachers can choose to put up classroom decorations that are funny. Teachers can designate a bulletin board to post humorous images, quotations, and jokes or hang up humorous posters around the room.
- **Schedule:** To consistently add humor to the classroom, teachers can consciously incorporate humor into the schedule. For example, a teacher may choose to begin her first period class each Monday with a funny video to get students energized, ask students to wear funny clothing or accessories on Fridays, or choose a specific day for students to bring in jokes and share them.

Monitoring Element 38

Specific student responses and behaviors allow the teacher to determine whether this element is being implemented effectively and producing the desired effects.

- Students describe the teacher as someone who cares for them.
- Students describe the classroom as a friendly place.
- Students respond to the teacher's verbal interactions.
- Students respond to the teacher's nonverbal interactions.

Use this list to monitor student responses to element 38.

To monitor your own use of this element, use the scale in figure 9.2 in combination with the reproducible "Tracking Teacher Actions: Using Verbal and Nonverbal Behaviors That Indicate Affection for Students" (page 309). As with other proficiency scales, level 3 or higher is the goal.

4 Innovating	I adapt behaviors and create new strategies for unique student needs and situations.
3 Applying	I use verbal and nonverbal behaviors that indicate affection for students, and I monitor the extent to which my actions affect students.
2 Developing	I use verbal and nonverbal behaviors that indicate affection for students, but I do not monitor the effect on students.
1 Beginning	I use the strategies and behaviors associated with this element incorrectly or with parts missing.
0 Not Using	I am unaware of strategies and behaviors associated with this element.

Figure 9.2: Self-rating scale for element 38—Using verbal and nonverbal behaviors that indicate affection for students.

The following examples describe what each level of the scale might look like in the classroom.

- **Not Using (0):** A teacher may feel positively about his students but does not actively try to show that he likes his students as individuals.
- **Beginning (1):** A teacher uses verbal and nonverbal behaviors to indicate affection for some students. However, she does not use these behaviors to indicate affection for all the students in her class, thus making some students feel very welcome while alienating others.
- **Developing (2):** A teacher posts a photo bulletin board, attends after-school functions in which students participate, and tries to have informal conferences with each of his students to get to know them. However, he does not monitor the effects of his relationship-building efforts on students.
- **Applying (3):** A teacher tries a variety of strategies to indicate affection for students. The teacher monitors how students react to various strategies to determine which strategies work best for which students. For example, the teacher notices that one student seems to respond better to being given special responsibilities than he does to joking around.
- **Innovating (4):** A teacher actively seeks out students for informal conferences and uses the information she gathers to inform future interactions with students. She notices that some students need extra encouragement and interaction to feel welcome and comfortable in class, so she makes an effort to connect with those students about their interests more often.

Element 39: Understanding Students' Backgrounds and Interests

An effective teacher uses students' interests and backgrounds to produce a climate of acceptance and community. Research has shown that positive teacher-student relationships are associated with a decrease in classroom disruptions (Marzano, 2003). When teachers get to know students and seek to understand their interests and backgrounds, it creates an atmosphere of cooperation, rather than an "I-them" mentality (Plax & Kearney, 1990).

There are fourteen strategies within this element.

1. Student background surveys
2. Opinion questionnaires
3. Individual teacher-student conferences
4. Parent-teacher conferences
5. School newspaper, newsletter, or bulletin
6. Informal class interviews
7. Familiarity with student culture
8. Autobiographical metaphors and analogies
9. Six-word autobiographies
10. Independent investigations
11. Quotes
12. Comments about student achievement or areas of importance
13. Lineups
14. Individual student learning goals

The following sections will explore each strategy to provide you with guidelines to effectively implement this element. Read through each before creating a plan for your classroom. Teachers may use the strategies individually or in combination. Remember, these are not merely activities to be checked off; they are methods of creating a practice that combines your art with the science of understanding students' backgrounds and interests. Reflect on your use of each strategy by filling out the "Strategy Reflection Log" on page 331.

Student Background Surveys

Teachers should try to learn a little bit about each student at the beginning of the year to understand the backgrounds students are coming from and to obtain information on which to build relationships with students. One common way of obtaining such information is the student background survey—a questionnaire given at the start of the school year or beginning of a course containing questions relevant to students' lives. The survey could include questions about students' academic interests (favorite and least favorite subject in school), personal interests (hobbies, sports, lessons, art, books, video games, movies, and television shows), dreams, fears, family members, and family activities (traditions, vacations, and gatherings). Teachers can also provide sentence stems for students, such as, "During my free time I like to __________" or "Someday I'd like to be __________." Teachers can then use the information on the background surveys to inform interactions with students throughout the year.

Following are sample questions for student background surveys.

- Where were you born?
- How many brothers and sisters do you have?
- What are some things about your family that make you proud?
- What kinds of things did you do over the summer or on vacation that you enjoyed?
- What would you do if you knew you wouldn't fail?
- Do you have any hobbies (collecting things, artistic endeavors, building things)? If so, what are they?
- Do you participate in sports? If so, which sports? What do you like best about playing that sport?
- Do you take lessons of any kind (such as music, art, singing, dance, or speech)? If so, what kind?
- What is your favorite book, game, movie, video or computer game, or television show?

- If you had to describe yourself in a sentence or two, what might you say that would help others learn something about your personal interests?
- During my free time I like to __________.
- One thing I really like to do with my friends is __________.
- I really enjoy __________.
- My family enjoys __________.
- If I had a month of Saturdays, I'd spend most of my time __________.
- Someday I'd like to be __________.

Opinion Questionnaires

Teachers can use opinion questionnaires, like student background surveys, to better understand students' perspectives and backgrounds. However, opinion questionnaires generally focus on relevant classroom topics rather than more general information about the student. For example, a science teacher might create an opinion questionnaire that asks students the degree to which they find biology interesting, easy, and relevant. The science opinion questionnaire might also subtly gauge students' feelings of competence related with questions such as, How comfortable do you feel measuring exact quantities of liquid? How easy do you find memorization of long lists of names? How confident do you feel using a calculator to find the answer to basic algebraic equations?

Following are sample opinion questionnaire items.

- Which subject do you like the best? Why?
- Which subject do you like the least? Why?
- Would you rather work alone, in a small group, or in a large group?
- Where do you study or do your homework?
- What is the ideal environment for you to study?
- If you could improve in one way at school, what would it be?
- Name one thing that you think you do really well at school.
- When you're at school, how do you normally feel?
- What's one thing about school that you enjoy?
- What's one thing about school that you find frustrating?
- How often does an adult help you with your homework?
- To what degree do you find this subject interesting?
- To what degree do you find this subject difficult?
- To what degree do you find this subject important?
- Is it easier for you to learn something if you hear it, see it, or do it? Explain.
- Do you feel competent in your abilities with this subject? Explain.
- What is something that teachers have done in the past that you did like?
- What is something that teachers have done in the past that you did not like?
- What's something that the teacher could do that would help you learn?
- What has been your favorite assignment you've ever completed? Why?
- What would happen in your ideal class?
- What has been the most frustrating assignment you've ever been assigned? Why?

Individual Teacher-Student Conferences

Individual student-teacher conferences provide an opportunity for teachers to meet one on one with students and use probing questions to better understand students' backgrounds and interests. In an individual student-teacher conference, the teacher can cover both academic and nonacademic topics. For example, a teacher may begin a student-teacher conference by asking about the student's previous school experiences and home background. Over the course of the meeting, however, the teacher may transition into asking about the student's interests and perspectives on current issues.

Following are five steps to complete prior to the teacher-student conference.

1. Decide how you would like to schedule student-teacher conferences. A teacher could set aside a class period at the beginning or end of a unit, semester, or year to meet with students or create timeslots before and after school as well as during free periods for which students can sign up when convenient. A teacher should take care to verbally remind students about their appointments when he or she sees them during class.
2. Explain the purpose of conferences to students. A teacher should emphasize that the student-teacher conferences are an opportunity to better know each student and to check in academically. Reiterate that the meetings are to focus on the positive rather than the negative and also allow students an opportunity to voice their own concerns.
3. Consider where the conferences will be held and how long (approximately) each conference should last. If a teacher has set aside a class period to meet with students, determine the location that the conferences will be held (in the classroom, an open room, the hallway, and so on) and what students will do when they are not meeting with the teacher. If necessary, find another teacher to watch the class during individual student-teacher conferences and provide him or her with activities to engage students.
4. Organize and review academic materials for each student. Create a portfolio for each student that contains relevant assignments, assessments, and grades. A teacher should also create a list of topics that he or she wants to address with the student and write down thoughts related to each. Topics may include student progress, strengths, weaknesses, growth goals, opportunities, expectations, challenges, and concerns.
5. Consider questions about students' backgrounds and interests that you could ask during the conference. Because individual student-teacher conferences provide a rare opportunity to speak one on one with students, a teacher should take the opportunity to consider what he or she would like to know about each student and use the conferences as a way to strengthen relationships with each student.

Following are five steps to complete during the teacher-student conference.

1. Begin the conference by giving an overview of where the student stands academically and behaviorally. Focus on positive aspects of the student and provide examples of notable work the student has done. Use concrete examples of the student's past work or behaviors to reinforce each point. If the student has questions, be prepared to explain how scores (particularly those that may be lower than the student expected) were generated.
2. Allow students to voice their questions and concerns about the class, school, or teacher. Listen to students actively and respond consciously and respectfully. If the answer to a question is unknown, the teacher should plan to follow up with the student within a week. Particularly if a student seems heated or upset, remain sympathetic and objective in tone, even if the comments the student is making are directed negatively at the teacher.
3. Find out information about students' backgrounds. Ask students about their strengths, weaknesses, needs, learning style, goals, and so on. Also, take the opportunity to ask students about their lives outside of school—this may include any part-time jobs, family support available, hobbies,

extracurricular activities, siblings, interests, and so on. A teacher should take care to write down such information so it can inform later instruction and interactions.

4. Talk about areas that the student needs to work on. Have specific examples ready to illustrate these areas. Ask the student what he or she can personally do to improve in these areas, then ask the student about supports he or she may need from the teacher. Consider the tone of this segment of the conference and make sure that the conversation does not come off too critically, but rather as an opportunity for a student to grow academically or socially.
5. Create action plans with students if necessary. Identify short-term and long-term goals related to areas that could be improved upon, how such goals can be achieved, and commitments on the part of both the teacher and the student. Decide upon the necessity and frequency of progress check-ins as well as the availability of extra supports.

Following are three steps to complete after the teacher-student conference.

1. Remind students in class that you are available to address questions or concerns, and provide information about how they can contact you or times available for additional meetings if necessary. If specific information or resources were promised during student-teacher conferences, follow up in a timely fashion.
2. Follow up with students who missed their conferences and determine a time to reschedule.
3. Reach out to students as necessary outside of classwide student-teacher conferences. Particularly for students with whom an action plan was created or students who need extra support, find additional times to meet throughout the year.

Parent-Teacher Conferences

Parent-teacher conferences are a great opportunity for teachers to build relationships with their students' parents or guardians. They also provide a chance for teachers to better understand students, their backgrounds, and their recent life experiences. During parent-teacher conferences, teachers should keep an ear out for events of note—these might include family events or vacations, transition points for parents or siblings (such as births, deaths, graduations, marriages, divorces, or job changes), and plans to move to a new home or a different school.

Following are four steps to complete prior to the parent-teacher conference.

1. Send out invitations far in advance about parent-teacher conferences, the goals of the meeting, and options for scheduling. Options for dissemination of these materials include fliers and notices sent home by mail or with students, phone calls, emails, or announcements during community meetings.
2. Send out a reminder to parents about a week before the actual conference. The reminder should include the date, time, and location of each conference. You can choose to include a brief agenda for parents if desired.
3. Before the conferences, clean up the classroom and make sure it will be comfortable for incoming parents and guardians. For the meetings themselves, designate a more private or intimate space for the conferences and try to find adult chairs for parents to sit in (if they are not already present in the room).
4. Organize and review materials for each student. Create a portfolio for each student that contains relevant assignments, assessments, and grades. Create a list of topics that you want to address with parents and write down thoughts related to each. Topics may include student progress, strengths, weaknesses, growth goals, opportunities, expectations, challenges, concerns, content to be taught, upcoming school events, or parental support.

Following are five steps to complete during the parent-teacher conference.

1. Begin the conference by giving an overview of where the student stands academically and socially. If parents are unfamiliar, explain how student progress is measured against learning goals. Focus on positive aspects of the student and provide examples of notable work the student has done.
2. Allow parents to voice their questions and concerns. Listen to parents actively and respond consciously and respectfully. If the answer to a question is unknown, tell parents that you will find an answer and follow up in a timely manner after the conference.
3. Find out information about students' backgrounds. Ask parents about what they believe to be their student's strengths, weaknesses, needs, learning style, goals, interests, and so on. Furthermore, ask parents about their goals for their student and the ways in which you can help the student achieve those goals.
4. Talk about areas that the student needs to work on. Have specific examples ready to explain these areas to parents. After noting areas of improvement, explain what actions you are taking in the classroom to help the student and provide ideas for parental support. When talking about at-home supports, make sure to avoid language that parents or guardians might perceive as accusatory. Focus on using *we* instead of *they* or *you*.
5. Create action plans with parents or guardians when possible. If parents seem receptive to creating at-home supports for students, make commitments regarding what actions will be taken, how long such actions will last, and how often progress check-ins will occur. Determine preferred methods of communication (for example, phone calls, emails, letters home, and so on).

Following are three steps to complete after the parent-teacher conference.

1. Thank parents or guardians who attended parent-teacher conferences either by phone or by note. Remind them that you are available to address questions or concerns they may have, and provide contact information. If you promised to provide specific information or resources during the parent-teacher conference, send that information promptly.
2. Follow up with parents who did not attend parent-teacher conferences and ask if they are interested in meeting at an alternative time. Ask about preferences for communication to have on hand, even if they are not interested in meeting in person.
3. Continue to stay in touch with parents throughout the year. Notify them of opportunities for students and for parents as they come up. Furthermore, communicate and celebrate students' successes with parents when possible.

School Newspaper, Newsletter, or Bulletin

Many schools have publications, either for students or for parents, that showcase students' notable achievements. Teachers can read these publications to become aware of students' involvement in athletic events (such as track or swim meets; basketball, baseball, football, or other games; and awards ceremonies), debates, club events, school performances, and volunteer activities. Teachers can also create their own classroom newspapers, newsletters, or bulletins to send home to parents. Teachers could choose to showcase a few students per issue and ask them to volunteer information about their interests, goals, and accomplishments. Once aware of students' achievements, either through reading or compiling newsletters, the teacher can mention them to students to show that they are on the teacher's radar.

When creating a classroom newsletter, teachers should consider including the following information.

- **Featured student section:** Choose a few students each month and ask them to fill out a questionnaire that asks academic, personal, and silly questions. For example, academic questions might include, What has been your favorite project to date this year? What's your favorite subject? What work are you most proud of? Personal questions might include, How many siblings do you have? What are the names of your pets? What's your favorite book? Finally, silly questions might include, If you could have a superpower, what would it be? Would you rather have a year's supply of cookies or a year's supply of ice cream? If you had a time machine, when would you travel to? Compile students' answers to a few of these questions and publish them in the newsletter.
- **Upcoming events:** Provide a little bit of information about events on the horizon. Events addressed could include tests, long-term assignments, field trips, birthdays, holidays, sporting events, or other events that may hold importance for students.
- **Previous events:** Similar to upcoming events, teachers can use newsletters and newspapers to address events that have already occurred. Teachers might want to congratulate students on finishing testing, address a behavioral issue that occurred, or recap the results of extracurricular events.
- **Quotations:** Incorporate quotations into a classroom newsletter. Quotations could be inspiring quotes from famous people or humorous quotes from students.
- **Questions:** Place a questions section in the newsletter that addresses frequently asked questions on the part of students or parents (especially before a special event like a field trip). Alternatively, the teacher could designate a question box in his or her classroom and let students write questions and submit them. The teacher could draw a few questions for each issue and answer them.
- **Classroom rules and procedures:** Use the newsletter to post changes to rules and procedures, to remind students of existing rules and procedures, or to explain or clarify new rules and procedures as needed. Teachers can also feature a rule or procedure in each issue and emphasize its importance, what it looks like when adhered to, and why it was created.
- **Content:** Incorporate academic content into the newsletter or bulletin. This can be done in numerous ways. For example, provide fun or interesting facts about the content, provide an overview of what the class will be covering in the upcoming weeks, provide a review of what the class has previously covered, or list student learning goals being addressed.

Informal Class Interviews

Informal class interviews occur when a teacher asks students to share information about what is happening at school or in their lives that the teacher should be aware of. The teacher asks specific questions that prompt students to talk about their lives. For example, before starting direct instruction on a Monday, the teacher might ask the class to share what they did over the weekend. Alternatively, if students seem particularly unsettled or fidgety before a class period, the teacher might ask students directly about their behavior and if there is a root cause for their distraction.

Following are examples of informal class interview questions to start class.

- How is everyone doing so far today?
- How was everyone's weekend?
- What are you doing over the weekend? Anyone have exciting plans?
- What are you most looking forward to in the upcoming month?
- What were your thoughts on the homework for last night? Was it difficult?

- Did anyone see [television show] last night? What did you think?
- Who watched [school or professional sporting event]? What did you think of the game?
- Did anything eventful happen at [class or lunch period]?
- How would you describe your current mood? Why?
- How would you describe your current energy level? Why?
- Does anyone have an important event coming up this week the class should know about?
- Does anyone have plans for [holiday or day off]? What are they?

Familiarity With Student Culture

The teacher talks with students and becomes familiar with popular cultural phenomena students are interested in. This may include popular music, movies, television shows, and specific actors, singers, or bands (see figure 9.3 for a sample worksheet). The teacher can also become familiar with specific local events that draw large student attendance and popular places where students often gather outside of school hours. The teacher can also pay attention to the slang terms and phrases students use, and either look up their meaning on the internet or directly ask students about their meaning. The teacher may also seek to understand existing social dynamics within the school and how his or her students fit into these dynamics.

Familiarity With Student Culture Worksheet

When I'm not in school, I like to go to:

____

My favorite local event is:

____

My favorite musicians I like to listen to are:

____

The most popular song right now is:

____

My favorite movie I saw this year was:

____

My favorite television show is:

____

I think my group of friends could best be described as:

____

These are current slang words I think everyone should know:

____

Source: Marzano Research, 2016.

Figure 9.3: Worksheet for familiarity with student culture.

Visit **go.SolutionTree.com/instruction** *for a free reproducible version of this figure.*

Autobiographical Metaphors and Analogies

In this strategy, students construct metaphors that compare academic content with their own lives. These can be simple and concrete, or they can involve more complex patterns and processes. This strategy is helpful, as it provides a teacher with knowledge about students' backgrounds while simultaneously strengthening students' understanding of the content. Students can also construct analogies between the content and their lives. These may or may not accompany nonlinguistic representations. For example, a fifth-grade teacher, during a unit on the solar system, might ask students to create metaphors that relate what they have been taught thus far to their own lives. A student might compare members of his family to various celestial bodies (for example, my mother is like the sun because she controls our movement and makes sure we all get where we need to go), which strengthens the student's understanding of the unique characteristics of objects in the solar system while giving the teacher a glimpse at the student's familial relationships.

A worksheet like figure 9.4 can help guide students' use of this strategy.

Autobiographical Metaphors and Analogies Worksheet

Name: ______________________________

Class: ______________________________

______________________________ (something in my life) is like ______________________________ (content) because ______________________________.

The content being taught relates to my life because:

The content being taught is important for me to learn because:

Metaphor: ____________________ is ____________________.

Analogy: ____________________ is to ____________________ as ____________________ is to ____________________

Source: Marzano Research, 2016.

Figure 9.4: Worksheet for autobiographical metaphors and analogies.

Visit **go.SolutionTree.com/instruction** *for a free reproducible version of this figure.*

Six-Word Autobiographies

Six-word autobiographies are by no means new. Perhaps most famously, Ernest Hemingway, when asked to write a story in six words, wrote, "For sale: baby shoes, never worn." Students can also write autobiographies of themselves in exactly six words, and the teacher can lead a discussion in which students share and explain their biographies. The six-word autobiographies can be either a disparate list of six words (particularly for K–2 students) or a functioning sentence. For example, a student in elementary school might create the following six-word biography: "silly, nice, loves running and animals." This student might have considered these four characteristics as most important to understand his or her temperament. As students get older, however, the teacher might put a restriction on the assignment so that the autobiographies function more as a sentence. For example, older students might create the following six-word biographies: "School is fine; weekends are better" or "At least I think math's cool." Such autobiographies can show a lot about a student's temperament and give students an opportunity to distinguish themselves from one another.

Following are resources for six-word autobiographies. Visit **go.SolutionTree.com/instruction** to access live links to the websites mentioned in this book.

- Smith Magazine. (Ed.). (2009). *I can't keep my own secrets: Six-word memoirs by teens famous and obscure.* New York: HarperTeen.
- Saunders, J. M., & Smith, E. E. (2014). Every word is on trial: Six-word memoirs in the classroom. *The Reading Teacher, 67*(8), 600–605.

- *SMITH Magazine*, News From Schools (www.smithmag.net/schools)
- *A Teaching Guide for Six-Word Memoirs: Not Quite What I Was Planning* (www.smithmag.net/share/pdf/six-word-teachers-guide-first-book.pdf)
- Six Words (www.sixwordmemoirs.com)
- "Illustrated Six-Word Memoirs by Students From Grade School to Grad School" (www.brainpickings.org/2013/01/09/six-word-memoirs-students)

Independent Investigations

Independent investigations allow students to research a topic of interest and then report back to the class about what they have found and learned. These investigations can be related to content being taught or driven by students' nonacademic interests. For example, a teacher might ask students to choose one aspect of the content to research further (for homework or during part of a class period) and then bring students back together to share what they have learned. During this discussion, the teacher should query students about why they chose their topics and how the topics are relevant to their backgrounds or interests.

A worksheet like figure 9.5 can help guide students' use of this strategy.

Independent Investigations Worksheet

Name: ______________________ Date: ____________

Topic: ______________________

Three new things I learned about this topic from my investigation are:

1. ______________________
2. ______________________
3. ______________________

Something interesting I learned about this topic:

This topic is important to the content being taught because:

I think this topic is interesting because:

This topic relates to my life because:

Source: Marzano Research, 2016.

Figure 9.5: Worksheet for independent investigations.

Visit **go.SolutionTree.com/instruction** *for a free reproducible version of this figure.*

Quotes

Collecting and sharing quotes can be a fun way to better understand students' personalities and interests. A teacher can ask students in the class to collect quotes that they feel express their personality traits, interests, or aspirations and then have students share the quotes they have found. When discussing quotes, the teacher should make sure that students connect the reason they chose the quote to the quote itself. A teacher can model this strategy by sharing with the class quotes that he or she finds representative of the class, the content, or the teacher him- or herself.

There are many websites that provide libraries of quotations that students can search or browse by subject or author. Consider the following such websites. Visit **go.SolutionTree.com/instruction** to access live links to the websites mentioned in this book.

- The Quotations Page (www.quotationspage.com)
- The Quote Garden (www.quotegarden.com)
- BrainyQuote (www.brainyquote.com)
- ThinkExist (www.thinkexist.com)
- Wikiquote (www.wikiquote.com)
- SearchQuotes (www.searchquotes.com)

Comments About Student Achievement or Areas of Importance

Once a teacher has some background knowledge about students' values and interests, he or she can notice and comment on individual accomplishments and important events in their lives. In terms of individual accomplishments, a teacher might point out students' achievements in clubs or athletics, academic recognitions, artistic and dramatic accomplishments, or assignments done well. The teacher might comment on a student's outside-of-school activities, such as community service, volunteer work, or awards received. When commenting on important events in students' lives, the teacher should notice important events—such as family weddings, vacations, birthdays, and so on—and changes in students' families—such as a move, birth, death, marriage, divorce, or parent's transition in employment.

Lineups

In this strategy, a teacher uses specific questions that ask students to line up or sit in groups in ways that reveal their likes, dislikes, and preferences. Questions can be silly and serve as a fun activity to get to know the personalities of students, academically oriented and help the teacher better understand students' learning preferences, or both. For example, the teacher might ask a silly question in the form of "Would you rather . . . ?" and designate one side of the classroom to represent one answer to the question and the other side of the classroom to represent the other. Following a silly question, the teacher could include a more serious question about learning preferences by reading a statement such as "I prefer to work in groups" and using the four corners of the room to represent the answers I strongly agree, I agree, I disagree, and I strongly disagree.

Following are sample sentence stems for lineups.

- Would you rather __________ or __________?
- Do you agree or disagree with the following statement? __________.
- To what extent do you agree with the following statement? __________. Strongly agree, agree, disagree, or strongly disagree.
- How often do you __________? Never, rarely, sometimes, often, or always.
- How difficult is __________ for you? Difficult, neutral, or easy.
- Which of the following words best represents you: ________, ________, ________, or ______?
- Which of the following is your favorite: ________, ________, ________, or ________?
- Stand here if you like __________ and stand here if you don't like it.

Individual Student Learning Goals

With individual student learning goals, students identify something that interests them during instruction and create their own personalized learning goals during a unit. The teacher should help students connect their personalized learning goals to teacher-identified learning goals. Students can state their learning goals in the following formats.

- When this unit is completed, I will better understand __________.
- When this unit is completed, I will be able to __________.

A scale like the one in figure 9.6 can help students track their progress on individual learning goals.

4 = I did even better than the goal I set.
3 = I accomplished my goal.
2 = I didn't accomplish everything I wanted to, but I learned quite a bit.
1 = I tried, but I didn't really learn much.
0 = I didn't really try to accomplish my goal.

Figure 9.6: Student self-assessment scale for individual learning goals.

Figure 9.7 can help guide students' use of this strategy.

Monitoring Element 39

Specific student responses and behaviors allow the teacher to determine whether this element is being implemented effectively and producing the desired effects.

- Students describe the teacher as someone who knows them or is interested in them.
- Students respond when the teacher demonstrates understanding of their interests and backgrounds.
- Students say they feel that their teacher values them.
- Students say they know their peers.

Use this list to monitor student responses to element 39.

To monitor your own use of this element, use the scale in figure 9.8 in combination with the reproducible "Tracking Teacher Actions: Understanding Students' Backgrounds and Interests" (page 310). As with other proficiency scales, level 3 or higher is the goal.

The following examples describe what each level of the scale might look like in the classroom.

- **Not Using (0):** A teacher knows relatively little about students' backgrounds or interests. What background information she does know she found out by accident. As such, the teacher does not use students' backgrounds and interests to inform instruction or interactions with students.
- **Beginning (1):** A teacher sporadically seeks out information about some students and their lives outside of the classroom. However, he does not use this information to improve interaction with students.
- **Developing (2):** A teacher has an understanding of students' backgrounds and interests and uses this knowledge to inform instruction. However, the teacher pays little attention to whether students feel welcome and supported as a result of her actions.
- **Applying (3):** A teacher has a good understanding of his students' backgrounds and interests and regularly applies this knowledge to his lessons and in his interactions with students. The teacher

Individual Student Learning Goals Worksheet

Name: ____________________

Student-identified learning goal: ____________________

Initial score: ____________________

Goal score: ____________________ by ____________________ (date)

Specific things I am going to do to improve: ____________________

Score	a	b	c	d	e	f	g	h	i	j
4										
3										
2										
1										
0										

Date

a. ____________________ f. ____________________

b. ____________________ g. ____________________

c. ____________________ h. ____________________

d. ____________________ i. ____________________

e. ____________________ j. ____________________

4	3	2	1	0
I did even better than the goal I set.	I accomplished my goal.	I didn't accomplish everything I wanted to, but I learned quite a bit.	I tried, but I didn't really learn much.	I didn't really try to accomplish my goal.

Source: Marzano Research, 2016.

Figure 9.7: Worksheet for individual student learning goals.

Visit **go.SolutionTree.com/instruction** *for a free reproducible version of this figure.*

4 Innovating	I adapt behaviors and create new strategies for unique student needs and situations.
3 Applying	I understand students' backgrounds and interests, and I monitor the extent to which my actions affect students.
2 Developing	I understand students' backgrounds and interests, but I do not monitor the effect on students.
1 Beginning	I use the strategies and behaviors associated with this element incorrectly or with parts missing.
0 Not Using	I am unaware of strategies and behaviors associated with this element.

Figure 9.8: Self-rating scale for element 39—Understanding students' backgrounds and interests.

monitors students' attitudes and behaviors in class and specifically reaches out to students with whom he has strained relationships or who seem to be disengaged.

- **Innovating (4):** A teacher seeks to better understand the backgrounds and interests of students who need additional support. For example, she first uses student background surveys and opinion questionnaires to get an idea of the backgrounds and interests of the students in her class. Once she identifies students who do not get as much support from home, she takes care to actively comment on those students' achievements whenever possible and uses this information to inform her comments during parent-teacher conferences.

Element 40: Displaying Objectivity and Control

An effective teacher behaves in an objective and controlled manner. Research has shown that teachers who objectively viewed their students as young learners (as opposed to friends or enemies) produced greater achievement gains than teachers who were overly warm or overly cold toward students (Brophy & Evertson, 1976; Nelson, Martella, & Galand, 1998; Soar & Soar, 1979). Teachers should maintain a balance of dominance (leadership) and cooperation in the classroom (Brekelmans, Wubbels, & Creton, 1990; Marzano, 2018; Wubbels, Brekelmans, den Brok, & van Tartwijk, 2006; Wubbels, Brekelmans, van Tartwijk, & Admiral, 1999; Wubbels & Levy, 1993).

There are nine strategies within this element.

1. Self-reflection
2. Self-monitoring
3. Emotional triggers
4. Self-care
5. Assertiveness
6. A cool exterior
7. Active listening and speaking
8. Communication styles
9. Unique student needs

The following sections will explore each strategy to provide you with guidelines to effectively implement this element. Read through each before creating a plan for your classroom. Teachers may use the strategies individually or in combination. Remember, these are not merely activities to be checked off; they are methods of creating a practice that combines your art with the science of displaying objectivity and control. Reflect on your use of each strategy by filling out the "Strategy Reflection Log" on page 331.

Self-Reflection

The teacher self-reflects about consistency when enforcing the positive and negative consequences associated with the established rules and procedures. Some questions the teacher might consider include the following.

- Did I provide proper acknowledgment when students followed the rules and procedures?
- Did I use proper consequences when students did not follow rules and procedures?
- Did I take every opportunity today to provide positive and negative consequences for student behavior?
- Did I strike a nice balance between positive and negative consequences as needed?
- In my dealings with students, what should I seek to improve?

The teacher should also consider how to progressively increase expectations for students to control their own behavior.

Self-Monitoring

The teacher monitors his or her emotions in the classroom to avoid displaying counterproductive emotions such as anger, frustration, or hesitation. Before class each day, the teacher mentally reviews all of his or her students, noting those who might cause problems. The teacher should then identify specific negative thoughts and emotions the teacher might hold toward those students by asking, "How do I feel about [student's name]?" The teacher tries to identify events in the past that may be the source of negative thoughts and feelings toward the specific students by asking, "Why do I feel that way?" Finally, the teacher seeks to reframe negative beliefs about the students. For example, the teacher might recognize that student misbehavior usually has little to do with a specific teacher or identify explicit reasons the student might have misbehaved in the past in a way that does not imply disrespect or aggression toward the teacher. Visit **go.SolutionTree.com/instruction** for the reproducible "Self-Monitoring" for more questions to help guide your use of this strategy.

Emotional Triggers

The teacher considers sources of stress and other emotional triggers that make it hard to maintain emotional objectivity. Such triggers might be personal events, certain times of the school year, or specific student or faculty behaviors that make the teacher feel a certain way. For example, a teacher might become short-tempered toward the end of the semester because he perceives students' inability to concentrate as a sign of disrespect rather than excitement. Alternatively, the teacher may be anxious about his parents-in-law coming to town and allow this anxiety to affect his demeanor with students. Once the teacher identifies these triggers and why they make him feel the way he does, the teacher tries not to let those feelings affect his interactions with students. The teacher might also take extra steps to provide self-care, recognizing that when he feels relaxed and in control, he acts in a more objective manner with students.

A guide like figure 9.9 can help identify emotional triggers.

Emotional Trigger Identification Guide

Emotion that elicits a strong reaction: ________________________________

When I feel this emotion, I act in the following way:

I react this way when I feel this emotion because:

In the past, when reacting to this emotion, the following negative results have occurred:

Outside of school, I feel this emotion when:

In school, I feel this emotion when:

In the future, the following events, times of year, or behaviors might trigger this emotion:

I can take the following steps to ensure this emotion doesn't negatively affect my interactions with students and colleagues:

Notes:

Source: Marzano Research, 2016.

Figure 9.9: Identification guide for emotional triggers.

Visit **go.SolutionTree.com/instruction** *for a free reproducible version of this figure.*

Self-Care

Self-care includes intentional actions or practices that an individual partakes in to ensure his or her physical, mental, or emotional health. To engage in self-care, the teacher identifies activities that he or she finds to be rewarding and engages in the activities as needed to mitigate negative feelings. Self-care varies greatly between teachers depending on their needs. For example, if a teacher feels overwhelmed during the school day, she might take a moment to sit by herself, gather her thoughts, practice deep breathing, and identify things from her day that she is grateful for. A different teacher in the same situation might feel the need to give himself some type of reward to help maintain a healthy perspective. However, self-care is not just limited to teachers' actions during the school day. Self-care also encompasses activities that teachers may engage in outside of school that ensure they feel good and are optimistic about their lives and their careers. As such, self-care also encompasses getting a good night's sleep, exercising regularly, and partaking in relaxing activities (which could range from watching television, eating out at a nice restaurant, or seeing friends and family on a regular basis). Finally, teachers should also take actions to maintain healthy senses of humor so that they react positively when faced with negative events.

The following list provides examples of strategies that a teacher can immediately implement when he or she feels negatively during the school day.

- Experimenting with stress reduction techniques (such as deep breathing, meditation, and visualization)
- Removing him- or herself from a negative situation, even if it's only for a few minutes, to regroup and gather his or her thoughts
- Giving him- or herself a reward after a hard interaction or at the end of a difficult day
- Finding inspirational quotes, movies, and stories about teaching
- Finding humorous quotes, movies, and stories that will make him or her laugh
- Talking through or venting frustrations with someone
- Reflecting on the positive aspects of the day
- Considering his or her expectations for the day and whether they are realistic and modifying them if they are not

The following strategies provide examples of preventive actions teachers can take over longer periods of time to support physical, mental, and emotional health.

- Getting enough sleep
- Eating healthy meals
- Exercising regularly
- Finding rewarding hobbies
- Maintaining positive social relationships
- Using positive affirmations and self-talk to challenge negative thought patterns
- Engaging in reflective practices (such as journaling) to help process emotions
- Celebrating successes regularly
- Creating routines that make them feel accomplished at the end of the day
- Giving yourself permission to feel emotions (whether good or bad)
- Avoiding mood-altering substances such as drugs, nicotine, and alcohol

If short-term and long-term self-care strategies do not help your mood, consider talking to a health care professional.

Assertiveness

When considering interactions with students, a teacher may be assertive, passive, or aggressive. Ideally, a teacher should aim to be assertive—able to assert his or her own needs without ignoring or violating the rights of his or her students. As such, an assertive teacher navigates classroom relationships in a way that shows respect for students while still demonstrating that he or she has control. Furthermore, the teacher communicates his or her needs to students and does so in a way that makes it difficult for students to ignore or circumvent. For example, an assertive teacher, upon realizing that students are having a conversation during a lecture, would not ignore the problem. Rather, the teacher would take action to ensure that the students stop but would do so in such a way that shows that he or she respects and cares for the students.

When interacting with students and leading a classroom, a teacher often falls into the following three categories: (1) passive, (2) aggressive, or (3) assertive. Table 9.1 describes characteristics of being passive, aggressive, or assertive. It's important to determine what appropriate, assertive behavior looks like.

Table 9.1: Comparison of Passive, Aggressive, and Assertive Teaching Styles

	Passive	Aggressive	Assertive
General beliefs	Feels positively about external factors, places fault or blame on himself or herself, willing to violate own beliefs, may not be good at defining or communicating thoughts or beliefs	Feels positively about himself or herself, places fault or blame on external factors, stands up for beliefs in a way that violates the rights of others	Feels positively about himself or herself and external factors, finds a way to defend own beliefs without violating others'
Demeanor	Lacking self-confidence	Superior to others	Open and honest
Relationship with students	Fine or poor—students recognize the teacher's lack of control and may take advantage	Poor—students harbor negative feelings toward the teacher (such as fear or resentment)	Good—the teacher and students maintain a relationship of mutual respect
Consequence application	Finds it difficult to apply consequences to the class, chooses to ignore disciplinary problems	Punishes students in a way that makes students feel attacked	Willing to listen to students and compromise, though knows when to put his or her foot down
Verbal cues	Uses noncommittal phrases (like "um" and "maybe"), apologizes or uses justifications often, quiet or unwilling to speak up, can be dull or indirect in communicating feelings	Raises voice at students, tone may come off as harsh or sarcastic, addresses students inappropriately (uses threats or put-downs), treats opinions as facts	Firm but relaxed tone, seems sincere, uses "I" statements to express beliefs, uses cooperative statements to show students' opinions are valued, avoids statements that blame others or tell them what to do
Nonverbal cues	Avoids eye contact, poor posture, fidgets, reserved, crossed arms	Scowls, enters others' personal space, uses aggressive gestures like clenching fists or pointing at students, crossed arms	Active listening, direct eye contact, open body language, allows emotions to show appropriately (smiles when happy, frowns when upset)

A Cool Exterior

A teacher who maintains a cool exterior remains calm and collected when dealing with conflicts in the classroom. Maintaining a cool exterior includes using assertive body language, self-monitoring facial expressions, speaking in a calm and respectful tone of voice, actively listening to reasonable explanations, and avoiding engagement with students who argue, deny, or blame others for their conduct. For example, if a teacher often reacts poorly to students interrupting him, the teacher makes an active choice to address an interrupting student in a calm and professional manner. The teacher might pay particular attention to his tone, volume, and language; take a deep breath before asking the student to stop the unwanted behavior; and describe the student's actions as inappropriate but not make assumptions about the student based upon the repeated action.

Use the following guidelines to remain calm and cool when dealing with conflict.

- Use assertive body language (for example, eye contact, erect posture, and appropriate distance from listeners).
- Match facial expression with the content of the message you're presenting to students.
- Use an appropriate tone of voice that does not indicate emotion (use a pitch slightly but not greatly elevated from normal classroom speech).
- Listen to legitimate explanations.
- Avoid being diverted by students who deny, argue, or blame others for their conduct.

When addressing a particularly agitated student, use the following suggestions.

- Speak in a calm and respectful tone of voice.
- Use active listening and speaking strategies.
- Maintain an appropriate distance from the student.
- Seek to project a neutral facial expression.
- Comment on the student's behavior rather than the student's perceived motives.
- Avoid behaviors that provoke fear and anger from students, such as pointing a finger or shaking a fist, raising the voice, moving toward or hovering over the student, squinting the eyes, glaring or staring at the student, or ridiculing the student.

Active Listening and Speaking

An effective teacher listens to students without agreeing or disagreeing. The teacher should focus on what the student is saying and try to understand the student's viewpoint. The teacher demonstrates neutral body posture, gestures, and facial expressions. When the student is finished speaking, the teacher acknowledges that he or she heard the student ("I think I understand how you feel") and then prompts the student to go on ("What else is bothering you?"). The teacher repeats this process until the student can't think of anything else to say and is calmer. Finally, the teacher summarizes what he or she heard the student say. At the end of the summary, the teacher asks, "Am I right? Did I hear you completely?" The student will either say yes or correct the teacher. If the student corrects the teacher, the teacher should restate the summary with the correction incorporated.

Following is a nine-step process for active listening and speaking.

1. Maintain eye contact to show interest in what the other student is saying.
2. Consider facial expressions and body language for neutrality.
3. Acknowledge the student's comments verbally (for example, saying "I understand" or "I hear you").
4. Prompt the student to continue to speak his or her mind (for example, saying "Is there anything else you want to say?" or "What else are you feeling?").
5. Repeat steps 3 and 4 until the student does not have anything else to say.
6. Summarize what the student has said to the best of your abilities.
7. Ask the student to confirm the accuracy of the summary.

8. If the student disagrees with the summary, ask the student to make corrections. Restate the summary based on the student's corrections.
9. Respond to the student's comments in a calm, controlled manner. Avoid making judgments about the student's feelings or opinions.

Communication Styles

There are many different types of communication styles, and the style with which a teacher communicates affects his or her relationships with students as well as his or her ability to manage a classroom effectively. Generally, communication styles fall into the following five categories: (1) assertive connector, (2) apathetic avoider, (3) junior therapist, (4) bulldozer, and (5) hider. Teachers should be aware of various communication styles, determine the communication style he or she uses the most, and assess how this style affects the relationships in the classroom. Generally, the communication style of the assertive connector is favored, as it communicates respect to students while allowing the teacher to remain in control of the classroom. The teacher should also assess the communication styles of students and work to help them communicate assertively and effectively.

1. The assertive connector:
    - Uses consistent eye contact
    - Shows he or she understands others' emotions by mirroring them
    - Spends equal time speaking and listening
    - Expresses emotions appropriately
    - Asks questions respectfully and uses questions to get clarification or elaboration
    - Repeats what others have said to ensure understanding
    - Can express agreement, disagreement, or neutrality
    - Intends to connect with other people and resolve issues when communicating
    - Sends the overall message "I value our relationship and what you have to say"
2. The apathetic avoider:
    - Ignores the other person's presence or attempts to speak
    - Does not reply, waits too long to reply, or replies insufficiently
    - Interrupts while others are speaking
    - Gets distracted when working with others and shows distraction verbally or nonverbally
    - Appears apathetic or detached
    - Uses body language that is inconsistent with what is being said
    - Turns away, looks away, or walks away
    - Experiences anxiety when trying to connect with another person
    - Avoids relationships with other people
    - Sends the overall message "I don't want much of a relationship with you and will put minimal effort into it"
3. The junior therapist:
    - Assumes that he or she is better able to speak for an individual than that person is
    - Talks for other people and tells them about their own feelings or actions
    - Tends to talk about others rather than him- or herself
    - Decides how the other person should be and responds only when that person acts in accordance with that perception
    - Uses knowledge of the other person's background to justify an analysis of why the person thinks, feels, or acts in specific ways

- Uses knowledge of the other person's background to distort that person's point of view
- Sends the overall message "I know you better than you know yourself; I know you better than I know myself"

4. The bulldozer:
    - Focuses on his or her own topic
    - Ignores topics others bring up
    - Repeats the same thing over and over again
    - May speak in a louder-than-necessary voice or shout
    - Engages in aggressive behaviors such as attacking, criticizing, intimidating, or mocking others
    - Tries to harm others' self-esteem or point of view to "win" the conversation
    - Uses or threatens violence to get his or her way
    - Sends the overall message "I will do whatever it takes to get my way"
5. The hider:
    - Speaks very softly and is sometimes difficult to hear
    - May make comments that lack substance (talks in unclear or paradoxical sentences)
    - Uses contradictory or unclear language
    - Pulls away from the listener or uses body language that conveys fear
    - Doesn't respond to personal questions
    - Has incongruent body language, voice tone, and message, as the person tries to pretend he or she feels differently than what is being said
    - Assumes he or she will "lose" the conversation so avoids engaging
    - Sends the overall message "I am afraid of you and don't want you to know about me"

Unique Student Needs

There are five types of students who may challenge a teacher's ability to remain objective and in control: (1) students who are passive, (2) students who are aggressive, (3) students who have attention problems, (4) perfectionistic students, and (5) students who are socially inept. Teachers should consider students in their classes and identify students who may have unique needs. Once a teacher identifies these students, he or she should take proactive steps in remaining objective and in control during interactions with these students. For example, if a perfectionistic student repeatedly turns in work late, rather than becoming frustrated with the student, the teacher may want to remind himself or herself of the student's unique needs and take steps to help the student overcome his or her anxieties related to perfectionism.

Table 9.2 offers characteristics of the five types of students.

Monitoring Element 40

Specific student responses and behaviors allow the teacher to determine whether this element is being implemented effectively and producing the desired effects.

- Students feel settled by the teacher's calm demeanor.
- Students describe the teacher as someone who is in control of himself or herself and in control of the class.
- Students say that the teacher does not hold grudges or take things personally.

Use this list to monitor student responses to element 40.

Table 9.2: Characteristics of the Five Types of Students

Type of Student	Indicators	Teacher Consideration During Interaction
Passive	Avoids social interactions for fear of having a negative interaction or being dominated by others; afraid of criticism, ridicule, or rejection	This student is probably fearful of negative interactions, and a teacher's actions should remind this student that the classroom is a safe space.
Aggressive	Interrupts during class; lashes out; intimidates other students physically or verbally; rude or disrespectful to teacher; experiences relatively few successes	This student is disrespectful because his or her esteem needs are not met, and a teacher's actions should show that he or she values him or her as both a student and an individual.
Attention problems	Inattentive; distracted easily by unusual events; difficult to re-engage or get on task; late or incomplete work; difficulty with organization, remembering, or listening	This student has difficulty concentrating, and a teacher's actions should help him or her finish tasks and stay focused rather than getting frustrated, which is not productive in a teacher's interactions with this student.
Perfectionist	Holds him- or herself to unnecessarily high standards; motivated by fear of embarrassment rather than intellectual curiosity; unwilling to participate if there is a chance of failure	This student is afraid to make mistakes or fail, and a teacher's actions should show that mistakes are part of learning and that he or she should not be afraid to try.
Socially inept	Has few or no friends; seems unaware of how his or her actions affect others; seems unaware of subtle social cues; struggles to keep up natural conversations; appears anxious when interacting with others; considers him- or herself a loner	This student does not have the same social skills as other students, and a teacher's actions should encourage this student's social growth rather than holding him or her to the same social expectations as other students.

To monitor your own use of this element, use the scale in figure 9.10 in combination with the reproducible "Tracking Teacher Actions: Displaying Objectivity and Control" (page 311). As with other proficiency scales, level 3 or higher is the goal.

4 Innovating	I adapt behaviors and create new strategies for unique student needs and situations.
3 Applying	I display objectivity and control, and I monitor the extent to which my actions affect students.
2 Developing	I display objectivity and control, but I do not monitor the effect on students.
1 Beginning	I use the strategies and behaviors associated with this element incorrectly or with parts missing.
0 Not Using	I am unaware of strategies and behaviors associated with this element.

Figure 9.10: Self-rating scale for element 40—Displaying objectivity and control.

The following examples describe what each level of the scale might look like in the classroom.

- **Not Using (0):** The teacher does not regulate his emotions during class and allows them to affect his interactions with students. For example, if the teacher is having a bad day, the teacher takes out some of his frustrations on students or is more short-tempered than usual.
- **Beginning (1):** The teacher begins to assess the degree to which she displays objectivity and control in the classroom. However, while she is aware that she sometimes inappropriately

expresses emotions and often reflects on what happened, she does not know how to adjust her actions to prevent these issues.

- **Developing (2):** The teacher uses self-care strategies after particularly difficult days to help himself unwind and decompress. However, the teacher does not monitor whether using self-care strategies allow him to have better interactions with students or make him feel more optimistic in the long term.
- **Applying (3):** The teacher uses a combination of strategies including active listening and speaking, assertiveness, and maintaining a cool exterior. Since she began using these strategies in tandem, she has noticed that students seem to respect her more and she gets less frustrated by student misbehavior.
- **Innovating (4):** The teacher identifies students who trigger a negative reaction for her. Whenever she interacts with these students, she makes sure to interact in a positive way and follows up to ensure that the students respond positively.

Action Steps

Use the "Tracking Teacher Actions" reproducibles that follow (pages 309–311) to monitor your implementation of each element in this chapter.

Additionally, visit the appendix (page 329) for the reproducible "Tracking Progress Over Time" (page 330), which helps teachers set goals related to their proficiency with each element and track their progress toward these goals over the course of a unit, semester, or year. Also, the "Strategy Reflection Log" (page 331) in the appendix provides a space to write down your thoughts and reflect on the implementation process for specific strategies related to each element. Finally, visit **go.SolutionTree.com/instruction** for both student surveys and teacher surveys, the results of which provide feedback about your proficiency with each element.

Tracking Teacher Actions: Using Verbal and Nonverbal Behaviors That Indicate Affection for Students

The teacher can use this form to plan his or her usage of strategies related to the element of using verbal and nonverbal behaviors that indicate affection for students.

Check Strategies You Intend to Use	Strategies	Description of Instructional Plan
	Greeting Students at the Classroom Door	
	Holding Informal Conferences	
	Attending After-School Functions	
	Greeting Students by Name Outside of School	
	Giving Students Special Responsibilities or Leadership Roles in the Classroom	
	Scheduling Interaction	
	Creating a Photo Bulletin Board	
	Using Physical Behaviors	
	Using Humor	
	Other:	
	Other:	

Source: Adapted from Marzano Research. (2016). Marzano compendium of instructional strategies. *Centennial, CO: Author.*

Tracking Teacher Actions: Understanding Students' Backgrounds and Interests

The teacher can use this form to plan his or her usage of strategies related to the element of understanding students' backgrounds and interests.

Check Strategies You Intend to Use	Strategies	Description of Instructional Plan
	Student Background Surveys	
	Opinion Questionnaires	
	Individual Teacher-Student Conferences	
	Parent-Teacher Conferences	
	School Newspaper, Newsletter, or Bulletin	
	Informal Class Interviews	
	Familiarity With Student Culture	
	Autobiographical Metaphors and Analogies	
	Six-Word Autobiographies	
	Independent Investigations	
	Quotes	
	Comments About Student Achievement or Areas of Importance	
	Lineups	
	Individual Student Learning Goals	
	Other:	
	Other:	

Source: Adapted from Marzano Research. (2016). Marzano compendium of instructional strategies. *Centennial, CO: Author.*

Tracking Teacher Actions: Displaying Objectivity and Control

The teacher can use this form to plan his or her usage of strategies related to the element of displaying objectivity and control.

Check Strategies You Intend to Use	Strategies	Description of Instructional Plan
	Self-Reflection	
	Self-Monitoring	
	Emotional Triggers	
	Self-Care	
	Assertiveness	
	A Cool Exterior	
	Active Listening and Speaking	
	Communication Styles	
	Unique Student Needs	
	Other:	
	Other:	

Source: Adapted from Marzano Research. (2016). Marzano compendium of instructional strategies. *Centennial, CO: Author.*

CHAPTER 10

Communicating High Expectations

CONTEXT

The final design area to develop an effective context for learning is to communicate high expectations for all students. In effect, teachers must pay special attention to students for whom educators wittingly or unwittingly have developed low expectations. It is not so much that these students need dramatically different strategies to feel valued and respected, but sometimes teachers don't use typical instructional strategies as rigorously or completely with these students as they do with other students.

The goal of this design area is for reluctant students to feel valued and to not hesitate to interact with the teacher or their peers. Teachers are able to meet this goal by answering the question, What strategies will I use to help typically reluctant students feel valued and comfortable interacting with me and their peers? The three elements and associated strategies in this chapter help the teacher do just that.

Element 41: Demonstrating Value and Respect for Reluctant Learners

An effective teacher exhibits behaviors that demonstrate value and respect for reluctant learners. Research has shown that teachers' interactions with high-expectancy students (those from whom they expect high achievement) are more positive than their interactions with low-expectancy students (those from whom they expect low achievement or those who might be described as reluctant learners; Chaiken, Sigler, & Derlega, 1974; Cooper, 1979; Kester & Letchworth, 1972; Marzano, 2018; Page, 1971). When interacting with low-expectancy students, teachers usually praise them less (Babad, Inbar, & Rosenthal, 1982; Brophy & Good, 1970; Cooper & Baron, 1977; Firestone & Brody, 1975; Good, Cooper, & Blakey, 1980; Good, Sikes, & Brophy, 1973; Martinek & Johnson, 1979; Page, 1971; Rejeski, Darracott, & Hutslar, 1979), seat them farther away (Rist, 1970), are less friendly to them (Babad et al., 1982; Chaikin et al., 1974; Kester & Letchworth, 1972; Meichenbaum, Bowers, & Ross, 1969; Page, 1971; Smith & Luginbuhl, 1976), smile at them less, and make eye contact with them less often than they do with high-expectancy students (Chaikin et al., 1974; Marzano, 2018).

There are three strategies within this element.

1. Identifying expectation levels for all students
2. Identifying differential treatment of reluctant learners
3. Using nonverbal and verbal indicators of respect

The following sections will explore each strategy to provide you with guidelines to effectively implement this element. Read through each before creating a plan for your classroom. Teachers may use the strategies individually or in combination. Remember, these are not merely activities to be checked off; they are methods of creating a practice that combines your art with the science of demonstrating value and respect for reluctant learners. Reflect on your use of each strategy by filling out the "Strategy Reflection Log" on page 331.

Identifying Expectation Levels for All Students

The first step toward demonstrating equal value and respect for all students is to identify any pre-existing differences in expectations of students. To do this, the teacher identifies the expectation level for each student by imagining that each student has completed a comprehensive assessment that covers some of the more difficult content addressed in class. On a class list, the teacher writes the level at which he or she expects each student to perform on such an assessment: high, average, or low.

A log like figure 10.1 can help guide your use of this strategy.

Identifying Expectations Log			
Student Name	**Expectation Level**		
	High	Average	Low
	High	Average	Low

Source: Marzano Research, 2016.

Figure 10.1: Log for identifying expectations.

Visit **go.SolutionTree.com/instruction** *for a free reproducible version of this figure.*

Identifying Differential Treatment of Reluctant Learners

To identify any indication of differential treatment, it's good practice for a teacher to track his or her behavior for several days. Some behaviors associated with affective tone are as follows.

- Tone of voice
- Proximity
- Gestures
- Eye contact
- Smiles
- Playful dialogue
- Physical contact
- Range of questions

Some behaviors associated with quality of interaction are as follows.

- Providing feedback
- Probing for more complex information
- Coaching for an answer
- Calling on students
- Assessing the level of questions
- Assessing the level of response required for a reward (verbal or otherwise)

The teacher then uses the data collected to generate conclusions about differential treatment of reluctant learners. The teacher should identify specific students who seem to be receiving differential treatment. For example, a teacher might notice that he or she uses a distant or annoyed tone of voice with reluctant learners but a more conversational or engaged tone with high-expectancy students. The teacher might also examine whether he or she has generalized low expectations for certain groups of students because of ethnicity, appearance, verbal patterns, or socioeconomic status. If this is the case, the teacher should actively seek to behave in an unbiased manner. If biased patterns of thought are present, the teacher might try to ascertain the origin of those patterns and seek to suppress the behaviors.

Using an informal observation log (such as figure 10.2), the teacher can keep track of his or her affective tone and quality of interaction with specific students.

Identifying Differential Treatment Log																		
	Affective Tone										Quality of Interaction							
Student Name	Positive Tone	Negative Tone	Close Proximity	Physically Distant	Eye Contact	Avoiding Eye Contact	Smiles	Negative Facial Expressions	Playful Dialogue	Stilted Conversation	Calling on Student	Not Asking Student to Participate	Asking In-Depth Questions	Asking Only Basic Questions	Probing for More Complex Information	Accepting Basic Answers	Coaching Toward Correct Answer	Rejecting Incorrect Answers Without Helping

Source: Marzano Research, 2016.

Figure 10.2: Log for identifying differential treatment.

Visit **go.SolutionTree.com/instruction** *for a free reproducible version of this figure.*

Using Nonverbal and Verbal Indicators of Respect

The effective teacher uses eye contact, smiling, proximity, hand and body gestures, physical contact, and playful dialogue to communicate value and respect for all students. If a teacher recognizes different treatment for reluctant learners, the teacher should make an effort to use both verbal and nonverbal indicators to show respect and value for reluctant learners.

The ultimate goal of demonstrating value and respect for reluctant learners, and indeed for all students, is to make them feel comfortable and welcome in the classroom. While the types of gestures and verbal indications presented in this strategy provide diverse options and a good starting point for teachers who wish to be more intentional about demonstrating value for all students, it is essential to note the importance of differentiation within this strategy. Different students will have different preferences when it comes to how their teachers interact with them. For example, one student might feel uncomfortable with physical gestures such as a pat on the back or a high five. Another student might appreciate subtle gestures and positive facial expressions more than playful dialogue in front of the rest of the class. These likes and dislikes may be based on students' cultural backgrounds and upbringing, past experiences, or simple personal preferences. Using indicators of value and respect that a student dislikes or is not comfortable with will have an effect opposite of what was intended—the student will feel uncomfortable and disrespected in class. In short, methods of demonstrating value and respect for students cannot be used universally. This strategy requires that teachers know their individual students and pay attention to the effects these methods have on them.

Monitoring Element 41

Specific student responses and behaviors allow the teacher to determine whether this element is being implemented effectively and producing the desired effects.

- Students say the teacher cares for all students.
- Students treat each other with respect.

Use this list to monitor student responses to element 41.

To monitor your own use of this element, use the scale in figure 10.3 in combination with the reproducible "Tracking Teacher Actions: Demonstrating Value and Respect for Reluctant Learners" (page 326). As with other proficiency scales, level 3 or higher is the goal.

4 Innovating	I adapt behaviors and create new strategies for unique student needs and situations.
3 Applying	I exhibit behaviors that demonstrate value and respect for reluctant learners, and I monitor the impact on reluctant learners.
2 Developing	I exhibit behaviors that demonstrate value and respect for reluctant learners, but I do not monitor the effect on students.
1 Beginning	I use the strategies and behaviors associated with this element incorrectly or with parts missing.
0 Not Using	I am unaware of strategies and behaviors associated with this element.

Figure 10.3: Self-rating scale for element 41—Demonstrating value and respect for reluctant learners.

The following examples describe what each level of the scale might look like in the classroom.

- **Not Using (0):** A teacher realizes that he has differing expectations for his students, but he does not do anything to treat students more equitably.
- **Beginning (1):** A teacher is generally friendly and respectful to all students. She notices that she does not have as many personal interactions with the reluctant learners in her class, yet she does not change her behavior.
- **Developing (2):** A teacher has consciously begun to identify her expectations of various students and adjust her behavior to demonstrate value and respect for all students, but she has not collected any evidence of the impact this might be having on her reluctant learners.
- **Applying (3):** A teacher uses words and gestures to affirm his value and respect for all his students. He keeps track of behaviors from reluctant learners that indicate they are becoming more comfortable in the classroom, as well as instances in which students treat one another with respect. He is able to see that both these indicators are increasing as he becomes more proficient with this element.
- **Innovating (4):** A teacher uses verbal and nonverbal indicators to make all her students feel welcome and valued in her class. She often high-fives students or gives a pat on the back as encouragement. She notices, however, that one reluctant learner seems uncomfortable with this, so she modifies her implementation with that student to give him the personal space he needs.

Element 42: Asking In-Depth Questions of Reluctant Learners

An effective teacher asks questions of reluctant learners with the same frequency and depth as with high-expectancy students. Research has shown that, compared to high-expectancy students, low-expectancy students (those who could be described as reluctant learners) are less frequently called on to answer questions (Mendoza, Good, & Brophy, 1972; Rubovits & Maehr, 1971), allowed less time to answer questions (Allington, 1980; Taylor, 1979), and more frequently "given" answers to questions (Brophy & Good, 1970; Jeter & Davis, 1973; Marzano, 2018). If a low-expectancy student cannot answer a question, teachers usually call on a different student instead of helping the low-expectancy student answer (Brophy & Good, 1970; Jeter & Davis, 1973; Marzano, 2018).

There are eight strategies within this element.

1. Question levels
2. Response opportunities
3. Follow-up questioning
4. Evidence and support for student answers
5. Encouragement
6. Wait time
7. Response tracking
8. Inappropriate reactions

The following sections will explore each strategy to provide you with guidelines to effectively implement this element. Read through each before creating a plan for your classroom. Teachers may use the strategies individually or in combination. Remember, these are not merely activities to be checked off; they are methods of creating a practice that combines your art with the science of asking in-depth questions of reluctant learners. Reflect on your use of each strategy by filling out the "Strategy Reflection Log" on page 331.

Question Levels

Effective teachers ask questions that require students to analyze information, evaluate conclusions, or make inferences. For example, a teacher might present a short reading and then ask students to determine whether the author has given sufficient evidence for the conclusion. These types of questions are more complex than questions that test recognition or recall of correct answers. The teacher should ensure that he or she frequently asks reluctant learners complex questions, even if these students may need help or encouragement to respond.

An effective way to ensure that students are exposed to in-depth questions is to use questioning sequences rather than individual questions. Questioning sequences are a more reliable method for eliciting higher-order thinking from students than individual questions. A questioning sequence is a series of questions that lead from basic information to complex and rigorous thinking. Questioning sequences have four phases: (1) detail questions, (2) category questions, (3) elaboration questions, and (4) evidence questions. The *detail phase* asks students to recall discrete facts and information as a way of activating their existing knowledge about a topic. Types of details about a topic include people, objects, places, events, human constructs, and so on. The *category phase* focuses the sequence on a particular category of content and asks students to create connections by identifying examples within the category, coming up with general characteristics of the category, and making comparisons within and across categories. The *elaboration phase* asks students to make a claim about the characteristics they identified in the category phase by explaining reasons, describing effects, and making predictions. The *evidence phase* asks students to support their claims by identifying sources, explaining reasoning, qualifying conclusions, finding errors in reasoning, and examining elaborations from various perspectives.

Questioning sequences are flexible in that teachers can use them in a brief period of time, like one lesson or part of a lesson, or over a longer span of several lessons. In either case, the teacher uses scaffolding and support to guide students through the sequence toward complex thinking about the topic.

Response Opportunities

Teachers can reinforce high expectations for all students by giving them equal response opportunities. That is, no student should have significantly more or fewer opportunities to answer a question than any other student. There are many ways to give opportunities to respond and to increase overall response rates; this strategy focuses on equitable distribution of those opportunities. Teachers can use group and individual response strategies to provide students with opportunities to respond.

Following are such group response strategies.

- **Near partners:** Students stand up and walk at least seven steps from their seat to find a partner. Partners take turns sharing their responses.
- **Table groups:** Students work with others at their table or desk group to create or share responses.
- **Give one, get one:** Students write down their response, then find a partner and take turns sharing answers.
- **Jigsaw:** Students form groups and assign numbers within the groups. Then, the student numbered 1 in each group meets with the 1s from all the other groups, 2s meet with 2s, and so on. Each number group learns a different piece of the content. Finally, students go back to their original groups and share what they learned in their number groups.
- **Peer instruction:** Pose a question, and have students consider the answer individually. Then, students form groups and each member tries to convince the rest that his or her answer is correct. See how many students have changed their minds, then discuss the correct answer as a class.
- **Vote with your feet:** Students move to different locations depending on which answer they choose. Groups discuss their answers and choose a spokesperson to share with the rest of the class.

Following are individual response strategies.

- **Random names:** Write each student's name on a slip of paper, popsicle stick, or other item. When asking a question of the class, draw a name. That student answers the question. Return the student's name to the cup so that students' chances of being called on are always equal.
- **On your own:** Students think of an answer individually and write it down.
- **Response chaining:** Call on a student to answer a question. Select a second student to elaborate on or respond to the first's answer. Continue the chain as long as needed.
- **Whip around the room:** Each student quickly shares an answer or a piece of information with the class.
- **Exit slips:** Students write down an answer and turn it in before leaving class.

Follow-Up Questioning

If a student is having trouble answering a question, the teacher restates the question, encourages collaboration, gives hints and cues, or allows the student to opt out temporarily. For example, if the teacher asks a question about the traits of a character from a story and a student isn't sure of the answer, the teacher might ask the student to think about it in terms of comparing that character to another. If the teacher does allow the student to opt out, it is important to follow up with the student using a different question or in a one-on-one conversation at a later time. Visit **go.SolutionTree.com/instruction** for the reproducible "Follow-Up Questioning Log" to use with this strategy.

Evidence and Support for Student Answers

To reinforce high expectations for all students, the teacher requires similar levels of evidence and support for answers from every student. If a student makes a claim, the teacher asks him or her to provide grounds and backing for that claim, regardless of whether or not the student is typically a reluctant learner. If a student must make inferences in order to answer a question, the teacher asks the student to explain these inferences, even if the teacher has generally low expectations of the student.

In terms of evidence, *sufficiency* refers to there being enough evidence to reasonably support the claim. For example, one temperature reading on one day in one city is probably not enough evidence to support a larger claim about the climate of the state. *Relevance* has to do with whether the evidence is truly related to the claim. For example, facts about the population of a state are not relevant to claims about the climate. One way to help students concretely determine the relevance and sufficiency of their evidence is to diagram their argument. See figure 10.4 for an example.

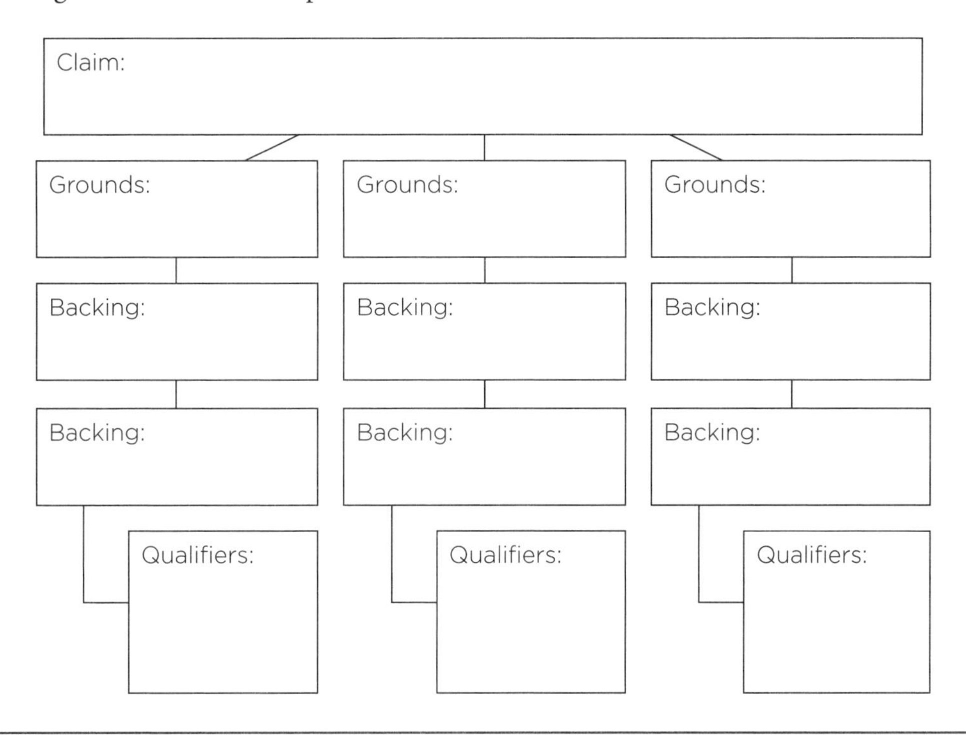

Figure 10.4: Diagramming an argument.

As shown, an argument has three parts: (1) claim, (2) grounds, and (3) backing. The claim is the opinion or conclusion that the argument seeks to defend. Grounds are reasons for the claim. Backing is evidence (often facts and data) that supports the grounds. Diagramming an argument in this manner forces students to make explicit connections and enables them to see where the argument is well supported and where it is not.

Encouragement

To encourage participation from all members of the class, the teacher attributes ideas and comments to those who offered them. The teacher also thanks each student who asks a question or provides an answer, even if the answer is incorrect. If a student does answer incorrectly, the teacher acknowledges any correct portions of the response and then explains how the incorrect portion could be altered to make it correct. Alternatively, the teacher states the question that the incorrect response would have answered.

Teachers can use phrases and sentence stems such as the following to encourage all students to participate.

- "Thank you for your contribution, [student name]."
- "[Student name], thanks for asking that question."
- "As [student name] pointed out earlier, __________ [reference or explain student's earlier contribution]."

- "I appreciate your response, but that's not quite what I was looking for." (Call on another student.)
- "I can tell you've been thinking hard about this; can I give you a slightly different perspective?" (Explain correct response.)
- "Might it instead be that __________ [explain correct response]?"
- "You said __________ [paraphrase correct parts of response]. That's exactly right. However, let's talk more about __________ [paraphrase incorrect parts]."
- "I like the way you expressed __________ [paraphrase correct parts of response], but I'd like to tweak the other part of your answer." (Paraphrase incorrect parts and explain correct response.)
- "If I had asked __________ [question that the incorrect response would have answered], that would be absolutely correct. But let's try to answer __________ [repeat question]." (Let student retry or call on another student.)

Wait Time

It's important for the teacher to provide appropriate wait time after asking a question and appropriate pause time between student answers to allow all students to process information and formulate responses. To use wait time, a teacher would pose a question, wait several seconds depending on the complexity of the question, and then call on a student to respond. Wait time also applies when a student pauses to collect his or her thoughts while speaking and between individual answers when multiple students are responding.

Teachers often feel awkward standing in silence for a few seconds when giving wait time, especially if they are new to the strategy. The following list gives examples of what a teacher might do to occupy him- or herself during wait time and reduce awkwardness.

- Count the number of seconds.
- Make eye contact with students around the room.
- Move from one place in the room to another.
- Take several deep breaths.
- Scan the classroom for student engagement.
- Think of three good answers to the question.
- Think of a cue or hint to give if a student answers incorrectly.

Response Tracking

An effective teacher ensures that all students have fairly equal opportunities to respond by calling on any student instead of only selecting those who raise their hands. The teacher also keeps track of which students have answered or been asked questions, perhaps by placing a checkmark or tally mark next to their names on the class chart. To focus on specific students, the teacher circles those students' names on a list or seating chart and then tracks how often they ask or respond to questions throughout a class period.

Inappropriate Reactions

The teacher encourages reluctant learners to answer questions and share their thoughts by avoiding inappropriate negative reactions to student responses. The teacher should avoid any of the following responses.

- Telling students they should have known the answer to a question
- Ignoring a student's response
- Making subjective comments about incorrect answers
- Allowing negative comments from other students

Instead of telling students they should have known the answer to a question, teachers can:

- Prompt them to try again by saying, "I'd like to give you a little more time to think about that."
- Remind them that they've learned the content by saying, "Think back to [day, time, or lesson when content was covered]. Remember when we talked about [topic]?
- Direct them to the answer by saying, "Look at [page or section of resource]. Where it says [content related to question], what do you think that means?"

Instead of ignoring students' responses, teachers can:

- Make eye contact
- Smile
- Thank them for their contributions
- Explain why the answer is incorrect

Instead of making subjective comments about incorrect answers, teachers can:

- Parse answers into correct and incorrect parts
- Make comments about students' effort
- Thank students for their contributions
- State the question an incorrect response would have answered
- Give students another chance by saying, "I must have miscommunicated what I was asking. I meant to say, [rephrase question]."

Instead of allowing negative comments from other students, teachers can:

- Establish classroom expectations or norms around respect and politeness
- Clearly and firmly convey that negative comments are unacceptable
- Enforce consequences for negative comments

Monitoring Element 42

Specific student responses and behaviors allow the teacher to determine whether this element is being implemented effectively and producing the desired effects.

- Students say the teacher expects everyone to participate.
- Students say the teacher asks difficult questions of everyone.

Use this list to monitor student responses to element 42.

To monitor your own use of this element, use the scale in figure 10.5 in combination with the reproducible "Tracking Teacher Actions: Asking In-Depth Questions of Reluctant Learners" (page 327). As with other proficiency scales, level 3 or higher is the goal.

4 Innovating	I adapt behaviors and create new strategies for unique student needs and situations.
3 Applying	I ask questions of reluctant learners with the same frequency and depth as with high-expectancy students, and I monitor the quality of participation of reluctant learners.
2 Developing	I ask questions of reluctant learners with the same frequency and depth as with high-expectancy students, but I do not monitor the effect on students.
1 Beginning	I use the strategies and behaviors associated with this element incorrectly or with parts missing.
0 Not Using	I am unaware of strategies and behaviors associated with this element.

Figure 10.5: Self-rating scale for element 42—Asking in-depth questions of reluctant learners.

The following examples describe what each level of the scale might look like in the classroom.

- **Not Using (0):** A teacher avoids asking in-depth questions of reluctant learners.
- **Beginning (1):** A teacher tries to make sure she calls on all of her students, even the reluctant learners. However, she does not do this consistently and often finds herself simply asking another student when the first person she calls on doesn't give the right answer.
- **Developing (2):** A teacher asks in-depth questions of reluctant learners with the same frequency as he does other students. He intentionally uses follow-up questions and wait time to make sure they have a chance to answer, but he hasn't tried to figure out if these techniques are having the desired effect.
- **Applying (3):** A teacher uses effective questioning techniques to ask in-depth questions of reluctant learners. He also monitors their responses and is able to see that their confidence is increasing over time and they are more likely to give complete answers with less prompting.
- **Innovating (4):** A teacher is utilizing various strategies and monitoring their effects. She sees success with most of her reluctant learners by using encouragement and follow-up questions, but one student is still struggling. To help this student succeed, the teacher implements extra scaffolding when asking for evidence and support.

Element 43: Probing Incorrect Answers With Reluctant Learners

An effective teacher probes incorrect answers with reluctant learners in the same manner as he or she does with high-expectancy students. Research has shown that teachers are more willing to probe an incorrect answer with high-expectancy students than with low-expectancy students (students that could be described as reluctant learners; Brophy, 1983; Cooper, 1979; Marzano, 2018). Teachers also give low-expectancy students less feedback about their answers (Brophy & Good, 1970; Cooper, 1979; Cornbleth, Davis, & Button, 1972; Good et al., 1973; Jeter & Davis, 1973; Willis, 1970) and spend less time trying to uncover the logic and structure of low-expectancy students' answers to questions (Brophy & Good, 1970; Jeter & Davis, 1973; Marzano, 2018).

There are four strategies within this element.

1. Using an appropriate response process
2. Letting students off the hook temporarily
3. Using answer revision
4. Using think-pair-share

The following sections will explore each strategy to provide you with guidelines to effectively implement this element. Read through each before creating a plan for your classroom. Teachers may use the strategies individually or in combination. Remember, these are not merely activities to be checked off; they are methods of creating a practice that combines your art with the science of probing incorrect answers with reluctant learners. Reflect on your use of each strategy by filling out the "Strategy Reflection Log" on page 331.

Using an Appropriate Response Process

The effective teacher responds appropriately to incorrect or incomplete responses from reluctant learners by first demonstrating gratitude for the student's response. Next, the teacher points out what is correct and what is incorrect about the student's response. Whenever possible, the teacher should emphasize what was correct and acknowledge that the student was headed in the right direction. If the student's response was completely incorrect, the teacher identifies the question that the incorrect response would have answered. Finally, the teacher helps the student answer correctly or complete his or her previous answer by giving the student more time to think, using hints or cues, modifying or restating the original question, or finding a simpler question within the one initially asked. The teacher might also provide the answer to the student and ask the student to elaborate on it, restate it in his or her own words, or provide an example of the answer.

Following are the three steps of the appropriate response process.

1. Express appreciation for the student's response.
    - "Thank you for that answer!"
    - "I appreciate your willingness to share."
    - "Thank you for bringing up those ideas."
2. Identify the correct and incorrect parts of the answer.
    - "When you said [correct portion of response], that was exactly right. However, I want to talk more about [incorrect portion]."
    - "You were headed in the right direction with [correct portion], but you took a bit of a detour with [incorrect portion]. Let's see if we can get back on track."
    - "Actually, your response about [incorrect portion] would have answered a different question, such as [question the response would have answered]."
3. Help the student correct his or her response.
    - "Let me rephrase the question: [restatement of question]?"
    - "Let's start by thinking about [smaller or simpler part of the question]."
    - "Would you like more time to think about it?"
    - "Think about what we know about [hint or cue]. How does that change your answer?"
    - "Can you explain the thinking behind your answer?"

Letting Students Off the Hook Temporarily

If a student becomes flustered, confused, or embarrassed while answering a question, the effective teacher lets the student pass temporarily. However, as noted previously, the teacher should return to the same student at a later time (in either a whole-class or one-on-one context) and ask this student to answer a different question or assist him or her with thinking through the initial question when the student feels calmer. Teachers should keep track of the student and the question the student opted out of. Visit **go.SolutionTree.com/instruction** for the reproducible "Temporary Opt-Out Tracking Log" to use with this strategy.

Using Answer Revision

The teacher can use elaborative interrogation techniques to help a student probe his or her answer until the student realizes that it is not defensible. The teacher might respond to a student's incorrect answer with questions such as the following.

- "How did you arrive at that answer?"
- "What makes you think that's true?"
- "What evidence supports your answer?"
- "Is there another conclusion your evidence might support?"
- "Could you draw a different conclusion from the same evidence?"
- "Can you explain the reasoning behind your answer?"
- "If someone challenged your answer, how would you defend it?"
- "Can you think of other possible answers to the question?"

Using Think-Pair-Share

Frank Lyman (1981) originally developed think-pair-share. In this strategy, the teacher uses this structure to allow reluctant learners time to rehearse and correct answers before sharing them in front of the class. First, the teacher asks or displays a question and students briefly think about the answer individually. Then, students form pairs and tell their partners their best answers to the question. Pairs discuss and come to a consensus about their answer. The teacher then asks pairs to share their answers with the class.

A worksheet like figure 10.6 can help guide students' use of this strategy.

My answer:	My partner's answer:
If I had to share our discussion with the class, I would say:	

Source: Marzano Research, 2016.

Figure 10.6: Worksheet for think-pair-share.

Visit **go.SolutionTree.com/instruction** *for a free reproducible version of this figure.*

Monitoring Element 43

Specific student responses and behaviors allow the teacher to determine whether this element is being implemented effectively and producing the desired effects.

- Students say the teacher lets them off the hook temporarily.
- Students say the teacher won't give up on them.
- Students say the teacher helps them think deeply about the content.
- Students say the teacher helps them answer difficult questions successfully.

Use this list to monitor student responses to element 43.

To monitor your own use of this element, use the scale in figure 10.7 in combination with the reproducible "Tracking Teacher Actions: Probing Incorrect Answers With Reluctant Learners" (page 328). As with other proficiency scales, level 3 or higher is the goal.

4 Innovating	I adapt behaviors and create new strategies for unique student needs and situations.
3 Applying	I probe incorrect answers with reluctant learners in the same manner as with high-expectancy students, and I monitor the level and quality of responses of reluctant learners.
2 Developing	I probe incorrect answers with reluctant learners in the same manner as with high-expectancy students, but I do not monitor the effect on students.
1 Beginning	I use the strategies and behaviors associated with this element incorrectly or with parts missing.
0 Not Using	I am unaware of strategies and behaviors associated with this element.

Figure 10.7: Self-rating scale for element 43—Probing incorrect answers with reluctant learners.

The following examples describe what each level of the scale might look like in the classroom.

- **Not Using (0):** A teacher simply calls on a different student if someone in his class gives an incorrect answer.
- **Beginning (1):** A teacher gives reluctant learners an opportunity to try again if they give an incorrect answer, but she doesn't provide scaffolding or leading questions to help in the process.
- **Developing (2):** A teacher helps reluctant learners revise incorrect answers by asking questions that help them identify and re-examine their errors. However, he does nothing to determine if this strategy is having a lasting impact on his reluctant learners.
- **Applying (3):** A teacher probes incorrect answers to help reluctant learners self-correct their errors. He informally monitors how his reluctant learners respond when he asks them challenging questions. Over time, he notices that students seem more comfortable attempting to answer questions they are unsure about as well as working through the probing questions to correct their errors.
- **Innovating (4):** A teacher helps reluctant learners find the correct answer to a question when they initially present an incorrect answer, and she monitors the effect this has on students. While most students are successful in response to these strategies, one student continues to be particularly uncomfortable with responding to probing questions in front of the rest of the class. To support this student, the teacher creates a worksheet with a set of general probing questions. When she would normally ask probing questions verbally, she gives the student the worksheet and lets her off the hook temporarily to think about the questions on her own.

Action Steps

Use the "Tracking Teacher Actions" reproducibles that follow (pages 326–328) to monitor your implementation of each element in this chapter.

Additionally, visit the appendix (page 329) for the reproducible "Tracking Progress Over Time" (page 330), which helps teachers set goals related to their proficiency with each element and track their progress toward these goals over the course of a unit, semester, or year. Also, the "Strategy Reflection Log" (page 331) in the appendix provides a space to write down your thoughts and reflect on the implementation process for specific strategies related to each element. Finally, visit **go.SolutionTree.com/instruction** for both student surveys and teacher surveys, the results of which provide feedback about your proficiency with each element.

Tracking Teacher Actions: Demonstrating Value and Respect for Reluctant Learners

The teacher can use this form to plan his or her usage of strategies related to the element of demonstrating value and respect for reluctant learners.

Check Strategies You Intend to Use	Strategies	Description of Instructional Plan
	Identifying Expectation Levels for All Students	
	Identifying Differential Treatment of Reluctant Learners	
	Using Nonverbal and Verbal Indicators of Respect	
	Other:	
	Other:	

Source: Adapted from Marzano Research. (2016). Marzano compendium of instructional strategies. *Centennial, CO: Author.*

Tracking Teacher Actions: Asking In-Depth Questions of Reluctant Learners

The teacher can use this form to plan his or her usage of strategies related to the element of asking in-depth questions of reluctant learners.

Check Strategies You Intend to Use	Strategies	Description of Instructional Plan
	Question Levels	
	Response Opportunities	
	Follow-Up Questioning	
	Evidence and Support for Student Answers	
	Encouragement	
	Wait Time	
	Response Tracking	
	Inappropriate Reactions	
	Other:	
	Other:	

Source: Adapted from Marzano Research. (2016). Marzano compendium of instructional strategies. *Centennial, CO: Author.*

Tracking Teacher Actions: Probing Incorrect Answers With Reluctant Learners

The teacher can use this form to plan his or her usage of strategies related to the element of probing incorrect answers with reluctant learners.

Check Strategies You Intend to Use	Strategies	Description of Instructional Plan
	Using an Appropriate Response Process	
	Letting Students Off the Hook Temporarily	
	Using Answer Revision	
	Using Think-Pair-Share	
	Other:	
	Other:	

Source: Adapted from Marzano Research. (2016). Marzano compendium of instructional strategies. *Centennial, CO: Author.*

Appendix
Reproducibles

The following two reproducibles will support your implementation of the forty-three elements. "Tracking Progress Over Time" (page 330) helps teachers set goals related to their proficiency with each element and track their progress toward these goals over the course of a unit, semester, or year. The "Strategy Reflection Log" (page 331) provides teachers a space to write down their thoughts and reflect on the implementation process for specific strategies related to each element.

See *The Marzano Compendium of Instructional Strategies* (Marzano Research, 2016) for a rich, frequently updated online resource for K–12 teachers, instructional coaches, teacher mentors, and administrators to fully implement *The New Art and Science of Teaching* framework.

Tracking Progress Over Time

Use this worksheet to set a goal for your use of this element, make a plan for increasing your mastery, and chart your progress toward your goal.

Element: ______________________________

Initial score: ______________________________

Goal score: ____________________ by ____________________(date)

Specific things I am going to do to improve: ______________________________

____

____

____

Score on Element										
4										
3										
2										
1										
0	a	b	c	d	e	f	g	h	i	j

Date

a. ______________________________ f. ______________________________

b. ______________________________ g. ______________________________

c. ______________________________ h. ______________________________

d. ______________________________ i. ______________________________

e. ______________________________ j. ______________________________

Source: Adapted from Marzano Research. (2016). Marzano compendium of instructional strategies. *Centennial, CO: Author*

Strategy Reflection Log

Use this worksheet to select a strategy, set a goal, and reflect on your use of that strategy.

Element: __________

Strategy: __________

Goal: __________

Date	How did it go?

Source: Adapted from Marzano Research. (2016). Marzano compendium of instructional strategies. *Centennial, CO: Author*

References and Resources

Alexander, P. A., White, C. S., Haensly, P. A., & Crimmins-Jeans, M. (1987). *Training in analogical reasoning.* Tech. Report. College Station, GA: College of Education, Texas A&M University.

Allington, R. L. (1980). Teacher interruption behaviors during primary-grade oral reading. *Journal of Educational Psychology, 72*(3), 371–377.

Anderman, E. M., & Wolters, C. A. (2006). Goals, values, and affect: Influences on student motivation. In P. A. Alexander & P. H. Winne (Eds.), *Handbook of educational psychology* (pp. 369–389). Mahwah, NJ: Erlbaum.

Anderson, J. R. (1982). Acquisition of cognitive skills. *Psychological Review, 89*, 369–406.

Anderson, J. R. (1995). *Learning and memory: An integrated approach.* New York: Wiley.

Anderson, L. M., Evertson, C. M., & Emmer, E. T. (1980). Dimensions in classroom management derived from recent research. *Journal of Curriculum Studies, 12*(4), 343–356.

Arlin, M. (1979). Teacher transitions can disrupt time flow in classrooms. *American Educational Research Journal, 16*(1), 42–56.

Armento, B. J. (1978, February). *Teacher behavior and effective teaching of concepts.* Paper presented at the annual meeting of the American Association of Colleges for Teacher Education, Chicago.

Babad, E., Inbar, J., & Rosenthal, R. (1982). Pygmalion, Galatea, and the Golem: Investigations of biased and unbiased teachers. *Journal of Educational Psychology, 74*(4), 459–474.

Baker, W. P., & Lawson, A. E. (1995). *Effect of analogical instruction and reasoning level on achievement in general genetics.* Tempe, AZ: Department of Zoology.

Bangert-Drowns, R. L., Hurley, M. M., & Wilkinson, B. (2004). The effects of school-based writing-to-learn interventions on academic achievement: A meta-analysis. *Review of Educational Research, 74*(1), 29–58.

Bangert-Drowns, R. L., Kulik, C.-L. C., Kulik, J. A., & Morgan, M. T. (1991). The instructional effects of feedback in test-like events. *Review of Educational Research, 61*(2), 213–238.

Bangert-Drowns, R. L., Kulik, J. A., & Kulik, C. C. (1991). Effects of classroom testing. *Journal of Educational Research, 85*(2), 89–99.

Becker, W. C. (Ed.). (1988). Direct instruction: Special issue. *Education and Treatment of Children, 11*, 297–402.

Bettencourt, E. M., Gillett, M. H., Gall, M. D., & Hull, R. E. (1983). Effects of teacher enthusiasm training on student on-task behavior and achievement. *American Educational Research Journal, 20*(3), 435–450.

Black, P., & Wiliam, D. (1998). Assessment and classroom learning. *Assessment in Education: Principles, Policy and Practice, 5*(1), 7–74.

Bloom, B. S. (1976). *Human characteristics and school learning.* New York: McGraw-Hill.

Bloom, B. S. (1984). The search for methods of group instruction as effective as one-to-one tutoring. *Educational Leadership, 41*(8), 4–17.

Bowen, C. W. (2000). A quantitative review of cooperative learning effects on high school and college chemistry achievement. *Journal of Chemical Education, 77*(1), 116–119.

Brekelmans, M., Wubbels, T., & Creton, H. A. (1990). A study of student perceptions of physics teacher behavior. *Journal of Research in Science Teaching, 27*(4), 335–350.

Broadhurst, A. R., & Darnell, D. K. (1965). An introduction to cybernetics and information theory. *Quarterly Journal of Speech, 51*(3), 442–453.

Brookhart, S. M., & Nitko, A. J. (2007). *Assessment and grading in classrooms.* Upper Saddle River, NJ: Pearson Education.

Brophy, J. E. (1983). Research on the self-fulfilling prophecy and teacher expectations. *Journal of Educational Psychology, 75*(5), 631–661.

Brophy, J. E. (1996). *Teaching problem students.* New York: Guilford Press.

Brophy, J. E. (2006). History of research on classroom management. In C. M. Evertson & C. S. Weinstein (Eds.), *Handbook of classroom management: Research, practice, and contemporary issues* (pp. 17–43). Mahwah, NJ: Erlbaum.

Brophy, J. E., & Evertson, C. M. (1976). *Learning from teaching: A developmental perspective.* Boston: Allyn & Bacon.

Brophy, J. E., & Good, T. L. (1970). Teacher's communication of differential expectations for children's classroom performance: Some behavioral data. *Journal of Educational Psychology, 61*(5), 365–374.

Brown, J. S., & Burton, R. R. (1978). Diagnostic models for procedural bugs in basic mathematical skills. *Cognitive Science: A Multidisciplinary Journal, 2*, 155–192.

Butler, D. L., & Winne, P. H. (1995). Feedback and self-regulated learning: A theoretical synthesis. *Review of Educational Research, 65*(3), 245–281.

Cahill, L., Prins, B., Weber, M., & McGaugh, J. (1994). Beta-adrenergic activation and memory of emotional events. *Nature, 371*(6499), 702–704.

Carleton, L., & Marzano, R. J. (2010). *Vocabulary games for the classroom.* Bloomington, IN: Marzano Research.

Chaikin, A. L., Sigler, E., & Derlega, V. J. (1974). Nonverbal mediators of teacher expectancy effects. *Journal of Personality and Social Psychology, 30*(1), 144–149.

Clement, J., Lockhead, J., & Mink, G. S. (1979). Translation difficulties in learning mathematics. *American Mathematical Monthly, 88*(4), 286–290.

Coats, W. D., & Smidchens, U. (1966). Audience recall as a function of speaker dynamism. *Journal of Educational Psychology, 57*(4), 189–191.

Cooper, H. (1989). *Homework.* White Plains, NY: Longman.

Cooper, H. M. (1979). Pygmalion grows up: A model for teacher expectation communication and performance influence. *Review of Educational Research, 49*(3), 389–410.

Cooper, H., & Baron, R. (1977). Academic expectations and attributed responsibility as predictors of professional teachers' reinforcement behavior. *Journal of Educational Psychology, 69*(4), 409–418.

Cooper, H., Robinson, J. C., & Patall, E. A. (2006). Does homework improve academic achievement?: A synthesis of research, 1987–2003. *Review of Educational Research, 76*(1), 1–62.

Cornbleth, C., Davis, O., & Button, C. (1972). *Teacher-pupil interaction and teacher expectations for pupil achievement in secondary social studies class*. Paper presented at the annual meeting of the American Educational Research Association, Chicago.

Crismore, A. (Ed.). (1985). *Landscapes: A state-of-the-art assessment of reading comprehension research: 1974–1984. Final report*. Washington, DC: U.S. Department of Education.

Crooks, T. J. (1988). The impact of classroom evaluation practices on students. *Review of Educational Research, 58*(4), 438–481.

Cross, K. P. (1998). Classroom research: Implementing the scholarship of teaching. In T. Angelo (Ed.), *Classroom assessment and research: An update on uses, approaches, and research findings* (pp. 5–12). San Francisco: Jossey-Bass.

Csikszentmihalyi, M. (1990). *Flow: The psychology of optimal experience*. New York: Harper & Row.

Csikszentmihalyi, M., & Nakamura, J. (1989). The dynamics of intrinsic motivation: A study of adolescents. In R. Ames & C. Ames (Eds.), *Research on motivation in education: Goals and cognitions* (pp. 45–71). New York: Academic Press.

Dansereau, D. F. (1988). Cooperative learning strategies. In C. E. Weinstein, E. T. Goetz, & P. A. Alexander, *Learning and study strategies: Issues in Assessment, Instruction, and Evaluation* (pp. 103–120). New York: Academic Press.

Darnell, D. (1970). "Clozentropy": A procedure for testing English language proficiency of foreign students. *Speech Monographs, 37*(4), 36–46.

Darnell, D. (1972). Information theory: An approach to human communication. In R. W. Budd & B. D. Ruben (Eds.), *Approaches to human communication* (pp. 156–169). New York: Spartan.

de Bono, E. (1999). *Six thinking hats*. New York: Back Bay Books.

Deci, E. L., Koestner, R., & Ryan, R. M. (2001). Extrinsic rewards and intrinsic motivation in education: Reconsidered once again. *Review of Educational Research, 71*(1), 1–27.

Deci, E. L., Ryan, R. M., & Koestner, R. (2001). The pervasive effects of rewards on intrinsic motivation: Response to Cameron. *Review of Educational Research, 71*(1), 43–51.

Dweck, C. S. (2006). *Mindset: The new psychology of success*. New York: Ballantine.

Dwyer, T., Blizzard, L., & Dean, K. (1996). Physical activity and performance in children. *Nutrition Review, 54*(4), 27–31.

Dwyer, T., Sallis, J., Blizzard, L., Lazarus, R., & Dean, K. (2001). Relation of academic performance to physical activity and fitness in children. *Pediatric Exercise Science, 13*, 225–237.

Ebbinghaus, H. (1987). Regarding a new application of performance testing and its use with school children. *Journal of Psychology and Physiology, 13*, 225–237.

Eisenhart, M. (1977, May). *Maintaining control: Teacher competence in the classroom*. Paper presented at the American Anthropological Association, Houston, TX.

El-Nemr, M. A. (1980). Meta-analysis of outcomes of teaching biology as inquiry. *Dissertation Abstracts International, 40*, 5813A.

Emmer, E. T., & Gerwels, M. C. (2006). Classroom management in middle and high school classrooms. In C. Evertson, C. M. Weinstein, & C. S. Weinstein (Eds.), *Handbook of classroom management: Research, practice, and contemporary issues* (pp. 407–437). Mahwah, NJ: Erlbaum.

Emmer, E. T., Evertson, C. M., & Worsham, M. E. (2003). *Classroom management for secondary teachers* (6th ed.). Boston: Allyn & Bacon.

Emmer, E. T., Evertson, C., & Anderson, L. (1980). Effective classroom management at the beginning of the school year. *Elementary School Journal, 80*(5), 219–231.

Emmer, E. T., Sanford, J. P., Clements, B. S., & Martin, J. (1982). *Improving classroom management and organization in junior high schools: An experimental investigation* (R & D Report No. 6153). Austin: Research and Development Center for Teacher Education, University of Texas.

Emmer, E. T., Sanford, J. P., Evertson, C. M., Clements, B. S., & Martin, J. (1981). *The classroom management improvement study: An experiment in elementary school classrooms* (R & D Report No. 6050). Austin: Research and Development Center for Teacher Education, University of Texas.

Epstein, J. A., & Harackiewicz, J. M. (1992). Winning is not enough: The effects of competition and achievement orientation on intrinsic interest. *Personality and Social Psychology Bulletin, 18*(2), 128–138.

Evertson, C. M., & Emmer, E. T. (1982). Preventive classroom management. In D. L. Duke (Ed.), *Helping teachers manage classrooms* (pp. 2–31). Alexandria, VA: Association for Supervision and Curriculum Development.

Evertson, C. M., Emmer, E. T., & Worsham, M. E. (2003). *Classroom management for elementary teachers* (6th ed.). Boston: Allyn & Bacon.

Evertson, C. M., Emmer, E. T., Sanford, J. P., & Clements, B. S. (1983). Improving classroom management: An experiment in elementary classrooms. *Elementary School Journal, 84*(2), 173–188.

Evertson, C. M., & Weinstein, C. S. (Eds.). (2006). *Handbook of classroom management: Research, practice, and contemporary issues*. Mahwah, NJ: Erlbaum.

Feltz, D. L., & Landers, D. M. (1983). The effects of mental practice on motor skill learning and performance: A meta-analysis. *Journal of Sport Psychology, 5*, 25–57.

Firestone, G., & Brody, N. (1975). Longitudinal investigation of teacher-student interactions and their relationship to academic performance. *Journal of Educational Psychology, 67*(4), 544–550.

Fitts, P. M., & Posner, M. I. (1967). *Human performance*. Belmont, CA: Brooks/Cole.

Fraser, B. J., Walberg, H. J., Welch, W. W., & Hattie, J. A. (1987). Synthesis of educational productivity research [Special issue]. *International Journal of Educational Research, 11*(2), 145–252.

Frederick, W. C. (1980). Instructional time. *Evaluation in Education, 4*, 117–118.

Fuchs, L. S., & Fuchs, D. (1986). Effects of systematic formative evaluation: A meta-analysis. *Exceptional Children, 53*(3), 199–208.

Ganske, L. (1981). Note-taking: A significant and integral part of learning environments. *Educational Communication and Technology: A Journal of Theory, Research, and Development, 29*(3), 155–175.

Gettinger, M., & Kohler, K. M. (2006). Process-outcome approaches to classroom management and effective teaching. In C. Evertson, C. M. Weinstein, & C. S. Weinstein (Eds.), *Handbook of classroom management: Research, practice, and contemporary issues* (pp. 73–95). Mahwah, NJ: Erlbaum.

Gick, M. L., & Holyoak, K. J. (1980). Analogical problem solving. *Cognitive Psychology, 12*, 306–353.

Gick, M. L., & Holyoak, K. J. (1983). Schema induction and analogical transfer. *Cognitive Psychology, 15*, 1–38.

Gijbels, D., Dochy, J., Van den Bossche, P., & Segers, M. (2005). Effects of problem-based learning: A meta-analysis from the angle of assessment. *Review of Educational Research, 75*(1), 27–61.

Good, T. L., & Brophy, J. E. (2003). *Looking in classrooms* (9th ed.). Boston: Allyn & Bacon.

Good, T. L., Cooper, H. M., & Blakey, S. L. (1980). Classroom interaction as a function of teacher expectations, student sex, and time of year. *Journal of Educational Psychology, 72*(3), 378–385.

Good, T. L., Sikes, J., & Brophy, J. (1973). Effects of teacher sex and student sex on classroom interaction. *Journal of Educational Psychology, 65*(1), 74–87.

Graue, M. E., Weinstein, T., & Walberg, H. J. (1983). School-based home instruction and learning: A quantitative synthesis. *The Journal of Educational Research, 76*(6), 351–360.

Guzzetti, B. J., Snyder, T. E., Glass, G. V., & Gamas, W. S. (1993). Promoting conceptual change in science: A comparative meta-analysis of instructional interventions from reading education and science education. *Reading Research Quarterly, 28*(2), 116–159.

Haas, M. (2005). Teaching methods for secondary algebra: A meta-analysis of findings. *NASSP Bulletin, 89*(642), 24–46.

Hahn, C. L. (1998). *Becoming political: Comparative perspectives on citizenship education.* Albany: State University of New York Press.

Hall, L. E. (1989). The effects of cooperative learning on achievement: A meta-analysis. *Dissertation Abstracts International, 50*, 343A.

Haller, E. P., Child, D. A., & Walberg, H. J. (1988). Can comprehension be taught?: A quantitative synthesis of "metacognitive" studies. *Educational Researcher, 17*(9), 5–8.

Hamaker, C. (1986). The effects of adjunct questions on prose learning. *Review of Educational Research, 56*(2), 212–242.

Hardré, P. L., & Reeve, J. (2003). A motivational model of rural students' intentions to persist in, versus drop out of, high school. *Journal of Educational Psychology, 95*(2), 347–356.

Harris, M. J., & Rosenthal, R. (1985). Mediation of interpersonal expectancy effects: 31 meta-analyses. *Psychological Bulletin, 97*(3), 363–386.

Hattie, J. A. (1992). Measuring the effects of schooling. *Australian Journal of Education, 36*(1), 5–13.

Hattie, J., Biggs, J., & Purdie, N. (1996). Effects of learning skills interventions on student learning: A meta-analysis. *Review of Educational Research, 66*(2), 99–136.

Hattie, J., & Timperley, H. (2007). The power of feedback. *Review of Educational Research, 77*, 81–112.

Henk, W. A., & Stahl, N. A. (1985). *A meta-analysis of the effect of notetaking on learning from lecture.* Paper presented at the 34th annual meeting of the National Reading Conference, St. Petersburg Beach, FL.

Hess, D. E. (2009). *Controversy in the classroom: The democratic power of discussion.* New York: Routledge.

Hofstetter, C. R., Sticht, T. G., & Hofstetter, C. H. (1999). Knowledge, literacy, and power. *Communication Research, 26*(1), 58–80.

Jennings, P. A. (2015). *Mindfulness for teachers: Simple skills for peace and productivity in the classroom.* New York: Norton.

Jensen, E. (2005). *Teaching with the brain in mind* (2nd, rev. and updated ed.). Alexandria, VA: Association for Supervision and Curriculum Development.

Jeter, J., & Davis, O. (1973). *Elementary school teachers' differential classroom interaction with children as a function of differential expectations of pupil achievements.* Paper presented at the annual meeting of the American Educational Research Association, New Orleans, LA.

Johnson, D., Maruyama, G., Johnson, R., Nelson, D., & Skon, L. (1981). Effects of cooperative, competitive, and individualistic goal structures on achievement: A meta-analysis. *Psychological Bulletin, 89*(1), 47–62.

Johnson-Laird, P. N. (1983). *Mental models: Towards a cognitive science of language, inference, and consciousness.* Cambridge, MA: Harvard University Press.

Johnson-Laird, P. N., & Byrne, R. M. J. (1991). *Deduction.* Hillsdale, NJ: Lawrence Erlbaum.

Jonas, P. M. (2004). *Secrets of connecting leadership and learning with humor.* Lanham, MD: Scarecrow Education.

Kagan, S., & Kagan, M. (2009). *Kagan cooperative learning.* Melbourne, Australia: Hawker Brownlow Education.

Kester, S., & Letchworth, G. (1972). Communication of teacher expectations and their effects on achievement and attitudes of secondary school students. *Journal of Educational Research, 66*(2), 51–55.

Kirsch, I. (1999). The response expectancy: An introduction. In I. Kirsch (Ed.), *How expectancies shape experience* (p. 7). Washington, DC: American Psychological Association.

Kluger, A. N., & DeNisi, A. (1996). The effects of feedback interventions on performance: A historical review, a meta-analysis and a preliminary intervention theory. *Psychological Bulletin, 119*(2), 254–284.

Kounin, J. S. (1983). *Classrooms: Individual or behavior settings?: Micrographs in teaching and learning* (General Series No. 1). Bloomington: Indiana University, School of Education.

Kumar, D. D. (1991). A meta-analysis of the relationship between science instruction and student engagement. *Education Review, 43*(1), 49–61.

Land, M. L. (1980, February). *Joint effects of teacher structure and teacher enthusiasm on student achievement.* Paper presented at the annual meeting of the Southwest Educational Research Association, San Antonio, TX.

Larson, R. W. (2000). Toward a psychology of positive youth development. *American Psychologist, 55*(1), 170–183.

Lee, A. Y. (n.d.). *Analogical reasoning: A new look at an old problem.* Boulder: University of Colorado, Institute of Cognitive Science.

Linden, D. E., Bittner, R. A., Muckli, L., Waltz, J. A., Kriegekorte, N., Goebel, R., et al. (2003). Cortical capacity constraints for visual working memory: Dissociation of FMRI load effects in a fronto-parietal network. *Neuroimage, 20*(3), 1518–1530.

Lipsey, M. W., & Wilson, D. B. (1993). The efficacy of psychological, educational, and behavioral treatment. *American Psychologist, 48*(12), 1181–1209.

Lott, G. W. (1983). The effect of inquiry teaching and advanced organizers upon student outcomes in science education. *Journal of Research in Science Teaching, 20*(5), 437–451.

Lovelace, M. K. (2005). Meta-analysis of experimental research based on the Dunn & Dunn model. *Journal of Educational Research, 98*(3), 176–183.

Lou, Y., Abrami, P. C., Spense, J. C., Paulsen, C., Chambers, B., & Apollonio, S. (1996). Within-class grouping: A meta-analysis. *Review of Educational Research, 66*(4), 423–458.

Luiten, J., Ames, W., & Ackerson, G. (1980). A meta-analysis of the effects of advance organizers on learning and retention. *American Educational Research Journal, 17*(2), 211–218.

Lyman, F. (1981). The responsive classroom discussion: The inclusion of ALL students. In A. S. Anderson (Ed.), *Mainstreaming digest: A collection of faculty and student papers* (pp. 109–113). College Park: University of Maryland.

Lysakowski, R. S., & Walberg, H. J. (1981). Classroom reinforcement in relation to learning: A quantitative analysis. *Journal of Educational Research, 75*(2), 69–77.

Lysakowski, R. S., & Walberg, H. J. (1982). Instructional effects of cues, participation, and corrective feedback: A quantitative synthesis. *American Educational Research Journal, 19*(4), 559–578.

Martinek, T. J., & Johnson, S. B. (1979). Teacher expectations: Effects on dyadic interaction and self-concept in elementary-age children. *Research Quarterly, 50*(1), 60–70.

Marzano Research. (2016). *Marzano compendium of instructional strategies.* Centennial, CO: Author.

Marzano, R. J. (1992). *A different kind of classroom: Teaching with dimensions of learning.* Alexandria, VA: Association for Supervision and Curriculum Development.

Marzano, R. J. (2003). *Classroom management that works: Research-based strategies for every teacher.* Alexandria, VA: Association for Supervision and Curriculum Development.

Marzano, R. J. (2006). *Classroom assessment and grading that work.* Alexandria, VA: Association for Supervision and Curriculum Development.

Marzano, R. J. (2007). *The art and science of teaching: A comprehensive framework for effective instruction.* Alexandria, VA: Association for Supervision and Curriculum Development.

Marzano, R. J. (2010). *Formative assessment and standards-based grading.* Bloomington, IN: Marzano Research.

Marzano, R. J. (2017). *The new art and science of teaching.* Bloomington, IN: Solution Tree Press.

Marzano, R. J. (2018). *The research base supporting* The New Art and Science of Teaching. Bloomington, IN: Marzano Research.

Marzano, R. J., Brandt, R. S., Hughes, C. S., Jones, B. F., Presseisen, B. Z., Rankin, S. C., et al. (1988). *Dimensions of thinking: A framework for curriculum and instruction.* Alexandria, VA: Association for Supervision and Curriculum Development.

Marzano, R. J., & Brown, J. L. (2009). *A handbook for the art and science of teaching.* Alexandria, VA: Association for Supervision and Curriculum Development.

Marzano, R. J., Gaddy, B. B., Foseid, M. C., Foseid, M. P., & Marzano, J. S. (2005). *A handbook for classroom management that works.* Alexandria, VA: Association for Supervision and Curriculum Development.

Marzano, R. J., Gnadt, J., & Jesse, D. M. (1990). *The effects of three types of linguistic encoding strategies on the processing of information presented in lecture format.* Unpublished manuscript. Denver: University of Colorado at Denver.

Marzano, R. J., & Heflebower, T. (2012). *Teaching and assessing 21st century skills.* Bloomington, IN: Marzano Research.

Marzano, R. J., & Marzano, J. S. (2015). *Managing the inner world of teaching: Emotions, interpretations, and actions.* Bloomington, IN: Marzano Research.

Marzano, R. J., & Simms, J. A. (2014). *Questioning sequences in the classroom.* Bloomington, IN: Marzano Research.

Mastin, V. E. (1963). Teacher enthusiasm. *Journal of Educational Research, 56*(7), 385–386.

Mayer, R. E. (1979). Can advance organizers influence meaningful learning? *Review of Educational Research, 49*(2), 371–383.

Mayer, R. E. (1989). Models of understanding. *Review of Educational Research, 59*(1), 43–64.

Mayer, R. E. (2003). *Learning and instruction.* Upper Saddle River, NJ: Merrill/Prentice Hall.

McCaslin, M., Bozack, A. R., Napoleon, L., Thomas, A., Vasquez, V., Wayman, V., et al. (2006). Self-regulated learning and classroom management: Theory, research, and consideration for classroom practice. In C. Evertson, C. M. Weinstein, & C. S. Weinstein (Eds.), *Handbook of classroom management: Research, practice, and contemporary issues* (pp. 223–252). Mahwah, NJ: Erlbaum.

McCombs, B. L. (2001). Self-regulated learning and academic achievement: A phenomenological view. In B. J. Zimmerman & D. H. Schunk (Eds.), *Self-regulated learning and academic achievement: Theoretical perspectives* (2nd ed., pp. 67–124). Mahwah, NJ: Erlbaum.

McConnell, J. W. (1977, April). *The relationship between selected teacher behaviors and attitudes and achievement of algebra classes.* Paper presented at the annual meeting of the American Educational Research Association, New York.

McDaniel, M. A., & Donnelly, C. M. (1996). Learning with analogy and elaborative interrogation. *Journal of Educational Psychology, 88*(3), 508–519.

McVee, M. B., Dunsmore, K., & Gavelek, J. R. (2005). Schema theory revisited. Review of *Educational Research, 75*(4), 531–566.

Meichenbaum, D., Bowers, K., & Ross, R. (1969). A behavioral analysis of teacher expectancy effect. *Journal of Personality and Social Psychology, 13*(4), 306–316.

Mendoza, S., Good, T., & Brophy, J. (1972). *Who talks in junior high classrooms?* (Report No. 68). Austin: Research and Development Center for Teacher Education, University of Texas at Austin.

Michaels, S., O'Connor, M. C., & Hall, M. W. (2010). *Accountable Talk® sourcebook: For classroom conversation that works.* Pittsburgh, PA: University of Pittsburgh.

Moriarity, B., Douglas, G., Punch, K., & Hattie, J. (1995). The importance of self-efficacy as a mediating variable between learning environments and achievement. *British Journal of Educational Psychology, 65*(1), 73–84.

Moskowitz, G., & Hayman, J. L., Jr. (1976). Success strategies of inner-city teachers: A year-long study. *Journal of Educational Research, 69*(8), 283–289.

National Research Council & Institute of Medicine. (2004). *Engaging schools: Fostering high school students' motivation to learn.* Washington, DC: The National Academies Press.

Natriello, G. (1987). The impact of evaluation processes on students. *Educational Psychologist, 22*(2), 155–175.

Nelson, J. R., Martella, R., & Galand, B. (1998). The effects of teaching school expectations and establishing a consistent consequence on formal office disciplinary actions. *Journal of Emotional and Behavioral Disorders, 4*(3), 153–161.

Nesbit, J. C., & Adesope, O. O. (2006). Learning with concept and knowledge maps: A meta-analysis. *Review of Educational Research, 76*(3), 413–448.

Nuthall, G. (1999). The way students learn: Acquiring knowledge from an integrated science and social studies unit. *Elementary School Journal, 99*(4), 303–341.

Nuthall, G., & Alton-Lee, A. (1995). Assessing classroom learning: How students use their knowledge and experience to answer classroom achievement test questions in science and social studies. *American Educational Research Journal, 32*(1), 185–223.

Ogle, D. M. (1986). K-W-L: A teaching model that develops active reading out of expository text. *Reading Teacher, 39*(6), 564–570.

Ormrod, J. E. (2008). *Educational psychology: Developing learners* (6th ed.). Upper Saddle River, NJ: Pearson.

Ormrod, J. E. (2014). *Educational psychology: Developing learners* (8th ed.). Upper Saddle River, NJ: Pearson.

Page, S. (1971). Social interaction and experimenter effects in a verbal conditioning experiment. *Canadian Journal of Educational Psychology, 25*(6), 463–475.

Paschal, R. A., Weinstein, T., & Walberg, H. J. (1984). The effects of homework on learning: A quantitative synthesis. *Journal of Educational Research, 78*(2), 97–104.

Perry, N. E., Turner, J. C., & Meyer, D. K. (2006). Classrooms as contexts for motivating learning. In P. Alexander & P. Winne (Eds.), *Handbook of educational psychology* (pp. 327–348). Mahwah, NJ: Erlbaum.

Pflaum, S. W., Walberg, H. J., Karegianes, M. L., & Rasher, S. P. (1980). Reading instruction: A quantitative analysis. *Educational Researcher, 9*(7), 12–18.

Plax, T. G., & Kearney, P. (1990). Classroom management: Structuring the classroom for work. In J. A. Daly, G. W. Friedrich, & A. L. Vangelesti (Eds.), *Teaching communication: Theory, research, and methods* (pp. 223–236). Hillsdale, NJ: Erlbaum.

Popova, M. (n.d.). *Illustrated six-word memoirs by students from grade school to grad school.* Accessed at www.brainpickings.org/2013/01/09/six-word-memoirs-students on April 24, 2018.

Powell, G. (1980, December). *A meta-analysis of the effects of "imposed" and "induced" imagery upon word recall.* Paper presented at the annual meeting of the National Reading Conference, San Diego, CA.

Raphael, R. E., & Kirschner, B. M. (1985). *The effects of instruction in compare/contrast text structure in sixth-grade students' reading comprehension and writing products* (Research Series No. 161). Lansing, MI: The Institute for Research on Teaching.

Redfield, D. L., & Rousseau, E. W. (1981). A meta-analysis of experimental research on teacher questioning behavior. *Review of Educational Research, 51*(2), 237–245.

Reeve, J. (2006). Extrinsic rewards and inner motivation. In C. Evertson, C. M. Weinstein, & C. S. Weinstein (Eds.), *Handbook of classroom management: Research, practice, and contemporary issues* (pp. 645–664). Mahwah, NJ: Erlbaum.

Reeve, J., & Deci, E. (1996). Elements of competitive situations that affect intrinsic motivation. *Personality and Social Psychology Bulletin, 22*(1), 24–33.

Rejeski, W., Darracott, C., & Hutslar, S. (1979). Pygmalion in youth sport: A field study. *Journal of Sports Psychology, 1*(4), 311–319.

Rist, R. (1970). Student social class and teacher expectations: The self-fulfilling prophecy in ghetto education. *Harvard Educational Review, 40*(3), 411–451.

Roeser, R. W., Peck, S. C., & Nasir, N. S. (2006). Self and identify processes in school motivation, learning, and achievement. In P. Alexander & P. Winne (Eds.), *Handbook of educational psychology* (pp. 391–424). Mahwah, NJ: Erlbaum.

Rosenshine, B. (1970). Enthusiastic teaching: A research review. *School Review, 78*(4), 499–514.

Rosenshine, B. (2002). *9: Converging findings on classroom instruction.* Accessed at http://nepc.colorado.edu/files/Chapter09-Rosenshine-Final.pdf on May 21, 2012.

Rosenshine, B., & Furst, N. (1973). The use of direct observation to study teaching. In R. Travers (Ed.), *Handbook of research on teaching* (2nd ed., pp. 263–298). Chicago: Rand McNally.

Rosenshine, B., & Meister, C. C. (1994). Reciprocal teaching: A review of the research. *Review of Educational Research, 64*(4), 479–530.

Ross, J. A. (1988). Controlling variables: A meta-analysis of training studies. *Review of Educational Research, 58*(4), 405–437.

Rovee-Collier, C. (1995). Time windows in cognitive development. *Developmental Psychology, 31*(2), 147–169.

Rubovits, P., & Maehr, M. (1971). Pygmalion analyzed: Toward an explanation of the Rosenthal-Jacobson findings. *Journal of Personality and Social Psychology, 19*, 197–203.

Sanford, J. P., & Evertson, C. M. (1981). Classroom management in a low SES junior high: Three case studies. *Journal of Teacher Education, 32*(1), 34–38.

Saunders, J. M., & Smith, E. E. (2014). Every word is on trial: Six-word memoirs in the classroom. *The Reading Teacher, 67*(8), 600–605.

Schunk, D. H., & Cox, P. D. (1986). Strategy training and attributional feedback with learning disabled students. *Journal of Educational Psychology, 73*(3), 201–209.

Schwanenflugel, P. J., Stahl, S. A., & McFalls, E. L. (1997). Partial word knowledge and vocabulary growth during reading comprehension. *Journal of Literacy Research, 29*(4), 531–553.

Scott, D., & Marzano, R. J. (2014). *Awaken the learner: Finding the source of effective education.* Bloomington, IN: Marzano Research.

Skinner, C. H., Fletcher, P. A., & Hennington, C. (1996). Increasing learning rates by increasing student response rates. *School Psychology Quarterly, 11*, 313–325.

Smith, F. J., & Luginbuhl, J. E. (1976). Inspecting expectancy: Some laboratory results of relevance for teacher training. *Journal of Educational Psychology, 68*(3), 265–272.

Smith Magazine. (Ed.). (2009). *I can't keep my own secrets: Six-word memoirs by teens famous and obscure.* New York: HarperTeen.

Smith Magazine. (n.d.). *A teaching guide for six-word memoirs: Not quite what I was planning.* New York: HarperPerennial.

Smith, H. A. (1985). The marking of transitions by more and less effective teachers. *Theory Into Practice, 24*(1), 57–62.

Soar, R. S., & Soar, R. M. (1979). Emotional climate and management. In P. L. Peterson & H. J. Walberg (Eds.), *Research on teaching: Concepts, findings, and implications* (pp. 97–119). Berkeley, CA: McCutchan.

Stage, S. A., & Quiroz, D. R. (1997). A meta-analysis of interventions to decrease disruptive classroom behavior in public education settings. *School Psychology Review, 26*(3), 333–368.

Stahl, S. A. (1999). *Vocabulary development.* Cambridge, MA: Brookline.

Stahl, S. A., & Fairbanks, M. M. (1986). The effects of vocabulary instruction: A model-based meta-analysis. *Review of Educational Research, 56*(1), 72–110.

Stipek, D. J., & Weisz, J. R. (1981). Perceived personal control and academic achievement. *Review of Educational Research, 51*(1), 101–137.

Stone, C. L. (1983). A meta-analysis of advanced organizer studies. *Journal of Experimental Education, 51*(4), 194–199.

Sweitzer, G. L., & Anderson, R. D. (1983). A meta-analysis of research in science teacher education practices associated with inquiry strategy. *Journal of Research in Science Teaching, 20*(5), 453–466.

Taylor, M. (1979). Race, sex, and the expression of self-fulfilling prophecies in a laboratory teaching situation. *Journal of Personality and Social Psychology, 37*(6), 897–912.

Taylor, W. L. (1953). "Cloze procedure": A new tool for measuring readability. *Journalism Quarterly, 30*(4), 415–433.

Tennenbaum, G., & Goldring, E. (1989). A meta-analysis of the effect of enhanced instruction: Cues, participation, reinforcement, and feedback and correctives on motor skill learning. *Journal of Research and Development in Education, 22*(3), 53–64.

Tennyson, R. D., & Cocchiarella, M. J. (1986). An empirically based instructional design theory for teaching concepts. *Review of Educational Research, 56*, 40–71.

Toulmin, S. E. (2003). *The uses of argument* (Updated ed.). Cambridge, United Kingdom: Cambridge University Press.

Toulmin, S., Rieke, R., & Janik, A. (1981). *An introduction to reasoning.* New York: Macmillan.

Walberg, J. H. (1982). What makes schooling effective? A synthesis and critique of three national studies. *Contemporary Education Review, 1*, 23–24.

Walberg, H. J. (1999). Productive teaching. In H. C. Waxman & H. J. Walberg (Eds.), *New directions for teaching practice research* (pp. 75–104). Berkeley, CA: McCutchen.

Weiner, N. (1967). *The human use of human beings.* New York: Avon.

Weinstein, C. S. (1977). Modifying student behavior in an open classroom through changes in the physical design. *American Educational Research Journal, 14*(3), 249–262.

Weinstein, C. E., Goetz, E. T., & Alexander, P. A. (Eds.). (1988). *Learning and study strategies: Issues in assessment, instruction, and evaluation.* San Diego: Academic Press.

West, L. H. T., & Fensham, P. J. (1976). Prior knowledge or advance organizers as affective variables in chemical learning. *Journal of Research in Science Teaching, 13*(4), 297–306.

Williams, R. G., & Ware, J. E., Jr. (1976). Validity of student ratings of instruction under different incentive conditions: A further study of the Dr. Fox effect. *Journal of Educational Psychology, 68*(1), 48–56.

Williams, R. G., & Ware, J. E., Jr. (1977). An extended visit with Dr. Fox: Validity of student satisfaction with instruction rating after repeated exposures to a lecturer. *American Educational Research Journal, 14*, 449–457.

Willis, B. (1970). The influence of teacher expectation on teachers' classroom interaction with selected children. *Dissertation Abstracts, 30*, 5072A.

Wise, K. C., & Okey, J. R. (1983). A meta-analysis of the effects of various science teaching strategies on achievement. *Journal of Research in Science Teaching, 20*(5), 415–425.

Wubbels, T., Brekelmans, M., den Brok, P., & van Tartwijk, J. (2006). An interpersonal perspective on classroom management in secondary classrooms in the Netherlands. In C. Evertson & C. S. Weinstein (Eds.), *Handbook of classroom management: Research, practice, and contemporary issues* (pp. 1161–1191). Mahwah, NJ: Erlbaum.

Wubbels, T., Brekelmans, M., van Tartwijk, J., & Admiral, W. (1999). Interpersonal relationships between teachers and students in the classroom. In H. C. Waxman & H. J. Walberg (Eds.), *New directions for teaching practice and research* (pp. 151–170). Berkeley, CA: McCutchan.

Wubbels, T., & Levy, J. (Eds.). (1993). *Do you know what you look like? Interpersonal relationships in education*. London: Falmer Press.

Wyckoff, W. L. (1973). The effect of stimulus variation on learning from lecture. *The Journal of Experimental Education, 41*(3), 85–96.

Index

O

P

Q

R

S

T

U

V

W

Solution Tree's mission is to advance the work of our authors. By working with the best researchers and educators worldwide, we strive to be the premier provider of innovative publishing, in-demand events, and inspired professional development designed to transform education to ensure that all students learn.

ASCD is a global nonprofit association dedicated to the whole child approach that supports educators, families, community members, and policy makers. We provide expert and innovative solutions to facilitate professional development through print and digital publishing, on-site learning services, and conferences and events that empower educators to support the success of each child.